The Works Tigers

The Works Tigers
1964 to 1966

The development and competition history of the Works Tigers, including a detailed account of each event, FIA Homologations and the performance figures of the rally cars. Contains previously unpublished factory build records from the Competition Department and new photographs from the archives of the 1964 Le Mans attempt.

Foreword by Ian Hall

To another 'works car' owner,
With best wishes
Graham Rood

Graham Rood

The Works Tigers

This book is published by:

Mercian Manuals Ltd
353 Kenilworth Road
Balsall Common
Coventry
West Midlands
CV7 7DL
01676 533304
www.mercianmanuals.co.uk

Distribution worldwide by the same.

© Graham Rood 2007

ISBN 978 1 903088 39 5

All rights reserved. No part of this publication may be reproduced, stored in a retrieval system, or transmitted, in any form or by any means, electronic, mechanical, photocopying, recording or otherwise, without the prior written permission of the publishers.

CONTENTS

Introduction 5

Acknowledgements 7

Foreword: Ian Hall 9

Chapter 1: The Beginnings 11
Chapter 2: The Tiger in embryo 23
Chapter 3: Le Mans 1964 33
Chapter 4: The Prelude 57
Chapter 5: Geneva Rally 1964 63
Chapter 6: RAC Rally 1964 79
Chapter 7: Monte Carlo Rally 1965 91
Chapter 8: Tulip Rally 1965 125
Chapter 9: Scottish Rally 1965 133
Chapter 10: International Police Rally 1965 135
Chapter 11: Alpine Rally 1965 141
Chapter 12: Targa Florio 1965 169
Chapter 13: RAC Rally 1965 179
Chapter 14: Monte Carlo Rally 1966 183
Chapter 15: Tulip Rally 1966 199
Chapter 16: Acropolis Rally 1966 211
Chapter 17: Gulf London Rally 1966 221
Chapter 18: The build of the works rally cars 227
Chapter 19: Obituary and Reflections 257

Appendix 1: Le Mans Aerodynamics report 261
Appendix 2: Le Mans Tiger development notes 271
Appendix 3: Details of the Rally cars 277
Appendix 4: Summary of results by rally 287
Appendix 5: Events and cars by Driver/Co-driver 289
Appendix 6: FIA Homologation details and USA 'homologation' notes ... 291
Appendix 7: Appendix J Regulations relevant to the Tiger 353
Appendix 8: Performance figures of the works rally cars 359
Appendix 9: The Press – Impressions of the Rally cars 365
Appendix 10: Works rally car build sheets 383
Appendix 11: Competition options from Humber Road and USA ... 405
Appendix 12: Tiger production figures 411

The Works Tigers

INTRODUCTION

This book is intended to contain an accurate history of the works rally Tigers and those details of works build etc, which either get lost with time or become inaccurate through serial reporting, with original mistakes being perpetually reported.

Every effort has been made to be strictly accurate and checks have been made on the surviving works Tigers; ADU311B (Peter Riley & ex-Author), ADU312B (ex-Don Pither) and the last of the works build FRW668C (Author), and with the competition managers, works drivers, co-drivers team managers and mechanics - many of whom, seemingly naturally, are still involved with rallying at all levels.

Whilst not strictly works drives in the true sense of the word, the drives of the Rev. Rupert Jones on the 64 RAC, Peter Harper and Rupert Jones on the Targa Florio, and John Gott with his Police Rally win, have all been included, since they were undertaken in works cars of some sort or other in the timescales of the works Tiger lifespan. Also included is the effort by the Competition Department to tackle the Le Mans 24 hour Endurance Race, this event being the competition debut of the Tiger in Europe

Along with the Healey 3000, the Tiger really represented the last of the "big bangers" –with the possible exception of the Datsun 240/260 series - and gave some interest at the big-engined end of the rallies. However, the more nimble Mini-Cooper 'S', the Imp, the Cortina GT and Lotus Cortina were beginning to make their mark, and Rootes soon turned to their 875 and 998 Imps, and BMC away from the Healey 3000 to the 1071 and 1275 Cooper 'S', to provide their front line rally cars.

But, for just two years, the Tiger added stimulation to International competition – particularly in tarmac events – and a well-driven Tiger provided serious competition in its class and did as well on ice and snow (Monte Carlo 65) as it did on tarmac (Alpine 65) and in the dust and rocks of the Acropolis.

Early into this new century the nostalgia for that era of rallying is growing and the Healeys and Tigers are again rallying in the many historic events - what wonderful sounds are returning!

Graham Rood

Bentley, Hants

The Works Tigers

The Tiger's successes 1964-65

1965 Salt Lake City National Points Races, Utah 1st outright.
1965 Santa Barbara Road Races, California 1st Class B production race.
1965 Player's 200 Meeting, Mosport, Ontario 1st after 15 laps, finishing 8 seconds ahead of nearest competitor.
1965 Stockton, California, Road Races 1st Class B production race.
1965 International Scottish Rally 1st over 2,500 cc. GT class.
1965 International Police Rally, Belgium 1st outright, without a single penalty point.
1965 Monte Carlo Rally 1st and 2nd Over 2,500 cc. GT class. 4th Overall.
1964 Geneva Rally 1st, 2nd, 3rd Over 2,500 cc. GT Class.
1964 Pacific Divisional Championships, Willow Springs, California 1st in Class B production event.
1964 US 200 Mile National Sports Car Race, Elkhart Lake 1st in Class, 2nd Overall.
also Dutch National 24-hour speed record at Zandvoort Circuit 9th February 1965
V8 4.2 litre engine, 0.60 mph in 9.2 seconds, acceleration from 20 mph in top gear, top speed over 120 mph, 164 bhp.

It's easy enough to make a car look sporty. It's not difficult to give it an exciting sound. But proving by performance that it's worthy of being called a sports sensation – that's where actions speak louder than words. The Sunbeam Tiger has been getting in on the action in rallies and races all over the world, and collecting winner's laurels with a regularity that's far from monotonous. That's why when you settle behind the wheel of a Tiger, whether you are going to gun it at full throttle on a motorway or tootle in traffic at 20 mph in top gear (yes, 20 in top !), you know positively that the performance has been proved. The excitement you can take for granted. Price ex-works **£1445.10.5** inc £250.10.5 pt.

London Showrooms and Export Division Devonshire House Piccadilly London W1

ACKNOWLEDGEMENTS

Grateful acknowledgements are given to all of those rally correspondents in Autocar, Motor, Motoring News, Autosport, Classic Car, Motor Racing and Motor Sport for their detailed and lucid reporting; to the following for their excellent photographs – LAT/Motoring News, Autosport, Coventry Transport Museum, Photo Plage, Photo Junior, Photo Wasserman, Photo Erpe, Foster & Skeffington, Birmingham Post & Mail, United Press, Michael Cooper, Car & Driver, Atlas Photographic for the Rootes Photographic Archive - and Graham Robson at Autocar for the interesting and productive times spent in their photographic libraries. Many individuals contributed photographs and documents and thanks are due to John Clegg, Don Barrow, Geoffrey Goddard, Dave McDermott, Robert Clayson, Mike Kempley, Alan Clegg, Mike Taylor for information in his book 'Tiger' and to Michael Turner for his fine Police Rally painting. Particular thanks are due to Robin Turvey, Andrew Cowan, Des O'Dell and Derek Hughes for access to their mine of information and the numerous fact-finding discussions, the majority, seemingly, either travelling to rallies, during rallies at service points or huddled in the cold beside the road waiting - sometimes fruitlessly - for our respective rally cars to arrive. Most of the managers, crews and mechanics retained their direct involvement with rallying and my thanks go to those who have added the valuable little pieces of vital information and to those who have supplied personal photos from their Tiger days. Paul Burch, a long time Rootes competitor and team manager kindly supplied many of the photographs used in the 'The Beginnings'.

The drafts were reviewed by many of those involved with the competition history of the Tiger, numerous suggestions were proffered and most taken up. Particular thanks in this area are due to Ian Hall for his reading of the original script, his memories of the events - all of which were included - his penning of the excellent foreword and the use of his rally photos. Thanks in this area are due to Mike Taylor and his Tiger book, from which much of the early production history of the Tiger was gleaned, and to Graham Vickery of the Sunbeam Tiger Owners Club who sourced a publisher and gave much useful information along with production figures. Also the Club itself for providing material from their archives. A generous vote of thanks must go to Peter and Richard Shimmell, from Mercian Manuals Ltd, who were prepared to take the risk of publishing a fairly specialist narrative. Thanks also go to John Dandy, Chairman of the Sunbeam Tiger Owners Club, for proof reading the text. My final thanks go to Judith Fields who spent much time sorting out my computer literacy and scanned in many of the photographs and text files.

Many of the personnel you will now find becoming increasingly active in the rise in interest of Historic Rallying – where the Tiger qualifies in the Historic Class.

I hope the wait for the book was worth it!

The Works Tigers

FOREWORD

I was delighted to be asked by Graham Rood to write a few introductory words to his wonderfully researched new book on the Works Tigers.

When I started to think back to the "Tiger years" it came as a real shock to realise that the period when we were competing in International Rallies in the Tigers is much further back in time now than were the "Bentleys at Le Mans" when I first read the Tim Birkin and Sammy Davis Bentley books as a teenager. The ensuing sense of perspective puts me firmly in my place as a relic of the past!

I can imagine some younger readers, who may well be modern Tiger dicers, looking back on the road rallies of the 1950s and 1960s and wondering what all the fuss is about. After all, what's so difficult about averaging 30mph, or even 40mph, with a car like a Sunbeam Tiger? Good question and it deserves an answer, which is of course rooted in the difference between modern roads and the even worse ones of the period. To all intents and purposes there were no motorways, and certainly no joined up network even when a motorway, autobahn or autoroute did exist. Even dual-carriageways were few and far between and the everyday traffic was often slow and cumbersome, which didn't exactly help a rally crew in a hurry. An added problem was that the average motorist simply didn't expect to be overtaken between two lorries downhill on a 'B' road by a rally car travelling at very high speed!

Then there was the relentless pressure of the Rally Time Schedule. On the Monte Carlo Rally, for example, competitors started from a selection of different capital cities (Paris, Oslo, Athens, Glasgow etc) and drove for three days and two nights on specified routes with regular Time Controls before joining up at an Alpine town for the third night, which consisted of a virtual road race through the French Alps to the finish in Monaco. This meant of course that if you were due, say, at Reims at 11 o'clock on Tuesday evening then you had to be at the Reims Control (which might be in the crypt of the Cathedral or similar unlikely spot in the City centre) ready to clock out at 11 o'clock or marks would be lost. No allowances were made for weather, traffic conditions, time to eat (sleep was unheard of), buy petrol, adjust brakes, ferry crossings or anything else. In other words you had to be on time everywhere all the

The Works Tigers

time for three days and nights and the only blessing compared with to-day was that we weren't cursed with overall speed limits, except, I think, in Denmark.

To take another example, the Alpine Rally. This was set at very high average speeds over the highest, twistiest and scariest roads in the Alps with numerous sections timed to the second. In other words, one second over your due time and all chance of a major award (the much-prized "Coupe des Alpes" for a penalty free run) was gone for good. These sections were all possible to do on time given a very good car and crew - but only just, and the ascent and descent of hair-pinned roads and passes was seemingly endless.

There is no doubt in my mind that the top International Rally drivers of that era were in all probability the fastest and safest road drivers in the World before or since.

I write this in all honesty because it simply isn't possible to drive like that on modern roads for such long periods. Drivers like Harper, Hopkirk, Elford, Makinen, Clark, Aaltonen, Carlsson, Pat Moss and a select few others could be guaranteed to get a car across Europe in virtually any conditions without damage (usually!) at speeds which the average driver probably wouldn't believe. From my point of view, co-driving Peter Harper in various Rapiers and Tigers was a unique privilege and the best driving lessons anyone could have. It was also flattering in the extreme that he would rest and even sleep when it was my turn to press on, albeit not quite so quickly!

When you have read Graham Rood's fascinating book then there will be little or nothing you don't know about those few short years when the Tiger made its mark in the Rally world. If the economic conditions of the time had been different who knows what might have developed in later years.

Ian Hall

THE BEGINNINGS

A brief dwell into the Rootes Competition Department's long history of competitive motorsport.

Whilst this book deals essentially with the Tiger period in the mid 60's, the Rootes Group had been successfully involved in competition - particularly rallying - for many years before the introduction of the Tiger. They had gained many successes with the Sunbeam Talbot Alpine and the Rapier, with a variety of drivers and in a variety of International rallies. They had rallied with such diverse cars as Hillman Huskys on the Safari Rally, the Humber Super Snipe on the Monte Carlo Rally, Sunbeam Alpines on, appropriately, the Alpine Rally, a Sunbeam Talbot 90 on the Monte Carlo as well as many other events. The Talbot Alpines and Rapiers had provided the lions' share including such classic events as the 1956 Mille Miglia.

The die was perhaps cast as far back as 1932, when a team of Talbot 105's had won the Coupe des Alpes, one of the team, in car No 9, being Norman Garrad. Norman had then competed in some small rallies, amongst them the Lands End Trial using a pre-war Sunbeam Talbot 2-litre - suitably modified for the occasion - winning a cup in the process. Further success came in the 1938 Monte Carlo Rally in a Talbot 10 with Sammy Davis, securing a fine 22nd place. The factory's (i.e. Garrad's) experience of pre-war rallying had also included assistance, and perhaps more, with Maurice Gatsonides' Hillman Minx in the 1939 Monte.

In the post war '47 Alpine Rally, the factory had an interest in the Sunbeam Talbot 2 litre (pre the 90) Tourer of D A Clease, and it was after this entry that Norman began to press for an official Competition Department. By this time the new Sunbeam Talbot 80 and 90 were arriving on the scene and Norman began to further formulate the idea of a Rootes Competition Department with increasing fervour. In this year he took his first 90, a late prototype, on the French Alpine Rally and the car, although finishing, had problems with sump damage, which he thought might have been avoided by different preparation.

Upon his return to the factory, Norman decided that it was time to set up a competition shop, which he duly did in the back of the sales department paint shop in Stoke. Supported by three mechanics - Jimmy Ashworth, Jerry Spencer and "Big Ray", a test driver in the form of Glen Johnson, and with Ernie Beck taking care of the engines, the department started building, testing, rebuilding and retesting the cars and generally making them more suitable for use in competition.

As the operation became more involved, the financial strains inevitably became greater and the money that Rootes alone were putting into the competition department became progressively more inadequate and Norman Garrad began to seek further afield for additional financial support. The fresh injection of cash came initially from Shell Oil and from some of the component manufacturers like Dunlop, Laycock etc.

With this further backing, the competition department set out to compete with the existing rally teams. After much testing, building and rebuilding, a team of three Sunbeam 80s were entered for the 1949 Monte Carlo Rally. Whilst all three cars finished (Peter Monkhouse 31st and 4th in class, Nick Haines 37th and George Hartwell 46th), it was decided to put all further effort into the 90, which was considered more suitable. This produced, after much work, better results and on the Alpine Rally in the summer of 1949 the team came 5th, 20th and 25th overall (Monkhouse/Hartwell, Douglas Clease of "The Autocar" and Norman Garrad himself, respectively).

The Beginnings

The Chairman of the Royal Automobile Club

requests the pleasure of the company of

Mr. J.N. Pearman

at a Luncheon at the Royal Automobile Club at 12.30 p.m. for 1.0 p.m.

on Friday, 20th March, to present the

DEWAR TROPHY to SUNBEAM-TALBOT LTD.

for the outstanding performance of a team of three Sunbeam-Talbot cars in the International Alpine Rally, 1952, and the Research and Development that made this possible.

R.S.V.P. General Manager,
The Royal Automobile Club,
85, Pall Mall, London, S.W.1.

P.T.O.

HOTEL MARTINEZ
CANNES

DINER

donné dans la Salle des Fêtes
de l'Hôtel Martinez
en l'honneur des Concurrents du
XV.e RALLYE INTERNATIONAL DES ALPES

Cannes, le 17 Juillet 1952

The Beginnings

The team winning Talbot '105' models which won the Coupe des Alpes in the 1932 Alpine rally. The team are, from the left, the Hon. Brian Lewis, 'Tim' Rose-Richards and Norman Garrad.

Things progressed, and in the 1950 Monte the Sunbeam Talbot 90's won the prize for the "best non-French team" with all three cars intact at the finish.

In the same rally there were two other competitors using Rootes cars - a Hillman Minx, which won the best-equipped prize, and a Humber Super Snipe (JHP 239) driven by the two Dutchmen - Maurice Gatsonides and K S Barendrecht. The weather, unlike the mild 1949 event, had been a normal snowy and icy Monte, yet Gatsonides had arrived back in Monaco secure in second place overall and without a single penalty point to his discredit. It was largely due to this result that, when Peter Monkhouse was sadly killed on the 1950 Mille Miglia, Maurice was called in by Norman Garrad to be team captain for the 1950 Alpine. At the halfway halt "Gatso" had worked his way up to first in class, with George Hartwell second. However, as the event progressed, fate intervened and Gatso's rear axle called enough and George Hartwell ran out of time after an accident on the road. George Murray-Frame, the third Rootes driver, was even more unfortunate having completed the route in time only to have his battery finally fail in Monte Carlo, with the loss of his Coupe des Alpes.

With the Rootes Team now showing a more competitive front, they were provided with a more suitable rally car - the Mk2 Sunbeam Talbot 90. Lessons learnt from the previous years of rallying had been incorporated into this model and with the "signing" of Stirling Moss in 1952, greater things were expected. In the Alpine Rally of that year the Sunbeam Talbot number one team, which included Moss, won three Coupe des Alpes, the Manufacturers team prize and the Marseilles and Provence AC Challenge Cup. The team continued through 1952 and with the coming of the Alpine again and with an entry this time of six cars for this 1953 event, the team gained more success. Of the six drivers four won Coupes - Moss, Frame, Sheila van Damm and Fitch - with Moss making sixth overall, whilst giving away 600cc to 1200cc to the three cars ahead of him.

The Beginnings

Norman Garrad and D Horton storm the Col de la Mendola during the second stage of the 1949 Alpine rally from Monte Carlo to Cortina d'Ampezzo – a 480 mile leg. (Rootes)

The Beginnings

George Murray-Frame, John Pearson in their Sunbeam Talbot for the 1950 Monte Carlo Rally. (Photo Junior)

The George Hartwell/ Chipperton Sunbeam tests the suspension on the last test in Marseilles at the end of the 1950 Alpine Rally. Both front wings and lights look well used and the rear nearside wheel parts company with 'terra firma'. (Rootes)

The Beginnings

T.H. Wisdom driving Hillman Minx on the Col de Valberg which completed the 2,000 miles course - taken on one of the many hair-pin bends which, for speedy travel, call for very skilful handling!!

By courtesy of The Motor.

The Beginnings

Maurice Gatsonides – 'Gatso' – brings his Dutch registered Sunbeam Talbot to meet some of the English contingent on the 1951 Monte Carlo Rally. (Rootes)

Ronnie Adams and John Pearson in pristine form at the start of the 1953 RAC Rally in Hastings. (Rootes)

The Beginnings

1954 provided more good results, the team prize on the Monte and for Stirling Moss yet another Coupe on the Alpine. However, all this was put in the shade by the result of the 1955 Monte - an outright win by the Norwegian Per Malling in his Mk 3 - and Sheila van Damm compounded the success by winning the Coupe des Dames. In October 1955 the debut was announced of a car that was to provide - after a few years of development - a highly competitive rally car - the Sunbeam Rapier. Its debut in competition proper was the 1956 Mille Miglia with a driver whose connections were to become virtually synonymous with Sunbeam - Peter Harper.

Born in 1921, Peter had been rallying since 1947 - then with a Sunbeam Talbot 2 litre (0-60mph in some 30secs and a top speed of 72mphll) and competed as a works driver in the Sunbeam Talbot 90's and ST 90 Alpines, and had given the Rapier its competition debut in the 1956 Mille Miglia with Sheila van Damm.

The crew and car finished the gruelling 1000-mile event in 15.5 hours, an average of 65mph, and, along with the private entry of Wisnewski/Bosmiller, finished first and second in the 1600cc Special Touring Class. The Tulip Rally followed, with all four cars finishing in the top ten and privateer John Melvin providing a class win. In buoyant mood from these successes, the Alpine Rally was tackled with five Rapiers. Unfortunately only two cars finished, Harper/Humphrey at 23rd and the Dean/Sparrow car at 28th, the remaining three having accidents.

Like the results of the Alpine, the 1957 season was somewhat disappointing with some successes in two events, the Tulip (in which the Jimmy Ray / Ian Hall privately owned and prepared car won the best British car award) and the Mille Miglia, but it was with the introduction of the 1958 model Rapier Series 2 that more regular success were to be achieved. The RAC Rally at that time, 1958, was held in March and the season started well for Rootes when the Harper/Dean combination won the event outright. Further successes followed - first and second on the Circuit of Ireland, team prize-winners on the Tulip, outright winners of Uganda's Mount Elgon Rally, outright winners of the London Rally. The culmination arrived on the Alpine Rally where the Rapiers finished 1-2-3-4-5 in class, won the Coupe des Alpes and were third in the Coupe des Dames. Altogether a season of note!

1959 was even better. The team had been joined by Paddy Hopkirk, then 26, who had been driving for five years with Standard-Triumph - his best result to date being an outright win on the 1958 Circuit of Ireland, his home event, in a TR3. Along with Peter Harper and Peter Jopp the team excelled themselves. Fifth overall and "best British" in the Monte, third overall in the Alpine for Hopkirk/Jack Scott with the Jopp/Leston car in 6th position and a noteworthy result on one of the rallying classics, the Liege-Rome-Liege where only 14 of the 97 entries finished, the Jimmy Ray/Mike Cotton car finishing 11th overall.

For the 60's the Series 3 Rapier was introduced with many of the lessons learned from the Series 2 rally cars incorporated, and after a lacklustre RAC Rally with the old Series 2's, the team prepared for the Monte with their Series 3's. These five cars with their distinctive registration numbers YWK1 to YWK5, provided another good season.

The Harper/Raymond Baxter car, YWK5, finished fourth overall on the Monte and won the "best British" award for the third year running - the Monte was becoming a speciality with Rootes. The team also competed on the Acropolis Rally, with the car being driven by Harper and Procter, who won not only their class but also the Acropolis Cup. This was followed by a class win on the Alpine.

In the early 1960's the Monte Carlo Rally was an event that was highly considered by British competitors and on the 1961 Rally, some 110 British enthusiasts entered with 21 of this number being in Rootes cars. Again Harper won the best British award, his class and the fastest lap overall on the Monaco Grand Prix circuit tests (2.51.1)

The Beginnings

Three of the six team Sunbeams on the 1953 Alpine. George Murray-Frame and John Pearman pose alongside MKV22, with Sheila van Damm/Anne Hall (MKV25) and the John Fitch/Peter Miller car (MKV24). (Rootes)

Part of the team for the 1954 Alpine Rally. The Murray-Frame/Pearman Sunbeam and the Stirling Moss/Cutts car line up alongside Rootes competition team 'boss' Norman Garrad. (Rootes)

The Beginnings

The George Murray-Frame/John Pearman Humber Super Snipe, well past the Grand Prix circuit chicane lines up the Tabac corner approaching the Monaco sea front on the 1954 Monte Carlo Rally. (Rootes)

The Peter Harper / Sheila van Damm Rapier in the 1956 Mille Miglia. In this event, the competition debut of the Rapier, two cars were entered in the 1600 cc special touring class and finished second and third. The car completed 1000 miles in 15 hrs 04 mins 37 secs followed by the Wisnewski / Bosmiller Rapier. (Stanley Paul publ)

The Beginnings

Peter Harper compresses the springs of his Rapier on the final stage of the 1958 Alpine Rally at the Parc de Borely in Marseilles. (Stanley Paul publ)

Whilst the works team compounded their success in Europe, a pair of interesting drivers were gaining success in the Rapier in Mexico. Pedro and Ricardo Rodriguez won a convincing 1-2 class victory in Mexico's major race meeting, Ricardo turning in a fastest lap at 69.9mph. On the other side of the world, in Africa, the 1961 East African Safari - a 3200 mile marathon across the lesser known bits of East Africa - provided a fourth overall for the Humber Super Snipe of Lee Talbot/Iqbal and a class win for the Rapier of Valumbia/Bakhsh. 1961 was also the first "rally of the forests" - the RAC Rally. Of 150 starters only 81 managed to finish, and the Rapier Team were very successful, the Peter Harper / Ian Hall car leading the success with a fine 3rd overall behind Eric Carlsson's Saab and Pat Moss's Healey 3000.

Running in parallel with the factory effort, the Sunbeam Alpine was being rallied in Europe and whilst the 1960 Monte resulted in a class win in the 1300 to 1600 GT class, and a third in class on both the Circuit of Ireland and Alpine rallies, the car was never particularly successful. After a further class win on the 1961 Monte and an outright win on the Scottish Rally of that year, the limited success of the Alpine became even more limited and Rootes fell back on the Rapier for its results.

Racing was, perhaps, a little more successful for the Alpine with probably the most notable result being at the 1961 Le Mans 24 hour race where the Harper/Jopp Harrington Alpine Series 2 (3000RW) won the prized Index of Thermal Efficiency. Rootes had been competing, and continued to compete, at Le Mans for a number of years with the Alpine, but had not had too much success.

Thus it was, as the Rapier came to the end of its illustrious rally career, and the Alpine was considered not suitable, the Rootes Competition Department turned towards the Tiger for its next competitive motor car.

The competition department's long involvement with, and support of, racing and rallying meant that the department was well founded, had the rally management organization with the right motor-sport contacts, the technical experience and expertise to provide well built and reliable motor cars, and the very necessary service back-up during the rallies proper.

The Beginnings

The Paddy Hopkirk/Jack Scott Rapier at full speed on the challenging Gavia Pass during the 1960 Coupe des Alpes, where they finished 6th in the Touring Category and 2nd in class. A closer look shows the high standard of preparation of the car and the fact that it remains undamaged a tribute to the skill of the driver. (Paddy Hopkirk)

THE TIGER IN EMBRYO

The Alpine morphs into the potent Tiger.

The Sunbeam Tiger owes its existence to the foresight of two men, Ian Garrad and Carroll Shelby. Ian Garrad (the son of the then Rootes Competition Manager - Norman Garrad - and the West Coast Manager of Rootes American Motors Inc) had long felt that there was an excellent market for a higher performance Sunbeam sports car to supplement the capable Alpine.

The Sunbeam Alpine had been introduced in 1959 and had achieved very good commercial sales in the all-important US market, helped along by competition success in the hands of Stirling Moss and Jack Brabham. Whilst initially designed to compete with the likes of the MGA, it was no match for the MGB and the big Healey. It was clear to Rootes that engine performance had to be lifted if volume sales were to be improved.

Whilst the Alpine engine responded well to tuning, as the Le Mans Alpines had shown, and Jack Brabham - of Grand Prix fame - had been selling tuning kits for the Alpine, Brabham realised that the successful way forward was to fit a larger engine and suggested to Garrad an American V8 as a successor to the 4 cylinder unit.

Rootes Coventry engineers had experimented with every engine in the Rootes portfolio. Initially the Humber Hawk engine was mooted and then the 1600cc Alfa Romeo engine and Daimler's 2.5 litre V8 unit but none of these could meet the requirements of an effective engine installation with minimum production body modifications, and the ideas were dropped.

Ian Garrad was well aware of these early attempts at up-rating the Alpine and in 1962, after watching Shelby's AC Cobras trouncing everything at Riverside, he was prompted to take up Jack Brabham's, and others', suggestion to install a US V8 in the humble Alpine. At first Garrad believed the answer lay with installing the small block Chrysler 216 cu in (3.5-litre) in the Alpine's chassis. Whilst this engine suited the commercial politics of Chrysler's recent investment in Rootes UK, it was too wide for the Alpine chassis.

Most Vee engines have a tendency to be wide at cylinder head level (apart from the few very narrow V engines of the Lancia type) and the replacement engine needed to be narrow enough to fit the width of the existing Alpine engine compartment. Fortunately, the Ford Motor Co. had just developed a new 221 cu in (3.6 litre) overhead valve V8 - the same basic powerplant that Shelby was putting in his early Cobras. Its outstanding feature was Ford's thin-wall casting which produced the lightest V8 in the industry. It was compact and had potential for enlargement, and was soon increased to 260 cu in (4.2 litre) that gave 164 bhp at 4400 rpm with an impressive 258 lb.ft torque at 2200 rpm – an engine that really would 'pull the skin off a rice pudding'. Critically, the Ford engine was just 20 inches across the cylinder banks - in comparison to the Daimler unit that was over 28 inches wide - and that 20 inches would just allow the engine to be slipped into the engine compartment with minimum modification.

The 260 cu in engine had been fitted originally to the Ford Falcon Sprint in late 1962/early 1963, replacing the standard basic 6-cyl in-line 144 cu in engine. This Ford Falcon Futura Sprint was the car that Ford entered for the 1964 Monte Carlo Rally with a 260 engine tuned to 260 bhp. Eight cars were entered and Bo Ljungfeldt was fastest on all of the stages, but was pipped to the overall win by Paddy Hopkirk (on handicap) in the 1071cc (65 cu in) Cooper S. One of the Falcon drivers was Peter Harper, who was perhaps getting in some V8 practice for the 1965 rally. If so, it was obviously time well spent – as his 1965 Monte Carlo result in a Sunbeam Tiger was to show.

The Tiger In Embryo

However, in early 1963, what was now needed was some impetus to initiate the development of the Alpine V8 and the right person to start the ball rolling. Having discarded the idea of using the Chrysler 216 cu in unit, Garrad talked to Doane Spencer and Ken Miles, West Coast racers and engineers familiar with installing V8's in British sports cars and the Ford 260 cu in (4.2-litre) was settled upon.

In February Ian telephoned John Panks – the director of Rootes Motors Inc, America – to expound the proposals. Panks was immediately enthusiastic and arrived in Los Angeles within a few days to mull over the concept with Garrad. The Alpine was racing in America at the time and reasonable results indicated that the chassis was effective but the performance was inadequate compared to the opposition in its class (Class F production). After discussing the sales potential and price estimates, the next step was to see if the engine would actually fit the space available. Following an introduction by the automotive journalist Bill Carroll, Ian turned to Shelby to help make reality the dream of a Sunbeam sports car with sufficient power to compete with E types, Healeys and Porsches.

Carroll Shelby was probably the most experienced exponent of fitting American V8s into English cars at the time and a meeting was set up with Shelby at his workshop at Princeton Drive in Venice, Los Angeles. A fundamental assessment using chalk marks and tape measures showed that it should work, and Panks and Garrad retired to their hotel to figure out a method of persuading the Rootes board to support the idea. Fortuitously, Brian Rootes was visiting San Francisco and it was decided to broach the proposal there and then, and Ian flew up to meet Brian. Their discussion was fruitful and the initial go-ahead was given. In March 1963 Garrad, with Brian Rootes discreet backing in his pocket, agreed an arrangement that in return for US$10,000 (liberated from a Rootes Inc advertising budget) and provision of a base SII Alpine, Shelby's workshop would turn the project around in eight weeks.

The intention then was to commission Shelby to produce the car, but his proposal was rather lengthy for this initial and quick 'look-see', so later that month another less expensive commission was agreed between Garrad and Ken Miles, who had his own workshop as well as racing and working for Shelby. Another SII Alpine was delivered to Miles's workshop for the conversion within the week. At this stage the scuttle, steering, suspension and rear axle were left unaltered, and very successful efforts were made to keep the car looking original. The result showed clearly that the engine would fit, but like all prototypes some work was still needed, the car being nose heavy and the undersized and weak wire wheels and tyres causing problems – mainly from the extra power transmitted to the road. Over the next few weeks of testing, the cooling was improved and the engine moved further back to improve the weight distribution and thus the handling. The rear leaf springs were also modified to prevent wind-up and axle-tramp on acceleration.

In the period that the Miles Alpine had been built and tested, the second prototype from Shelby was nearing completion and this car was meant to be closer to the proposed production standard. The work was given to George Boskoff one of Shelby's engine men and he started by fitting the standard 260 engine and clutch, a four speed manual box and a Ford Galaxie final drive, all connected with a special prop-shaft. The idea of using a worm and sector steering mechanism, as in the early Cobras, gave some problems and this was solved by the use of an MG rack & pinion unit from Doane Spencer's workshop. George Boskoff and later Phil Remington provided the lion's share of the effort on this second prototype and made the ideas work and, when finished, the car was demonstrated to Ian Garrad. The immediate failing was that the axle final ratios were too low and Doane Spencer replaced the Galaxie unit by a Studebaker Champion part, and this proved satisfactory. With the suspension suitably adjusted, Ken Miles took the car to Riverside Raceway for evaluation of the handling and ride, and this was followed by an extensive test schedule involving heavy traffic running and high temperature testing on the roads of the

The Tiger In Embryo

Mojave Desert. John Panks tested both cars at the end of April - both passed with flying colours - and he at once conveyed in a six page memorandum his intense excitement to Brian Rootes, in which he not only proposed several possible approaches to production but also the initial name of the Alpine V8 – The Thunderbolt. The next hurdle was to convince the head of the Rootes family of its suitability for a production vehicle.

The Shelby prototype Palo Alto 2006.

The Miles prototype pictured in 2006. Both cars remain in the U.S.A.

The Tiger In Embryo

In July 1963, a banana boat delivered the Shelby-built Alpine V8 to Southampton docks and Ian with his wife Laura Garrad flew to England to meet brother Lewis to escort the car to the end of its long journey to Coventry. To let Lewis take up the story. "On the Monday morning Ian and I drove the "Beasty" to the Ryton factory to meet Peter Ware the Engineering Director and his assistant Peter Wilson. Ware was not exactly a fan of the project which was quite understandable since he had no knowledge of it. However, he and a lot of other people soon changed their mind when Lord Rootes drove the car and shall we say 'popped his cork'. He loved it and everyone knew better than argue with his Lordship when he was in his enthusiastic mood". Lord Rootes', simple "All right, we'll make it" and his instruction to Engineering management "Make this a top priority " set the Alpine V8 on its way to production.

Having got over this critical hurdle, the problems associated with engine supply and the actual production of the car began. By mid-November 1963, the negotiations between Ford and Rootes were completed and the first 50 production engines were on their way. Also Jensen Motors had been sub-contracted to produce the car as they had the combination of engineering experience with prototype development work, the production capacity to build the car in sufficient numbers and last, but not least, had the space available.

As the two prototypes had been a 'cut-and-shut' build (but professionally accomplished) there were few, if any, drawings of the modifications. Jensen engineers started the work to produce a viable production car in September 1963, producing both drawings and body modifications, and the first project analysis vehicle (Project 870) was on the road by the 14th November 1963. The Project 870 car, now known as the "Alpine 260" was immediately taken on a continental test drive to Milan by Project Engineer Alec Caine and Development Engineer Don Tarbun but not before a short test run by Lord Rootes on 1st December. Later Peter Wilson and Kevin Beattie (Jensen Chief Engineer) drove the car back to Coventry. This testing led to the need for a few modifications, including the rear axle Panhard rod to reduce axle tramp and running the exhaust pipes through, rather than under, the chassis frame. Testing, modification and more testing of engine performance, cooling and fuel consumption continued and by the New Year, the Jensen prototype had covered over 5000 miles in the UK and Europe. The Project 870 car was later designated 'AF1' and delivered to Brian Lister in Cambridge as the basis for a development vehicle for Le Mans.

The second prototype – AF2 – also built up from a SIII Alpine had come through 500 miles of Pave' testing during February without major failure and by early March Jensen had a total of eleven prototypes in development.

In a progress report to Engineering dated 18th March, the status of each Jensen designation of these prototypes by AF (Alpine Ford) disclosed:

The Tiger In Embryo

> **AF1.** At Brian Lister's for Le Mans Conversion. Original engine returned to Jensen.
> **AF2.** 'Pave' now completed. Vehicle now with Service for preparation of Service literature.
> **AF3.** Shipped to Carroll Shelby, USA. Less engine and gearbox.
> **AF4.** Completed 15,000 endurance testing. Inspection now in progress.
> **AF5.** Completed 15,000 endurance testing. Partially stripped for inspection.
> **AF6.** Still in use by Jensen Planning.
> **AF7.** Vehicle transferred to Humber Experimental Dept for general development.
> **AF8.** Despatched to Ladbrooke Hall for preparation and shipping to the New York Show.
> **AF9.** The first pre-production car has now been built.
> **AF10.** The 2nd pre-production car progressing satisfactorily for completion by 20th March 64.
> **AF11.** This vehicle is proceeding in accordance with programme for R.H.D. manual.

Panks and Garrad had recognised early on the importance to prospective sales in the USA of publicity from racing and the Rootes hierarchy agreed that Carroll Shelby should be approached again to construct a race car suitable for Class 'B' production race events. AF3 was flown to California where Shelby's people installed a tuned 260 cu in engine and modified the suspension amongst much else. It seems the factory budget was quite generous on this occasion and reportedly some US $40,000 was spent in support of the car; even stretching to the car being repainted in yellow.

The initial promotion effort for the Shelby competition Tiger was an entry to the B Production Class of Pacific Coast SCCA championships. Unfortunately Shelby's team of engineers was fully stretched by the many demands of other race-car programmes. This meant the soon to be numbered '45 B' Tiger was not properly developed before its first outing in the hands of Lew Spencer at Tucson in April. Whilst observers marked the car out for future success it didn't achieve any at first. This came in June 1964 at Willow Springs where a Rootes press release claimed the "Sunbeam Tiger's First Kill" with these glowing words.

"The Sunbeam Tiger, Rootes' latest sports car won its first competition honours in the Pacific Coast Divisional Championship Races at Willow Springs, California. The Tiger, driven by Lew Spencer, won the Class "B" production event at an average speed of 89mph, finishing 12 seconds ahead of the Jaguar XKE in second place. The British cars fought off a vigorous challenge from strong contingents of Corvettes, Stingrays and Cobras".

To quote Mike Taylor (Tiger – The Making of a Sports Car) " In September of the same year, Lew drove the Tiger in the 200 mile National Sports Car Race at Elkhart Lake, where he finished second overall and first in class. Lew Spencer recalls, 'Apart from the cooling problems, the Tiger was always a little frightening to drive on a race track because of its short wheelbase."

Since the Ford Motor Company demands of Shelby were on the up and the mixed performance of the Tiger was disappointing to Ian Garrad, an approach was made to Doane Spencer to transfer the race team to the Hollywood Sports Car operation. Doane had prepared race-cars over many years and he agreed to take over Rootes US racing ambitions with effect from the 1965 season. The new car (55 B) went on to take the Californian racing scene by storm.

Rootes needed the Tiger to be exhibited and introduced to the American Press and public at the New York 9th International Motor Show in early April 64 – advanced publicity had already been issued to the Rootes distributors in the US – and since no production cars were available yet AF8 was prepared to show standard and shipped to the States.

The Tiger In Embryo

Laguna Seca- June 1964

Still known officially as the 'Sunbeam Alpine 260', all promotion literature and stand displays carried this name at first. Whilst the decision to finally name the car as the 'Sunbeam Tiger' had been made in England in the previous month this was not announced to the US press until 4th April, with the headline "Rootes Let Tiger Loose at Auto Show". Panks and Garrad were not overwhelmed however by the external appearance of the Tiger, due to its close similarity to the Alpine, but in the time available, only one small alteration was made, a horizontal stainless steel strip was added at waist height along with Tiger badging. Yet whilst the US press reviews were initially somewhat lukewarm, the Tiger was a complete success with the discerning public, and Tiger orders constituted a major part of the record Rootes sales figure of over £4 million.

Testing of the AF prototypes continued with two more Series I cars added to the development schedule; AF12 (the 2nd R.H.D. prototype with rear disc brakes) and AF14 (an automatic). Finally, the start of production began in early June 1964 with the first five production Tigers allocated to the Rootes Competition Department for the forthcoming European Rally programme. All initial production of the Tiger was built to export US L.H.D. specification. However, the 'Sunbeam Alpine 260' lived on, since Rootes lawyers had established that due to local brand protection (Panhard Tigre in France & Messerschmitt tg5000 in Germany) the name "Tiger" could not be used in any European country in which these two cars were distributed. So it was decreed in conjunction with Simca of France that the Sunbeam Tiger should be launched and marketed across Europe as the Sunbeam Alpine 260. Two thousand cars had been exported to America before the Tiger was released to the UK market in March 1965 – after an unveiling on the Rootes stand at the 49th International Motor Show at Earls Court in October 1964.

The Tiger In Embryo

The Rootes stand at the 1964 New York Auto Show with Tiger AF8 looking pristine. (Rootes)

AF development 'Tiger' based on SIV Alpine GT – with wire wheels & knock-ons. (Rootes)

The Tiger In Embryo

In the meantime, before the availability of the Tiger on the road in the UK, the Competition Department had been busy at work with the car and the Tiger had started its competition career in both International racing and rallying.

A rare photograph of the Tiger on the Jensen production line. (Birmingham Post & Mail Ltd)

The Tiger In Embryo

Carroll Shelby (left), Lee Iacocca, VP of the Ford Motor Company and John Panks (right), MD of Rootes Motors Inc., at the New York Motor Show. This press release photo text states that 'orders valued at over £ 2,500,000 have already been placed on this car.' (Rootes)

The Tiger In Embryo

Des O'Dell and Ian Garrad with the Sunbeam Tiger Owners Club 1980. (STOC)

Le Mans 1964

A potentially successful concept turns to ashes on the racetrack.

In a similar way that the Monte Carlo Rally was, at that time, the public epitome of rallying, the Le Mans 24 hour race was, undoubtedly, the equivalent in long distance racing. Run annually in early June the event uses the long developed road circuit situated to the south of the town.

The race has, of course, a long and illustrious history. The first 24 hour race, the Grand Prix d'Endurance (Coupe Rudge-Whitworth), was run on the 26 and 27th May 1923. The circuit was made up of the normal unsurfaced public roads of the period, and, typically for the period, was two lengths of ordinary main road, with a minor road joining them to make a rough triangle. The circuit was different to the modern evolvement mainly in the fact that the road continued on after the White House down to a hairpin at the village of Pontlieue, and then returned to meet the later circuit at Tetre Rouge – clearly still seen on the Michelin maps 232 and 517.

ADU 180B photographed just prior to its retirement with a broken crankshaft. (Rootes)

Le Mans 1964

In 1923 the race was won by a 3 litre Cheynard-Walcker, which covered 1372.94 km at an average speed of 57.2 kph. In 5th place overall was a 3 litre Bentley of John F Duff and F C Clement, who returned the following year to win outright. In 1928, and the two following years, the English Bentleys made a habit of winning and established the legend of the Bentleys and Le Mans. However, it took until 1953 for English cars to win again with the 3.4 litre Jaguar C type and the later D types, although the British had always been, like the Monte Carlo Rally, enthusiastic and numerous participants in the event.

Rootes and the Competition Department had been involved with Le Mans for a number of years. In 1961 they had used the Sunbeam Alpine with the attractive Harrington hardtop and had won the much prized, particularly by the French, Index of Thermal Efficiency. This efficiency prize was based on a ton/miles per gallon formula and had been regularly the prize of the smaller engined French cars- the DB Panhards, Alpine-Renaults etc. In that race the Sunbeam Alpine had started with a race weight of 2149.506 lbs and had completed the course at an average fuel consumption of 17.8 mpg and an average speed of 90.919 mph – giving an Index of 1.07 (that is 7% above its target figure). It had finished 16th overall and had beaten the Lotus Elite and DB Panhard into second and third places, both of these with an Index of 1.03.

In 1962 Rootes had entered two Sunbeam Alpines driven by Harper/Procter and Hopkirk/Jopp. The Peter Harper car had finished in a creditable 15th place overall, but the Paddy Hopkirk car had foundered at the 17th hour with engine maladies. The following year two Alpines were again running, driven by Lewis/Ballisat and Harper/Procter again. This time the Harper car lasted only 12 hours, retiring with a blown head gasket and the Lewis/Ballisat car followed 6 hours later with crankshaft problems.

During the early development of the Tiger, Norman Garrad – who had been transferred to the Sales Department from Competitions in February 1964 – had seen the competition potential of the car and, having discussed the idea with Timothy Rootes, drew up a list of events in which he thought the car would be competitive and bring in good publicity – one of which was the Le Mans 24 hour race.

On the basis of the Tigers running in the 'big-boys' class – the Prototypes – and the potential publicity from a good result to help launch the Tiger in America, the Rootes Board had been persuaded into supporting the running of two Tigers for the 1964 race.

The immediate questions for the Competition Department to answer in late December 1963 and into January 1964 were what type of body and who was to be the constructor, who will do the engines and transmission and how much time and money have we got to get it all together?

The first consideration was body shape. One of the Rootes body stylists, Ron Wisdom, had sketched out a most attractive body based closely on the anticipated production Tiger shape, and during January had used the MIRA wind-tunnel with a ¼ scale model to refine the detailed shape. Wisdom used the frontal styling of the Alpine / Tiger up to the 'A' post and with a raked windscreen allowing for a lower profile, designed a fast back body, probably inspired by earlier Harrington designs, and completed the car with a Kamm rear end. The primary aims of the wind tunnel tests were to minimise the drag – without too much modification of the frontal aspect – ensure directional stability up to a speed of 170 mph and in a 30 mph crosswind (which represents a 10 degree yaw in effective head-on wind direction), make sure that engine, rear axle and brake cooling were adequate and that the ventilation of both the driver and engine compartment were acceptable.

From a series of 20 experimental test conditions that were used in the wind-tunnel, there were a number of changes in the cars' dimensions and detail shapes, the shape and protrusion of the windscreen, the blanking of the cooling ducts, the fitting of a rear spoiler and the possible use of flush wheel discs.

Le Mans 1964

Measurements allowed the calculation of the drag and lift coefficients (Cd and CL respectively) at both zero degrees and 10 degrees yaw. To ensure the dynamic stability of the car in crosswinds the aerodynamic centre of pressure (CofP) was calculated as a percentage of the wheelbase aft of the front wheel centreline. As long as the Centre of Gravity (CofG) remains ahead of the CofP of the car, the vehicle remains, inherently stable. As the CoP moves forward and approaches the CofG, and perhaps ends up forward of the CofG, the cars moves from being inherently stable to unstable and this forward movement of the CofP is often a result of crosswinds.

In the Tigers final aerodynamic state, with a four inch spoiler, the full-size car estimate of drag coefficient (Cd) was 0.369 and a Lift Coefficient (CL) of –0.051. At the estimated maximum speed of 170 mph into a direct headwind, this resulted in a drag force of 484 lbs and aerodynamic vertical forces of + 95 lb (lift) on the front axle and –162 lbs (down-force) on the rear. This led to an estimated weight distribution, at 170 mph, of 1253 lbs front and 1418 rear against a static weight distribution of 1348 lb and 1256 lb respectively.

From these tunnel tests and other calculations, the plot of overall drag against engine power (260 bhp) predicted a maximum speed of some 170 mph – a useful speed on the Mulsanne straight.

In 1964, high speed car aerodynamics was still a relatively new 'science', and the airflow engineers at Rootes understood that lift on the rear body, caused by a reduction in pressure from the flow over the rear bodyform, could cause a lightening of the rear end at speed. The use of the small and discrete detachable spoiler was designed to both reduce the drag and assist in the traction of the Tiger. The weight on the rear of the Tiger without the spoiler was 1283 lb and with the spoiler 1418 lb – at 170 mph - showing clearly the increase in dynamic loading. More load on the back of the car to improve traction also meant a lifting of the nose (a loss of only 7 lb load) and the detachable spoiler was meant to be used to determine the best balance during testing of the Tiger at speed. The detailed results of the Rootes Experimental Department Report, dated 4th February 1964 are contained in Appendix 1.

Brian Lister had been chosen as the prime contractor for the work, with Williams & Pritchard shaping the aluminium, and had recommended, as a result of his previous racing experience as a builder and constructor, that a light space frame be built and covered with an aluminium shell closely resembling the production Tiger – to minimise the gross weight. Rootes, however, were insistent that the cars were to be kept as original as possible, even if it meant a resultant weight penalty. Three Tigers were to be built by Ken Hazlewood, "Mr Brian's" project engineer the first of which was to be the development vehicle and the other two were to be the race cars, and all were to be right hand drive cars. Since prototyping of the Tiger had only just commenced the 'Project 870' (AF1) car – 7734 KV - was pressed into a second life and despatched to Lister's to form the basis of the development 'Mule', still bearing its 'Alpine' insignia as the eventual marque name of 'Tiger' was still some months away from being decided upon.

As the Competition Department had no experience at that time of building or running the V-8 engine, four engines had been ordered at the outset from Carroll Shelby, the US racer and manufacturer of the Cobra, who was well experienced in competition preparation of the Ford V-8 engine, and who had been intimately involved in the prototype road cars. He had recommended the standard size 260 cu inch engine to keep the race car as close to the original Tiger production car as possible - in line with the Rootes policy - but modified to give in the region of 275 bhp – over the 164 bhp of the standard car. This had been achieved by the use of twin four-barrel Carter carburettors on a twin intake competition manifold, and a modified camshaft with solid, as distinct from hydraulic cam followers. The cylinder heads were cleaned and modified and a dual-point distributor fitted to allow the engine to rev higher. This was coupled to a Borg Warner T.10 aluminium cased close ratio gearbox with a 3.7: 1 back axle ratio. At the time this represented a pretty standard way of gaining more power without the loss of reliability – of high importance in a 24 hour race.

Le Mans 1964

7734 KV - the 'mule' development car. The neat, and detachable, spoiler is just above the number plate and the car sits well on its 15 inch Dunlop alloy wheels and Dunlop racing tyres. It carries an 'Alpine' script which appears to have been partially obscured on the negative. (Rootes)

Critical issues around cooling had challenged the Jensen development programme for the production car from the outset and extensive Experimental Department reports had been made by Rootes development engineer Don Tarbun on cooling and temperature surveys of the first prototype from as early as December 1963. This was to occupy Lister's Ken Hazlewood's attention as well and at the outset he fitted an oil cooler and a larger radiator core together with under-body air scoops.

As had been the case for the Tour de France Automobile, the use of the standard 13 inch wheel would have resulted in unacceptable tyre stresses, a combination of car weight and tyre linear velocity during the long high speed Mulsanne straight and a 15 inch diameter rim was specified as acceptable. Dunlop had access to a 15 inch magnesium alloy wheel and 32 were purchased by Marcus Chambers, at £38 each – a fairly high price compared to the Minilite wheel later used for the rally cars at around £15 a piece. To these were fitted Dunlop L15 R6 tyres – 6.00 front and 6.50 rear. Hazlewood had also fitted larger 11" Girling disc brakes.

By mid-March Lister's had the development car running and soon afterwards the first Shelby engine arrived for the "Mule" (later to be briefly named 'The Thunderbolt') with a test curve peaking at 275 bhp.

On the 14th April the development car, 7734KV, was collected from Brian Lister's establishment at Cambridge and, next day, given a shakedown at Mallory Park by Keith Ballisat. The Tiger was running 144 lb/inch front springs and 115 lb/inch rear springs, a 13/16 inch rear roll bar and was fitted with the Le Mans Dunlop 6.5L wheels on R6 racing tyres. Apart from adjusting tyre pressures, finding axle tramp during starts, excessive roll in corners and front-end float, there was very little else that could be accomplished in the timescale. The engineers recognised that damper settings needed some urgent work, as did the need to increase spring rates to counter the roll problem and a rear roll bar to help reduce tramp – but in the timescale this would have to be completed during the Le Mans test session in a few days time.

Le Mans 1964

An overhead shot of the 'mule' showing the clean and classic lines developed in the wind-tunnel. (Rootes)

The 'mule' at speed during its first testing at Mallory Park. Keith Ballisat, the competition manager of Shell, conducts this testing session. (Rootes)

Le Mans 1964

A windswept Marcus Chambers, the Rootes Competition Manager, discusses the wayward handling characteristics of the Tiger with Keith Ballisat, prior to tackling the range of problems. (Rootes)

On the 17th, the car left the Coventry Works for Hurn Airport, and, on arriving in France, the Tiger was driven to Le Mans in convoy with the rest of the team. The next morning the team arrived at the pits in good time to start the testing at 10.00am. Peter Procter and Keith Ballisat were the drivers and soon had the car lapping the circuit. Peter Procter takes up the story in the STOC's 'Cats Whiskers'.. "The cars were just finished in time for the test weekend and I set out on a few laps to settle the car in. The cars looked superb. Brian Lister had done a first class job and I was very happy with the driving position. However, the car felt, and was, very heavy. I found I had to work very hard in the faster corners to keep the car balanced and vicious oversteer occurred coming out of the slower corners such as Arnage and Mulsanne. The brakes soon started to overheat and lock up, worse still, the oil pressure disappeared on the slower corners. On reporting these problems, I was surprised to be told by Marcus that perhaps I was pushing the car too hard, even though in all my previous test experience that had been the object. Sadly, in the race week proper, these problems were still manifest."

Mike Parkes, a former Rootes employee, and now driving for Ferrari had wandered across to the Sunbeam pit, no doubt to renew old acquaintances, and had offered to take the Tiger out, and, in view of his wide experience on the circuit, Marcus took up the generous offer. Parkes turned in a time of 4min 26.4 sec, against that of 3 min 47.1 sec of his Ferrari, and confirmed the opinion of the Rootes drivers of poor handling and brakes. Peter Procter had turned in a respectable time of 4 min 33 sec and had been reaching 6000 revs down Mulsanne, which was over 150 mph. Oil pressure problems still persisted and the car was still overheating – which had been improved by a bigger radiator. Mike Parkes

Le Mans 1964

had been polite about the car but inferred that, as the Tiger was no longer in the Alpine class, but now running with the Prototypes, there was much to do to become even marginally competitive.

At the start of the tests, the front spring rates on the Tiger had been increased to 170 lb/inch, by the use of ex-competition Rapier units and the rears remained the same as the Mallory Park test, as did the front roll bar. In spite of these changes the previous problems of excessive roll, axle tramp and front end float persisted.

There was obviously still much to accomplish and with the results of the testing under their belt, the team left on Monday to complete the sorely needed testing at Snetterton, with its long straight and closer proximity to Lister's in Cambridge, or on the banked track at MIRA at Nuneaton – close to the competition department.

On the 29th April the Tiger was taken to Snetterton with Keith Ballisat doing the driving, and the engineers from Rootes and Lister's in attendance, including Brian Lister, Ken Hazlewood, John Goff, (competition engineer), P.D. Joyce (chassis engineer) and numerous engineers and mechanics from both organisations. For this test session a number of changes had been made. Like the later rally cars, the rear spring rates had been raised to 187 lb/inch by the use of the Hillman Husky parts bin, the fronts remaining at 170 lb/inch.

During the tests the dampers were changed to Koni adjustables. After some running the Panhard-rod location was lowered by two inches, with the overall result that the axle tramp was significantly reduced. Keith Ballisat then put in a lap time of 1 min 50 secs without extending the car and thought that a 1 min 45 was on the cards. Mike Parkes had lapped Snetterton in 1 min 39 secs, so the deficit was being reduced. Further testing ensued with more weight lower down in the tail, by the use of a sandbag to simulate a revised petrol tank position, and with the projected use of six inch tyres on the front, a stiffer roll bar and higher rate front springs, some optimism reigned.

The clean and aerodynamic lines of the Le Mans Tiger are an eloquent expression of the design skills of the engineers of Rootes Experimental Department. (Rootes)

Le Mans 1964

The development Le Mans car sitting, in its original aluminium and with wing mirrors, outside the competition department at Humber Road. (Rootes)

Sitting alone in the pits in the wet – perhaps during the fabled French lunch hour – the 'mule' Tiger again shows its classic lines. The three sliding vents on the bonnet have appeared since the early prototypes and were, presumably, to assess whether permanent cooling vents were needed. This was not carried over to the race cars. (Rootes)

Le Mans 1964

The three test drivers - Keith Ballisat, Claude Dubois and Peter Procter - pose with the car in the competitors' parking lot behind the Le Mans pits. (Rootes)

The drivers discuss progress under the watchful eye of the French officials and the press. (Rootes)

Le Mans 1964

Mikes Parkes, watched by L to R. Marcus Chambers, John Rowe, Alec Caine and Peter Wilson, climbs into the Tiger to test the car at the Le Mans test session on the 18th April 1964. A former Rootes employee, Parkes was now a works driver for Ferrari and was testing at the circuit on the same days. (Rootes)

On the 12th May, with one month left before Le Mans, John Goff collected the 4th engine from Shelby and various Cobra parts from Gatwick airport.

On the 14th May, Bernard Unett, a long-time Rootes driver, along with Keith Ballisat, ran the car at Silverstone with the higher rate front springs fitted (200 lb/inch) and a range of anti-roll bars were available. After fitting the 1-inch front anti-roll bar and even higher rate front springs (244 lb/inch), and some spirited driving, Bernard turned in a 1 min 52.2 sec lap, which was considered adequate as the axle ratio was not suitable for Silverstone, but was still not over-impressed with the roadholding. The handling, however, had been greatly improved compared to the previous Snetterton test. From these trials the specification for Le Mans proper was set, and this is presented in Appendix 2, which shows the Rootes Experimental and Engineering Departments report dated 12th August 1964 for the five week development period evaluating handling characteristics and road holding.

Further tests continued at MIRA, on the high-speed banking, and whilst the engine cooling was shown to be effective there were still concerns about high oil temperature and low oil pressures.

On the 4th June, Marcus travelled to Cambridge to review the state of build of the two race cars. Rear axles with a smaller track, to prevent the tyres fouling the rear body, had been requested from Salisburys, and whilst the first had been fitted to the development car, the two for the race cars were running late. This had set Listers back some two weeks, leaving very little time to complete the two cars and deliver them to Coventry to trim the interiors and finish all of those minor, and often not so minor, difficulties that always seem to arise – even in the best prepared of teams.

On Monday, June 15th, the two race cars were

Le Mans 1964

loaded onto the transporter and, after the almost inevitable delays in ensuring that everything is in place, the service cars and team arrived at Hurn Airport, near the south coast resort of Bournemouth, at around 10 am. The race cars and transporter were shipped across to Cherbourg. Lunch was taken south of Cherbourg and upon reaching Le Mans that evening the cars were garaged in the village of Arnage, with the mechanics lodged nearby and the rest of the team in the Hotel de Paris in Le Mans centre. Scrutineering took place next morning on the 16th, Tuesday, and the only minor problem was that car 8 (ADU 179B) had the wrong engine number on the RAC certified paperwork, but this was soon sorted by a representative of the RAC vouching for the authenticity of the Tiger. The fuel tanks were drained in order for the ACO to verify the tank capacity and these turned out at 137 litres and 135 litres for the two cars.

Next day the cars were taken for practice and ADU179B ran its bearings after only one and a half laps, so that was sent off for an engine change. ADU 180B also had some problems, Peter Procter complaining of lack of performance and the continuing lack of oil pressure.

That evening, after the engine change on 179B, Marcus Chambers, along with Jim Ashworth, took the car out on a road test along the long straights of the N23 from Le Mans to La Fleche and in Marcus's words "We went down to the end a couple of times and managed an indicated 150 mph a couple of times, which, at any rate, proved that the headlights were adequate."

However, all of these problems, the lack of much needed development time, the potential difficulties with low oil pressure and high temperatures and the added fact that the cars were 66 lbs heavier than the standard Tiger (2640 lb) and 160 lb heavier than the competition - in the form of the Shelby Cobras (with the 289 cu in engine and 100 bhp more) - led to a feeling of disquiet and disappointment in the team.

Three mechanics/fitters apply finishing touches to the 'No 8' car still to get its Tiger badges. (Rootes)

Le Mans 1964

The two race cars are fitted and fettled at the Competition Department in Humber Road prior to being transported to Le Mans for scrutineering and the 24 hour race proper. (Rootes)

Le Mans 1964

The race cars are completed in the Competition Department after their return from Listers and a final engine tune on the Crypton overseen by Jimmy Blumer and Jim Ashworth. The cars have sprouted footwell vents since the Le Mans test day. (Rootes)

The engine compartment of the race cars showing the twin Carter carburettors. (Rootes)

Le Mans 1964

In order to try and minimise the poor publicity that would seem to be looming, Marcus Chambers rang Peter Wilson in Coventry to discuss the possible withdrawal of the cars before the start. The answer was that, with the time and money already spent on the venture, it would be preferable to start, whatever the outcome.

For the race, the cars were to be driven by the pairings of:

Keith Ballisat and Claude Dubois
ADU 179B   (Car No 8)

Peter Procter and Jimmy Blumer
ADU 180B   (Car No 9)

Both Peter Procter and Claude Dubois had competed previously at Le Mans, Peter with Peter Harper in the 1961 Sunbeam Alpine success and in both '62 and '63, and both of the others had International rallying and racing experience.

On the race day the cars were aligned in their position along the pit counter, ready for the start at 4.00pm, and, as Marcus Chambers plaintively noted, "the best thing that could be said of our cars was that they looked well turned out."

The Ballisat/Dubois car, ADU179B, lasted only 3 hours into the race, retiring with a broken piston, and, although it had reached a speed of 161.6 mph down the Mulsanne straight, was never placed higher than 26th.

ADU 180B had started well and was lapping consistently in the mid field, rising to 20th in the 5th hour. Peter Procter continues: "My co-driver was Jimmy Blumer, a fellow Yorkshireman whom I had known for many years. I elected to start the race (contrary to the Raymond Baxter commentary on the video of Le Mans) and made a good start. In those days, of course, we had to run across the track first; those starts were wonderful. 1964 was my fourth Le Mans and I had learnt in the first year that the crafty ones, like Stirling Moss, stared running about five seconds before the count finished and they never brought you back. To go howling through Dunlop and that heart-stopping spring down to the Esses with a great gaggle of Ferraris, Masers and all sorts was beyond words. Then to drive flat out down the Mulsanne straight and try to get into a five-point seatbelt whilst still overtaking and being overtaken was something else. After one lap though, things settled down, and the car behaved very well. I had got used to number 9's vices and adjusted to suit. The main concern was the engine. As the car drifted through the slower corners, the oil pressure was minimal.

"I handed the car over to Jimmy and gave him as much info as possible whilst the car was being refuelled. Things were going quite well and after a few more changeovers I thought, maybe, we could get a result. It was not to be. I had come through the very tricky White House corner with as much speed on as possible in top. A fast exit here meant that you could pull a lot more revs for about a mile past the pits and Dunlop into the Esses. I was passing the pits flat out in the dark when there was a big explosion and flames shot out from under the bonnet. I stood on the brakes and found that I couldn't turn the steering wheel. I learned afterwards that the blast had jammed the steering with its knuckle joints. In those days, there was no barrier between the track and pits, only a painted line, but it was a very serious offence to cross this. Old number 9 crossed the line and ran up the pit counter taking the door handle off and graunching the side-panels. By a miracle there were no cars in the pit lane being refuelled, otherwise a major disaster would have occurred. Had the explosion occurred anywhere else on the circuit, it would have been a big moment.

"As the car was, by this time, tightly wedged into the pit counter, I climbed out of the nearside door only to be met by a very angry chief pit marshal who shall remain nameless. "Pierre" he said, "You are een terrible trouble, you ave crossed ze line, you cannot do zat. But first we must move ze car." "OK," I said, " you drive and I'll push." He jumped in and then said "But she will not steer!" "Now you know why I parked the ******* thing there in the first place!" I replied.

Le Mans 1964

I then left the scene and made for the nearest bar!"

The Tiger had lasted some 9 hours into the race before the dramatic retirement with a broken crankshaft. At an average speed of around 107 mph, 123 laps had been completed and a speed of 162.2 mph clocked on the Mulsanne straight – close enough to the predicted 170 mph. This far into the race it had risen to 18th position overall, which, perhaps, was a loose indication of its potential.

The failure of the Shelby prepared engines was attributed to slack tolerances, which Marcus Chambers thought also caused the low oil pressures. Marcus notes in his book "We eventually got a refund from Shelby and that was, no doubt, used to buy engines for the rally Tigers."

The Tigers here in the pits ready for the 4 pm start. (Rootes)

Le Mans 1964

The two Tigers take their place in the pits ready for the 4 pm start. (Rootes)

Lining up the Ballisat /Dubois Tiger in the pits beside the 1570cc Alfa Romeo TZ of Biscaldi/ Sala - which finished in 15th place - Ernie Beck keeps an eye on the back of the car. (Rootes)

Le Mans 1964

Peter Procter, Marcus Chambers & Jimmy Blumer await the start at 4 pm. (Rootes)

Claude Dubois and Keith Ballisat similarly wait in the pits prior to the start. (Rootes)

49

Le Mans 1964

ADU 180B sweeps past the 1147cc Hobbs / Slotemaker Triumph Spitfire under the Dunlop Bridge. Both cars were running in the Prototype Class and the Spitfire finished in 21st place. (Rootes)

Le Mans 1964

Claude Dubois brings the Tiger in for, presumably, an unscheduled stop. Peter Procter, from the retired car contemplates the cause - as does engine man Ernie Beck. No pit-wall in the 1960's - only a white line to be crossed at the wrong time under considerable penalty. (Rootes)

Le Mans 1964

In the end ADU 179B and 7734 KV were sold in early 1965 and ADU 180B was kept and loaned by Marcus Chambers to Bernard Unett. With some serious modification, to the rear suspension amid much else and an engine swap for a 289 unit in mid season, the Tiger was very successfully raced in the 1965 Autosport Championship. The season was completed, having competed against the Ginettas, Porsches, Ron Fry's 250LM Ferrari and the Red Rose lightweight E-type of Brian Redman, with Unett achieving 11 wins and 9 second places a 1st in class and 2nd overall in the Championship.

The Le Mans episode had not been a particular success, but, like all competition, within this 'failure' a lot had been learned – the main lesson being that time is needed to be able to produce a good competition car from a standard production vehicle. Adequate finance is also a pre-requisite – but time, unfortunately, cannot be purchased. Rootes had the technical ability, the engineering experience, and the access to the requisite driver testing skills but, as this chapter clearly shows, the available time was just too short.

Marcus Chambers, the incoming Competition Manager, with all his motorsport experience, had been reticent about the ambitious timescales of the programme, but, with the pressure coming from the need for publicity for the launching of the Tiger in the USA, had inherited a fait accompli.

The rally programme had always been the primary target of the Competition Department for the Tiger, and this had been started in a timely fashion, and, of course, was less complex (at least in the build of the vehicle) than the Le Mans cars. The Le Mans cars were in the prototype class, which allowed a wider range of modification to the standard vehicle, whilst the rally cars were classed as a production car and the modifications allowed were more heavily restricted by the FIA for international competition – and, therefore, easier to handle in a shorter time.

Much experience had been assimilated, both negative and positive, and, no doubt, the lessons learned – one of which must have been to keep more control 'in house' - were fed into the forthcoming rally programme.

The end for the Dubois/Ballisat car, clouded in oil smoke from a broken piston. The car had only completed three of the 24 hours and was in 32nd position at its demise. (Michael Cooper)

Le Mans 1964

Pos.	No.	Make and type	Group	cc	Team	1	2	3	4	5	6	7	8	9	10	11	12	13	14	15	16	17	18	19	20	21	22	23	24
1	20	FERRARI 275 P	P	3299	Guichet–Vaccarella	5	3	3	4	2	2	2	2	2	2	1	1	1	1	1	1	1	1	1	1	1	1	1	1
2	14	FERRARI 330 P	P	3972	Bonnier–G. Hill	4	4	4	3	4	3	3	3	3	3	3	5	3	2	2	2	2	2	2	2	2	2	2	2
3	19	FERRARI 330 P	P	3972	Bandini–Surtees	2	1	1	1	1	1	1	1	1	1	2	2	2	3	3	3	3	3	3	3	3	3	3	3
4	5	COBRA FORD Daytona	GT	4727	Gurney–Bondurant	6	7	8	8	8	5	5	4	4	4	4	3	4	5	5	4	4	4	4	4	4	4	4	4
5	24	FERRARI GTO	GT	2953	«Beurlys»–L. Bianchi	18	17	20	18	13	10	12	10	9	7	9	8	7	5	6	6	6	6	5	5	5	5	5	5
6	25	FERRARI GTO	GT	2953	Ireland–Maggs	15	15	15	13	9	8	9	9	8	10	7	10	9	8	7	7	7	6	6	6	6	6	6	6
7	34	PORSCHE 904/4 GTS	GT	1967	Buchet–Ligier	23	22	22	21	18	15	15	14	13	13	12	11	11	9	9	8	8	8	8	7	7	7	7	7
8	33	PORSCHE 904/4 GTS	GT	1967	Ben Pon–Van Zalinge	22	21	23	22	19	16	16	15	15	14	13	13	13	12	11	10	9	9	10	9	9	8	8	8
9	27	FERRARI GTO	GT	2953	Tavano–Grossman	10	18	16	14	10	9	10	8	12	9	8	7	6	6	5	4	4	5	7	7	8	8	9	9
10	31	PORSCHE 904/4 GTS	GT	1967	Koch–Schiller	39	28	27	25	22	19	18	18	16	15	14	14	15	12	11	10	9	10	10	9	10	10	10	10
11	35	PORSCHE 904/4 GTS	GT	1967	Muller–C. Sage	25	26	26	26	23	22	20	20	19	17	17	17	16	16	15	16	15	17	15	14	14	13	12	11
12	32	PORSCHE 904/4 GTS	GT	1967	«Franc»–Kerguen	27	25	25	29	28	24	21	21	19	18	16	16	14	14	13	13	13	12	12	12	13	12	13	12
13	57	ALFA ROMEO TZ	GT	1570	Businello–Deserti	28	29	29	28	25	26	22	22	21	20	18	18	18	15	15	14	14	14	14	13	13	14	14	13
14	1	ISO RIVOLTA Chevrolet	P	5354	Berney–Noblet	16	16	17	15	11	12	13	11	10	11	10	9	13	18	21	19	18	17	16	16	16	16	16	14
15	41	ALFA ROMEO TZ	GT	1570	Biscaldi–Sala	30	31	30	30	27	27	23	23	22	21	19	19	17	17	16	16	16	15	15	15	15	15	15	15
16	23	FERRARI 275 LM	P	3286	Dumay–Langlois	14	14	13	12	16	20	17	16	14	17	15	14	11	8	12	15	15	12	11	11	11	11	11	16
17	46	ALPINE RENAULT M64	P	1149	Delageneste–Morrogh	32	32	33	31	29	28	25	23	22	20	20	19	18	19	18	19	18	17	17	17	17	17	17	17
18	64	A.C. COBRA FORD	GT	4727	De Mortemart–Fraissinet	34	35	36	33	32	30	27	26	25	24	22	23	21	20	19	21	21	19	18	18	18	18	18	18
19	37	M.G. B	GT	1801	Hedges–Hopkirk	35	36	38	36	34	32	28	27	24	23	21	23	22	22	22	22	22	20	19	19	19	19	19	19
20	59	ALPINE RENAULT M63	P	1001	Masson–Zeccoli	52	50	49	46	41	40	37	33	29	25	24	24	23	23	23	23	23	21	20	20	20	20	20	20
21	50	TRIUMPH Spitfire	P	1147	Hobbs–Slotemaker	38	41	41	39	36	37	31	29	27	26	25	25	24	24	25	24	23	22	22	22	21	21	21	21
22	43	LOTUS Elite	GT	1216	C. Hunt–Wagstaff	43	42	40	37	40	35	34	30	31	34	32	31	29	27	27	27	27	25	24	24	24	24	23	22
23	52	RENÉ BONNET Aérodjet	GT	1108	Farjon–S. Lelong	46	46	45	43	40	39	36	32	30	28	26	25	26	24	24	22	24	22	21	21	21	22	22	23
24	53	AUSTIN-HEALEY Sprite	P	1101	Baker–Bradley	41	44	42	41	38	36	32	34	33	31	38	27	26	26	26	26	25	26	26	24	23	23	23	24
25	47	ALPINE RENAULT M63	P	1001	M. Bianchi–Vinatier	33	34	35	32	45	43	40	36	35	32	29	29	30	28	28	28	28	28	28	26	25	25	25	25
	30	PORSCHE 904/8	P	1984	Davis–Mitter	12	11	11	11	7	7	7	7	7	6	6	8	7	13	16	12	12	11 clutch						
	18	ASTON MARTIN DB4	GT	3751	Salmon–Sutcliffe	11	6	14	17	14	11	12	12	12	11	12	10	10	9	11	11 disqualified (oil)								
	48	RENÉ BONNET Aérodjet	P	1150	Bourbon Parme–Bouharde	31	33	34	34	31	31	26	28	26	25	23	22	21	20	20	20 gear box								
	16	JAGUAR E	GT	3781	Lindner–Nocker	19	19	19	20	21	25	33	38	36	35	33	33	31	29	29 blown gasket									
	54	ALPINE RENAULT M63	P	1001	Vidal–Grandsire	45	40	37	35	30	29	29	37	32	30	28	32	32	30 transmission										
	10	FORD GT 40	P	4181	P. Hill–McLaren	44	38	28	23	17	13	8	6	5	5	5	4 gear box												
	65	TRIUMPH Spitfire	P	1147	Marnat–Piot	42	43	43	42	39	35	35	30	28	27	24	27	28 accident											
	45	CD 3 PANHARD	P	1191	P. Lelong–Verrier	51	48	48	47	44	41	38	35	33	31	30	30 transmission												
	21	FERRARI 275 P	P	3294	Parkes–Scarfiotti	50	49	44	45	37	33	39	39	38	36	34 oil pump													
	29	PORSCHE 904/8	P	1981	E. Barth–Linge	9	8	10	10	6	6	6	5	6	8 clutch														
	6	COBRA FORD Daytona	GT	4727	Amon–Neerpasch	13	12	9	9	5	4	4	17	17	16 disqualified (battery)														
	9	SUNBEAM Tiger Ford	P	4267	Blumer–Procter	24	24	24	24	20	21	19	19	18 engine															
	44	CD 3 PANHARD	P	1191	Berthaut–Guilhaudin	48	47	47	50	47	45	41	40	37 engine															
	26	FERRARI GTO	GT	2953	Hugus–Rosinski	21	23	21	19	15	14	14	13 back axle																
	2	MASERATI 151/3	P	4941	Simon–Trintignant	17	10	7	7	3	18	24	24 short circuit																
	17	JAGUAR E	GT	3781	Lumsden–Sargent	20	20	18	16	12	17	34 gear box																	
	3	A.C. COBRA	GT	4727	Sears–Bolton	7	13	12	27	24	23 accident																		
	22	FERRARI 275 P	P	3290	Baghetti–Maglioli	54	53	51	49	42	38 left the road																		
	55	RENÉ BONNET Aérodjet	P	1001	Beltoise–Laureau	49	51	50	48	43	44 fuel pump																		
	56	RENÉ BONNET Aérodjet	P	1001	P. Monneret–Rudaz	36	37	39	37	33	42 engine																		
	11	FORD GT 40	P	4181	Ginther–Gregory	1	2	2	2	26 gear box																			
	60	RENÉ BONNET Aérodjet	P	1150	Basini–Charrière	37	39	46	44	44 engine																			
	15	FERRARI 330 P	P	3969	P. Rodriguez–Hudson	3	5	5	5 blown gasket																				
	12	FORD GT 40	P	4181	Schlesser–Attwood	8	9	6	6 fire																				
	40	ALFA ROMEO GTZ	GT	1570	Masoero–Rolland	29	30	31	38 left the road																				
	48	SUNBEAM TIGER FORD	P	4260	Dubois–Ballisat	26	27	32 engine																					
	49	TRIUMPH Spitfire	P	1147	Rothschild–Tullius	40	45 accident																						
	42	DEEP SANDERSON 301	P	1293	Lawrence–Spice	47	52 overheated																						
	38	LOTUS Elan	P	1593	Gele–Richard	53	44 overheated																						
	58	FERRARI 275 LM	P	3286	Piper–Rindt	oil pipe																							

The hour by hour running history of the 1964 Le Mans. (from 'The Le Mans 24 hr Race' Christian Moity)

Le Mans 1964

Keith Ballisat

Claude Dubois & Keith Ballisat

The Competition Manager for the oil company Shell International, Keith had been involved with competition since 1949, starting in motorcycle trials. He competed in the Scottish Six Day Trials in the early '50s, and won the Newcomer's Award on a 500T Norton.. Continuing his motor-cycling - a works Ariel in '53 - he transferred to four-wheels in a Morris Minor in '54 and then on to a TR2 in 1955 – his driving skills in this car leading to a place in the Triumph works team. He entered the 1958 Alpine Rally in his TR3 and partnered by Alain Bertaut, finished in fourth place overall behind three Alfa-Romeo Giuliettas, and winning a coveted Coupe des Alpes. In 1959 he finished second on the Tulip and sixth in the Liege-Rome-Liege, but rallying was clashing with work and he took to the less time consuming circuit racing with a Formula 2 Cooper-Climax. Ken Tyrell signed him for a FJ drive in 1960 and in that year he also drove a Triumph TRS at Le Mans. Rallying, however, was still in his blood and links with Rootes were forged at a time when the Rapiers were starting to become un-competitive. In spite of this handicap he still managed fifth place on the Acropolis, seventh in the Alpine and a fifth place Touring Car award, and first in class, on the 1962 Tour de France – with 'Tiny' Lewis. With these levels of experience he was a natural for Marcus Chambers to use to help develop the Le Mans Tigers and to compete in the race proper.

Claude Dubois

Claude Dubois began racing in 1953 and in a career spanning 14 years he drove on eight occasions at Le Mans. He won his first race at Spa in his own Triumph TR2. Claude drove for several teams including the Belgian National Race Team, Ecurie Francochamps, Ecurie de Montaigu and several manufacturers – Triumph, Abarth, Renault and Rootes. His introduction to Rootes cam through his racing association with Shell Oil and it was Keith Ballisat who asked Claude to co-drive with him the No 8 Tiger at Le Mans. He was the sole distributor for the Benelux countries of AC cars, Shelby Cobra, Ford GT40 and de Tomaso and he went on, later, to to establish Chrysler Belgium.

Jimmy Blumer

Jimmy Blumer's competition life began at the age 18 with an entry of a 1938 Morris 10 in the 1950 Monte Carlo. In the 50's he drove in the Monte in various cars before moving onto sprints and hill climbing and becoming a circuit racer in the ex-Moss Cooper 1100 Bobtail in 1957. Throughout the 50's Jimmy drove numerous cars and had many wins and places, including in 1958 doing the first 100 mph lap in an Lotus X1 1100cc chasing Jim Clark in the D Type at Full Sutton. Approached by Daniel Richmond to drive the then unseen small BMC for 1960 he had tremendous fun with the early 850cc Mini doing a lot of development races in Minis and later that year in the new Cooper Monaco 2 litre in which he had numerous victories across Europe before joining Ecurie Ecosse to drive their 2.5 Monaco and the Tojeiro EE. In 1963 he was asked by Alan Mann to drive the new Cortina GT and this led in 1964 to Marcus Chambers inviting Jimmy to drive one of the Lister constructed Tigers at Le Mans.

Le Mans 1964

Peter Procter

Peter started racing in 1955 with an Aston Martin DB24. He then bought a Cooper Norton 500 and enjoyed several wins at a National level. He has driven for some famous names such as Ken Tyrell Team Lotus, Alexis and Gemini. In 1964 he drove the Team Lotus F2 car to 2nd place at the Berlin Grand Prix. He also scored a fifth place at Clermont Ferrand. Furthermore in 1964 he won the Tour De France in a Mustang with Andrew Cowan. He also competed at Le Mans between 1961 and 1964 driving for the Rootes team. Most notably winning in 1961 the much coveted "Index of Thermal Efficiency" with Peter Harper in a Sunbeam Alpine Harrington. Other endurance races included the Sebring 12hrs both in 1961 and 1962. He was also 1st with Sir John Whitmore in the 6hr Saloon Car Championship. Peter also competed in rallying and drove a Sunbeam Rapier for the Rootes Group in the Monte Carlo and also drove for the Ford Motor Company. He took part in many international events including the Monte Carlo (8 times), RAC (7 times), Alpine, Tulip, Liege-Sofia-Liege and the Acropolis.

Prior to motor racing, Peter was a professional and celebrated cyclist. He rode for Great Britain in two World Championships and won many events including the British Hill-Climb Championship ('King of the Mountains').

In 2002 Peter again drove the No 9 Le Mans '64 entry Tiger in the Le Mans Classic as well as in the Goodwood Revival "TT". Peter is the Honorary President of the Sunbeam Tiger Owners Club.

Le Mans 1964

Peter Procter - Woodcote Chicane
Goodwood Revival Meeting - TT, 2002
Copyright: Michael Cooper

The Le Mans Tigers live on in Historic Racing

Top to Bottom:

ADU180B
ADU179B
7734KV 'The Mule'.

The Prelude

The Tiger's first steps into rallying, suitably hidden from prying eyes.

Within the time available before competing as a Rootes Team in the Geneva Rally at the end of October of that year (1964), and whilst the first rally cars were being built from the first production cars (ADU 311B, AHP293B, 294B & 295B were all built in June 1964, but were not available for test due to minor problems in build), Marcus Chambers wanted to carry out an appraisal trip to get an early idea of the capability of the cars for rallying and to assess any potential weaknesses. Because the early rally cars were not available, a development car was used and on the 12th July Marcus Chambers, Peter Riley, Tiny Lewis, John Goff (the engineer) and Gerry Spencer, in the estate car, travelled initially to Dover to catch the 23.00hrs boat to Dunkirk, en route to Grenoble for the first tests on the Col de Menee and Col de Rousset. Apart from a little panel beating on the front wings to clear the tyres and the panhard-rod bracket weld failing, the tests were considered successful and the team pushed on to Die for breakfast. Despite being Bastille day (14th July), a garage was found in Carpenteras where the panhard-rod bracket was reunited with its chassis and the car and team were ready for an early start for Mont Ventoux, the classic hill climb featured in the European Mountain championship. In these series of climbs the primary purpose was to assess the efficacy of the engine cooling, for which there was some concern, and during the runs from Bedoin up to the summit, where the control for the Coupes des Alpes rally is traditionally situated, the engine temperature continued to rise during the whole of the run. But, by removing the bar across the radiator surround and a fog lamp, the temperature dropped by some 8 deg C, which was considered acceptable without any drastic alterations to the cooling system - that was to come later! By lunchtime the tests were complete, after a number of runs up the mountain and the team left for an overnight stop at Le Logis-de-Pin.

An early 4.30 start next morning saw Marcus Chambers and Gerry Spencer leaving for Sigale with the Tiger arriving from Entrevaux half an hour after the estate car, and the team discussed the plans for the day over breakfast in the cafe in the Church Square. More tests were carried out and the team returned to the previous night's residence, the Ferme Napolean, after dropping John Goff at Nice Airport for a return flight to London.

Yet another early start at 5.00am - early starts seemingly a definitive requirement of rallying, either during testing or in anger - led to a two hour run to the Col d'Allos (2240m) for further runs up and down the Col. One decision at that point was that the axle ratio was too high, but the test was terminated by Tiny Lewis and Peter Riley making head on contact with a Renault Dauphine on a blind hairpin, with no more serious consequences than a written-off Dauphine. Several hours were lost whilst Tiny & Peter called out a recovery vehicle from a garage in St Andre-les-Alpes, before sorting the Tiger and continuing through Barcolonette for lunch and thence to Briancon overnight. The next day was a series of tests over the Col de Lauteret (2058m), the Galibier (2640m) and the Col du Telegraphie (1570m) before heading for St Claude via Frangy and Bellegarde for the overnight stop.

A final day's testing on the Ballon d'Alsace, reached through the Col de Bussang and Col de Bramont, finished the testing schedule and the convoy returned to the channel ports, and England the next day, and consolidated their thoughts on the strengths and weaknesses of the Tiger for International Rallying.

To start the rallying programme, it had been proposed that the Tour de France, run in late September of that year, would be a suitable rally debut for the Tiger, with good potential for public-

The Prelude

ity if the event provided the right results. Ian Hall, nominated as the rally co-ordinator, was told to start the organisation of the booking of hotels, working out the recce schedules, opening negotiations with potential crews and also to start to prepare a team of three Tigers.

However, this years' Tour included eight circuit races of between 1 and 2 hours duration, as well as nine hill climbs, including Mont Ventoux. With rapid circuits like Le Mans, Monza, Reims, Cognac, Albi, Pau and Clermond Ferrand, a large percentage of the circuit running would be at full throttle. Within the Tiger's Touring Class were the Ford Mustangs driven by the rally team's future crewmembers Peter Harper, Andrew Cowan and David Pollard. Whilst the Tiger would have undoubtedly competed well, Peter Riley, who had competed in the Tour de France previously, considered that the problems of engine cooling may well have limited the Tiger's performance, particularly with the amount of full throttle driving. The nail in the coffin, however, was a combination of the Tiger's 13-inch wheels, the potential top speed in its homologated form and a gross weight of between 23 and 25 cwt. With such small wheels, the continuous high speeds and the elevated tyre contact loads from the substantial weights, Dunlop were unable to sanction the use of their tyres on the circuit sections, due to worries of unreliability and safety, and consequently the scheme was abandoned. Unfortunately the Tigers Le Mans wheels (15 inch) could not be used as the Tiger was only homologated for rallying on 13-inch rims.

'Tiny' Lewis looks pleased at the Tiger's performance. (via Ian Hall)

The Prelude

The result of the Touring Category in the Tour de France bode well in some way for the Tiger team, however, as Andrew Cowan & Peter Procter won the class in their Mustang, with the Peter Harper/ David Pollard Mustang a very close second. Had it not been for a 15km penalty for Harper for a parc-ferme push-start, he would have just pipped the Procter car by just some 5km in some 2000km of competitive motoring - just one quarter of one percent in almost a week's motoring.

Since the Tour de France was a non starter, Marcus Chambers decided that it would be appropriate to do a low key entry into another rally before the Geneva as an experimental baptism of (low key) fire for the Tiger.

At the same time as the Tour de France, in the Italian Dolomites, around Cortina d'Ampezzo, the first international rally of the San Martino di Castrozza was being inaugurated on the 12th to 14th September. An entry in this rally would not only prove a useful evaluation under true rally conditions in the mountains, but if it failed no one would notice, and if it succeeded it would boost the teams credibility. Ian Hall also noted.... "Even better, this Dolomites rally finished a week or two before the Geneva so we could recce that on the way home....."

The car to be used was the first rally car built (ADU311B), complete with wing vents (à la Healey) and the new TechDel Minilite magnesium wheels.

A relaxed Ian Hall waits for the "off". (via Ian Hall)

The Prelude

'Tiny' Lewis and Ian Hall take on the Italian opposition in the Dolomites. (via Ian Hall)

Ian Hall takes up the story...."thus Tiny (IDL) Lewis and I took ADU311B via Ostende to the Dolomites. The car was prepared very hurriedly but proved fast and reliable except for one important detail. A 20-gallon tank had been homologated for the rally cars, and the first of the new tanks was put in the boot about a day before departure. At the last minute (there were a lot of last minutes in the Competition Department in those days!), it was realised that the standard fuel gauge would need modifying. This was done at the last minute, but not calibrated properly as it turned out; and 'Tiny' and I shot off to the ferry with the assumption that when the gauge showed empty there was still something like 8 gallons in the new tank. We monitored this on the way down and felt that we had got the hang of it just about the time it ran out of petrol on the Autobahn near the Austrian border. A fully organised passing Beetle owner sold us 5 litres which got us to a pump.

"Problem number two came when the organisers didn't like our homologation form, which I think was a primitive photocopy of the draft one submitted to the RAC. Down Cortina way they had never heard of a Sunbeam Tiger V8 and not surprisingly were most suspicious.

"We knew that in fact the RAC had approved the papers a few days before and, in truth, it was as legal as anybody else's homologation papers in those days. Numerous 'phone calls to Coventry, London, Milan and Geneva (not so easy in 1964!) finally got the matter sorted out. Someone must have put in a lot of work to do this back in the UK on a Friday afternoon.

"The rally was super – short sharp sections over steep minor alpine tracks and a very tight schedule. The only opposition in the big GT class was an unsuitable amateur big Yank, a Studebaker Avanti, I think, which crashed out very early on. Sadly no Ferraris, but the 1600 Alfa-Romeo Tubolaris' crews were totally demoralised by the Tiger's performance as they clearly thought that it was a pushrod Sunbeam Alpine; an impression we did nothing to discourage." Ian

The Prelude

continues..."during this first night of furious motoring the Tiger slid into a control with about 59secs to spare. One of the Alfas (1600, twin-cam, dual Webers, bright red, alloy wheels, racing tyres etc. etc...) slides to a halt beside us, and the pilot shouts something in Italian to me. I only half hear and then we're gone.... I think over what I've heard..."Mille seicento, mille seicento ???" Clearly he thinks this is an Alpine. Next control - same performance. He gets away in front of us. 'Tiny' overtakes him uphill between two lacets at about 5,500 in 2nd. Next time we stop I nod amiably and say "Si, si, mille seicento!" Italian goes pale, mouth drops open, hands in the air and last seen shouting "Mama mia, mille seicento!"

"Sadly, after about seven hours or so of this, our rally came to an end. You've guessed it - we ran out of fuel when fully wound up and going well, the gauge still resolutely showing around the quarter full mark. My recollection is that we coasted some 14km downhill to get some benzina before heading off to bed. A sad end, but quite a lot had been learned about the new car.

"Thus to Geneva where we picked up the route book and did a seven day detailed recce of the whole route, start to finish, and then straight back to Coventry after dropping 'Tiny' off in Bristol.

"I remember stopping from about 110 mph at a traffic census near Amesbury or somewhere. Asked where we had come from I said "Geneva." The man said "No, today sir?" I said "Geneva." He enquired my destination. I said "Coventry." He looked down the road to the West Country, looked back at me and said "I see sir." I hope it helped his census."

On the return to Coventry, the diagnosis of the San Martino di Castrozza was discussed and the final preparations made for the Geneva rally for a team of three Tigers and the supporting service and management crews.

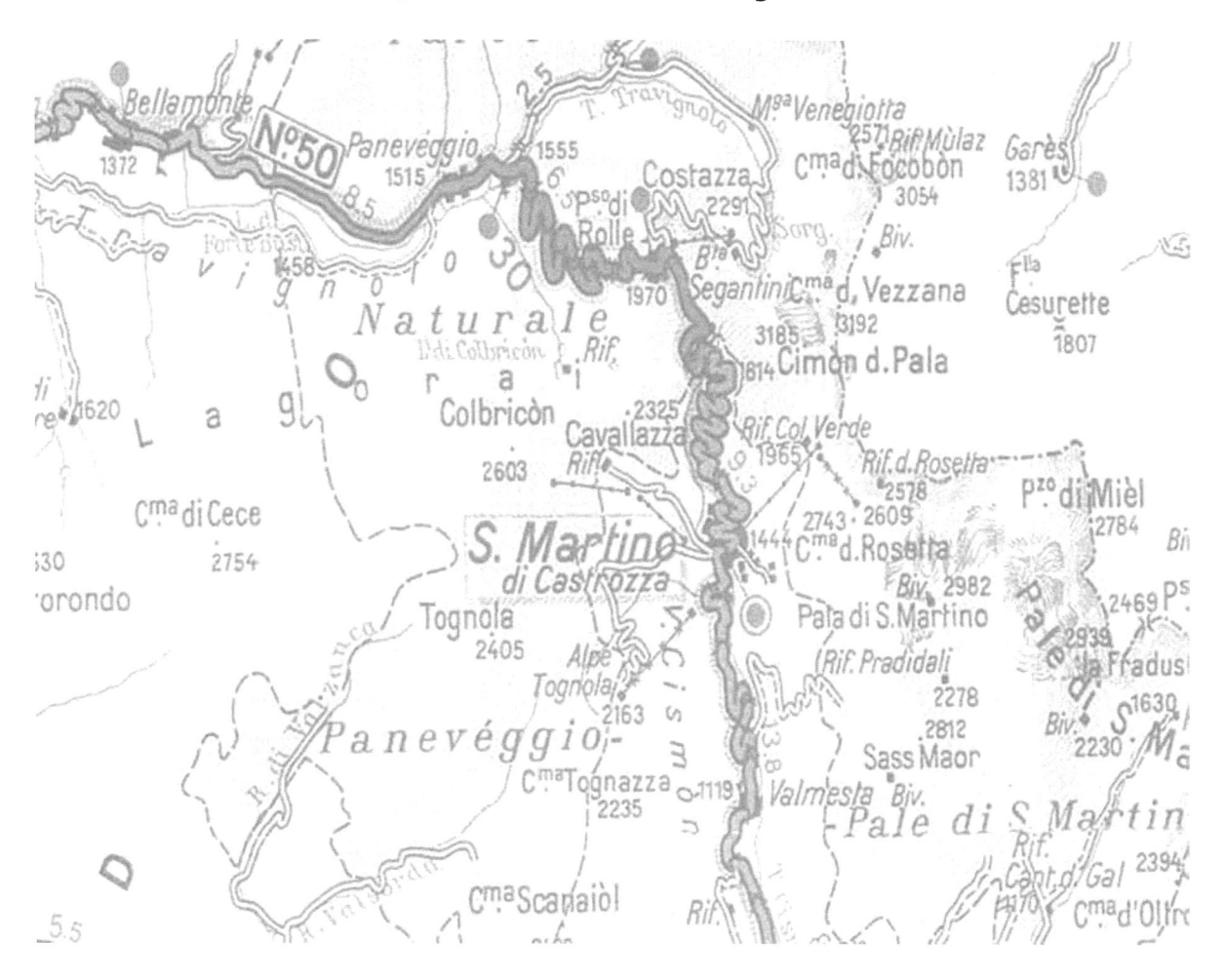

The Prelude

'Tiny' Lewis

A motor engineer and garage owner from Bristol, 'Tiny' (Ian) started competing from a young age and found that the love of motorsport had exceeded his strong interest in his business – not an unusual occurrence at this time in the motorsport arena. Nicknamed 'Tiny' for the usual reasons, this 6ft 3in driver drove a wide range of cars in his career, although he remained basically true to the Rootes marque, and he led the team year after year. Marcus Chambers remembers 'He had all the qualities that go to make a good team driver and test driver. He was also blessed with a good sense of humour, even in adversity'. Prior to his involvement with Rootes he drove the Triumph Herald on several Tulip rallies – finishing 38th on the 1960 event – before changing to a Rapier. On the 1963 RAC Rally he finished 4th overall – in spite of a damaged front wishbone – and led the Rapiers to a and 1st and 2nd in the 1000 to 1600 cc class for Touring cars. His San Martino, Geneva and Alpine rallies in the Tiger were followed by drives in the early rally development of the Imp, which was crowned in 1965 by a 2nd overall on the Tulip rally - co-driven by David Pollard - behind the Rosemary Smith/ Val Domleo Imp.

Geneva Rally 1964

A 1-2-3 in class for the Tiger on its International debut.

Robin Turvey and Peter Riley await the start of the Geneva Rally 1964. (Rootes)

Aptly described by Stuart Turner as one of the most underrated rallies on the calendar, with brisk road sections interspersed with several tests, the Geneva Rally of 1964 was not only the last but one rally counting for the European Championship, but also included the national championships of Switzerland, France and Germany, thus ensuring a good entry.

A route, some 2000km in length, ran through the French and Italian Alps using many of the famous hill climb sections, and, being October, the weather forecast was for rain and light snow during the rally - a forecast which, unfortunately, proved accurate. For the Tiger, this rally was its European debut and was welcome in that it provided a new contender in the big GT class, which had long been dominated by the successful Austin Healey 3000. Three Tigers had been entered from Humber Road and were fitted with Shelby engines, a Holley carburettor, polished heads and a higher performance camshaft with solid cam followers to allow the engine to rev above its normal maximum.

On the 12th October the three Tigers and two service cars were airlifted from Baginton Airport, Coventry, to Calais, prior to an overnight halt at

Geneva Rally 1964

The 'Tiny' Lewis/Barry Hughes Tiger waits to have the honour of being the first car away on the 1964 Geneva Rally, followed by the Riley/Turvey Tiger. (Photo Wasserman)

Troyes, with Geneva the final destination next day. In spite of the excellent preparation, and as inevitably found on the best prepared rally car, there were several minor, and not so minor, problems before the rally. On the run down, Peter Riley's car started misfiring, and this was quickly traced to the dual point distributor contact set problems, which was rapidly solved. But a more serious problem was found on 'Tiny' Lewis's car when a drive fault was diagnosed as a clutch problem and the linings were found to be burnt out. A not usual overnight session was spent by the mechanics on the car, and the clutches on this car, and the other two, were changed well in time for scrutineering at 14.00hrs on the Thursday and the start at 17.00hrs.

72 crews left the start at Plainpalais, near the hall where the Geneva Motor Show is held, 23 in the GT class and the remainder in the Touring category, and, in the late afternoon, followed a devious route around the Southern half of the city in cold, light rain and grey skies to the first test at the Col de Marchairuz. This test was a hill climb of 5.5km in length and very wet with the almost perfect tarmac surface quite slippery. Fastest up the hill was Heinz Schiller in his Porsche 904, with Peter Riley's Tiger putting up the next fastest GT class time followed closely by the Spitfires of Terry Hunter and Jean-Jaques Thuner.

The route now led directly into France for the second test on the Col de la Faucille, an 11km stage tackled in heavy rain. Fastest time was made by Henri Greder in his 4.7 litre V8 Ford Falcon in 7min 33secs (with the enlarged version of the engine in the Tiger). Thuner in his Spitfire, who knew the hill well, put up a time of 7min 52secs, which was well matched by Peter Riley in the Tiger. The handicap system, however, penalised the large GT cars like the

Geneva Rally 1964

Tiger and favoured the more nimble, but smaller engined, Spitfires and also cars like the Group 1 Ford Falcon of Greder. Schiller was again fast up the hill in his Porsche, but he retired immediately after these two hills and John Davenport noted in his report in Motoring News that "it was rumoured that he just liked to go out and show that he could go up these two hills faster than anyone else" - but this did mean one less, however, in the Tiger class.

Peter Riley and Robin Turvey provide some potential competition in the big-engined class on the Geneva Rally, but were limited in their overall success partially by the handicapping system, which favoured the Group 1 cars. (Photo Wasserman)

Geneva Rally 1964

Barry Hughes and 'Tiny' Lewis before the start of the Geneva, after their overnight clutch change. Not a racing overall in sight! (Rootes)

The next épreuve was just off the main road near Nantua at Les Neyrolles, a stage that will be remembered by many drivers for its first hairpin, which is concealed by a slight browl In the GT class Terry Hunter was fastest at 5mins 28secs. A tight road section from Hautville, followed by a more relaxed section leading into Chambery then ensued, with the route leading through St.Lauret du Dont via Quaix and over the Charmette. From St.Lauret the cars motored on in the evening to St.Jean En Royans where the 21km "circuit" to the Cime du Mas was to be tackled. The weather had meanwhile improved and the conditions were now fine and dry. Although the road through the woods at the top of the climb was still wet, Greder easily put up the faster time, with 15secs in hand on his set time. Leaving St.Jean, the route led down the Rousset to Die and along the main road to Recoubeam, where an extremely rapid section over the Col de Pennes was scheduled. The ascent through Jansac was very gritty and several cars left the road. The three Tigers, however, completed this section without trouble and the following short run through the rising dawn for a one-hour neutralisation halt at Bedoin, which lay at the foot of Mont Ventoux.

Immediately following this short breakfast break - typically French, with its rolls and coffee - the hill climb ran up to the turn off Chalet Reynard, a distance of 14.5km. From the top of Ventoux, and perhaps for reasons of daylight, the pace on the road sections eased considerably and the route led from its most southern most point over the Alpes through Laragne and Guillestre towards the Italian frontier and the épreuve using the Cesana-Sestriere hill climb.

Geneva Rally 1964

Rosemary Smith at the start control with Margaret Mackenzie, head down, hard at work. (Rootes)

The Rosemary Smith Tiger tackles the last hill climb of the event, La Muraz in the wet and with the bonnet held closed by a non-production item - two rubber bungys. (Photo Wasserman)

Geneva Rally 1964

However, the route had been changed at Guillestre to by-pass the section over the Col d'Isoard which was blocked by snow, and re-routed along the main N94 road through Briancon and over the Col de Montgenevre, which, at 1850m, is some 510m lower than the Isoard. There followed a long and easy run to Almese, to the west of Turin, and whilst it was a relatively easy road section, there were some difficulties with the timing and situation of the time controls, so virtually everyone treated it as a flat out section - compared by one competitor to a game of Russian roulette - but as the final control was where it was supposed to be, everyone had time in hand. From this control the autostrada was used to Aosta, and then over the St.Bernard Pass (or through the newly opened tunnel as some confusion arose through differing instructions) to the Champex special stage and a tight road section where each minute of lateness resulted in a 100-point penalty. This section was only 21km long and apart from a short section on reasonably surfaced roads, the remainder was on unsurfaced roads, liberally sprinkled with hairpins. 'Tiny' Lewis was one of the few who completed this difficult road section without penalty, a notable achievement. The rally now returned to France and over the snow covered Col de la Forclaz for a seven-hour neutralisation halt at Chamonix, where the crews could grab some food and sleep.

Just before the control at Chamonix, 'Tiny' Lewis made an important discovery. The Tigers had still been experiencing overheating problems, in spite of the work in improving the airflow to the radiator, and the additional fitment of a larger radiator and high flow water pumps. However, at this time, 'Tiny' found that above engine speeds of around 4000 rev/min, the flow from the big water pump created such a pressure reduction that the bottom hose collapsed, thus diminishing the coolant flow through the radiator, a problem solved by getting the mechanics to fit a copper-wire coil inside the hose - a solution which greatly alleviated the overheating problems.

At three o'clock in the morning and after a service of all three Tigers, the cars pulled out of Chamonix for the third time and the final leg back to Geneva. The first test at St Joux de Vertes at Montriond was cancelled due to heavy falls of snow - and the crews embarked on a long re-route that took them south of Geneva to the foot of Mount Revard. Whilst there was snow at the top of the climb, it was not sufficient to stop the climb going ahead, and as the snow was only on the last 2.5km, it was not considered worth fitting studded tyres. Whilst Henri Greder put up the fastest overall time, as distinct from handicap time, of 7mins 47secs, 'Tiny' Lewis pulled out all the stops and returned the fastest GT class time of 7mins 54secs, which was equalled only by Meyer in his Porsche Carrera. An easy road section to Beafort led to a section that was rumoured to be tight as well as icy - and although it was not as icy as expected, many competitors had minor excursions into the scenery, especially on the descent to the Barrage de Roselund. Snow also caused a few problems on the next section, which although easy, led over the snow covered Col de la Colombiere. Peter Riley and Robin Turvey ground to a halt in their Tiger, wheels spinning, but persuaded two Italian spectators to sit on the boot until they reached the top of the Col. Meanwhile Rosemary Smith and Margaret Mackenzie, who were moving along with no problems, stopped to help and then found themselves immobile. However, luck (and skill) was on their side and they managed to get going again. One remaining tight section round Mont Saxonne, made even tighter by a mistake in the Shell navigation notes, led to the final épreuve of la Muraz which led up the back road to the top of Mont Saleve.

The final run into Geneva and the finish was something of a road-race, as had been many of the other road sections - even in daylight - since virtually all of the foreigners had no idea as to where the Stadium was situated. This led to the navigators' nightmare of getting lost in towns - Willy Cave regularly carried a relevant Michelin Guide to help ameliorate this problem - and Margaret Mackenzie unfortunately fell foul to this easily occurring problem and lost a place in the final order as well as the Manufacturers' Cup. As Rosemary Smith noted "Marcus was

Geneva Rally 1964

jumping up and down at the finish."

However, the Tigers were classified in the first three places of the big GT class (over 2500cc) – a significant success.

Of the 37 finishers, 'Tiny' Lewis and Barry Hughes were in 11th place overall with 571 penalties, one place ahead of Barry Williams and John Davenport in their 1071 Cooper 'S'. Peter Riley and Robin Turvey finished in 15th position with 1150 penalties with the final Tiger of Rosemary Smith and Margaret Mackenzie finishing in 20th place.

So in their first international outing the Tigers had performed reliably and consistently, winning their class well, but as was to be found in later continental rallies, the handicap system was against them. The handicap required that the larger engined cars or cars entered in the higher groups (e.g. the GT group) - or in the case of the Tigers, both - needed to achieve considerably faster times than their smaller engined contemporaries to avoid penalties. Thus the Group 1 cars had the advantage and the Group 1 Ford Falcon of Henri Greder with its 4.7 litre V-8 engine was the expected, but no less worthy, winner.

The class winning crews, with competition manager Marcus Chambers in the background. (Rootes)

Geneva Rally 1964

Rosemary Smith

A resident of Dublin, Rosemary started business with her own fashion design business and one of her first commissions was for a lady driver who competed in Irish Rallying and liked to have tailored jump-suits made for the purpose of driving. She soon asked Rosemary to navigate in a local rally where it soon became apparent that navigating was not Rosemary's forte and they switched places. Taking part in the 1960 RAC rally followed – with little success – but the following year, with Sally Cooper, she competed in the Monte Carlo Rally and they finished in the top five. This caught the eye of the then Rootes Competition Manager, Norman Garrad, and Rosemary was offered a place in the works team to replace Mary Handley-Page. Following her inclusion in the team, she regularly won the Coupe des Dames Trophies as well as many class and outright wins. In 1965 she won the Tulip Rally outright but she was robbed of the 1966 Monte Carlo Ladies Cup when, along with the BMC Mini Cooper team and others, she was disqualified in the 'lighting row'.

Rosemary Smith helps publicise the Tiger win at the 1964 49th International Motor Show at Earls Court. Rootes also gained 2nd place in the Manufacturers Team Prize.

Geneva Rally 1964

The drivers view of the Geneva Rally: the following seven pages contain the comments on the rally from Peter Riley in the post rally questionnaire - with a combination of excellent punctuation and some interesting thoughts.

ROOTES GROUP

COMPETITIONS REPORT FORM

File. Rally Misc

RALLY... Geneva 1964............... APPROX. MILEAGE... 3500 Kms......

CAR...... Sunbeam Tiger........   STATE OF TUNE..... Group III......

DRIVER... Peter Riley..........   CO-DRIVER......... Robin Turvey...

Engine

1. Was the power sufficient and the torque range satisfactory?

    The power reaching the back wheels does not feel anything near the quoted 200+ b.h.p. I don't think the car stayed in tune consistently and I suspect that the Powr-lok differential absorbed a fair quantity of power. We have a great deal less acceleration than the 4.7 litre Group I Ford Falcon.

    The torque range is magnificent.

2. Was any work carried out on the engine? No

3. What was fuel consumption? 6 m.p.g special stages - approx. 10 m.p.g overall

4. What was oil consumption? ½ gall for 2000 miles (4000 m.p.g)

5. Was the oil pressure affected by any particular condition?
    Not appreciably

6. Any oil leaks? No

7. Any comments or suggestions?

    How about consulting an American engine tuning specialist such as Alan Mann or Holman Moody.

Carburation and Fuel Supply

8. Were any flat spots or carburettor blow-back apparent?

    The state of carburettor tune appeared to vary considerably with temperature and altitude. The tick-over varied between stalling and 1600 r.p.m. The inside of the exhaust pipes varied in colour between black and pale grey. In fact the carburation was only satisfactory when running steadily on main roads.

Geneva Rally 1964

9. Was any fuel vapourisation or carburettor icing apparent? No

10. Was the fuel pump satisfactory, or did any fuel leaks appear?

    Fuel pump O.K. No fuel leaks.

11. Was the auxiliary fuel tank satisfactory, together with the change-over taps and piping? Yes

12. Was the throttle control accurate and smooth at the pedal?

    No. If the engine was taken above 5000 r.p.m on full throttle the accelerator pedal remained down for a full second after removal of the driver's foot. Due to the poor carburation one never knew exactly what would result from a given depression of the pedal. Sometimes the response was immediate and smooth, sometimes a flat spot, sometimes half power. Altogether a poor set-up.

13. Any comments or suggestions?

    How about a Holley carburettor.

Electrical System

14. Did you have any generator or battery troubles?

    Yes. On the first night the fan belt stretched so much that the generator speed dropped too low to sustain the ignition and one fog lamp. The charging rate and/or battery capacity appears to be too low to cope with any fall off in generator performance. It would never have dealt with a conventional lighting system; the only way we managed at all is because 2 quartz-iodine headlamps give sufficient light for fast motoring on winding roads.

15. How often did you have the battery topped up?

    Never. It is very difficult to get at since the spares box has to be unscrewed from the boot floor to inspect the battery. This should be rearranged.

16. Did the ignition system and sparking plugs work satisfactorily?

    After 800 miles the points closed up and the car misfired badly. We re-set the points by eye after which the engine ran on all eight cylinders.

17. Any problems with the fan belt drive or distributor drive?

    We consumed 4 fan belts. The reason for the overload on this drive is now known to be flattening of the bottom radiator hose.

18. Did the starter operate without trouble?

   Due to poor carburation and small battery capacity the car was an uncertain starter.

19. Was the lighting system trouble free and satisfactorily laid out with regard to types and position of lamps?

   The iodine/block lens headlamps were superb. We should prefer dipped headlamp units in the small bonnet mounted lamps. The fog lamp position was unsatisfactory in that jacking the car up meant bending back the fog lamps. They had to be re-set after each "jack-up" and the jack winding handle even then rapped the fog lamp glass on each revolution.

20. Was the instrument lighting satisfactory? Yes

21. Any comments or suggestions? No

Cooling and Heating

22. Did you suffer any cooling troubles or radiator leaks?

   Radiator temperature was 200°F - 220°F continuously. Now known to be caused by bottom hose flattening under pressure above 4000 r.p.m.

23. Was the water temperature much affected by any particular conditions?

   Continuously too high.

24. Did the heating and demisting equipment work well?

   There is no ram effect with speed. The demisting with blower in operation is just satisfactory. Not a very powerful system by modern standards.

25. Any comments or suggestions? Fit armoured radiator hoses.

Clutch, Gearbox and Transmission

26. Was the clutch trouble-free? Yes

27. Did you suffer clutch slip on any occasion? No

28. Did the gearbox give any trouble, was it silent in all gears?

   Pretty good box.

29. Did the gear lever work smoothly or was there any lever chatter? Yes

30. Were the gear ratios satisfactorily spaced for your purpose?

Yes, this gearbox seemed to be a very fair compromise. But it will be easier to judge it when the engine is giving consistent and increased power.

31. Did the back axle give any trouble or leak?   No trouble

32. Was the axle ratio suitable for your purpose?   Yes

33. Any comments or suggestions?   No

Road-holding, Steering and Ride

34. Was the road-holding balance good and the car easy to control?

One of the most encouraging features was the excellent balance of the car. The only difficulty was on sharp slow corners when the limited-slip differential tended to make the car understeer strongly. This improved as the rally progressed. Please don't overhaul or reset the differential.

35. Did you suffer from wheel hop, or shock absorber failure?

No shock absorber trouble. The wheel hop was quite manageable when driving hard; in fact it is only apparent on light or trailing throttle.

36. Was the springing and ride satisfactory?   The ride was particularly good for this type of rally car.

37. Was the rear wheel traction satisfactory?   Yes

Normally on dry or wet, tarmac or gravel roads the traction was excellent. On ice and snow at very low speeds it was extremely bad, not helped by a low speed flat spot at higher altitudes and lower temperatures. The traction improved as the speed rose.

38. Was the steering light and accurate at all speeds?

No. Here lies the biggest room for improvement. As the front wheels get closer to break-away point the steering becomes heavier and more insensitive. When travelling fast on a narrow winding road it is not possible to move the steering wheel fast enough to take advantage of the car's good balance and road holding. It will put up much higher average speeds if the steering was lighter on lock and higher geared. The steering geometry wants a very careful scrutiny. I would be prepared to sacrifice some directional stability to obtain lighter steering on lock.

39. Was the underbody protection suitable?   None fitted. We touched the centre of the chassis cruciform on the road surface on one bump, without damage.

-5-

40. Any comments or suggestions?   No

Braking

41. Did you suffer any form of brake fade?

   Yes. On fast descents the braking power declined considerably. The drum expansion of the rear brakes increased the pedal travel when hot, and even on the second or third pump when a solid pedal was obtained the stopping power had deteriorated badly.

42. Did you suffer any form of fluid boiling?

   No. The new HP brake fluid withstood very abnormal temperatures without boiling. The car stood for about 2 minutes in one control with smoke and smell gushing from under the wheel arches and yet the fluid did not boil. Quite remarkable.

43. Did you suffer from any fluid leakage?   No

44. How often were the brake pads/linings changed during the event?

   1 set front pads, 1 set rear leading shoes replaced, which was my fault in trying to take up the rear brake drum expansion with the hand brake and overdoing it on one occasion.

45. Any comments or suggestions?   We should have a 4 disc conversion for rallying.

Tyres

46. Was the tyre type and size satisfactory?   Yes

47. What pressures did you use?   F...31... R...31...

48. What was the approximate rate of wear?

   One tyre change at half distance was needed. The rears more worn than the fronts.

49. Any comments or suggestions?   No

Body Furniture and Fittings

50. Were the seats comfortable and easy to adjust?   Very good. (Microcell Contour 6 driver's seat. Standard passenger seat)

51. Were the main controls easy to reach and operate?

   The 2" set back of the gear knob increased the ease of gear change. With this modification the car was well laid out.

Geneva Rally 1964

52. Was the safety harness comfortable and easy to adjust? Yes

53. Were the minor controls (i.e. switches etc) easy to understand operate? Yes

54. Did any of the body furniture break or rattle? No trouble

55. Any comments or suggestions? The most civilised and comfortable of any rally G.T. car I have ever driven.

Car Preparation

56. Was the car delivered to you in perfect condition? Yes

57. Did you carry out any work prior to the event?

    I believe misfiring developed on the way to Geneva which was due to wear on the heel of the distributor cam closing points.

58. Did you personally check the equipment carried in the car? Yes

59. Any comments or suggestions? No

Rally Service

60. Were the service points well planned and sufficient in quantity?
    Satisfactory

61. Was there any lack of spares or tools at any service point? No

62. Any comments or suggestions? No

Comparison with Competitors

63. How did your car compare with its competitors in the rally? Please refer especially to vehicles of similar type and price.

    It was faster than the one E type Jaguar and one DB4 Aston Martin entered, which were both privately entered and driven. It was a great deal slower than the 904 Porsche which is the car which now sets the standard in the G.T. Category of current International Rallying. It was also considerably (10 secs in 4 mins) slower than the Group I 4.7 litre Falcon. In scratch performance on varying types of hill it was approximately the same in performance as the latest Triumph Spitfire.

64. Where did you finish in the results? 15th Overall (Handicap)
    2nd in class
    4th in G.T Category

-7-

65. If you failed to finish, what circumstances caused your retirement?

7 mins lost on the road (1 min. battery run down, 2 mins not going fast enough, 4 mins navigation)

66. Any comments or suggestions?

This car with development is quite capable of winning outright. It has all the basic specification required and I am sure will prove Rootes' most successful rally car ever.

General

67. Have you any suggestions for the future improvement of this car, with competitions in mind?

A great deal more power is required and I am sure advice can be obtained from the American exponents. The braking must be improved with 4 discs. The steering should be more responsive.

68. Have you any further points not covered in this report that you wish to raise? No

Geneva Rally 1964

Peter Riley

Peter started his rallying as a bachelor of independent means who raced and rallied for the pure fun of it – beginning his rallying in a Healey Silverstone in 1950. Later he married Ann Wisdom who navigated and co-drove Pat Moss to many of their victories – including the outright win on the 1960 Liege-Rome-Liege in the Healey 3000. His talent at driving soon bought him to the attention of the rally team managers and he drove for Ford before joining the BMC works team in 1959. Living in Abingdon, to be close to the Competition Department, he was an engineer with a degree in Mechanical Engineering and, as such, had a good mechanical 'feel' for his cars. He excelled on the 1959 Liege-Rome-Liege finishing first in the GT class in the Healey 3000, second in class on the 1960 Tulip in an Austin A105 and competing with both the 3000 on other rallies – including the 1961 Acropolis - and the new Mini-Minor in the 1961 Tulip. He joined Rootes for the Geneva Rally of 1964.

Sunbeam Tiger in racing trim

GENEVA RALLY   OCTOBER 1964

SUNBEAM Tiger

1ST Tiny Lewis / Barry Hughes
2ND Peter Riley / Robin Turvey
3RD Rosemary Smith / Margaret Mackenzie

GRAND TOURING CARS—OVER 2,500 c.c.

and **2ND MANUFACTURERS' TEAM PRIZE**

also REPRESENTING GREAT BRITAIN **2ND NATIONS' CUP**

SUBJECT TO OFFICIAL CONFIRMATION

In its first international rally in Europe

the new 4.2 litre Sunbeam Tiger showed it was bred to success. Over a 1,250 mile route, mostly in the French Alps and taking in parts of Switzerland and Italy, three of the new models proved themselves in the face of Europe's hottest competition. The Tiger finished 3rd and 4th in the G.T. Category—based on handicap on engine size. Only 38 cars finished of over 100 starters. Three Sunbeam Tigers started; all three finished. No mean achievement in a new car—and proof positive of the race and rally breeding of Sunbeam cars which have figured prominently in International motor sport for over a decade.

SUNBEAM TIGER See it at Earl's Court Motor Show. Available for U.K. delivery early 1965

ROOTES MOTORS LTD.
LONDON SHOWROOMS & EXPORT DIVISION: ROOTES LTD, DEVONSHIRE HOUSE, PICCADILLY, LONDON W.1

RAC Rally 1964

The Reverend manages the only finish of a 'works' Tiger in the forest.

After the works success in the Geneva rally, the factory decided to put its effort into running three 998 Imps and a Rapier on the RAC, leaving it to a semi-works effort to provide the debut of the Tiger, firstly in Great Britain and secondly on a forest event.

AHP483B had been registered in August 1964 and a discussion between the Rev. Rupert Jones and Marcus Chambers, old friends from the Cambridge University Car Club's long distance record breaking days, led to the loan of a vehicle for the Reverend and John Clegg to drive, with the entry being taken care of by Vitafoam - who had been supporting Rupert Jones' racing Mini previously - and Rootes taking care of the preparation.

The car had been prepared in a similar way to the Geneva cars, but the engine had been bought direct from Ford at Detroit. Two engines had been purchased, one for 483B and the other for AHP 295B. Slightly more power was coaxed out of the engines with modified cylinder heads, reprofiled cam and solid lifters, the net result being that one engine gave 211bhp at 5200 rev/min and the other 217bhp at 5000 rev/min during bench testing. To assist with engine cooling, an oil cooler had been fitted behind the front valence and the bonnet was propped open at the rear to allow more air to escape from the engine compartment. To help with forward vision during the bleak winter nights, four 5-inch fog and driving lights had been fitted, the 5 inch Lucas fog lights being bracket mounted on the front bumper, as in the Geneva cars. Run in November, the RAC rally usually has its fair share of desolate weather, including rain, snow, ice and fog and for this rally two windscreen heaters were fixed to the inside of the windscreen in front of each crew member. Minilite wheels were not used, the standard steel wheels sufficing, fitted with either the universally used Dunlop SP3 tyres for the road or tarmac stages or Dunlop SP44 for the gravel stages.

This year the rally started on November 8th at the Duke of York Barracks in Chelsea, running immediately into the West Country and thence into Wales from south to north. By 2pm on November 9th the Oulton Park stage was due to be tackled with the crews then threading their way into the Lake District and into Scotland for an overnight stop in Perth. From Scotland the next day's running brought the rally south through the North of England into Norfolk for a stage at Snetterton before the final run into the finish in London at 7pm on the 12th November.

Overall the route covered a circular 2528 miles for which 165 cars had entered, the Rupert Jones/John Clegg Tiger starting at number 43. Since the car was unlikely to be amongst the front runners in the forests on its first event on the loose, the reverend gentleman's strategy was to make a maximum effort to be in the top six on the three tarmac stages at Porlock Hill and the Oulton Park and Snetterton racing circuits, whilst maintaining a sensible, and hopefully trouble free, run in the forests.

One piece of advice given to the crew from the Rootes service mechanics, before the start, was concerning the problems of the Tigers' exhaust pipes being long and close to the ground. Often, on rough stages or poor tarmac – or when the shock absorbers weakened allowing contact with the ground over bumps - they became flattened with the obvious consequences on engine breathing.

79

RAC Rally 1964

Rupert Jones and John Clegg with the Vitafoam entry for the 1964 RAC Rally. (Rootes)

The pristine Jones/Clegg Tiger in the Bramshill Forest stage near Camberley. (Author)

RAC Rally 1964

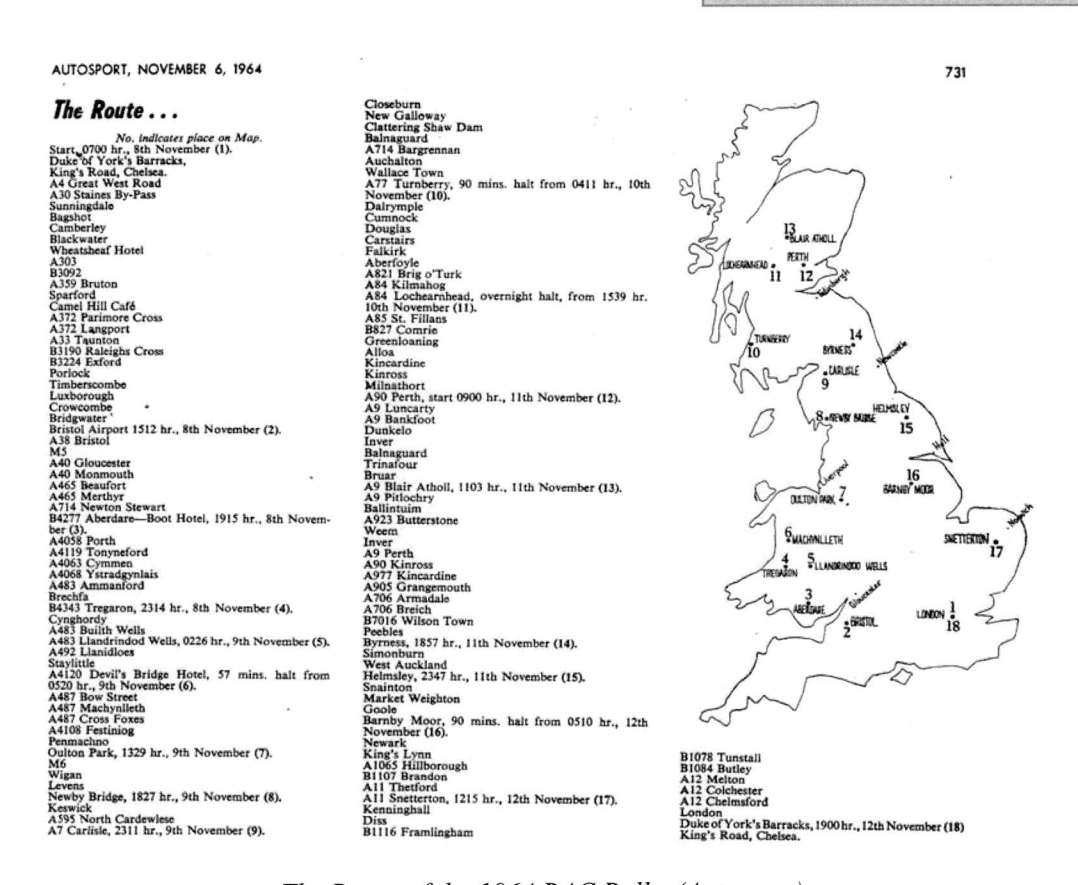

The Route of the 1964 RAC Rally. (Autosport)

Determined not to suffer from this problem, the crew stopped, soon after the start, at a local hardwareshop and bought a broom handle that was carefully carried in the Tiger at all times. John Cleggs' job, apart from navigating and co-driving, was to insert the broom handle, at every suitable opportunity, up each exhaust pipe in turn, to check for any restriction. No doubt it caused some interest, if not mirth, to the many spectators.

The first stage in Bramshill forest went smoothly enough as did the remaining forests before the descent of Porlock Hill on the old toll road. Rupert was to put a maximum effort into this stage and the beginning was exemplary, with the car going very quickly down the first open part - and then the road tightens up as it comes into the trees. As Rupert noted in one of his magazine articles "It was a good job that there was a car park on the apex of the bend with spectators to help the car back on the road." The spectators had been getting in some practice, however, as he was not the only Rootes driver to blot his copy book at this point. 'Tiny' Lewis and Robin Turvey had arrived in their works Imp at great speed and had gone head over heels in their car and had lost some time when Robin had had to run back up to the initial impact point, where the front screen had gone missing, to pick up his road book. Luckily the route then passed close by 'Tiny' Lewis's garage in Bristol and he was able to have the bodywork refurbished and the glass replaced in record time. At least the Tiger stayed on its wheels – and, in spite of this indiscretion, the stage time was very reasonable!

As the rally wended its way into Wales and darkness, the temperature dropped and in addition to the fog and mist, the ice became another problem. In the rough forests, tyre problems manifested themselves and the Tiger suffered some punctures due to the large amounts of engine torque moving the tyres on the rims under hard acceleration and pulling the valves off the inner tubes, with the obvious results. At the control in

RAC Rally 1964

Devil's Bridge in mid-Wales the Tiger made a spectacular entrance as "the spare was flat, and both rear tyres were flat and one on fire as we scratched our way down the hills to the control leaving a pall of black smoke hanging over the mountains." A discussion with the Dunlop Service van and a change of tyre size to prevent slippage provided a solution to this particular tyre problem. The next major effort was made at Oulton Park where the rally used six laps of the full circuit, the only problem being that the fog was so thick that it wasn't possible to see the pits from the centre of the paddock.

Rupert takes up the story "As we approached Oulton Park it began to get foggy. We were to do five laps as a stage rather than a race, so no pit signals. I stuck pieces of tape on the dash, one to be removed each time I passed go, and set out at high speed, knowing the circuit well. The fog had really come down and to start with I had to weave around the slower cars. Coming out of the Esso hairpin the boot was really down and 120 mph came up; now where was the 300 yard marker board? I must have missed it. I hadn't... there were no boards out as it was a rally. Oops, there was Knicker Brook and this was too fast... a big one-eighty spin job and backwards uphill... flicked her round forward again as taught on the skid-pan, and pressed on through the fog. No more suprises, and third fastest, until the stage was abandoned because of the fog." The time for the Tiger was excellent, the crew being, by the official results, fourth fastest with a time of 14mins 12secs, only 20secs behind the quickest competitor. This test was on scratch with the fastest crew setting the bogey time and this turned out to be the Paddy Hopkirk/Henry Liddon Cooper 'S' with a time of 13mins 52secs (with an incredible 2 min 12 sec best flying lap), followed closely by the Henry Taylor Ford Cortina GT.

As the route led north into the Lake District, the fog became patchy and then cleared to give a fine, clear, frosty night for the Lake District stages. An unplanned excursion into a ditch on the Grizedale stage, whilst being chased by John Sprinzel in his Sprite, led to a maximum penalty for the stage and some rapid work by the service crew, who had to weld the front bumper back on, led onto the Dodd special stage on the north side of Bassenthwaite Lake. When run East to West, the finish is at the end of a steep downhill long straight. Rupert explains "...we triggered over the top in the Tiger, going rather fast. I have never fallen off a cliff, but I am sure that I know what it feels like...... and those marshals running the control deserve a very high honour for bravery and devotion to duty." As dawn broke the crew entered Scotland and as the Tiger left special stage 34 the ignition refused to work and some road time was lost in sorting out the fault, which apparently turned out to be a disconnected low-tension lead from the coil to the distributor. Writing in 'Collectors Car' Rupert Jones describes the next 30mins vividly -"A feature of my rally-

OULTON PARK

1	P.Hopkirk/H.Liddon	Cooper S	13.52
2	H.Taylor/B.Melia	Cortina GT	13.59
3	V.Elford/D.Stone	Cortina GT	14.10
4	R.Jones/J.Clegg	Tiger	14.12
5	T.Makinen/D.Barrow	Healey 3000	14.33
6	R.Aaltonen/A.Ambrose	Cooper S	14.43

RAC Rally 1964

The less than pristine Tiger - note the dent in the navigator's door - tackles the dry forest stages. (LAT)

ing has been that some of the faster parts turn out to be road sections. Now started such a section. Twenty miles to the time control at the Turnberry Hotel and minus five minutes to do it."

After a most welcome night in bed, the rally restarted on a loop north from Perth with the classic Scottish stages in Craigvinean and Drummond Hill, and the only trouble on this loop was a stuck starter motor that was soon cured. During the section south of Perth, which ran down to Hexham a further minor problem arose which is described again by Rupert Jones - "A monumental navigational error in southern Scotland saw us head towards Gretna instead of Hexham. There ensued another of those high-speed road sections over the moors to correct the error. We filled up with petrol and made it with five minutes to spare, but could not persuade our service crew that we had just been taking our time....they looked at the temperature gauges..." From the Kielder forest complex, heading further south through the classic Yorkshire stages of Cropton, Pickering, Staindale and Dalby, the Tiger was beginning to get a bit tired and the pounding that the suspension had taken had caused the shock absorbers to weaken and the car became difficult to hold in a straight line, some of the faster straights being taken in a series of long drifts. Also the look of the car was changed when somewhere in the forests the welds on the bumper fatigued and the bumper, complete with two fog lamps, disappeared forever. As dawn broke, the remaining competitors started a long run south caused by the cancellation of three stages, the route leading through Kings Lynn and Thetford to the Snetterton Circuit.

RAC Rally 1964

The Tiger suspension at full droop, Rupert Jones takes a 'flat over brow' on one of the faster sections of a forest stage. (via John Clegg)

This was the third, and last, maximum effort stage and Rupert again takes up the story. "Competitors were to join the circuit just after the hairpin at the end of Norwich straight, and start in pairs. My other half was Timo Makinen in the Healey 3000 and I was determined to give him a really good run. I knew the circuit well. As we went through the gate to the start line the Tiger went onto seven. I tried everything with the throttle to clear it - but no way - and Timo pulled away from me.

"She was going well enough to make things interesting and I took the Esses well and suddenly we were on all eight again. I tried desperately to catch Timo and drove with great abandon to the point of making a photographer and two marshals, on the inside of Coram, take avoiding action. They need not have worried, I was loving it and had my eye well and truly in. She was at an indicated 127 mph at the end of the Norwich straight, and I seem to remember we were well on the leader board for this stage." With the remembered advice of Archie Scott-Brown, given some years earlier, that it was advisable to enter the Esses slowly and then it was virtually flat-out to the end of the pits straight and Riches Corner, an excellent time had ensued, the crew and car putting up fourth fastest time overall. The stage was on scratch timing again with Timo Makinen being fastest in the Healey 3000 in a time of 11mins 26secs with the Tiger on 12.39.

RAC Rally 1964

SNETTERTON

1	T.Makinen/D.Barrow	Healey 3000	11.26
2	D.Morley /E.Morley	Healey 3000	11.37
3	M.Gibbs /R.Morgan	Cortina	12.36
4	R.Jones /A.Clegg	Tiger	12.39
5	P.Moon /B.Culcheth	Cooper	12.50

'Are you OK?' Rupert Jones gives the 'thumbs-up' to his previous BMC Team-mates – Donald & Erle Morley – in their sidelined Healey 3000. (via John Clegg)

The Tiger arrives at a Control on its Dunlop SP3s. By the time the Tiger had lost its front bumper and accompanying lights, but the sumpguard still looks as new. (via John Clegg)

RAC Rally 1964

Not all of the RAC stages used smooth forest tracks – here the Tiger negotiates some 'three-ply', two wheel-tracks with a centre ridge, which keeps the sumpguard in regular use. (Foster & Skeffington)

Rupert Jones grapples with the wildly understeering Tiger on Snetterton Racing Circuit. (via John Clegg)

RAC Rally 1964

Rupert Jones, perhaps after one of his more rapid road sections, waits whilst John Clegg sprints for the time clock at a control on the RAC rally. (Rootes)

A final stage at Rendlesham Forest followed, where Makinen set the fastest time of 7.20 against the set time of 7.36, and the run back into London through Colchester and Chelmsford completed the circuitous route.

Out of the 165 entries, only 89 finished with the very tired Tiger finishing a creditable 45th overall. Rupert's own analysis of the finishing position estimated that "...without the off on Grizedale and the road penalties in Scotland caused by the loss of electrics, we could have been about twelfth."

There had been problems, some mechanical, some otherwise induced, but the factory had learned of some of the weaknesses of the Tiger on its first outing on the loose which were to help in the later development of the car.

But on its first outing on the RAC Rally the crew had got the car round a laborious route under difficult weather conditions to provide the first finish for a Tiger - and what was to prove to be the only finish for a works Tiger - on the RAC.

RAC Rally 1964

John Clegg removes his helmet and contemplates the stage times in a control at the end of a stage. The off-side door looks a bit secondhand as do the rally numbers. (Rootes)

In the 1960's, the need to get good stage times did not preclude a brief stop to see if compatriots were OK.

RAC Rally 1964

The Rev. Rupert Jones & John Clegg.

Rev. Rupert Jones

From a motoring family Rupert had competed as a navigator for his father whilst at school and, during his National Service, had persuaded his CO to sanction the formation of a motorcycle trials team – which he organized as a competing member. Having decided at school that his vocation lay within the church, the 'Bishop' studied at Cambridge University and got involved with BMC in the seven-days endurance records with the CU team in an A-35 in 1957 at Montlhery. His talents were rapidly recognized by Marcus Chambers and he soon joined Peter Riley to co-drive on the 1959 Liege- Rome- Liege – finishing tenth overall and first in the big GT class - out of only 14 finishers. Later he competed with John Gott in another Healey 3000 in the 1960 Liege to finish tenth and help gain the coveted the team prize – this was the Liege where the Pat Moss/Ann Riley Healey 3000 won outright. Later competition in the early 850cc Minis on the Monte Carlo provided some exciting and memorable times finally led to his involvement with Goodliffe Racing and hence the RAC and Targa Florio in the Tiger.

John Clegg

An early participant in motorsport from the age of 16, John - a relative of the Mini tuner and racer Harry Ratcliffe - found a niche in navigating on the night rallies of the Motoring News series. His membership of the Knowldale Car Club enabled him to gain success with many of the clubs drivers – Mike Sutcliffe, Phil Crabtree, Don Grimshaw, Derek Astle – most of whom continued with Ford and BMC works drives.

When Rupert Jones came as a curate to a parish in Rochdale, he naturally joined Knowldale and persuaded Vitafoam – in nearby Middleton – to sponsor his motorsport activities and John got involved in this operation. His first international rally, with Rupert on the Tour de France in a Mini-Cooper, led to the co-drive in the Tiger. This started with the loan of a practice car – to get used to the Tiger handling and performance – and then the collection of the rally car from Rootes Competition Department on the way to the start in London – after a long lunch with Marcus Chambers!

RAC Rally 1964

Monte Carlo Rally 1965

Snow storms in the mountains decimate the Monte Carlo runners, but the Tigers finish 4th & 11th overall and win the GT class.

Of all the rallies in the international calendar, the Monte Carlo Rally has, undoubtedly, the glossiest image with the public and press alike. Perhaps it is the image of the international rally driver gambling on the Casino roulette tables, basking in the warm Mediterranean sun (although it is often raining) and sipping champagne; whilst in the next instant he sits, steely-eyed, in his rally car, ready to do battle with the elements of the Alpes Maritimes. But, whatever the image, the rally attracts considerable amounts of publicity valuable to the Motor Industry, and, in the event of an outright win, potential increases in car sales (as with the Mini Cooper S).

The mixture of high life and hard work is appealing, at least mentally, but rallying, of course, is not quite like that, and whilst the Monte has its attractions, it is one of the most difficult rallies in terms of team organisation and is a nightmare in terms of tyre usage and choice. The combination of dry roads, wet roads, icy roads and snow covered roads (to any depth) and, of course, any combination of those four basic conditions plus any in-between circumstances, makes the correct choice of tyre paramount to returning a good performance. In addition to the tyre problem, changing stage conditions are a major headache. It is not uncommon to start a stage on dry tarmac, which as it progresses up the Col goes into wet tarmac, then into the same wet tarmac but with patches of ice (especially in the shady corners protected from the sun), then onto packed ice and snow and finally when the top is eventually reached, it may well be covered in soft snow, perhaps freshly fallen. Then, of course, the process is reversed on the descent.

Probably on each of these road conditions a different tyre is needed for optimum performance, from a dry tarmac racer to a fully studded snow tyre, but the team manager and driver have to make a single choice – even with the help of ice-note crews. Having now made the choice, the next nightmare is changing weather conditions, which can be very rapid in the Alpes Maritime, with road surface conditions changing drastically from the passing of the first cars to the last. So it was in this year's event, and it was to have a very significant effect on the pattern of results.

In the end it was essentially to be determined by the place of starting, always a gamble on mainly weather conditions on the long run-in on the common route. The starting point also determines the start number and thus the position in which the competitor runs from the journey of the common routes, over the selectives to Monaco.

Rootes had originally intended to enter two Rapiers but, because of the strong showing on the Geneva, switched the entry to two Tigers, and with two Imps, had opted for the London start at the Duke of York Barracks in Chelsea. The other start points were scattered throughout eight other capitals in Europe, being Paris, Frankfurt, Lisbon, Athens, Warsaw, Stockholm, Minsk and Monte Carlo itself. The London starters were allocated numbers between 93 and 145, with the Andrew Cowan/Robin Turvey Tiger at 103 (AHP295B) and the Peter Harper/Ian Hall car (ADU312B) at number 107.

The route from London led direct to the control at Dover and the cars would embark on the 'Lord Warden' for the channel crossing to Boulogne. The cars then ran direct to Liege where they met up with the Paris entrants (Numbers 176-211) and the Frankfurt starters (Numbers 147-170). Looping north through Holland, the cars drove, via Boulogne - again for the London starters - through Moyan and Rennes, to join the Lisbon crews (Numbers 219-229) and those from Monte Carlo (239-261).

Monte Carlo Rally 1965

Ian Hall and Peter Harper, dressed in appropriate Monte clothing, discuss eligibility with the RAC scrutineer at the London Start. The position of the Heuer Clocks and the Halda trip can be seen, as can the fitting of the Rev Counter into the top padding on the dash. (Rootes)

Winding on around the Guyenne region of France through Angouleme, Montauban and Mauriac, the route joined the two sole Athens starters (273 and 274) in St.Flour. Both these starters were works Mini Cooper S's of Rauno Aaltonen/ Tony Ambrose (1275cc) and Geoff Mabbs/John Davenport (970cc). The latter had the dubious distinction of being the last car in the rally and, as it later showed, to be a distinct disadvantage this year. Then into the Massif Central through Mont Brison and Bourg to St. Claude, a little town in the Jura mountains about 35 miles north west of Geneva, where the competitors finally met the remainder of the entrants from Stockholm (34-68), Minsk (72-91) and Warsaw (2-29). From this town onwards, the common route for all starters, in numerical order, ran through Le Poizat, Chambery and Gap, finally emerging some 550 miles - and five stages later - in Monte Carlo.

Peter Harper, who was a well-proven Monte specialist – it was his 15th Monte – was not particularly enamoured with the rally as his comments on a television interview indicate "... the reason I don't like it is because it's such a lottery as regards weather. I mean from first to last car it's roughly about six hours, so the first cars can get good weather and the cars half-way through can get atrocious weather and the cars at the end can have good weather again. Also this business of making the route known, because you drive - there are some thing like eighty or ninety miles of special stages this year - two and a half thousand miles and then the whole rally is decided on those – just eighty or ninety miles. It makes nonsense of rallying. If the weather was atrocious, terrible like

Monte Carlo Rally 1965

it was in 1958 where only five cars got through clean - it was so bad that you were sort of digging your way through and arrived a day late and won the thing - now that would be what I call a good Monte Carlo Rally."

Asked (perhaps prophetically) if he would like some bad weather this year, Peter replied "...Oh, yes, really deep snow. The thing, as I say, has become so professional and it's getting so fast and we practice all the stages, you might need a lightly studded tyre for one stage, or maybe just an ordinary dry road tyre, but then you've got to get off that tyre to your lightly studded tyre, maybe off that lightly studded tyre onto a heavily studded tyre – depending upon conditions that are being fed back to you - and for our two cars, I think that we've got something like sixty wheels scattered around France, and even that's not quite enough."

However like it or not, this rally would be the 8th time he had driven a Sunbeam into the top 12 ratings and this consistency would lead to an outright win of the Challenge Antony Noghes (won previously in 1962 & 63) for the best performance by a competitor who had completed at least 10 Montes.

Andrew Cowan and Robin Turvey talk their way through scrutineering at the start of the Monte at the London start. The foam padding holding the bonnet open at the rear is clearly visible, as is the "bedspring" to spring the bonnet open. Also visible are the wing vents, the in-line fuses for the forward lights and the de-icing bundy tube for the headlights. Robin takes the standard co-driver's approach at scrutineering of appearing to be completely confused with it all. (Rootes)

Monte Carlo Rally 1965

WARSAW
2, Leslie Brooke/Robert Freeborough (Mini-Cooper); 7, Johannes Ortner/Alexander Legradi (Steyr-Puch); 10, Nicolas Koob/Armand Weis (D.K.W.); 16, John la Trobe/David Bailey (Mini); 17, Joachim Springer/Jochen Neerpasch (Ford Taunus); 19, Sidney Broomfield/Geoffrey Speight (Mini); 20, Gerhard Bodmer/Erwin Moch (Glas); 21, Graham Warner/John Spiers (Volvo); 29, Sobiesław Zasada/Kazimierz Osinski (Steyr-Puch).

STOCKHOLM
34, Wolfgang Levy/Gerhard Gottlieb (B.M.W. 1800); 35, Picko Troberg/X (Mini-Cooper); 36, Bo Ljungfeldt/Fergus Sager (Ford Mustang); 38, Miss Laila Schou Nilsen/Miss Nancy Pettersen (Saab 96 Sport); 40, Eric Carlsson/Gunnar Palm (Saab 96 Sport); 45, Claude le Guezec/X (Renault); 47, Ove Andersson/Torsten Aman (Saab 96 Sport); 49, Mrs. Pat Moss-Carlsson/Miss Elizabeth Nyström (Saab 96 Sport); 52, Timo Makinen/Paul Easter (Mini-Cooper); 55, Mme. Thérèse Mahieuw/X (Alfa Romeo); 56, Paddy Hopkirk/Henry Liddon (Mini-Cooper); 57, Jean Laroche/J.-C. Bouly (B.M.W.); 58, Hans Walter/Werner Lier (B.M.W.); 68, Bengt Söderström/So Svedberg (Ford Cortina).

MINSK
72, Don Morley/Erle Morley (Mini-Cooper); 73, Guy Verrier/Bernard Pasquier (Citroën DS19); 75, Robert Neyret/J. Terramorsi (Citroën DS19); 77, Paul Coltelloni/X (Citroën DS19); 79, Lucien Bianchi/Jean Demortier (Citroën DS19); 82, Mlle. Lucette Pointet/Mlle. Françoise Houillon (Citroën DS19); 85, Jean-Paul Joly/Michel Nicol (Citroën DS19); 89, Miss Elizabeth Jones/Miss Pat Ozanne (Mini); 91, Raymond Baxter/Jack Scott (Mini-Cooper).

LONDON
93, Sydney Allard/Tom Fisk (Allardette); 94, Peter Bolton/Gordon Shanley (Triumph 2000); 95, David Pollard/Barry Hughes (Hillman Imp); 96, Claude Twigdon/Anthony Gorst (Mini); 97, Frederick Vivian/Mrs. Vivian Vivian (Sunbeam Rapier); 98, Brian Petch/Harold Miller (Mini); 99, Alex Griffiths/Stuart Turner (Reliant Sabre); 100, Joseph Lloyd/John Twigdon (Lotus Elan); 101, Joe Foster/Fred Sleight (Mini-Cooper); 102, Peter Fitzgerald/X (Ford Cortina); 103, Andrew Cowan/Robin Turvey (Sunbeam Tiger); 104, Roy Pinder/Charles Pollard (Jaguar E); 105, Horace Appleby/Dr. Robert McGhie (Mini-Cooper); 106, Miss Valerie Pirie/Miss Susan Reeves (Triumph Spitfire); 107, Peter Harper/Ian Hall (Sunbeam Tiger); 108, Georges Duviau/Julian Alderton (Sunbeam Rapier); 109, Norman Harvey/David Jones (Mini-Cooper); 110, Eric Brinkman/Ronald Clifford Brown (Ford); 111, Edwin Hodson/Ken Coffey (Ford Cortina); 112, Gordon King/Colin Sproxton (Ford Cortina); 113, Miss Rosemary Smith/Miss Margaret Mackenzie (Hillman Imp); 114, Michael Bausola/Dennis Furneaux (Morris Oxford); 115, Roy Kirkham/Roy Mapple (Mini-Cooper); 116, Dan Margulies/Julian Chitty (Ford Cortina); 117, Dennis Pratt/Douglas Gray (Ford Cortina); 118, Rob Slotemaker/Alan Taylor (Triumph Spitfire); 119, Michael Frostick/Maxwell Boyd (Ford Corsair); 120, Phil Walton/Eric Lynch (Mini); 121, Alex Cleghorn/William Cooper (Volvo); 122, Steve Neal/Norman Parrish (Mini-Cooper); 123, David Friswell/X (Mini-Cooper); 124, Tiny Lewis/Jose Culcheth (Hillman Imp); 125, Sidney Davey/Anthony Carter (Volkswagen 1500S); 126, Ken James/Mike Hughes (Rover 2000); 127, Colin Plummer/Stephen Silverthorne (Mini); 128, John Cuff/Douglas Anderson (Vauxhall); 129, James Bullough/John Middleton (Ford Cortina); 130, Kjell Gudim/X (Hillman Imp); 131, Terry Hunter/Patrick Lier (Triumph Spitfire); 132, William Clemens/Tim Bosence (Mini); 133, Raymond Joss/John Fitzpatrick (Mini-Cooper); 134, James Gardner/Colin Malkin (Mini-Cooper); 135, Albert Hill/James Shaw (M.G. 1100); 136, Roger Clark/Arnold Porter (Rover 2000); 137, Laurence Handley/Wilson Giles (N.S.U. Prinz); 138, Courtney Edwards/Tom Wisdom (Austin 1800); 139, "Tony"/"Gerry" (Ford Cortina); 140, Bill Ramsden/"Diz" Daymond (Ford Cortina); 141, Simo Lampinen/Jyrki Ahava (Triumph Spitfire); 142, Arnold Burton/George Humble (Lotus Ford Cortina); 143, William Robson/James Thompson (Ford Anglia); 144, Alan Allard/Robert Mackie (Ford Cortina); 145, Nicholas Rowe/Roger Doidge (Hillman Imp).

FRANKFURT
147, Herbert Linge/Peter Falk (Porsche); 150, Eugen Böhringer/Rolf Wütherich (Porsche); 155, Hartvig Conradsen/Kjeld Jorgensen (Mini-Cooper); 161, Giorgio Pianta/Giancarlo Mamino (Lancia Flavia); 163, Pauli Toivonen/X (Porsche); 170, Peter Jopp/X (Lancia Flavia).

PARIS
176, Harry Källström/Ragnvald Haakansson (Mini-Cooper); 177, Logan Morrison/Johnstone Syer (Rover 2000); 178, Gerald Dinwiddy/Michael Bowyer (Hillman Imp); 180, Raphaël Geminiani/Jacques Anquetil (Ford Mustang); 181, Leo Cella/Mario de Villa (Lancia Flavia); 184, Jean-Françoise Piot/X (Renault R8); 185, Henri Greder/Martial Delalande (Ford Mustang); 186, Maurice Gatsonides/Albert Ilcken (Sunbeam Tiger); 187, Richard Tilley/Charles Williams (Mini-Cooper); 190, Ivor Jones/John Brown (Mini); 195, David Piper/X (Lancia Flavia); 196, Henri Marang/Paul Coltelloni (Citroën DS19); 200, James Wood/Norman Thomas (Ford Cortina); 203, Hugues Hazard/André Bouly (Lancia Flavia); 204, John Wadsworth/Allan Cooke (Mini-Cooper); 205, Jean-Jacques Thuner/John Gretener (Triumph Spitfire); 209, Mrs. Anne Hall/Miss Val Domico (Rover 2000); 210, Ernest McMillen/Brian Waddell (Ford Corsair); 211, José Behra/Philippe Conso (N.S.U. Prinz).

LISBON
219, Jean Vinatier/Roger Masson (Renault R8); 220, Michel de Bourbon Parme/X (Renault R8);

228, Douglas Wilson-Spratt/Timothy Baker (Mini-Cooper); 229, Jacques Feret/Guy Monraisse (Renault R8).

MONTE CARLO
239, Eric Jackson/Kenneth Deacon (Ford Cortina); 241, Leslie Chamberlain/Alfred Oetterli (Ford Cortina); 242, René Trautmann/Jonny Rives (Lancia Flavia); 246, René Richard/X (Mercedes-Benz 300SE); 247, Vic Elford/David Stone (Ford Cortina); 249, Umberto de Bonis/Roberto Fusina (Fiat); 252, Henry Taylor/Brian Melia (Ford Cortina); 254, Mme. Annie Soisbault-Montaigu/Mme. Nicole Roure (Citroën DS19); 255, Jean Clement/Paul Condrillier (Renault R8); 257, Jean-Paul Colas/Jacques Dewez (Renault R8); 258, Esko Keinanen/Nils Helander (Ford Cortina); 261, Ewold van Bergen/Rex Wakely-Smith (Datsun); 262, David Seigle-Morris/Tony Nash (Ford Cortina); 264, Peter Procter/David Mabbs (Ford Corsair); 265, Mme. Claudine Bouchet/"Marie-Clemente Beaumont" (Lancia Flavia); 266, Roland Charrière/Paul Justamond (Renault R8).

ATHENS
273, Rauno Aaltonen/Tony Ambrose (Mini-Cooper); 274, Geoff Mabbs/X (Mini-Cooper).

Starting List for the 1965 Monte Carlo Rally. (Autosport)

Both Tigers had been prepared to the same specification by the Competition Department, with both cars being entered in the Group 3 Grand Touring (GT) class. Since the critical part of the rally, the 550 mile (885 km) run in from Saint Claude to Monte Carlo and the 379 mile (610km) Monte to Monte loop, all took place at night, then lighting was of primary importance. Both cars were now sporting a total of seven forward facing lights - including the two headlights in which iodine quartz bulbs were fitted and this was common with most works teams. The three upper lights comprised two 7 inch Lucas driving lamps with a central Lucas 7 inch clear spot - pointing straight down the middle of the road. The 5 inch fog lamps were mounted lower than on the cars for the Geneva rally, although still on a flat bracket at the ends of the front bumper, and all lamps were controlled independently of the head lamp system. In anticipation of the cold weather in store, although nobody at that point would imagine its unparalleled severity, much effort had been put into keeping the windscreen clear from ice and snow. Two windscreen heaters had been fitted

Monte Carlo Rally 1965

of the "Airflow De-froster" type that used a heated element to direct hot air onto the screen and heat the screen directly. In addition, to help the normal de-mist system, a perspex strip had been mounted along the front of the windscreen dash to concentrate the hot air onto the screen, a device that was also apparent on the works Mini Cooper S's. All of this was in addition to an "electrically heated" (in the 1964 meaning) windscreen and it was the power required for this and the lights that had necessitated the fitting of an alternator in place of the production dynamo. Also anticipation of the likely boreal conditions had hatched a novel idea for de-icing the driving lamps and a system was devised in the workshops that fed de-icing fluid to the lamps via a bundy tube, spraying the fluid directly onto the lamp glass.

The use of headlamp de-icing devices may well have been influenced by various tribulations on the 1963 Monte when, on the run-in through Germany, the Peter Harper/Ian Hall Rapier had encountered severe icing problems on the headlights, and as the lights grew dimmer and dimmer Peter thought that the battery was failing, but on stopping discovered half an inch of ice on the headlamp glass which had to be forcibly removed with a screwdriver. The weather had been so cold that the contents of the windscreen washer bottle had kept freezing in its usual position under the bonnet, and had to be kept by the navigators feet in the car – even then it had to be filled with neat methylated spirits - anti-freeze was not enough! 'Tiny' Lewis however, in the other car, was considerably more innovative; his was filled with gin and tonic! So for the Tiger, at least two lights, the driving spots, would be kept clear to enable adequate, if not ideal, illumination of the road ahead.

Andrew Cowan and an apparently bemused Robin Turvey go through scrutineering at the start of the Monte. The Trico representative awaits his chance to discuss wiper blades. The Tiger is already on studded Dunlop Weathermasters. (Rootes)

Monte Carlo Rally 1965

Ian Hall and Peter Harper take a final look at the engine compartment before the London start of the 1965 Monte Carlo. The plastic strip concentrating the hot air onto the screen can be seen, as can the supplementary electrical screen heaters. (Rootes)

As usual, 5.5 inch Minilites were fitted at both ends, and as a precaution both cars started on studded tyres. The Tigers ran exclusively on Dunlop tyres and the crews had, in addition, a choice of partly studded Weathermaster tread pattern in either radial ply or diagonal ply carcass. A second spare wheel was fitted to a carrier that allowed the wheel to be mounted externally on top of the boot lid, and this was to be a standard method of carrying two spare wheels for the remainder of the rallying life of the Tiger – where two spares needed to be carried.

Overheating was a problem that had continually plagued the standard road going Tiger and also continued to be a problem in the rally cars - although it was defeated later on. On the 1964 RAC, the bonnet had been raised at the trailing edge to allow hot air to escape out of the subsequent gap. This was in addition to the wing vents on these particular cars and, as on the Geneva rally cars, the grill bar had been removed.

Prior to the start - apart from the activity at Humber Road in building (and often rebuilding) the Tigers for the rally proper - the two crews had spent considerable time over the New Year testing tyres, making and checking pace notes and generally checking the route for timing. All four crew members had been out in the Haut-Alpes, centered on Gap, a small town of some 25,000 population and at an altitude of 2500ft - high enough to attract good snow falls for testing of tyres and studs - and central to the rally during the event itself.

Monte Carlo Rally 1965

These two images show the driving compartments of the Monte Carlo cars. Both pictures show the use of the standard steering wheel, the removal of the standard rev counter and filling the hole with a panel – held on with four screws – onto which two switches have been added - one a standard Lucas toggle switch and the other a pull-push type. Also both cars have a card-holder fitted on the gearbox tunnel which acts as an 'aide-memoire' for the navigation route notes when the co-driver drives and the driver rests on the long run-ins to the competitive sections. The lower picture shows the use of four switches on the arm rest/central glove pocket, which, presumably are used for the rally lights and maybe for the wipers (as on the later FRW668C). The lower picture looks like it was taken during the build – no Heuer Clocks – while the upper picture appears to be taken during scrutineering or at a time control, as behind the Tiger there appears to be a BMC Mini with its door open. (Rootes)

Monte Carlo Rally 1965

Ian Hall notes "...we had done very serious practice for this rally and Harper and I did a full road book recce from Chambery to Monte Carlo for all the cars in December. We then, Imp and Tiger crews, did our own pace notes for the Épreuves (speed sections) between Chambery and Monaco and then for the final Mountain Section for the top hundred or so finishers. On one of these recces we had a service car and crew and we made a point of practicing at more or less the right time of day – that is doing the night stages after dark. Peter and I had done this before with Rapiers and looking back now it does seem to be a rather dodgy thing to have been doing as we were always on our own without service or any other form of back-up. On one practice run we stuffed chief engineer Des O'Dell into the space behind the seats so he could see at first hand what it was like to be in a rally car in anger. He was a bit quiet afterwards but we got the impression that his previous racing experience with Aston Martin suddenly seemed quite tame! After Christmas, Harper and I, with Andrew Cowan and Robin Turvey in another Tiger, went out again for some final pace note checking and practice. One thing I should mention is that I think this was the first time we had an intercom for the crew which made reading pace notes much more relaxed."

Each crew had made their own pace notes in the practice cars over the various special stages, Peter Harper/Ian Hall in ADU311B and Andrew Cowan/Robin Turvey in AHP294B. Both crews used the standard Rootes pace note notation of Hairpin, Slow, Medium, Quick or Flat with plus (+) or minus (-) signs suffixed as a further refinement - normally added during the second and subsequent runs over the stages. This notation had originated from Peter Procter and as all the drivers used the same method it was possible, if not ideal - as events in the future would show - for one driver to make notes and the others to use them.

Mr Stevenson flags away the Harper/Hall Tiger from the London start. Like its sister Tiger, it is anticipating snow and ice and is already on studded Dunlops. (Rootes)

Monte Carlo Rally 1965

The Harper/Hall Tiger pulls away from the start at the Duke of York Barracks in Chelsea. In 1965 crews still wore ties to rally in. The electrical heaters are clearly visible on both sides of the windscreen. (LAT)

Having made their preparations, the team loaded the service cars, put the finishing touches to the Tigers and journeyed to London to set out on the 34th Rally Monte Carlo. At the unearthly hour of 3.20 on Saturday morning, January 16th, the first crews fired up their engines and A.K.Stevenson flagged away the first of the 49 London starters, a job he had carried out at the British end of the Monte since the 1920's. Both Tigers had an uneventful run through South London and along the Maidstone by-pass in Kent on dry and empty roads to arrive in Dover with plenty of time in hand. Andrew Cowan's Tiger needed a new speedometer cable, a fiddly job at the best of times, and after a thorough check over of both cars the mechanics retired for breakfast before joining the 'Lord Warden' for the channel crossing.

Unfortunately, a full gale was blowing by then and there had been talk of a 12 hour delay in sailing, but, due to the Monte participants, the boat finally sailed. Onboard, the seats and chairs were securely battened down, but finally - and not too soon for some entrants who were not naturally sailors - Boulogne was reached and, in addition to the high winds, the rain started! After a short halt, the Tigers left Boulogne for the 616 mile route in a loop through Belgium and Holland arriving back in Boulogne early on Sunday morning, some 18½ hours later. The weather remained inclement on this loop, as it was to be for the next 28 hours. Apart from the problems of heavy rain and difficult side winds, petrol workers in Belgium were on strike and there was some anxiety over fuel shortages, but the service crews managed - as usual - and both Tigers swept into Bolougne in the early hours of Sunday morning at the end of the loop, having joined the starters from Paris and Frankfurt near Liege. Amongst the

99

Monte Carlo Rally 1965

Paris starters, running at number 186, was the Dutch veteran Maurice Gatsonides driving in his 20th Monte Carlo Rally, an event he had won outright in 1953. With his historical connections with Rootes he had borrowed one of the Tiger recce cars (AHP294B). Whilst he was most impressed with its performance, he complained only that it was too fast to keep its numbers on, and at this control his co-driver, Albert Ilken, was replacing them with good old-fashioned paint. Presumably the problem didn't reoccur!

Having fettled their charges, the service crews loaded up their vehicles and left for the next service point whilst the Tigers lined up ready to leave at one minute intervals for the route to Monte Carlo via the common meeting point at St. Claude.

The run to St.Claude was generally uneventful for both Tigers, the only difficulty being in Andrew Cowan's Tiger and concerned the handbrake. The standard handbrake was being used which needed the button to be depressed to unlock the brake. In order to get the tail of the Tiger out around hairpins, Andrew was using the handbrake, but it was locking on, causing a few anxious moments. They found a garage and had the button drilled so that a pin could be inserted enabling it to be used as a 'fly-off' brake, but, of course, it now wouldn't lock 'on'. This was another field modification that would last the life of the rallying Tigers. The event was the first time that Andrew Cowan had entered the Monte in a competitive car, and like Peter Harper, it was the first time they had driven the Tigers 'in anger'. Peter Harper, however, had the advantage of being a regular competitor on the Monte, having driven his first event in 1950 in a Hillman Minx as a privateer.

At St.Flour, en route to St.Claude, the rally procession met the contingent from Athens, the two Cooper S's who, on their route had passed over the mountains through Sestrière and Gap, and Gap was the town that was to be used on the later run into Monte. At Sestrière they had run into a blizzard and

Four minutes earlier the Cowan / Turvey car had been flagged away from the London start-line by the enthusiastic Mr Stevenson. (LAT)

Monte Carlo Rally 1965

The Cowan/Turvey Tiger at the Dover control before boarding the "Lord Warden" for a stormy crossing of the English Channel to Boulogne. The Tiger is flanked on both sides by the works Triumph Spitfires. A youthful Simo Lampinen (Triumph Spitfire) passes behind Robin Turvey. (Rootes).

snow drifts and had changed onto studded tyres to enable them to reach control and continue over the Col de Mont Genevre to the town of Gap and then to the control at St.Flour via Crest. In the control the works Ford team, who had started en masse from Monte Carlo, were discussing the icy roads they had come over which had necessitated using studded tyres. Even the main road up to the common control in St.Flour, which was at an altitude of 2800ft, was a mixture of pure ice and packed snow with alternating patches of virtually dry tarmac.

Perhaps an indication of what was to come now occurred on the run from St.Flour to St.Claude, where, between Bourg and St.Claude, a distance of some 73km, snow falls reduced visibility to thirty feet or less. Of the 237 starters, 211 crews wearily arrived at St.Claude, 26 having retired for various reasons and of those 211, 25 had incurred road penalties. The cars now ran in numerical order on the final leg to Monte Carlo, a distance of 550 miles that included five difficult stages timed to the second, which, with the road penalties, would determine the starting order on the Mountain section next day from Monte Carlo. Already it was raining in Monte Carlo, a sure sign to the locals that that there was snow in the mountains. The route from the St.Claude control to Monaco, which included the five classification stages in its 550 miles, ran initially over mainly minor roads to Chambery, where a half hour was allowed for service, fuel and tyres, before setting out on the serious part of the rally over the stages to Monaco. This 120km run to Chambery was usually considered easy for most competitors, even on snow covered roads, and indeed this was the case for the early numbers, and for the Warsaw starters (Numbers 2-29), the sun even shone in places. But such are the vagaries of the weather in the Alps that, in spite of weather forecasts to the contrary, for the Tigers in the London starting group and those from Frankfurt, night had fallen and snow was beginning to fall and settle and getting progressively worse by the minute. Robin

Monte Carlo Rally 1965

The Harper/Hall Tiger awaiting loading at Dover Docks with a works Spitfire of the Dutchman Rob Slotemaker/Alan Taylor on one side and the Works Imp of David Pollard/Barry Hughes on the other. The Tiger sports one of its lightly studded spare wheels on the boot lid - a works modification. (Rootes)

Turvey swore that the snow was falling in substantial lumps rather than the more usual flakes!

By the time the later numbers had arrived on the scene, a blizzard was raging and up to 1.5ft of snow was to fall on the roads. All down the road to Chambery the weather was getting worse. Just north of Chambery near Aix-les-Baines, heavy snow drifts were forming on the Col du Chat and, in Chambery itself, the strong wind was forming the snow-storms very quickly into drifts. It was in these blizzards that the works Ford Cortinas lost an average of 20mins each and the Renault team disappeared to the last man (and car). Ian Hall recollects "... suddenly in the Massif the weather started to turn nasty but we were on studded SP44 tyres so this wasn't too much of a problem though they were getting a bit worn. As we approached the Time Control at Chambery, where the serious stuff started, it began to snow in anger and Harper really flew the thing past the evening traffic down the N.201 to get as much servicing time as possible before the Mountain Stages. A quick check over, new fully studded tyres and we were off into the dark night on pace notes to tackle the 'three cols' towards Grenoble."

John Davenport, who was co-driving the last car on the road - writing later in 'Motor Sport' - described the route "...already many of the road signs were obscured by the snow and the fresh falls did nothing to help matters, so that many, many cars simply got lost..." Generally the first one-third of the entry, up to number 136, were relatively lucky as they reached Chambery be-

Monte Carlo Rally 1965

fore the main blizzard, although they had found progressively heavier falling snow as they approached the roads closer to Chambery. For the Tigers the conditions were bad, but both had had fully studded tyres fitted at St.Claude. Andrew Cowan to this day still doesn't know why he chose full studs - but in spite of some amusement from some other competitors, the choice was obviously the right one.

A further problem for both Tigers and other competitors in the same group of numbers was that one road high in the hills above Le Poizat had been snowed over since the first cars had passed through; and so Peter Harper and Andrew Cowan found themselves taking a detour of around 6km before rejoining the official route, but in spite of this unplanned detour Peter Harper arrived at the control in time.

The Cowan/Turvey Tiger hustles through the flat and wet French landscape at the junction of the N42 and the D224 just north of Nabrinken. (Rootes)

The Harper/Hall Tiger at a control complete with pillow for the long common route. (LAT)

Monte Carlo Rally 1965

The Cowan/Turvey Tiger leaves the Boulogne control in the rain on the way to join the Frankfurt and Paris starters in Liege on the loop through Arnhem, La Haye and Anvers before returning to Boulogne. (Rootes)

The Paris start of Maurice Gatsonides and Albert Ilken. (Via Ian Hall)

Monte Carlo Rally 1965

Maurice Gatsonides, a long time Rootes competitor, approaches the Alps in his borrowed Cowan/ Turvey recce Tiger, with his co-driver Albert Ilken apparently asleep. The car has an interesting lighting set up with a light shield over its spot lights - something Gatsonides fitted regularly to his rally cars - and externally mounted electric horns. The Tiger remains on steel wheels but carries an (European production) Alpine wing motif and a corresponding 260 badge. (Rootes)

At this stage in the rally Ian Hall was struck with an occurrence of the navigators malaise, normally experienced when running head down in the maps – a bout of motion sickness. In spite of this inconvenience Ian was his usual professional self and the only mistake to which he would confess was that at a control - many of which punctuate the route - he was in such a hurry to clock in that he rushed over to the control and offered his Michelin map instead of his roadbook.

Five km south of Chambery came the first of the special stages which used the narrow and twisty D912 road over the Col du Granier, running through St.Pierre d'Entremont, up the Col de Coucheron and down into the little mountain village of Le Sappey en Chartreuse, high above Grenoble. Whilst the road up to the first tunnel on the Granier was clear, the majority of its 47km was deep in snow and blizzards, and the stage produced virtually every combination of conditions. The weather was still deteriorating and, as a final blow, Le Sappey had a power failure! By this time the atrocious weather affected the whole field, or, at least, those who were left. Andrew Cowan and Robin Turvey had tackled this stage with alacrity and were rewarded with an 8th fastest time.

Timo Makinen and Paddy Hopkirk had produced the two fastest times, Makinen's an incredible 41mins 28secs, some 1min 43secs faster than Hopkirk, whilst Andrew turned in a very respectable 45mins 53secs being beaten only by the two Cooper S's, the three Citroens (all five front wheel drive) and the lone Cortina of Soderstrom (45.30).

Monte Carlo Rally 1965

Hustling through the French hairpins on the ascent of one of the many Cols on the route, the dirt and petrol stained Harper/Hall Tiger sports a clear-view panel on the rear window. (Rootes)

The Tigers burbled their way out of the stage and sped off through Grenoble along the D524 to Chamrousse, high in the Grand Alpes.

Here the service before the stage, vital for the correct choice of tyres, was chaotic - a small road jammed with spectators' cars, service vehicles who had nowhere else to stop and service, and finally, totally unrestrained spectators. With the winds still at gale force and the snow continuing to drift badly, the service crews worked their usual miracles, in the case of the Tigers there was very little to do, and rapidly the cars were away and into the 35.5km stage over the Chamrousse Pass, a twisty road covered in packed snow which finished back down on the main road near Uriage. Ian Hall remembers the night run "...the blizzard got worse and the whole night took on a surreal atmosphere with the entire scene a mass of whirling snow and the junctions just holes in snow banks. I vaguely remember meeting the service crews a couple of times but don't think the car needed any attention except clearing the packed snow from the wheel arches. Tyre and stud wear in these conditions was negligible. We met one of our Ice Note crews at the bottom of the Col des Lecques who thrust their notes into the car but we left sideways without a chance for conversation! We didn't need ice notes anyway – the whole road was snow and more snow. For some reason nothing went seriously wrong – Peter was at his awesome best with his remarkable eyesight and sensitive car control..."

A long road section over mainly D roads to Gap followed, which was followed by a rebate in the blizzards and in Gap only flurries of snow remained to remind the crews of the previous hours of blood, sweat and tears.

Monte Carlo Rally 1965

The Cowan/Turvey Tiger exhibits some understeer on its progress through the dry roads of France towards the snow in the mountains. (Rootes)

On the St.Apollinaire stage, the third of the night and set over 17km, over 6 inches of snow had fallen since 4pm and the road conditions were not always improved by the sometimes erratic progress of the snowploughs. The next stage over the 14km Col des Lecques was very much on. The wide roads were covered in deep snow, but the edges were visibly marked giving the drivers a clear idea of 'what was where', which is difficult on drift covered roads.

From the end of the stage the itinerary looped around to Barreme and then back into the mountains, with their fog of whirling snow, and towards the control at Pont Charles Albert, the last before Monaco.

The Tigers crossed the bridge and within 2km were at the last of the special stages, the steep climb up La Roquette to Levens. The road surface was dry all the way up and the correspondent from 'Autocar' described the scene "...the 'big bangers' in the rally, the Sunbeam Tigers of Cowan/Turvey and Harper/Hall looked and sounded on top of their form, the drivers using lots of throttle to swing the cars round the hairpins on the dry road..." Predictably, under these conditions, Bohringer's Porsche was quickest at 6mins 20secs for the 7km stage, but both Peter Harper (4th fastest at 6.58) and Andrew Cowan (8th overall at 7.02 - 4secs and 4 places! - and equalling Linge's time in the works Porsche 911) made the most use of the Tigers superiorities on tarmac. Now there was only the road section down the N202 to Nice and across the mountains to La Turbie and finally to the control at Monte Carlo - and sleep!

Monte Carlo Rally 1965

On this morning of the 19th, only 35 crews arrived at the final control in Monaco never having been more than one hour late anywhere along the route - 35 out of the 273 starters. Pat Moss-Carlsson, who was in 6th position overall and leading the ladies class, described it as the hardest she had ever competed in. The cars, having been fettled by their service crews previously in the hills above the Principality before the control, were inspected and put into Parc Fermé.

The Peter Harper and Ian Hall Tiger pulls away from a Time Control, almost certainly situated in the warmth of the Bar in the Café des Voyageurs in the background. (LAT)

Placings before the Monte-Monte Mountain Circuit:

1	Makinen/Easter	Cooper S	0	113.01
2	Bianchi/Demorrier	Citroen DS	120	121.24
3	Neyret/Terramorsi	Citroen DS	360	121.09
4	Bohringer/Wutterich	Porsche 904	240	128.30
5	Harper/Hall	Sunbeam Tiger	360	129.37
6	Moss-Carlsson/Nystrom	Saab 96 Sport	600	128.06
11	Cowan/Turvey	Sunbeam Tiger	1020	128.56

Monte Carlo Rally 1965

Timo Makinen and Paul Easter in their works Mini Cooper S led the field by a large margin, and were, incredibly, the only crew not to have collected road penalties, whilst the Citroens of Bianchi and Neyret were second and third respectively. Bohringer was fourth in his Porsche 904, an incredible drive in such a car, whilst fifth was the Peter Harper/Ian Hall Tiger, another excellent drive with a car with so much torque which inevitably makes it very touchy on snow and ice. In 11th place was the Andrew Cowan/Robin Turvey Tiger who, whilst having a faster aggregate time over the stages than the Harper/Hall Tiger, had incurred more road penalties. These had been acquired when both Tigers had arrived at a service point short of fuel. Peter Harper had arrived first and both fuel cans had been used to replenish his vehicle leaving Andrew Cowan to use a singularly tardy French roadside petrol-pump to fill the tank.

Both of the Tigers, as well as now being first and second in class, remained essentially undamaged and in good shape for the Mountain Circuit - even though Cowan's vehicle was missing both of its headlamp surrounds, a problem not unknown to more normal Tiger owners. With the lead that the Tigers had in their class, Marcus Chambers now decided to let Peter Harper go for the highest possible position overall, whilst Andrew Cowan was to consolidate his class position and thus, at least, enable a class win should any malady befall the Harper car. This course of action had also been coloured by a shortage of studded tyres and the decision was made to give Peter Harper new tyres and Andrew Cowan was to run on Peter's used tyres. Consequently, where studded tyres were to be used, this would slow Andrew as, in those days, studs became loose fairly quickly and after a hard driven stage many of the studs were missing.

This year, for the first time, there was to be no thrash around the Grand Prix Circuit, but a 380 mile supplementary test around the Lower Alpes behind Monaco, with the highest placed 120 cars competing. The Automobile Club had no problems in choosing the cars since only 35 had gained eligibility by actually arriving in Monaco, and these crews set out to cover the road section, set at an average speed of 37mph, and tackle the six stages in between the road sections. There were, in fact, only three stages with each being traversed twice, not necessarily in the same direction, and because of the conditions en route the maximum lateness had been increased to thirty minutes.

At 6.52pm the Makinen/Easter Cooper S was flagged away on the "Épreuve Complementaire Monaco-Monaco", commonly known as the Mountain Circuit, and five minutes later the Harper/Hall Tiger burbled away to be followed in a further six minutes by the Cowan/Turvey car. After a short run out of 37mins along the coast to Menton and up into the mountains over the Col de Castillon, Peter Harper opened the score convincingly over the first stage, from Sospel along the Gorges de Piaon to Moulinet, by recording the scratch fastest time of 6mins 29secs for the 11km, an average of 101.8km/hr (63.6mph), and beating Bohringer in the Porsche by three seconds. Twenty one seconds behind was the Cowan/Turvey Tiger and so competitive was the entry that these 21secs dropped them to 5th fastest behind the Porsches of Bohringer and Linge, Erik Carlsson in the Saab and, of course, Peter Harper and Ian Hall.

Ian remembers the re-start and run out from Monaco and the first stage "The following evening we lined up again under the arc lights by the Harbour. A very Gallic and excited PA announcer shouting about "Arpair et Ole dans Soonbeam Teegre avec un moteur le plus grand!" and we screamed off towards Menton, all lights full on, ignoring all speed limits and the French Highway Code, then inland up the Col de Castillon towards the Turini. The first épreuve is a short fast climb. It was also bone dry and our new studded tyres made the most incredible racket as Peter threw the Tiger up for the fastest time. The car was sideways all the time in a most un-Harper like manner. The rest of the night was ice and snow all the way but I don't remember much falling snow. The service crews were magnificent. Once we got a set of new spiked tyres and new front pads (pre-bedded - part of our preparation routine) and

Monte Carlo Rally 1965

Cowan and Turvey transverse a French Col on one of the drier parts of the route. (Rootes)

petrol was chucked in in double quick time."

Immediately came the second stage, starting at the other end of the village of Moulinet and across the infamous Col de Turini and down to la Bollene Vesubie – 37km of twisting, tight roads. The roads leading to the top of the Turini were dry except for the last few hundred feet – in the afternoon there had been a heavy fall of snow – and the Harper/Hall Tiger kept up the pressure, even though the steep roads with the many hairpins did not particularly suit the Tiger, clearing the stage in 25mins 51secs and recording fifth fastest scratch time. The Cowan/Turvey car was only 38secs behind, just over a second a kilometre. Both cars took a short service at La Bollene and hurried off for the 45km road section over the very minor roads of the Alpes Maritimes to St.Sauveur and the start of the third stage, a typical up and over col running through Roubion and over the Col de Couillole at 1678m to end in the little village of Beuil, a distance of 21km, but with road conditions considerably worse than the Turini.

Once again the Makinen/Easter Cooper S was fastest but the Harper/Hall Tiger was only 1min 38secs slower over the 21km, finishing in a time of 24.07, with Andrew Cowan close behind in 24.37. 78km down the road at the time control at Pont Charles-Albert, the service crews were beginning to set up their point, mainly for tyres and fuel, but with enough spares to carry out quite major repairs on the car, if necessary, and if time allowed.

As they were setting up, Peter Harper had joined the main road and entered the control at Puget-Theniers, looking very relaxed in the Tiger, the exhaust burbling away and Peter sitting quietly at the wheel, in distinct contrast to the marshals. An immediate turn off the main road and the steep twisty climb over the Col de St.Raphael and then along the very small D27 and over the Col-

Monte Carlo Rally 1965

let des Sausses led the Tigers towards the time control. At Pont Charles-Albert the cars had started to come through. John La Trobe in his Mini Cooper was short of fuel and stopped to beg fuel from the Rootes crews, who willingly gave him two gallons and he shot off into the night. Suddenly both Tigers and the Pollard/Hughes Imp all arrived together and all demanding fuel. After three minutes of strenuous activity all three cars were away into the night, Andrew Cowan unfortunately dropping a minute road penalty, leaving the service crews to rapidly pack and leave for the next point.

For the second time over the Turini, this time in reverse, both of the Tigers were predictably slower, as the Col is slower in this direction, Harper/Hall returning 28mins 11secs and being beaten by the Cowan/Turvey car that returned an excellent 27mins 59secs. However, on the St.Sauveur stage over the Col de Couille in the same direction both Harper (23.52) and Cowan (24.14) improved on their previous times, the Harper car being fifth fastest. The weary crews approached the sixth and final stage and with a final effort Harper finished the stage in 27mins 43secs, just 1min 11secs faster than Cowan.

As the crews approached Monte Carlo and the finish line, they pondered on difficulties of the Mountain Circuit that had turned out to be a very tough test with only 22 cars finishing within their 30 minute allotted lateness. During the night Bianchi in his Citroen had gone out dramatically when he destroyed his car against a tree, having been forced to run on badly worn tyres due to a service problem, whilst Neyret, third in Monte, had dropped four places in the night.

The Harper/Hall Tiger passes through the village outskirts of La Chaise Dieu on the Saint Flour - Montbrison leg under the watchful eyes of the Gendarmerie and locals. The N499 now is renumbered as the D999. (Rootes)

Monte Carlo Rally 1965

All the other front-runners had maintained their positions and Pat Moss-Carlsson had taken advantage of her front wheel drive (and the handicapping system) to pass Peter Harper into third place. Andrew Cowan had a good run too, and apart from minor damage to the left hand fog light and bumper, had maintained his position in both the overall classification and in the large capacity GT class.

Andrew also had a well deserved moment of glory later, when, after a change of tyres he won the driving tests, or the manoeuvring speed tests as the organisers liked to call it, on the Quai Albert 1er in Monte Carlo He recorded 57.4 secs with Peter just 0.5secs slower on 57.9 secs, and just beating Paddy Hopkirk on 57.95 secs in the Cooper S.

The Tigers made their mark in these tests and Autosport noted "the acceleration of the Tigers was reminiscent of dragsters, the red Rootes machines screaming down the long straight with smoking tyres."

Thus in only their second major attempt at rallying with the Tiger, Rootes had finished a fine 4th and 11th overall and captured the first two places in the GT class. The Harper/Hall Tiger also collected the RAC Challenge Trophy for the highest placed British competitor driving a British car and the London Starting Control award.

It is interesting to note that of the first seven places in the final results, five of those places were taken by "engine over the driving wheels" type of car (three front wheel drive and two rear wheel drive) whilst only two cars of the front engine rear wheel drive variety were in their number, Peter Harper's Tiger and the Rover 2000 of Roger Clark. It was also significant that out of the 237 starters, running, of course, in numerical order from the St.Claude control, all but one of the top ten finishers came from the top 150 numbers, only Henry Taylor in the works Cortina squeezing into 9th place; and looking further down the lists, 32 of the finishers were in the top 150 numbers and only 3 from 150-276.

Thus is rallying guided by the vagaries of the weather interspersed with large doses of luck! As a final indication as to how fast it is necessary to drive to be competitive on roads completely covered with ice and snow on the épreuves, Timo Makinen's Mini Cooper S averaged very close on 60mph on a road where, for most people, it would be difficult to average 45mph, even when it is dry! This puts even more into perspective the incredible performance by Eugen Bohringer and the classic drives of both Peter Harper and Roger Clark - all essentially in cars not particularly suited to the extreme conditions experienced in this year's Monte. Ian Hall, who was in the thick of it all, notes on the performance of Eugen Bohringer "...always demon quick he usually drove a works Mercedes but this time was in a Porsche 904 of the type more usually seen at Le Mans or the Targa Florio. Anything less suitable for a long fast rally in a blizzard would be hard to imagine and for my money this was one of the drives of the century."

An excellent result for the Tiger that was to prove to be a hard act to follow.

Monte Carlo Rally 1965

ROUTE OF THE MONTE CARLO — MONTE CARLO CIRCUIT RE-INTRODUCED THIS YEAR

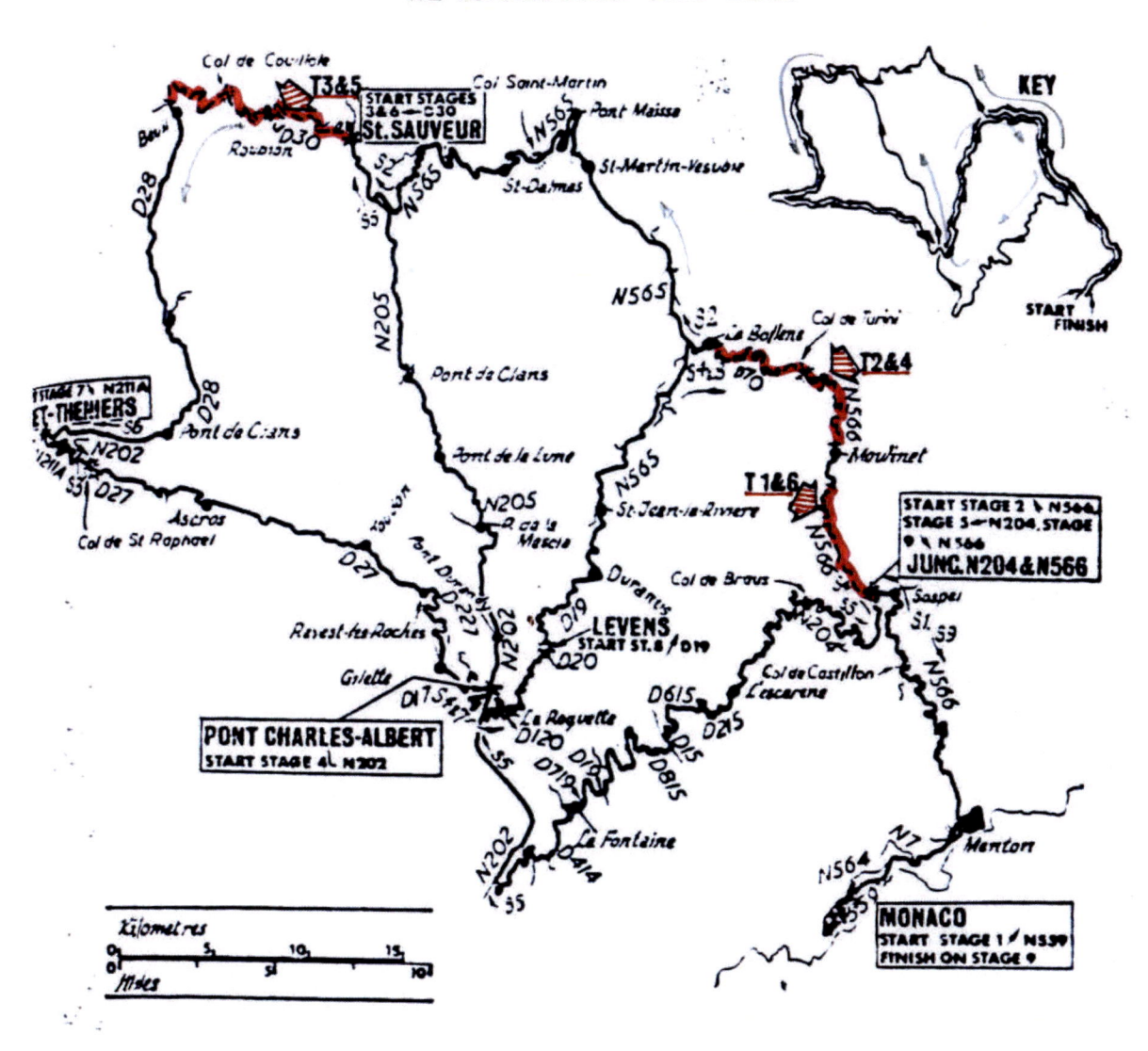

The route of the last night's Mountain Circuit, just six stages from Monaco to Monaco. (Autocar)

113

Monte Carlo Rally 1965

ÉPREUVE COMPLÉMENTAIRE MONACO-MONACO

1ʳᵉ Etape : MONACO–Bif. N 204/N 566 (Sospel) (34 km) – Temps idéal : 0 h 37

MONACO	N 559	
Bif. N 559/N 564	N 564	
Bif. 564/N 7	N 7	
MENTON	N 566	12
COL DE CASTILLON		27
SOSPEL	N 204	33
Bif. N 204/N 566		34

2ᵉ Etape : Bif. N 204/N 566 (Sospel)–SAINT-SAUVEUR-sur-TINEE (82 km)
Temps idéal : 1 h 30

Bif. N 204/N 566	N 566	
Première épreuve à moyenne spéciale chronométrée		Distance : 6 km environ (entre la Bifurcation N 204/N 566 et Notre-Dame de la Menour).
MOULINET	—	11
Deuxième épreuve à moyenne spéciale chronométrée		Distance : 26 km environ. DEPART : MOULINET N 566 ; COL DE TURINI D 70 ; ARRIVEE : LA BOLLENE
LA BOLLENE	D 70	37
Bif. D 70/N 565	N 565	40
SAINT-MARTIN-VESUBIE	—	53
PONT MAISSA	—	56
COL SAINT-MARTIN	—	61
SAINT-DALMAS V.	—	64
Bif. N 565/N 205	N 205	78
SAINT-SAUVEUR-sur-TINEE		82

3ᵉ Etape : SAINT-SAUVEUR-sur-TINEE – PONT CHARLES-ALBERT (99 km)
Temps idéal : 1 h 48

SAINT-SAUVEUR-sur-TINEE	D 30	
Troisième épreuve à moyenne spéciale chronométrée		Distance : 21 km environ. DEPART : SAINT-SAUVEUR-sur-TINEE D 30 ; ROUBION — ; COL DE LA COUILLOLE — ; ARRIVEE : BEUIL
BEUIL	D 28	21
PONT DE CIANS	N 202	43
PUGET-THENIERS	N 211 A	51
COL DE SAINT-RAPHAEL	—	
Bif. N 211 A/D 27	D 27	59
ASCROS	—	68
TOUDON	—	79,5
REVEST-LES-ROCHES	—	84,5
COL DE SAUSSE	—	
Bif. D 27/D 227	D 227	
GILETTE	D 17	92
PONT CHARLES-ALBERT		99

4ᵉ Etape : PONT CHARLES-ALBERT–Bif. N 566/N 204 (Sospel) (75,5 km)
Temps idéal : 1 h 23

PONT CHARLES-ALBERT	N 202	
Bif. N 202/D 120	D 120	
LA ROQUETTE	D 20	4,5
Bif. D 20/D 19	D 19	10,5
LEVENS	—	11,5
DURANUS	—	19,5
SAINT-JEAN-LA-RIVIERE	N 565	24,5
Bif. N 565/D 70	D 70	35,5
LA BOLLENE		38,5
Quatrième épreuve à moyenne spéciale chronométrée		Distance : 26 km environ. DEPART : LA BOLLENE D 70 ; COL DE TURINI N 566 ; ARRIVEE : MOULINET
MOULINET	N 566	64,5
Bif. N 566/N 204		75,5

A page from the route of the 1965 Monte Carlo Rally, showing the route mapped in the previous figure. The first Etape runs from Monaco to the junction of the N204 & N566 at Sospel, a distance of 34km. The next Etape contains two special stages, one from Sospel to Moulinet (11km) and the other immediately from Moulinet to La Bollene (26km), over the Col de Turini. The first Etape has a time allowance of 37 minutes and the second 1 hour 30 minutes, including the épreuves (special stages).

Monte Carlo Rally 1965

SPECIAL STAGE TIMES ON THE MONACO-MONACO SECTION

Crew and make	1st stage	2nd stage	3rd stage	4th stage	5th stage	6th stage	Total
S. Zasada/K. Osinski (Steyr-Puch)	7 m. 15 s.	27 m. 17 s.	26 m. 28 s.	27 m. 14 s.	25 m. 34 s.	27 m. 25 s.	141 m. 13 s.
P. Ekholdt/J. Haraldsen (Saab)	7 m. 6 s.	26 m. 59 s.	25 m. 59 s.	29 m. 11 s.	25 m. 56 s.	28 m. 14 s.	143 m. 25 s.
E. Carlsson/G. Palm (Saab)	6 m. 49 s.	25 m. 22 s.	24 m. 8 s.	26 m. 11 s.	23 m. 25 s.	25 m. 59 s.	131 m. 54 s.
O. Andersson/T. Aman (Saab)	7 m. 1 s.	25 m. 57 s.	24 m. 28 s.	26 m. 36 s.	23 m. 44 s.	26 m. 17 s.	134 m. 3 s.
H. Lund/B. Wahgren (Saab)	7 m. 14 s.	27 m. 16 s.	25 m. 57 s.	28 m. 34 s.	24 m. 52 s.	28 m. 3 s.	141 m. 56 s.
Pat Moss-Carlsson/Elizabeth Nystrom (Saab)	6 m. 50 s.	25 m. 50 s.	24 m. 48 s.	26 m. 49 s.	24 m. 15 s.	26 m. 1 s.	134 m. 33 s.
T. Makinen/P. Easter (Mini-Cooper)	6 m. 55 s.	24 m. 39 s.	22 m. 29 s.	25 m. 10 s.	22 m. 51 s.	24 m. 28 s.	126 m. 32 s.
H.-J. Walter/W. Lier (B.M.W.)	7 m. 4 s.	25 m. 50 s.	24 m. 34 s.	29 m. 3 s.	24 m. 2 s.	28 m. 8 s.	138 m. 41 s.
B. Söderström/S. O. Svedberg (Lotus Cortina)	7 m. 0 s.	26 m. 42 s.	24 m. 21 s.	27 m. 3 s.	24 m. 11 s.	26 m. 33 s.	135 m. 50 s.
G. Verrier/B. Pasquier (Citroën)	7 m. 21 s.	28 m. 15 s.	26 m. 44 s.	27 m. 33 s.	25 m. 14 s.	27 m. 54 s.	143 m. 1 s.
R. Neyret/J. Terramorsi (Citroën)	6 m. 59 s.	26 m. 33 s.	24 m. 34 s.	28 m. 33 s.	24 m. 39 s.	27 m. 38 s.	138 m. 56 s.
J.-C. Ogier/G. Servoz (Citroën)	6 m. 58 s.	26 m. 9 s.	24 m. 26 s.	28 m. 38 s.	24 m. 47 s.	27 m. 58 s.	138 m. 56 s.
D. E. Pollard/B. F. Hughes (Hillman)	7 m. 18 s.	27 m. 10 s.	25 m. 39 s.	28 m. 45 s.	26 m. 18 s.	28 m. 40 s.	143 m. 50 s.
A. Cowan/R. Turvey (Sunbeam)	6 m. 50 s.	26 m. 29 s.	24 m. 37 s.	27 m. 59 s.	24 m. 14 s.	28 m. 54 s.	139 m. 3 s.
P. Harper/I. Hall (Sunbeam)	6 m. 29 s.	25 m. 51 s.	24 m. 7 s.	28 m. 11 s.	23 m. 52 s.	27 m. 43 s.	136 m. 13 s.
Rosemary Smith/Margaret Mackenzie (Hillman)	7 m. 39 s.	27 m. 58 s.	25 m. 59 s.	28 m. 24 s.	25 m. 3 s.	28 m. 46 s.	144 m. 49 s.
R. Slotemaker/A. Taylor (Triumph)	7 m. 13 s.	26 m. 12 s.	26 m. 34 s.	27 m. 36 s.	25 m. 1 s.	26 m. 52 s.	139 m. 28 s.
R. Clark/A. Porter (Rover)	7 m. 9 s.	26 m. 36 s.	25 m. 28 s.	28 m. 42 s.	24 m. 56 s.	28 m. 48 s.	141 m. 39 s.
G. Selbach/W. Seelinger (Ford)	7 m. 10 s.	27 m. 47 s.	26 m. 14 s.	28 m. 36 s.	26 m. 16 s.	29 m. 1 s.	145 m. 4 s.
H. Linge/P. Falk (Porsche)	6 m. 40 s.	25 m. 31 s.	24 m. 21 s.	26 m. 42 s.	24 m. 26 s.	28 m. 0 s.	135 m. 40 s.
E. Böhringer/R. Wutherich (Porsche)	6 m. 32 s.	24 m. 47 s.	23 m. 44 s.	26 m. 35 s.	23 m. 15 s.	26 m. 7 s.	131 m. 0 s.
H. Taylor/B. Melia (Ford)	7 m. 2 s.	25 m. 48 s.	24 m. 44 s.	27 m. 20 s.	24 m. 34 s.	28 m. 5 s.	137 m. 33 s.

SPECIAL STAGE TIMES ON THE CHAMBERY-MONACO SECTION

Crew and make	1st stage	2nd stage	3rd stage	4th stage	5th stage	Total
J. la Trobe/D. Bailey (Mini-Cooper)	49 m. 58 s.	37 m. 9 s.	23 m. 32 s.	15 m. 2 s.	7 m. 55 s.	133 m. 36 s.
J. Nielsen/H. Henriksen (Volvo)	49 m. 42 s.	36 m. 37 s.	25 m. 49 s.	14 m. 57 s.	7 m. 53 s.	134 m. 58 s.
S. Zasada/K. Osinski (Steyr-Puch)	51 m. 17 s.	36 m. 37 s.	24 m. 56 s.	15 m. 2 s.	7 m. 48 s.	135 m. 40 s.
P. Ekholdt/J. Haraldsen (Saab)	53 m. 55 s.	36 m. 31 s.	24 m. 41 s.	15 m. 25 s.	8 m. 32 s.	139 m. 4 s.
E. Carlsson/G. Palm (Saab)	40 m. 0 s.	37 m. 28 s.	21 m. 18 s.	13 m. 51 s.	7 m. 13 s.	120 m. 30 s.
O. Andersson/T. Aman (Saab)	47 m. 16 s.	34 m. 6 s.	23 m. 13 s.	13 m. 54 s.	15 m. 2 s.	133 m. 31 s.
H. Lund/B. Wahgren (Saab)	47 m. 53 s.	36 m. 7 s.	22 m. 39 s.	14 m. 45 s.	7 m. 50 s.	129 m. 14 s.
Pat Moss-Carlsson/Elizabeth Nystrom (Saab)	47 m. 54 s.	34 m. 46 s.	22 m. 43 s.	14 m. 31 s.	7 m. 22 s.	127 m. 16 s.
T. Makinen/P. Easter (Mini-Cooper)	41 m. 28 s.	30 m. 25 s.	20 m. 32 s.	12 m. 47 s.	6 m. 59 s.	112 m. 11 s.
O. Vilkas/O. P. Paroma (Mercedes-Benz)	48 m. 12 s.	38 m. 51 s.	22 m. 51 s.	14 m. 50 s.	8 m. 32 s.	133 m. 16 s.
P. Hopkirk/H. Liddon (Mini-Cooper)	43 m. 15 s.	31 m. 45 s.	20 m. 45 s.	13 m. 59 s.	8 m. 11 s.	117 m. 51 s.
H.-J. Walter/W. Lier (B.M.W.)	45 m. 58 s.	35 m. 38 s.	25 m. 3 s.	14 m. 4 s.	7 m. 12 s.	127 m. 55 s.
A. Ingier/F. Jacobsen (Saab)	50 m. 4 s.	39 m. 12 s.	23 m. 23 s.	15 m. 37 s.	8 m. 17 s.	136 m. 33 s.
B. Söderström/S. O. Svedberg (Lotus Cortina)	45 m. 30 s.	35 m. 37 s.	21 m. 24 s.	13 m. 47 s.	7 m. 35 s.	123 m. 53 s.
D. Morley/E. Morley (Mini-Cooper)	46 m. 19 s.	35 m. 31 s.	21 m. 47 s.	14 m. 3 s.	6 m. 59 s.	124 m. 39 s.
G. Verrier/B. Pasquier (Citroën)	46 m. 18 s.	36 m. 11 s.	22 m. 56 s.	14 m. 54 s.	7 m. 51 s.	128 m. 10 s.
R. Neyret/J. Terramorsi (Citroën)	43 m. 12 s.	33 m. 33 s.	22 m. 23 s.	13 m. 55 s.	7 m. 26 s.	120 m. 19 s.
L. Bianchi/J. Demortier (Citroën)	43 m. 24 s.	34 m. 14 s.	21 m. 21 s.	13 m. 59 s.	7 m. 36 s.	120 m. 34 s.
Lucette Pointet/Françoise Houillon (Citroën)	45 m. 29 s.	34 m. 52 s.	22 m. 46 s.	14 m. 29 s.	15 m. 18 s.	132 m. 54 s.
J.-C. Ogier/G. Servoz (Citroën)	44 m. 1 s.	34 m. 41 s.	22 m. 49 s.	14 m. 26 s.	7 m. 25 s.	123 m. 22 s.
D. E. Pollard/B. F. Hughes (Hillman)	54 m. 58 s.	38 m. 37 s.	21 m. 41 s.	14 m. 36 s.	7 m. 36 s.	137 m. 14 s.
A. Cowan/R. Turvey (Sunbeam)	45 m. 53 s.	37 m. 43 s.	22 m. 11 s.	14 m. 29 s.	7 m. 2 s.	128 m. 1 s.
P. Harper/I. Hall (Sunbeam)	47 m. 4 s.	37 m. 39 s.	22 m. 24 s.	14 m. 42 s.	6 m. 58 s.	128 m. 47 s.
Rosemary Smith/Margaret Mackenzie (Hillman)	49 m. 25 s.	39 m. 5 s.	22 m. 0 s.	14 m. 29 s.	7 m. 58 s.	132 m. 57 s.
R. Slotemaker/A. Taylor (Triumph)	50 m. 58 s.	39 m. 41 s.	22 m. 52 s.	14 m. 43 s.	7 m. 1 s.	135 m. 15 s.
R. Joss/J. Fitzpatrick (Austin)	53 m. 18 s.	38 m. 38 s.	22 m. 24 s.	13 m. 41 s.	7 m. 55 s.	136 m. 56 s.
R. Clark/A. Porter (Rover)	49 m. 46 s.	36 m. 45 s.	21 m. 33 s.	14 m. 34 s.	7 m. 25 s.	130 m. 3 s.
C. Edwards/T. Wisdom (Austin)	55 m. 9 s.	39 m. 33 s.	23 m. 4 s.	15 m. 18 s.	7 m. 58 s.	141 m. 2 s.
S. Lampinen/J. Ahava (Triumph)	47 m. 39 s.	35 m. 44 s.	21 m. 28 s.	13 m. 36 s.	6 m. 49 s.	125 m. 16 s.
G. Selbach/W. Seelinger (Ford)	56 m. 0 s.	38 m. 34 s.	23 m. 33 s.	15 m. 23 s.	7 m. 29 s.	140 m. 59 s.
H. Linge/P. Falk (Porsche)	52 m. 40 s.	35 m. 10 s.	20 m. 36 s.	14 m. 14 s.	7 m. 2 s.	129 m. 48 s.
E. Böhringer/R. Wutherich (Porsche)	52 m. 55 s.	35 m. 5 s.	19 m. 55 s.	13 m. 25 s.	6 m. 20 s.	127 m. 40 s.
H. Marang/P. Coltelloni (Citroën)	55 m. 5 s.	38 m. 3 s.	24 m. 16 s.	14 m. 59 s.	7 m. 39 s.	140 m. 2 s.
J.-J. Thuner/J. Gretener (Triumph)	55 m. 17 s.	36 m. 59 s.	21 m. 45 s.	14 m. 30 s.	6 m. 45 s.	137 m. 16 s.
H. Taylor/B. Melia (Ford)	53 m. 32 s.	36 m. 8 s.	21 m. 29 s.	14 m. 5 s.	7 m. 47 s.	133 m. 1 s.

This table shows the actual times taken by the 22 crews who finished the whole of the Mountain Circuit test: Makinen was beaten only on one of the stages - the first - by Harper's Tiger. The factor of comparison has to be applied to these times to get the final figures. (Autosport)

Monte Carlo Rally 1965

Andrew Cowan and Robin Turvey power their way across the top of the Col de Turini special stage on the last night Mountain Circuit Monaco to Monaco leg. (Rootes)

At a service point, where seconds can prevent a road time penalty, Des O'Dell gives a hand at changing the front tyres on Peter Harper's Tiger on the 1965 Monte Carlo Rally. Note the innovative use of nut guns for rapid changes. (Mike Kempley)

Monte Carlo Rally 1965

Andrew Cowan keeps the dirt-stained Tiger in line and between the snow banks whilst Robin Turvey similarly keeps in line with the pace notes as they rapidly traverse a special stage on the Mountain Circuit. (LAT)

The Harper/Hall Tiger hustles through an "Épreuve Chronometrique" in the mountains before the finish in Monaco. (Rootes)

Monte Carlo Rally 1965

Peter Harper and Ian Hall speed through a special stage in the Alpes above Monaco. The Tiger has lost its right side headlamp surround and the left hand foglight has been replaced. Whilst giving a good fill-in of light, the fog lights were nevertheless very vulnerable to minor driving indiscretions in that position. Ian Hall uses the intercom to dictate the road notes. (LAT)

Peter Harper uses the power of the Tiger to good effect out of the hairpins on the drier roads of the La Roquette special stage en route to Levens. (LAT)

Monte Carlo Rally 1965

ADU312B accelerates hard, with the rear springs in full compression on the La Roquette stage. (Photo Junior)

Peter Harper and Ian Hall at speed on the top of the Col du Turini special stage, with Ian at similar speed on the road notes, essential under these draconian conditions. (LAT)

Monte Carlo Rally 1965

XXXIVᵐᵉ RALLYE AUTOMOBILE MONTE-CARLO JANVIER 1965

Robin Turvey & Andrew Cowan seem pleased after their return from the Mountain Circuit. (Photo Plage)

At the completion of the 1964 Rallye Monte Carlo, Andrew Cowan and Robin Turvey collect their well-deserved rewards at the Monaco Royal Palace for their 11th overall, second in class and fastest in the driving test. (Rootes)

Monte Carlo Rally 1965

Above: Peter Harper and Ian Hall, in formal pose during the prize-giving at the Palace, show their hard won cups.

Below: Ian Hall and Peter Harper in a more relaxed pose. A fine 4th overall and a 1st in the GT class were their just deserts. (Rootes)

Monte Carlo Rally 1965

The victorious Rootes team with their rally-worn Tigers after the prize giving at the Monaco Royal Palace, with the cars back on the road tyres used in the final "driving tests" on the sea-front in Monte Carlo. In those days the cars remained unwashed prior to the prize giving. (Rootes)

Monte Carlo Rally 1965

MARCH, 1965 — MOTOR SPORT

ROOTES SUCCESSES IN 1965 MONTE CARLO RALLY

SUNBEAM TIGER

1ST Peter Harper / Ian Hall

2ND Andrew Cowan / Robin Turvey

GRAND TOURING CARS OVER 2,500 c.c.

Peter Harper and Ian Hall also **4TH** overall

OTHER AWARDS
International Sporting Club Cup
R.A.C. Challenge Trophy
Challenge Antony Noghes

HILLMAN IMP

PROVES ITS PERFORMANCE AND RELIABILITY

2ND David Pollard / Barry Hughes

4TH Rosemary Smith / Margaret Mackenzie

ALSO SECOND COUPE DES DAMES

GRAND TOURING CARS UP TO 1,000 c.c.

RESULTS SUBJECT TO OFFICIAL CONFIRMATION

RELIABILITY – that's what it takes to win awards in the world's great rallies. And it's reliability that succeeds in the day-and-night endurance of the Monte's gruelling 2,600-mile run, to be followed by the ordeal of a twisting, tortuous 380-mile circuit deep in snow and often carpeted with black ice. Of the 237 starters, 35 cars arrived and only 22 survived in the mountains. Among the successful few were four of the five works-entered Rootes cars – two Sunbeam Tigers, two Hillman Imps. A remarkable performance in an event the top drivers have called *the toughest Monte ever!*

ROOTES MOTORS LIMITED
BY APPOINTMENT TO HER MAJESTY THE QUEEN
MOTOR VEHICLE MANUFACTURERS
ROOTES MOTORS LIMITED
LONDON SHOWROOM AND EXPORT DIVISION ROOTES LIMITED DEVONSHIRE HOUSE PICCADILLY LONDON W1

Monte Carlo Rally 1965

Peter Harper

One of Britain's all-time top-class drivers – and he had staked this claim before leading the competition department's forays with the Tiger – Peter had started his rallying career in 1947, aged 26, rapidly graduating from club events to the international circuit. His first Monte Carlo Rally was in 1950 in a Hillman Minx, his wife Mavis standing in at the last minute as the co-driver. His talent soon came to the attention of Norman Garrad and he was soon leading the works team of Sunbeam Talbot Alpines – with a wide range of success. Over his 20 year career he remained loyal to Rootes – apart from a brief event with Ford in a Ford V-8 Falcon on the Tour de France Automobile – and throughout his Rootes career he drove Sunbeam Talbots, Alpines and Rapiers before Tigers – mainly on rallies but also he had singular success at Le Mans winning the Index of Thermal Efficiency in 1961 in the Alpine. A regular competitor in the Monte – he was widely regarded as a Monte specialist (no doubt something he would deny) - he competed in some 15 events and won the Antony Noghes Trophy in 1965 for the highest placed driver with ten or more Montes to his credit. Retiring from works rallying in 1967 he took up rallycross in the Imps, driving for the Alan Fraser team and winning the 'World of Sport' championship in 1969.

Ian Hall

Ian Hall, the Rootes driver, co-driver and rally team co-ordinator was, in his own words "brought up in the hard school of navigation in British Rallies in the Lake District and Yorkshire in Morgans and TR2s." From these early 1955/56 days, he continued his primary rally career with the Rootes team, driving in the 1958/59 period with Norman Garrad as his boss. With the introduction of the Rapier, he both drove and navigated and started his co-driving with Peter Harper in the early 1960's. A lawyer by profession he fitted his career between rallying, but when Marcus Chambers joined Rootes as the Competition Manager, Ian was the first choice as Marcus's assistant and team leader, and his legal career went on 'hold'. He competed in a wide range and number of events, including co-driving for Bill Bengry on the infamous Marathon de la Route (the Spa–Sofia-Liege rally) finishing 14th overall and winning the Group 2 class.

Ian opened his career in Tigers with Peter Harper in their first Tiger rally – the 1965 Monte Carlo. Of the eleven international appearances of the competition department with the Tiger, Ian co-drove on three (Monte, Tulip & Acropolis) and drove on one (Alpine).

He remains fully involved in motorsport – much of it with the VSCC (Vintage Sports Car Club) - and has the eminent sense to have a Riley as his pre-war transport.

Tulip Rally 1965

Unseasonable weather dashes the Tigers' hopes - but still an excellent result for Rootes.

Spurred with their success on the Monte, and to capture fourth overall on any Monte - let alone one in which the weather conditions made it particularly difficult - is a good result, Rootes entered two Tigers and two Imps for the Tulip, starting on the 27th April, with 'Tiny' Lewis forsaking a Tiger drive to run in one of the favoured Imps, as he had on the Monte. The Tigers were entered for Peter Harper/Ian Hall (ADU311B), the same partnership as on the Monte and one of the pre-rally favourites, and Peter Riley/Robin Turvey (AHP294B). Peter Riley was having his second drive in a Tiger, and, apart from the Geneva, had worked previously with Marcus Chambers for many years in the BMC works team, driving a variety of cars including the Healey 3000 (winning his class in the 1959 Liege-Rome-Liege), Austin A105, MGA 1600, Mini-Minor (1961 Tulip and first in class) as well as driving for the Ford works team for a while, which, all in all, added up to a wealth of invaluable experience.

The Tulip had traditionally been a good continental rally for the privateer and especially for an entrant/owner to tackle his first International - and consequently the event always attracted a good number of participants. The rally usually consisted of relatively high-speed sections on tarmac, with easy, if often long, road sections. Traditionally the rally always started in Noordwijk-aan-Zee, near the Hague, the route then moving out of Holland, meandering through Belgium or Luxembourg or Germany perhaps and into the French Alps, returning the same way to finish at Noordwijk. All the eliminating tests, upon which the rally result was essentially decided, used mainly circuits and hill climbs, interspersed with road sections used as link sections only. So it was this year, with the rally starting on the 27th April in Noordwijk and travelling down through Germany into France. There were nineteen speed tests specified, but, in the event, only thirteen were used, a total of only 59km in a total route of some 3200km.

Both Tigers had been similarly prepared at the works, AHP294B still retaining its wing vents as well as keeping the bonnet partially open, and ADU311B also used these methods to assist in the cooling. Many of the eliminating tests were at night and Peter Harper had a total of seven forward facing lights, using the same set up as he had on the Monte, whilst Peter Riley did without the centre upper spot light and relied for additional illumination on the 7 inch Lucas driving lamps. Both cars had the same fog lamp set-up, as used on the Monte. Both cars had their lights masked and to warn spectators and others of their approach - as they were leading the field - had a pair of air horns fitted in addition to the normal horn. Since the event was all on tarmac, Dunlop racers (Green Spots) were generally used fitted to the normal 5½ inch Minilite wheels. However, Rootes had their complement of tyres reduced slightly when one of the mechanics accidentally put a drill through the spare tyre wall, when drilling the boot lid to fit the rally plate - not an auspicious start!

Whilst not auspicious, it was certainly an early start, at 6.45 in the morning, when Richard Burton, who was making a film in Holland, flagged car number 1, the Peter Harper/Ian Hall Tiger, away, with Peter Riley and Robin Turvey starting one minute later at number 2. Following the brace of Tigers were the Morley brothers in their works Healey 3000 who had been interviewed by Dutch radio and television.

When asked for an opinion of their chances, replied that it should be all right if they managed to put a couple of Tigers in their tanks! The first eliminating test at Circuit Terlaemen (Zolder) was unfortunately cancelled due to local difficulties and a leisurely run down through Holland by motor-

Tulip Rally 1965

Richard Burton, making a film in Holland, wishes good luck to the Peter Harper/Ian Hall Tiger at the start of the 1965 Tulip Rally - not one of the better rallies for the Competition Department Tigers. (Classic Cars/Autocar)

way and sideroads led to the Nurburgring in Germany. This relatively short 8.5km section of the famous Nurburgring circuit was tackled in the reverse direction from Adenau Bridge back to the grandstands.

Peter Harper used the power and torque of the big motor to its best advantage, and set the fastest time of 4mins 37secs, no doubt enjoying the bettering of the Morley brothers Healey by some 3secs, although the BMC team later fought back when the time was later equalled by Timo Makinen's works 1275cc Cooper S. All three of these cars were using racing tyres for these tests, as were the works teams from Ford England, Ford France, Volvo and Lancia, and it was to be this factor which, later in the rally, was to drastically affect the results.

Following this test, the route wound down through the traditional Tulip road sections towards the Vosges mountains, in which several more speed tests were run: the Col du Struthof (4km), the Col de Fouchy (4km) - marshalled efficiently by the London Motor Club - and the Trois Epis (4.5km), situated 12km west of the border town of Colmar.

On le Struthof, Donald and Erle Morley took their revenge and in the fading light took their Healey up this wide, fast climb in 2mins 23secs. Again on the Fouchy, where the road was dry, the Morleys put up fastest time overall. Following Trois Epis, the road section was routed over the Col de la Schlucht, but since this was blocked by snow, the competitors were diverted round to the time control at St. Maurice-sur-Moselle. At this control there were 128 cars still running out of the 180 entry list and the service crews, who had preceded the rally, were setting up shop in the town, a few kilometres north of Ballon d'Alsace which was the next speed section. This stage was over a distance of 9.1km and the test ran up to the sum-

Tulip Rally 1965

mit of the Col at an altitude of 1250m (4062ft). As midnight approached and the crews got ready to receive and fettle their cars, snow began to fall which gradually became heavier and heavier and finally the wet snow began to settle. Both Tigers arrived, were serviced and as they, and the first few cars, lined up for the test, word reached the officials that the top of the Col was blocked by over a foot of snow. With the first cars turning round and the later cars arriving, some chaos reigned and finally a decision was made to cancel the Ballon test and re-route the rally around the main roads.

This not only meant missing out a further climb at Bourbach le Haut, but caused a few problems for those running on BP fuel - it circum-navigated the mobile BP tanker - and several competitors had a few anxious moments as they reached deep into their fuel reserves. The route now led further south towards Geneva and the time control at Champagnole on the N5 which was due to be reached at around 5am. As the crews drove on towards the Swiss border and approached Geneva, the snow thickened. The route ran down the N5 from Champagnole through St.Laurent-en-Grandvaux to St.Claude, also the well-known control from the previous Monte. The road rises out of St.Claude towards Bellegarde and it was here that the first hold-ups occurred in the snow. The whole field had been caught in the snow either on racing tyres or on their touring equivalent. Only BMC, in the guise of their competition manager, Stuart Turner, and urged on by the very experienced Morley brothers, had had sufficient foresight to lay on racing tyres with pop-in studs for its two entries.

Peter Harper and Ian Hall pull onto the historic Nurburgring circuit for the first eliminating test of the 1965 Tulip Rally, the intended first test at the Circuit Terlaemen (Zolder) having been cancelled. The Tiger set the joint fastest time with the Timo Makinen works Cooper S. On the start line waiting for the off is the Peter Riley/Robin Turvey Tiger, followed by the number 4 works Healey 3000 of Donald and Erle Morley. (Classic Cars /Autocar)

Tulip Rally 1965

SURVEY OF THE TIME CONTROLS

Noordwijk aan Zee	27 apr 65	06.45—09.15 u
Zolder	27 apr 65	10.39—13.09 u
Nürburgring	27 apr 65	14.21—16.51 u
Flughafen Ensheim	27 apr 65	18.30—21.00 u
St. Maurice s/Moselle	28 apr 65	00.23—02.53 u
Champagnole	28 apr 65	04.55—07.25 u
Champagnole	28 apr 65	10.30—13.00 u
St. Maurice s/Moselle	28 apr 65	14.30—16.33 u
Sarrebourg	28 apr 65	18.05—20.35 u
Larochette	28/29 apr 65	21.28—23.58 u
La Roche-en-Ardenne	29 apr 65	00.39—03.09 u
Zolder	29 apr 65	05.31—08.01 u
Noordwijk aan Zee	29 apr 65	10.36—13.06 u

SURVEY OF THE ELIMINATING TESTS

1	Circuit Terlaemen (Zolder)	3.000 m
2	Nürburgring (Nordschleife)	8.200 m
3	Course de Cote du Struthof	4.000 m
4	Course de Cote Col de Fouchy	4.000 m
5	Course de Cote des Trois Epis	4.500 m
6	Course de Cote Ballon d'Alsace	9.100 m
7	Course de Cote du Mont-Saleve	8.300 m
8	Course de Cote de la Faucille	10.600 m
9	Course de Cote Ballon d'Alsace	9.300 m
10	Course de Cote du Col de Bramont	6.300 m
11	Course de Cote Col de Fouchy	3.600 m
12	Course de Cote de Breitenbach	4.500 m
13	Course de Cote Bourscheid—Moulin	3.200 m
14	Course de Cote de Kautenbach	3.000 m
15	Course de Cote de Dasbourg	3.500 m
16	Course de Cote la Roche-Samree	7.500 m
17	Circuit de Francorchamps	4.200 m
18	Circuit Terlaemen (Zolder)	3.000 m
19	Circuit Zandvoort	3.800 m

An extract from the regulations of the 1965 Tulip Rally defining the Time Control and the Eliminating Tests with their length. The Tulip had long road sections that were relatively relaxed (only if the weather was clement!), interspersed with the speed tests from which the results were calculated.

Tulip Rally 1965

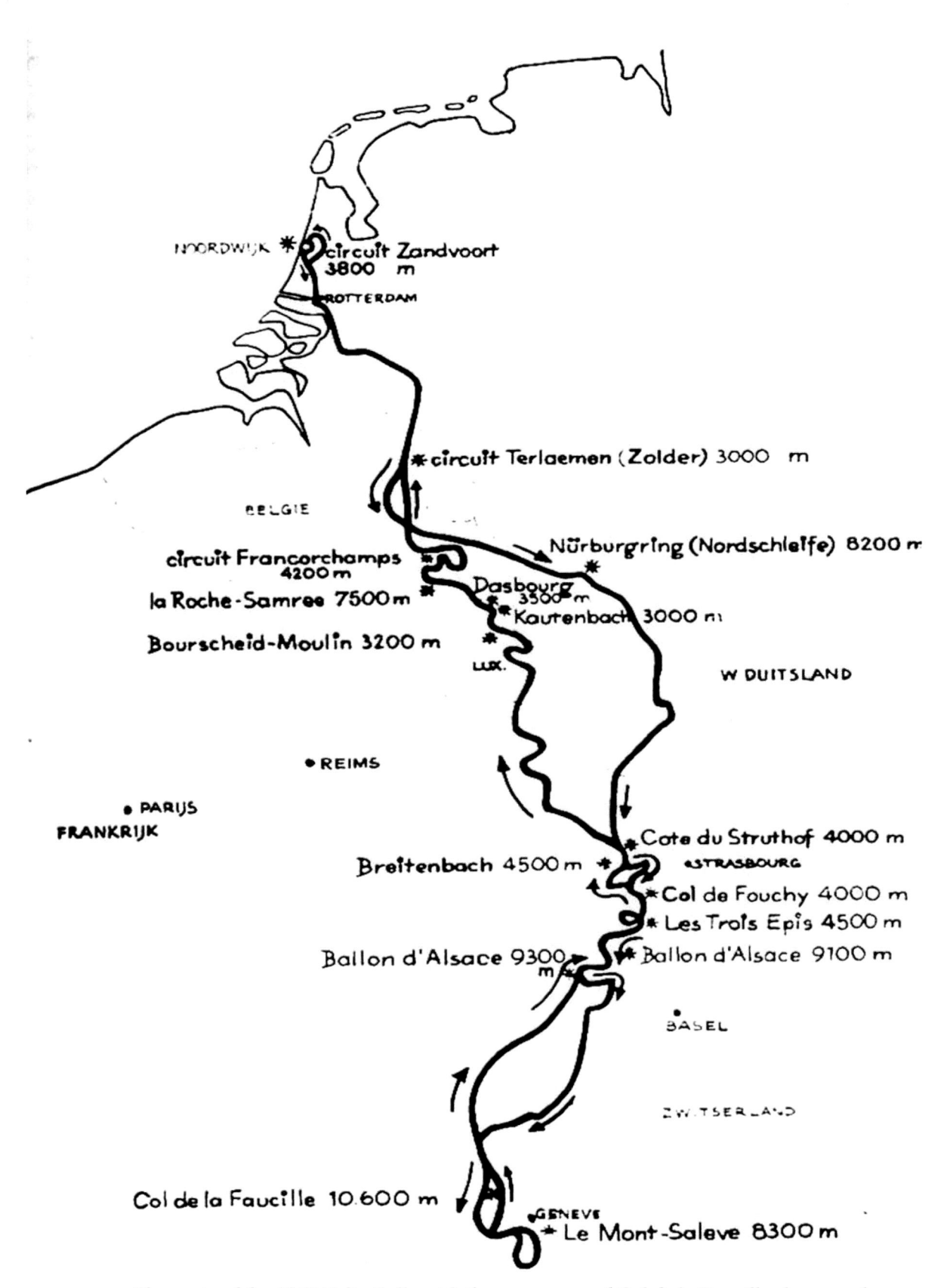

The route of the 1965 Tulip Rally with the snow covered Col de la Faucille shown and where the Tiger of Peter Riley / Robin Turvey departed the rally. (via Robert Clayson)

Tulip Rally 1965

The Peter Riley/Robin Turvey Tiger passes through St Laurent-en-Grandvaux on its way to the Col de la Savine, already suffering from the combination of unexpected snow and racing tyres - even Dunlops! (Rootes)

The Tigers could not get any suitable snow tyres for their 13 inch rims and many others, including the Imps, went round on Dunlop SP's. Jean-Jacques Thuner, who lives near Geneva, and was driving a works Triumph 2000, said that he could not remember conditions such as these ever happening before at this time of year. Ian Hall remembers that the Tiger was very difficult to get up the snow covered cols and running number one on the road, the combination of virgin snow and racing tyres made it virtually impossible. Ian notes "The snow made our progress up the Faucille very slow (racing tyres remember) with me bouncing on the back bumper and holding onto the extra spare wheel we had bolted to the boot lid. I can still feel the pain as my hands warmed up again back in the car. However get up the Faucille we did despite running No.1 in the rally and about 8 to 10 inches of virgin snow. This was due to the limited slip diff. and the sheer Harper genius."

The route then looped south of Geneva and took in the test at Mount Saleve, a test using the D41 road, which was originally 8.3km in length, but had been shortened to 6.4km to avoid snowfalls at the top of the test. The Morley brothers were again fastest on scratch in 5mins 47.8secs.

As the rally left the Mont Saleve test in the early morning, the test on the Col de Faucille, a distance of 10.6km, was between them and the control in Champagnole. Both Tigers were still on Dunlop Greenspot racing tyres and in an effort to make up time, Harper had an altercation when avoiding a van at the bottom of the Faucille near Gex. He had been on line for a fast corner when he met a French Camionette delivering on the wrong side of the road. Peter said it was a milk van, Ian Hall said it was wine and Robin Turvey thought it was bread; but the sum total was that Peter took to a ditch to avoid a head on accident, after which the Frenchman rapidly

Tulip Rally 1965

backed onto his correct side. The Tiger was firmly rooted in the ditch but undamaged, but when the straight-faced gendarmes arrived, they pointed out that the car must not be moved until a notary public or an equivalent functionaire arrived and committed everything to paper. Time was not, unfortunately, on Peter Harper's side and the Tiger and crew departed from the rally.

Both Tigers had been in severe trouble with their colossal torque and virtually smooth tyres, the snow filling the tread pattern - which was essentially a Dunlop dry racing design. Although the Faucille hill climb had been cancelled, it was still necessary to climb half of the snow covered hill to reach the route check and it was here that Peter Riley and Robin Turvey bowed out of the rally. Peter Riley notes "so we assayed the hill, which was extremely slippery, and the car wouldn't go up, wouldn't go up, wouldn't go up. That was the end of us as far as the rally was concerned. Turning the Tiger round to get out, it embedded itself in a snow bank. At which point I said "Lets see what happens in reverse", so we put it gently into reverse, with a very soft touch on the clutch, and it pulled itself out of the snow bank and up-hill! I shouted to Robin to jump in, and we proceeded, at 2.5 mph, gently up the Faucille – backwards! After about ¾ of a mile the car boiled, which was nothing unusual for a Tiger, but we managed to make the 9km to the top of the hill...." They were, however, in good company as the Ford Mustang of Henri Greder retired at the same spot, although, of course, it was of little comfort at the time. Both cars were, by now, OTL – over the time limit - and out of the rally.

Thus finished the Rally for the Tigers, but not for the Rootes team. At the finish, where 47 crews classified as finishers returned out of the 157 starters, the much modified Group 2 998cc Imps of Rosemary Smith/Val Domleo and 'Tiny' Lewis/David Pollard were declared first and second overall. A splendid win for Rootes in a Tulip Rally made particularly difficult by the unseasonable weather.

Peter Harper and Ian Hall pass through St Laurent-en-Grandvaux in the falling snow that was to cause so much havoc for the Tigers on this particular rally. (Rootes)

Tulip Rally 1965

Robin Turvey

Robin, like 'Tiny' Lewis, was a West Countryman and had been competing in the hectic club rallying scene before joining 'Tiny' to compete, with Rootes, in International rallies. His first International with Rootes was the 1963 RAC Rally when he competed with 'Tiny' in a Group 3 Sunbeam Rapier. An outing on the 1964 Tulip followed, with an early rally for the Imp but which led to a retirement. Later in the year he joined 'Tiny' Lewis again for the 1964 RAC Rally where they, and the car, survived the 'end-over-end' incident on the Porlock Toll Road in an Imp – losing only some 3 minutes - but were forced to retire later, just after the halt at Turnberry, with the failure of the universal joint in the drive train

His first rally in the Tiger was with Peter Riley on the 1964 Geneva Rally and he went on to compete in six events in the Tiger, one more with Peter Riley, one with Andrew Cowan and three with Peter Harper. He competed in the full rallying life of the Tiger from virtually the first rally (Geneva 1965) to definitely the last (Gulf London 1966). When not co-driving in the Tiger, his skills were used by Rootes in the Hillman Imp and he and 'Tiny' were entered in the 1965 RAC Rally in a 998cc Imp, finishing 12th overall and 3rd in class, behind the two works Saab Sports of Erik Carlsson and Pat Moss-Carlsson

After the Rootes period Robin was, almost naturally, further involved in the sport with Vauxhall/Opel, acting in the role of a Rally Co-ordinator in their UK National and International Rallying efforts.

Scottish Rally 1965

A short forest rally for Andrew Cowan - but a result for a Tiger.

Early in June, the competition department loaded a lone Tiger (ADU311B) and travelled north to Glasgow where the Scottish Rally was due to take place. It was an important event for Rootes since their Imps were built in Scotland and a lot of local support was apparent. Andrew Cowan, as Rootes resident Scottish driver, was to drive the car with Alan Redpath in the right hand seat. Apart from the 1964 RAC Rally, where the Rev. Rupert Jones had pedalled a semi-works Tiger through the forests, this was the first foray into the forests for a full works Tiger. All the previous rallies had been on tarmac, with the Tigers accounting well for themselves, and it was hoped that the Tiger would be as good in the forests. Although the rally headquarters was deep in the malt whisky country at Grantown-on-Spey, the event started at the offices of the Royal Scottish Automobile Club in central Glasgow.

The route led southwards in a loop leading firstly to stages using the large forests in the Peebles area of the southern uplands. Thence down to the forests around Dumfries and Kirkcudbright and back to Glasgow to complete the loop for the supper stop - the first main stop of the rally. The rally continued for the only night section down the Argyll Peninsula towards Bute, thence back towards Glencoe taking in ten hard stages on the way. A long run on Tuesday morning into the North East highlands and finally to Grantown completed the first leg. Two more days running in the highlands around Grantown with a final run back to Glasgow completed the 1660 mile route, of which 54 stages accounted for 20% of the total mileage, with a £200 prize for the eventual winner. The Scottish forests, varying in character from the slippery Peebleshire forests, the hard, rough stages in the Ayr and Wigtown area to the soft sandy forests of Banff and Moray, have never been known for their forgiving nature and it was with some justification that the BMC team called the rally "a Liege with thistles".... albeit a mini Liege.

Thus on Whit Monday morning on the 7th of June in a steady drizzle of rain, Andrew Cowan and Alan Redpath unlocked the Tiger after its night in the parc ferme, with perhaps a little trepidation, since the car had done little testing, but bearing in mind that there is no better testing than that "under fire" in actual rally conditions. As the first of the 102 starters fired up their engines and proceeded to the start ramp to be flagged away, the Tiger's engine refused to start and it was only after the car had been pushed around Blythswood Square for several minutes that it rumbled into life. Not a particularly propitious start and perhaps a portent of the future? Whilst the first few stages went well, the front suspension was taking a battering on the hard and rough stages, being magnified to some extent by the weight of the engine. The exhaust pipes had fallen off and in the night run down the Argyll peninsula the constant battering of the wishbones on the bump stops had caused the cross member to bend and the suspension to sag, and whilst temporary repairs had been made, more trouble was in store. The oil filter had slipped and hung down to rub on the universal coupling on the steering, which eventually wore its way through the filter casing and allowed the oil to escape in the middle of a stage. At that time, the engine was run on Super Shell, a vegetable oil, which apart from being rare on events at that time, could not be mixed with the more normally available mineral oil, as a mixture of the two types of oil turns into a buttery gel. There was, however, not much choice if the car was to continue. Andrew stopped a fellow Scot, Tommy Paton, borrowed some mineral oil, topped up the engine and continued. By this time the rally had progressed towards Glencoe and as there was a Rootes service point there, Andrew hoped to make that point where, no doubt, the

Scottish Rally 1965

service crews would work their usual wonders. Upon reaching the service point, Andrew was met by the Rootes team manager Marcus Chambers, who, having heard about the oil incident, assessed that the engine damage was probably terminal and that the suspension might collapse again and cause more damage or injury, and regretfully told Andrew that his rally was over.

The privately entered Tiger of John Melvin/Hamish Wilson (EGA65C), also had problems with a deranged suspension and steering, but in spite of these problems, a leaking sump and an off on one of the final stages, managed to keep the car in the rally and upheld Rootes honour by winning his class.

Subsequently to being refurbished at Glencoe, Andrew drove the Tiger around the rest of the route as a spectator and the car was returned to Coventry by Ian Hall and his wife without it missing a beat, although Ian notes that "It was a bit of a heap by then. En route to Coventry Rosemary Smith followed us in her Imp, and I decided to turn into a hotel drive with lunch in mind. Although I turned into the entrance at very low speed the surface was gravel, the Power-Lok diff. suddenly locked up and with the post-rally tick over at about 1200 rpm we under-steered smartly into a gatepost throwing Ros's (Ian's wife) head first into the Haldal I was not popular."

The Tiger that finished – the class winning John Melvin/Hamish Wilson car.

The International Police Rally 1965

The loan of a works Tiger produces a good dividend.

John Gott and D.Nicholson attract the attention of the spectators at the start of the 1965 International Police Rally. John Gott had used his previous driving record under the managership of Marcus Chambers to persuade Marcus to loan him a competitive car for this rally. It turned out to be a shrewd move by them both. (Rootes)

During early May, John Gott, the previous BMC competitions leader, driver and full time policeman, had persuaded Marcus Chambers, his old team manager in the BMC days, to loan him and Sgt.D.E.Nicholson a works Tiger to compete in the International Police Rally which took place annually in Belgium. The event was solely for police crews and Marcus agreed without much persuasion and it turned out to be an excellent decision. As a bonus, Marcus Chambers agreed to provide himself, a mechanic - Derek Hughes - and a service car to provide some support.

The car to be used was the Tulip recce car of Peter Harper and Peter Riley (AHP295B). The rally comprised a 690 mile circular route around the Belgian countryside and included military and civilian police teams from seven countries. AHP295B remained very much as it had during the Tulip recce, the only external change being the fitting of wire mesh stoneguards to the headlamps, a strategy that was to be kept later for the

The International Police Rally 1965

The Gott/Nicholson Tiger rounds one of the hairpins well surfaced with the continental cobble-stones (pavé); long lasting, but lethal in the wet. (Rootes)

Alpine rally.

The competition was quite fierce with four very hot Alfa Guilia Super TI's from Milan, three works Renaults, a BMW 1800 for Friedel/Oellerer (second last year) with a Weber carburettored engine producing over 160bhp and an innocuous looking VW from Liege, which turned out to be powered by a Porsche Carrera motor.

The event started and finished, in Liege, a town that John Gott knew well from his previous epic drives in the Liege-Rome-Liege marathon rallies. The opening 100 miles to the first test was through a maze of un-signposted roads north of Liege, and thanks to a well-completed recce none of the British lost any time.

The first test was a standing kilometre on the Masta straight at Francorchamps and the Gott/Nicholson Tiger set the fastest time of 28.9secs, with the BMW second on 30.3, closely followed by the Alfa of Milano/Angelli on 30.8secs. The next test was the hill climb at Neblon, where the Tiger again made the best time of 1min 31.8secs followed by the BMW on 1 min 34.6secs but, on this fast climb, the Alfa of Milano went out of the event with a spectacular crash. A road section of some 100 miles followed to the start of the last test, the international hill climb at Namur. Bathed in sun, the cobbles were extremely slippery and the Tiger was handicapped with large amounts of wheel-spin. Nevertheless an equal time (1 min 55.3secs) with the Mini Cooper of Sullivan/Bennet kept the Tiger in the overall lead. Only the Tiger and the 850 Mini of Heaver/Potter were without penalty at this point, since, in the speed tests, the fastest car in each class penalised the slower cars in the same class. Friedel's BMW came a close third on 1 min 56.2secs.

The International Police Rally 1965

A road section now ran from the French frontier near Givet, some 300 miles back to Liege. This turned out to be the most difficult part of the rally and the average speed over the many short sections of between 8 and 20 miles long - some extremely rough - varied from 37 to nearly 50 mph! It was in these sections when the battle between the Tiger and the BMW was finally resolved, when Friedel took a wrong slot which cost him 10secs at the next control, thereby dropping a whole minute. From the breakfast stop at Achouffe to the finish in Liege was accomplished without any road penalties, in spite of thick fog, and the Tiger completed the rally without any overall loss of road penalties. This professional performance by John Gott and Sgt ' Nich' Nicholson netted them the overall winner's spot - a well deserved victory.

It had turned out to have been a shrewd decision on the part of Marcus Chambers to loan the car to a highly competent crew and it had paid off well. As a spin off, Michael Turner produced one of his excellent paintings depicting the car in full flight on the event.

John Gott looks pleased with his efforts, whilst the Tiger still remains in pristine condition. (Rootes)

The International Police Rally 1965

The Gott/Nicholson Tiger works its way through the Belgian lanes towards the finish in Liege and victory. (Rootes)

The excellent Michael Turner painting of the Gott/Nicholson Tiger victory, which very effectively captures the essence of that era of rallying. (Michael Turner)

The International Police Rally 1965

Derek Hughes was the mechanic that Marcus Chambers took with him to service the Tiger on this rally. This letter, from John Gott to Derek, was typical of the close team relationships in rallying of that period. It also points out the undisputable fact that this was the first outright win for the Tiger on an International Rally. (courtesy of Derek Hughes)

The International Police Rally 1965

The Gott / Nicholson Tiger sets out for its win. This photo was sent to Derek Hughes as a memento for his help on the rally and is inscribed 'With thanks for all your help to make the victory possible' and signed by both crew members. (courtesy of Derek Hughes)

John Gott

The Chief Constable of Northants, John was the Captain of the BMC works team for six years and his broad and detailed knowledge of motoring was used to good cause by the whole team. Prior to joining BMC Competitions, his considerable experience in the world of International Motorsport was gained very much from rallying his own HRG and sharing drives in a Frazer Nash. These experiences had won him two Alpine Cups and, apart perhaps from Ian Appleyard in his XK120 Jaguar, he had more experience of rallies like the Alpine Rally than anyone who was not already in a works team. Being a policeman, he had a good memory, and writing everything down he amassed a formidable collection of information on competition details from all types of rally and used it all to ensure that the information was put at the disposal of the BMC team to enable the best result to be achieved. A top-level driver, he was well known for his drives on the Liege-Rome-Liege and Alpine rallies in both the Healey 3000 and the MGAs.

Alpine Rally 1965

A toughly fought class win disappears at post-event scrutineering with homologation discrepancies.

Apart from their European debut in the Geneva rally, the Alpine Rally, or to be more precise, the Coupe des Alpes, was the only rally where Rootes entered three Tigers. Hopes were high after the excellent Monte result and John Gott's outright win on the International Police Rally, and whilst a cruel stroke of luck had eliminated the cars on the Tulip, mechanical reliability was high and this was an event in which reliability was at a premium. Apart from the Scottish, a forest event, where mechanical maladies had stopped the car, no cars had failed to finish due to straight mechanical problems on a tarmac event. For the all important recce, where pace notes were checked on those hills and epreuves which had been used before, notes made for the navigationally difficult or dangerous sections of the selectives and road sections and the chore of new notes made on new épreuves and sections, Peter Harper and David Pollard took AHP 295B whilst AHP 293B and ERW 729C were used by the other two crews. AHP 295B, having just been returned by John Gott from its outright win on the International Police Rally had had the engine removed and passed to Ernie Beck for refurbishment, and the remainder of the car checked over. The checks, as usual, were thorough, and as well as routine changes of all the oils, the engine, gearbox and axle, the gearbox was opened through the top lid and when finished the gear linkage

Alpine Rally 1965

rods were checked and reset. A general spanner-check and an examination made for breakages and cracks on all the suspension and chassis followed, whilst the rear brake wheel cylinders were changed and new brake shoes fitted. Having checked both the rear hub end float and the front disc run out after the fitting of new wheel bearings, as well as a multitude of other important details, the car was despatched on Friday, 18 June to begin the recce. On the following Tuesday, the other two cars were driven into the workshop for their pre-recce preparation. AHP293B, chassis number 13, was one of the cars which had been built as a rally car along with ADU311B, ADU312B, AHP294B and AHP295B in June 1964, but was never actually used in anger in a rally before being sold. Apart from a good check over the car and chassis in general, which included an axle change, fitting of a competition clutch unit with a new clutch master cylinder and flexible clutch pipe, the brake pads were changed for DS11 front pads and VG95 rear shoe linings and after fitting the Heuer clocks and a single Halda Tripmaster, the car was despatched for the pre-rally contest with the French Alps. Whilst this Tiger was dealt with fairly quickly, ERW729C was a different matter! The car had been as a standard production car in March 1965 and first registered on April 1st and whilst some work had been done on the car, much remained to do. The engine, gearbox and axle were removed, the engine overhauled, fitting 289 cylinder heads in the process and the rear engine bulkhead modified for the fitting of a Holley carburettor. Both front and rear suspensions were stripped, modified and rebuilt, and a new 3.77 axle fitted. To cover the all-important lighting, iodine bulbs were fitted, with fog lights and a reverse light, the wiring being modified with line fuses in the appropriate parts of the loom. Since the problem of high under bonnet temperatures remained with the cars, special attention was paid to preventing the heat reaching the crew. All holes in the bulkhead were filled, aluminium paint was applied under the bulkhead and, as a final measure, the inside of the car was lined with tin-foil where neccessary.

A discussion in the Provence mid-day sun, perhaps on pacenotes, between Marcus Chambers, the competition manager (centre), the co-driver Don Barrow (his left) and the driver on this occasion, Ian Hall. (Rootes)

Alpine Rally 1965

Peter Harper and Mike Hughes take advantage of the time before the rally to rectify any minor problems on their Tiger and to take care of all the rally administrative paperwork and route amendments. The Tiger is already on Dunlop Green Spot Racers. (Rootes)

Finally, having completed the myriad of smaller items that are a vital necessity in a rally car prepared for international competition, and those small items which are peculiar to a particular rally driver, such as minor adjustments to the steering column, the car was pronounced ready for testing. On Wednesday 30th June, AHP295B returned from the recce - having been driven round the route by Peter Harper, whilst David Pollard made new pace notes and updated old ones - for rectification of those minor, and not so minor, differences that had arisen en-route. Minor overheating had occurred and by the fitment of a by-pass pipe, the removal of the pipe to the header tank and the fitting of a four-row radiator, it was hoped that these problems would be alleviated. A roughness in the engine at 4500 rev/min and above was investigated and the ignition contact points and ignition timing checked. Handling, also, had not been up to standard and the rear axle location was looked at, as it was suspected that the rear axle was steering the car. Finally, on the navigators' side, the Halda speed pilot was changed for a Twinmaster and with a final tidy of carpets and cockpit, the car was ready for another foray.

Meanwhile ERW729C, after the initial build and before leaving on the recce had been road tested and was returned on the 1st of July for the final rectification. Apart from minor servicing, and some rectification under the bonnet - where the bonnet had been rubbing on the oil cooler pipe - the shock absorbers were changed for Konis, the rev counter red lined at 6000 rev/min and, as other heating problems were still arising, the bonnet was held open at the rear with sorbo rubber and suitable modifications made to the bonnet

Alpine Rally 1965

pins. The car was now ready for 'Tiny' Lewis and Barry Hughes to take away for their recce.

In the meantime, on the 3rd July, AHP293B had been returned to Humber Road for minor rectification and apart from a change to Koni shock absorbers all-round, the fitting of the latest type of heater valve, a new set of wiper blades, the resetting of the clutch pedal ½ inch nearer the driver and a bleed of the clutch hydraulic system, the car was in excellent condition.

Having completed the recce car, some semblance of peace returned to the competition department and it wasn't until the Tuesday before the start of the rally that the final checks were carried out on ADU312B, the car allocated to Peter Harper for this rally. The normal servicing was carried out on the engine with the points, plugs and tappets checked, with special attention being paid to the recommendation that numbers 7 and 8 ignition leads should not run beside each other, and the starter motor changed. After a road test the car was found to be pulling to the left and the steering felt dead and stiff so the steering geometry was checked and the steering rack loosened, re-set and tightened. The final details were seen to - the rev counter red lined, a Ferodo fan belt fitted - and the car was ready for the rally proper along with ADU311B and AHP294B. Since much of the rally was held at night, lighting was important and all three cars had the same lamp arrangements as Peter Riley had used on the Tulip Rally. Each car had two 7 inch Lucas spotlamps fitted with driving lamp lenses and two 5 inch fog lamps fitted in the usual position on the front bumper.

Ian Hall discusses the rally with Rosemary Smith, driving a works Imp on this Alpine, before the start. From her light reading Rosemary obviously has some time in hand to enjoy the weather in the South of France. The French Esso camionette in the background sets the atmosphere for this challenge in the Alpes. (Rootes)

Alpine Rally 1965

Final preparations by Don Barrow and Ian Hall, both in good humour and relaxing in the Marseilles sunshine before the rally start. (Rootes)

A new departure was the fitting of stone-guards to the headlamps. They had been tried before on AHP295B on the International Police Rally by John Gott, and, of course on the Rapiers - and were fitted to all three cars for this event. A major change from normal practice, and a very distinctive feature of the Alpine cars, was a large air scoop fitted on the bonnet of each car, running from the very front edge and terminating over the carburettor inlet, the air being channelled into the Holley carburettor by this enormous scoop. The purpose of this device was to provide cool air direct to the carburettor and enhance the power output of the engine.

Under-bonnet temperatures in the normal Tiger were high and since this decreased engine power by the hot air being less dense and providing a lower density charge into the engine, the cooler air being fed directly into the carburettor mouth would provide a useful few more horsepower – perhaps vital on this tortuous and tight event. With regard to under-bonnet cooling, both ADU312B and AHP294B retained the traditional wing vents, whilst ADU311B had not been fitted with such contrivances and relied on the usual 'bonnet propped open' scheme – which incidentally both other cars used as well. Also on ADU311B, in order to help airflow through the radiator, a scoop was incorporated into the front valence. All cars were fitted with oil-coolers, the usual hedgehog type, to keep the engine oil temperatures to a reasonable level. All three cars were fitted with the usual Minilite magnesium alloy wheels and apart from reducing unsprung weight, they would help in dissipating the enormous amount of heat from the brakes, especially the discs, which was generated on an event like this where high speeds down the cols were equally as important as speed during the ascent. Dunlop tyres were again used, both of the SP3 type and racing tyres for the dry, with the spare

Alpine Rally 1965

The Rootes mechanics take on the tricky job of fitting the side numbers to the Ian Hall/Don Barrow Tiger, two mechanics to fit and one to supervise, whilst the crew enjoy the sun. The car sports stoneguards on the headlamps and is fitted with Dunlop SP3 pattern tyres on the standard 5½ inch rims. (Rootes)

sitting on the boot lid. Inside the driving compartment the usual Heuer clocks and Twin Halda dominated the co-driver's side, whilst on the driver's side the all-important rev counter had been sunk into the dash cover, just to the right of, and well in line with, the driver's view. An interesting quirk was the use of a non-lift wiper blade only on the driver's side of all three cars – perhaps it is not necessary for the co-driver to view the road in the rain! With the event being sponsored by Esso, 'Tiny' Lewis's Tiger (AHP294B) sported a modified Esso slogan, which, instead of proclaiming "I've got a Tiger in my tank", had been suitably modified to declare "I've got a tank in my Tiger". More than pertinent!

Scrutineering, held on the Old Port waterfront in the middle of Marseilles, was its usual thorough self and after a final series of checks and number fixing, the cars were ready for the start in the evening of Monday 19th July.

The route was divided into three main sections, an 879km (550 miles) run between Marseille and Grenoble; a 1288km (805 mile) section on a round-about route from Grenoble to Grenoble and a final 1433km (896 mile) excursion from Grenoble to the finish in Monte Carlo. As usual each leg had three kinds of road section; the most difficult mountain roads were chosen as selective sections which had to be attempted at a particularly high average speed and these 'selectifs' formed the basis for a Coupe des Alpes – the ambition of every serious rally driver – and any time lost - even one tenth of a second - on these selectives against the target time would incur the loss of a treasured Coupe.

Alpine Rally 1965

The 'Tiny' Lewis Tiger paraphrases the Esso slogan. (Rootes)

The second type, liaison sections linked the selectives. The final types were the épreuves, sections which required efforts of herculean proportions and which were timed to the nearest one-tenth of a second, for settling ties that may occur amongst those who might incur no penalties on the road. There were two long rest halts of 12 and 24 hours at Grenoble and a shorter 4-hour halt at Chamonix during the final leg.

The cars were divided into three categories, Touring (Groups 1 and 2), Grand Touring and, new for 1965, Sports and Prototype GT cars. The Tigers were, of course, running in the Grand Touring class along with their usual companions and competitors, the BMC works Healey 3000s. Average speeds on the selectives increased with engine capacity for the Touring cars, the highest capacity class (over 2500cc) being equated with the GT cars up to one litre.

The other two categories, the Prototype and GT classes shared a common average speed that was even higher still.

The final crew pairings for the Tigers were Peter Harper/ Mike Hughes (ADU312B), 'Tiny' Lewis/ Barry Hughes (AHP294B) and Ian Hall/ Don Barrow (ADU311B). Ian Hall was deputising for Peter Riley – an experienced Alpine driver - at very short notice as Peter's son was very ill.

At 9.30pm on the 23rd July the first car left the port of Marseilles, brightly lit for the start, on a dull, rather heavy, evening and travelled down the autoroute to the first hill climb at the Massif de St.Baume. The first section was a 5 mile climb to the top of the Col de l'Espigoulier and also a 'selectif' to the village on the other side, so it was important to go quickly in order not to lose time.

Alpine Rally 1965

Ian Hall had had some qualms about driving in such high-ranking company "...but I felt confident that I could cope although I had no delusions about quick times on the timed climbs in that company. My only concerns were that I didn't get much rest before the start and that I would be using Peter Harper's pace notes as I had, of course, had no opportunity to do my own, nor had I practiced the stages. A few miles from the start came the first timed section. The Morley brothers' works Healey was the next car behind me. They already had two Alpine Cups to their credit and I knew that they would catch me before the top, so I had a word with Donald and said that I would be fully aware that they would get past but I wouldn't move over until he let me know he was absolutely ready to pass by blasting the horns. He caught us in about 10 kms, closed up, blasted the horns and I let him by. I was happy enough to do this test without incident as two years before Harper had tipped our Rapier on its side in spectacular fashion and Hopkirk had put his big Healey over the edge!"

The Tigers completed this first series of tests with few problems, although not in the top ten. At the end of the next selective over the Col de Trebuchet there was a long liaison section through Colmars leading to the Col d'Allos which was both a hill climb and a selective. The route wound its way, overnight, northwards and eastwards up and down endless passes, towards the famous Quatre Chemins to Sigale selective beyond Castellane. The selectives in between followed in quick succession, leaving very little time for service or even refuelling between them. Over

Scrutineering of the Peter Harper/Mike Hughes Tiger on the Marseilles waterfront at the start of the 1965 Alpine Rally. Marcus Chambers discusses paperwork details in the background. The Tiger has a large air collector on the carburettor to focus the cold air from the bonnet scoop directly into the carburettor inlet. (Rootes)

Alpine Rally 1965

Marcus Chambers, the competition manager, points out to 'Tiny' Lewis and Barry Hughes some detail on the bonnet scoop construction, perhaps the mesh to prevent ingress of paper and grass into the carburettor. A Rootes mechanic carries out probably the most difficult pre-rally job - getting the numbers on straight and un-wrinkled. In the background a youthful Roger Clark and Jim Porter prepare to tackle the rally in the works Rover 2000. (Rootes)

Quatre Chemins and the selective over the Col du Bleine to Sigale, brake trouble caused the retirement of the 'Tiny' Lewis Tiger. The rear brake linings had become unbonded from the rear shoes, allowing the piston to pop out of the cylinder and spray hydraulic fluid over the hot drum, with the inevitable fire. In the resulting altercation, all the fire extinguishers were used up, finally putting out the fire but resulting in the retirement of the Tiger and crew.

Ian Hall recalls of this Quatre Chemins section

"... the following morning came a very tight section from Quatre Chemins to Sigale and then from Sigale to Entrevaux which we knew of old. The Morleys were now running in front of me on the road as the Alpine was timed section to section, but I did not expect to do these two on time. In fact, we did, passing a 904 Porsche on the way (no, not Bohringer!) and had a minute or so in hand. The Morleys were actually waiting at the Control to see if we did it and told us we were a minute up before Don clocked in!"

Alpine Rally 1965

'Tiny' Lewis and Barry Hughes wait for the scrutineer to finish marking the engine compartment components with paint to prevent the illegal changing of parts disallowed by the regulations. The hole in the bonnet feeding the cool air from the air scoop to the carburettor intake can be seen. (Rootes)

Ian Hall keeps the rally paperwork in his briefcase while Don Barrow has a final look at his side of the Tiger. The headlamp stoneguard hangs on its hinge, which allows cleaning of the lights. (Photo Junior)

Alpine Rally 1965

XXVI.ᵉ Coupe des Alpes 1965

The Ian Hall/Don Barrow Tiger prior to its altercation with the Armco on the Col d'Allos. After a promising start in Ian's first International drive, an interpretation of the available pace notes led to a minor accident, for which the frantic road time schedule left no time to rectify. (Photo Junior)

Alpine Rally 1965

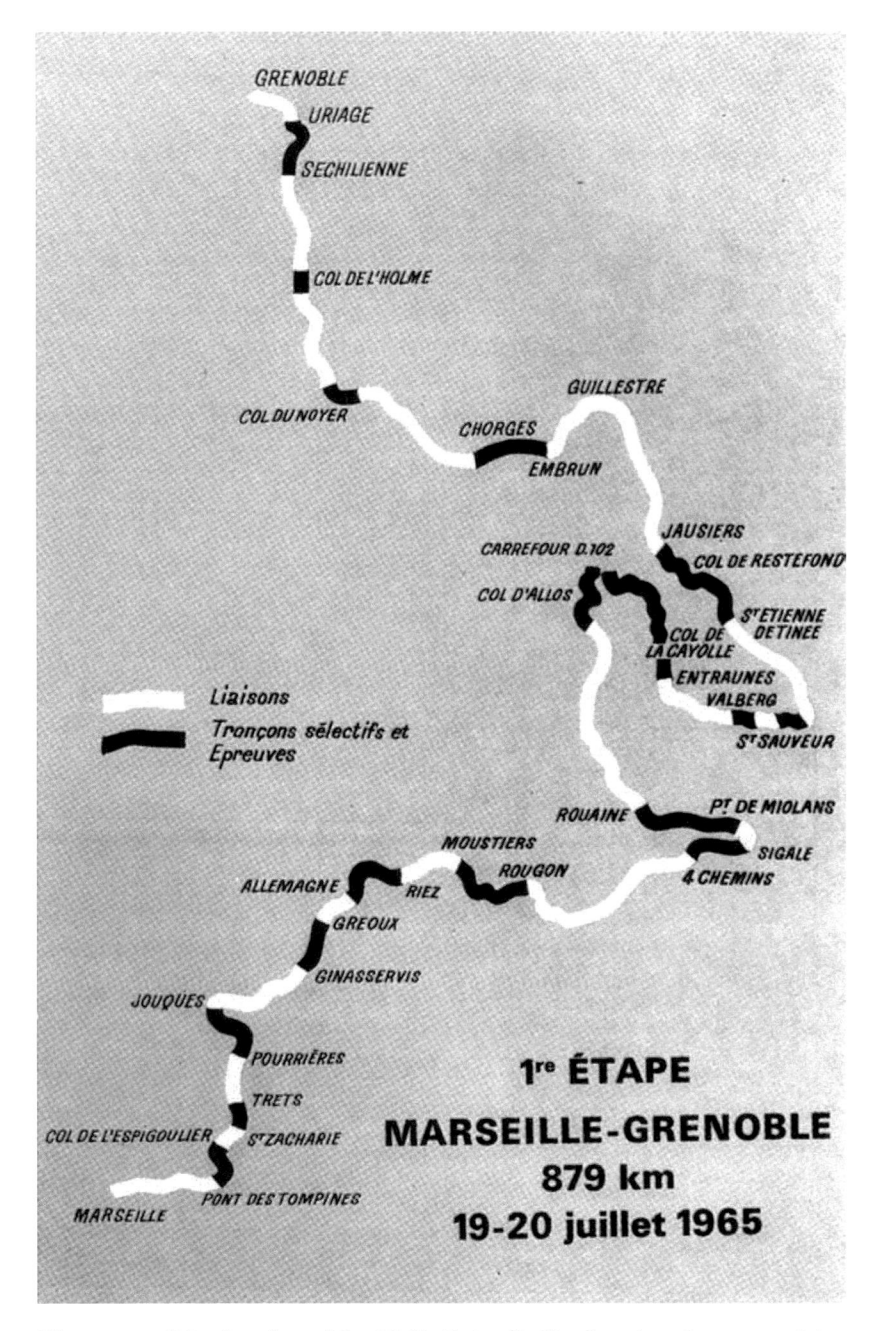

The route of the first leg of the 1965 Alpine Rally showing the competitive and linking road sections. (Rootes)

Over the tortuous but picturesque Allos, Peter Harper began to make his mark being 9th fastest, just 37.5secs slower than the fastest man, Pauli Toivonen, in his Porsche 904 and under 12secs slower than the Morley brothers in 6th place in their big Healey. Retirements over the Allos, however, were quite high, with Gunther Klass in his Porsche 904, and Ljungfelt in the Lotus Cortina - both from the top five. Another of the Rootes hopes disappeared at this point when Ian Hall and Don Barrow had a dispute with a wall which jumped out in front of the car on the descent of the Allos, partially due to dodgy brakes caused by an oil leak onto one of the front discs with the resultant loss of braking and partially due, perhaps, to a less than complete recce in the time available. Ian Hall remembers "Well into daylight by now, to a spectacular spot called Foux d'Allos at

Alpine Rally 1965

ADU311B, the Ian Hall/Don Barrow Tiger, carries on after its altercation with a wall. The Rootes mechanics have patched the car up enough to keep it running, but the right hand wing is flattened, the left spot light missing, the door numbers removed and the number plate repositioned as, presumably, the front bumper has been replaced. The Tiger is running on Dunlop Green Spot racing tyres. (Rootes)

the start of a timed climb to the top of the Col, with the selective section then continuing on the descent to the bottom near Barcellonette. At Foux d'Allos we had service and got new front pads and a new set of tyres. At the end of the timed climb on the Col I asked Don how long we had to get to the bottom, he started to work it out and I pressed on down the mountain. About half way down came a long left hander with a stone hut which I recognised from previous occasions but found myself going in much too fast. Harper's notes (which I no longer have) did not indicate anything particularly tricky about this corner and I suspect - I shall never know - that because of the prominent hut he had a mental note of it. This is not a criticism – I was using his notes at my risk. But that as it may, I understeered into some Armco beyond the hut and knocked the wing onto the tyre and slightly deranged the steering. As crashes go, it wasn't much of one but time was too tight to get it sorted and continue – particularly as the Col de Cayolle was immediately next. Don and I continued as an extra service car for the rest of the rally after getting the wing levered back off the tyre."

Simo Lampinen said to me after the rally "Don't you know White Hut corner on Allos?.... very tricky – we always have this corner marked as Slow on our notes." "No," I said, "but I do now!"

Whatever the cause, the result was that the Tiger rounded off the right hand front corner of the car and promptly retired. Immediately after the Allos came that épreuve over the Col de la Cayolle and a further épreuve over the Col de Valberg.

On the Valberg, Toivonen was fastest again with Harper being only some 32secs slower, and only 11secs slower than the Morley brothers, although

Alpine Rally 1965

Results at the end of the first leg (Marseille-Grenoble) were:

	Grand Touring Class: Epreuves		min	sec
1	Buchet/Marbaque	(Porsche 904)	31	44.4
2	Morley/Morley	(Healey 3000)	32	38
3	Harper/Hughes	(Sunbeam Tiger)	33	42.5
4	Hanrioud/Sage	(Renault Alpine)	34	25.5
5	Cowan/Coyle	(Rover 2000)	36	30.3
6	Smith/Taylor	(Hillman Imp)	37	39.4

on this test the Healey slid out a little too wide over a bridge and bent the back a little. As the rally wound its way north back to Grenoble and over the Col de Restefond, the highest in Europe, the weather worsened and it began to rain and it remained this way until the overnight stop in Grenoble, when the cars entered the parc ferme in brilliant sunshine.

After this, the shortest leg, only 54 of the 93 starters were still running. In the GT class only 5 out of the 15 surviving cars were clean on the road and of those five, Robert Buchet in his Porsche led from the Morley bothers, Peter Harper, Hanrioud in his Renault Alpine, Andrew Cowan and Brian Coyle in a Rover 2000 and Rosemary Smith/Sheila Taylor in an Imp. The Healey of the Morley brothers had lost time on a selective with the wire wheels breaking up and throwing off spokes.

After an overnight stop, the rally started out again at 5am, with vivid blue skies and dabs of cloud, but overnight storms had made roads difficult in places by washing down loose grit onto the smooth roads, a bit like driving on ball bearings. The route led directly to the hill-climb up the Chamrousse where the three Porsches of Toivonen, Buchet and Bohringer took the three top places without difficulty. Peter Harper, however was no slouch, putting up tenth fastest time, some 33secs behind the third quickest Porsche 904 of Bohringer. From the Chamrousse the field sped southwards via La Mure and Mens to yet another selective, this one being timed to the second, over the Col de Noyer. Over this test Harper was quicker than Toivonen in his 904 and no doubt the breakfast at the short halt in Gap tasted better for that! Two short selectives followed and a long road section to the foot of Mont Ventoux. On this climb Peter pulled out the stops and made fifth fastest time in 13mins 31.6secs, being only headed by the Morley brothers Healey in 13 22.4 and the usual trio of Porsches. Toivonen pressed on up the hill in a time of 12 15.4 for the 21.5km, setting an average of 105km/hr (65 mph) whilst Harper averaged close on 60 mph. At the other end of the scale the little DAF's needed more than 21 minutes to cover the same distance! - although they were a lot quicker downhill.

Further up the route in the town of Die the service crews had set up shop and established a service depot with the tyre companies, as the route went round in a loop returning to Die some four hours later. Piles of tyres lined the route, very largely Dunlop as most teams were using Dunlop SP covers although some, including the works Mini's, were on Dunlop racing tyres - Green Spots in both the wet and dry. After a 50 minute break, during which the cars were painstakingly tended to by the service crews, the cars embarked upon the energetic four hour loop embracing épreuves on the Col du Rousset and La Cime du Mass. Keeping up the pressure in the GT class, Harper recorded a time of 10 58.8 over the Rousset against the class leaders time of 10 11.4. Similarly for the next épreuve Harper was only 24secs off Buchet's

Alpine Rally 1965

time of 20.23.1. Back through Die for a necessary service, the cars now travelled north back towards a 24 hour stop in Grenoble.

This leg turned into one of the most difficult of the rally and the route ran over the Col du Menee on the D120/D7 to join the main road, the N75, just north of Clelles with an almost immediate turn off at St.Michel to tackle the Col de l'Allimas and Col de l'Arzelier before looping back to the main road. It was coming off this latter Col and down the slippery precipitous descent into St.Barthelemy at the end of the selective that the leader of the GT category, Robert Buchet, put his Porsche permanently off the road, handing the lead to Peter Harper's Tiger.

Three more tough selectives followed in quick succession, very testing since the weather was damp and misty and towards the end of the third selective, on the D280 via Prabert and Theys to St.Pierre d'Allevard, a layer of gravel on the road made the section extremely difficult and probably the most troublesome on the rally.

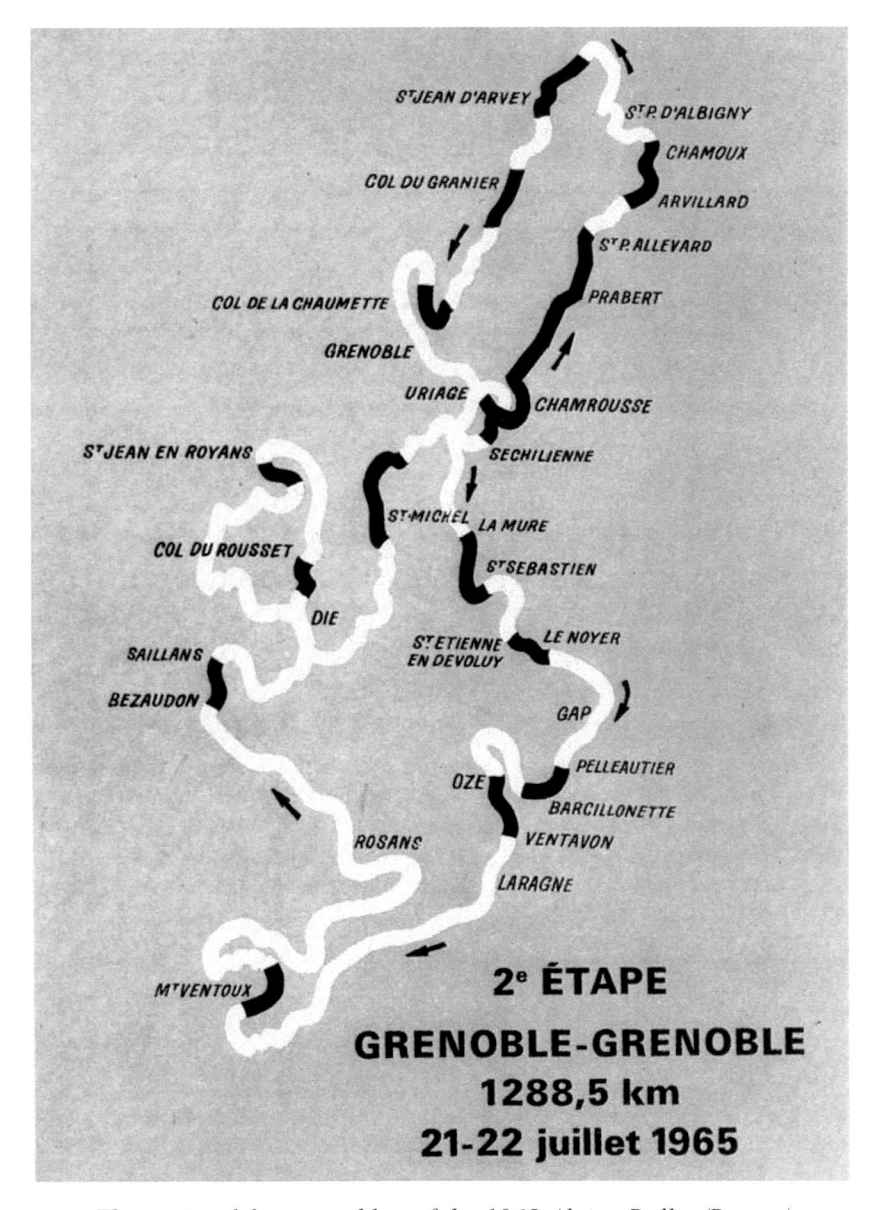

The route of the second leg of the 1965 Alpine Rally. (Rootes)

Alpine Rally 1965

Results at the end of the second leg (Grenoble - Grenoble) Grand Touring Class

Grand Touring Class: Epreuves			Penalties	min/sec
1	Harper/Hughes	Tiger	0	66m 58
2	Hanrioud/Sage	Alpine	0	69m 23.1
3	Cousten/Hebert	Alfa GTZ	60	67m 55.6
4	Cowan/Coyle	Rover 2000	60	74m 51.2
5	Morley/Morley	Healey 3000	180	64m 57.6
6	Smith/Taylor	Imp	180	78m 19.1

Only two drivers in the GT class cleaned this section, Peter Harper and Hanrioud in his Alpine - even Eugen Bohringer dropped a minute. A northern loop with a final dash over the Chaumette led the jaded competitors, and often more weary cars, back into Grenoble to a well needed service for the cars and a well deserved night's sleep for their crews.

In the Touring category there were no less than eleven Coupes, four with Renault, three with BMC, two with Ford and one apiece with Citroen and Lancia. Only Harper and Hanrioud were penalty free in the GT class whilst in the prototype category all had incurred some road penalty, clearly indicating the increasing severity of timing as the cars became more "sporting". Harper and Hughes were leading their class by an unassailable 2mins 25secs with a total time on the épreuves of 66mins 58secs. Less than half of the entry now remained and the surviving crews retired to bed before tackling the final 30 hour, 1433km leg to Monte Carlo.

Another 5am start on Friday morning led the 39 survivors out on a somewhat diversionary route over the Col du Granier to within sight of Geneva for a four hour halt in the afternoon at Chamonix. Having fought their way in and out of the tourist traffic going to the new Mont Blanc tunnel, both before and after Chamonix, the first really tight section after Chamonix was in the valley above Albertville, which the Tiger cleared with no problems, and the route sped southwards and over many smaller roads to the "piece de resistance" on the last night of the rally, a circuit over the Col d'Allos twice and back over the Cayolle. Over the Allos for the first time Harper put in a time of 14mins 59.2secs, and returned a time of 14 50.4 on the second loop-times which were to keep him well in the lead of the GT category.

Jean-Paul Hanrioud in his Alpine lost his Coupe over the Allos due to faulty spark plugs, leaving the Tiger as the only unpenalised GT car. Peter held his lead secure as the cars travelled over the last two selectives and épreuves to reach the finish at the Quai Albert Premier in Monte Carlo.

The Rootes team were more than pleased with the Tiger and crew, winning the GT class convincingly and returning the only clean sheet in that class - a really epic drive to win a treasured Coupe des Alpes. After the well-deserved celebrations the crews retired to bed whilst the Tiger sat in the Parc Fermé awaiting post-event scrutineering.

On Sunday morning, however, the scrutineers called Des O'Dell and Marcus Chambers to point out to them that the valve sizes on ADU312B did not comply with the homologation form and thus the car was to be disqualified and removed from the results. The valves were, in fact, smaller than those homologated and which had since been changed on the production car, but due to a mix up over later homologations by the competition department, the very fine drive by Peter Harper and Mike Hughes had come to nought (or almost) when the organisers had little choice but to exclude the Tiger and crew from the results.

Alpine Rally 1965

Des O'Dell had the unenvious task of waking Peter Harper and telling him the situation and whilst it was a shattering blow for the crew, they took it in good humour, partially because they were so tired, and at least it made Rauno Aaltonen rescind his promise to drive the Tiger into the swimming pool at the Hotel de Paris. Paddy Hopkirk commented in his Autosport column...... "It was hard luck on Peter Harper to be disqualified through no fault of his own - a bit naughty of the factory this. I know that if I won the Monte and the car was declared non-standard at the finish I wouldn't be very pleased with Stuart Turner!" John Davenport writing in his Alpine report in Motoring News, summed up the rally well when he reported that "this had been a rally of spectacular drives with Pauli Toivonen taking top honours in my book with Vic Elford, Peter Harper, Rene Trautman, Timo Makinen, Simo Lampinen, Andrew Cowan and Tony Fall not so far behind."

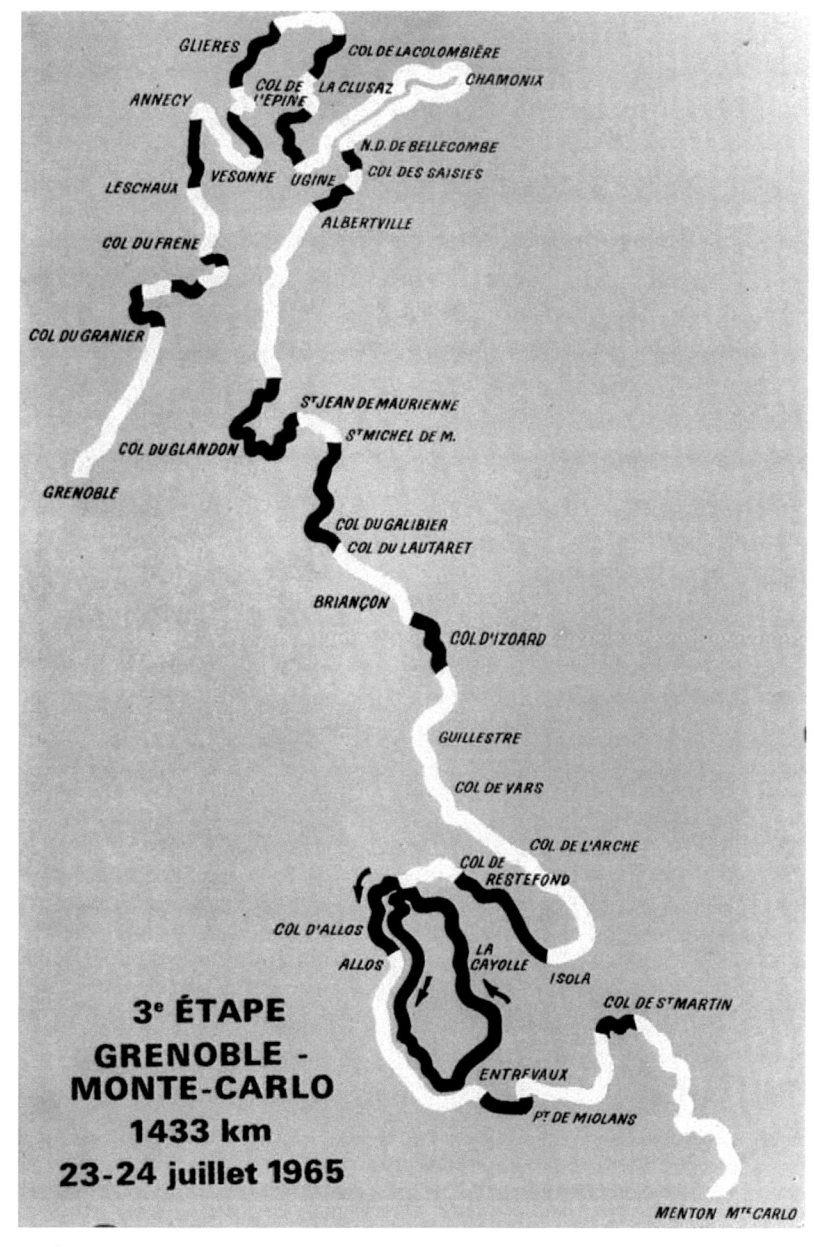

The route of the third and final leg of the 1965 Alpine Rally. (Rootes)

Alpine Rally 1965

With, no doubt, the front discs glowing, the Peter Harper/Mike Hughes Tiger carries out a rapid descent of a col, with little room left for error with the uncompromising hairpin walls and fading brakes. (LAT)

The Peter Harper/Mike Hughes Tiger pushes on up one of the many ascents of the cols on the daylight road sections between the épreuves. (Rootes)

Alpine Rally 1965

The Peter Harper/Mike Hughes Tiger tackles a climb up the twisty roads of the lesser roads of the Alps. (Rootes)

Peter Harper and Mike Hughes push-on over the Col du Restefond in worstening weather. (Rootes)

Alpine Rally 1965

Peter Harper swings the Tiger around one of the many tight hairpins in this rally, the dry tarmac roads putting high strain on the brakes and suspension, particularly with the high gripping power of the Dunlop Green Spot racing tyres and SP3 road tyres. (Rootes)

Mike Hughes contemplates his and Peter Harper's Tiger at the Time Control in St Etienne. At this stage the Tiger remained penalty free. (Rootes)

Alpine Rally 1965

The Peter Harper Tiger burbles past a disinterested gendarme on a liaison section. (Rootes)

Keeping tight in, the Peter Harper Tiger rounds one of the many bends on the Alpine Rally. (Motor)

161

Alpine Rally 1965

The valve size problem had arisen because the stated size of the inlet / exhaust valves in the original homologation form (FOR 176 from July 1964) was 49.25mm / 42.85mm, whilst the standard production car had valves of 42mm / 37mm diameter – a significant difference. The original valve diameters in the FOR 176 were the same as those entered in the Shelby Cobra ACC-US FIA recognition form of 30 November 1962, and it is almost certain that the Shelby figures were transferred, obviously without too much thought, directly to the FIA Homologation Form. The Shelby valve sizes were, however, somewhat larger than would fit directly into the original 260/289 head – although nowadays valve sizes of the 1962 Shelby quoted diameters are used in historic racing in the USA – but with a lot of re-working of the heads. The original Shelby valve sizes were probably a combination of an enthusiastic estimate of what might be possible (as this was prior to the 289 engine becoming available) combined with the seemingly inevitable rush to submit technical figures for a Form of Recognition for the coming season's racing. Hindsight - away from the frantic timescales and rush of competition - is a wonderful thing!

An interesting digression is that in the 1964 Sunbeam 260 Workshop Manual (Publication WSM 146) the inlet / exhaust valve diameters were given as 40.18mm / 35.07mm – a new set of figures, but these were the valve diameters for the 1962/3 head (C20E-F and C30E-B) while the 1964 head (C40E-B) had the later valve diameters of 42 / 37mm. However, whatever the complexities of changes in Ford engine production or other engine builders figures, the only important figure is that in the Form of Recognition. Pity the engineer who has the responsibility of filling in the homologation forms – particularly if the engine builders may be over 5000 miles away and out of your control, and engines aren't always available for directly checking component dimensions.

Marcus Chambers notes in his book that "It will be remembered that the first two engines that were fitted in the competition department at Coventry had been supplied by Carroll Shelby as replacements for the faulty Le Mans engines. Those engines, I suspect, were used by us to obtain the measurements for the homologation of the cars." He also noted "There was a small clause in the FIA Notice to Manufacturers which said that cars should be homologated in their highest state of tune. I read this as 'Always list the biggest valves', and the Le Mans cars were homologated with bigger valves. When we realised that the production engines were coming through with the smaller ones, we simply listed them as an option. The Alpine's organising club said that the smaller valves made the car more reliable! Now, having followed the Alpine – and Stuart Turner will bear this one out – it was difficult to go before a committee of the Commissaires Sportif and argue the exact meaning of the regulations. So we just said 'What the hell', we'd got a lot of publicity by being excluded, and we left it at that."

The official statement issued by the Rootes Publicity Department stated that "by the fitting of smaller valves to the Tiger, we certainly did not gain any advantage in performance, and this was only done to bring the rally car in line with that of the current models. The discrepancy arose because the initial production Tigers registered with the FIA were produced for the US market and employed larger valves than those currently fitted to the production models. Negotiations are in progress with the FIA to register the latest specification, but in any case we believe it was not vital to notify a modification which detunes engine performance."

In reality, the smaller valves would not have made the significant difference needed to beat the opposition, this was done by sheer driving skills and a competent rally car, but it was a dismal end to a classic rally for Rootes, where not only would have Harper and Hughes won the category and a Coupe des Alpes, but would have had their first victory of a Tiger over their traditional rival – the Healey 3000.

A moral victory, if not one to go down in the results - and a new set of homologation papers were rapidly produced.

Alpine Rally 1965

Alpine Rally • Report by Charles Bulmer : Pictures by George Moore

Moral Victory (but no Cup) to Harper ...undersize valves disqualify Tiger.

HARPER'S BIZARRE ALPINE DEFEAT

A snag in the Liège?

John Sprinzel comments from his column in Motor Racing.

Peter Harper, who took over the outright leadership on this final stage, had very little time in which to enjoy the spoils of a supposed victory. Shortly after the finish, the stewards removed the cylinder heads and found under-sized valves had been fitted to the Sunbeam Tiger. Naturally, they had no alternative but to exclude the entry, which seemed very hard on Peter, who had driven with skill and a great deal of care to be the only GT or Sports Prototype car able to manage the entire route without any loss of time. Harper and Mike Hughes took this disaster with very good tempers—if this had happened to most of the 'professionals' one feels they would have been banging on the Rootes door demanding compensation up to the equivalent of the large bag of prize money they had lost. Another 'unlucky' Alpine was the story of Jean-Pierre Hanrioud, driving a GT Renault-based Alpine. The only other GT to manage this very tight time schedule, he had ignition trouble during the last night and his Coupe too, remained in the organisers' huge store of unawarded trophies.

Alpine Rally 1965

The following three pages show the works movement sheet for the 1965 Alpine Rally – loaned from the Derek Hughes archives - which sets out all of the movements of the team members, rally cars and service cars ante- and post-rally.

The service cars were the Hillman Super Minx Estates, along with a Humber Super Snipe Estate and it is interesting to note that only three service vehicles were used on this long route along with a Commer 15cwt van to carry the heavier spares, wheels & tyres etc.

It can be seen that Ian Hall was originally down to drive the Super Snipe with Ernie Schofield and Dick Guy as travelling mechanics, but was deputed to drive ADU311B when Peter Riley had to pull-out at the last moment.

The team set up their pre-rally HQ at the Hotel Le Relais de la Magdeleine in Gemenos – a small town some 20 km east of the start in Marseiiles. Here, out of the hustle and bustle of the busy town, the pre-rally preparations for crew, mechanics and management could be carried out in relative seclusion.

Alpine Rally 1965

ALPINE RALLY 1965.

Three Sunbeam Tigers have been entered for the Alpine Rally with a view to winning the Manufacturers Team Prize, and three Alpine cups for unpenalised runs throughout the rally. One 998 cc. Hillman Imp fitted with experimental disc brakes has been entered for Rosemary Smith and the object being to win the Ladies Prize and the up to 1,000 cc. G.T. Class. It is not anticipated that a Group 3 Hillman Imp can complete the course without loss of marks and therefore we can not expect an Alpine cup for this entry.

RALLY CARS.

1.	PETER HARPER/DAVID POLLARD.	SUNBEAM TIGER	ADU 312 B	Category B	Class	5
2.	PETER RILEY/MICHAEL HUGHES.	SUNBEAM TIGER	ADU 311 B	" B	"	5
3.	TINY LEWIS/BARRY HUGHES.	SUNBEAM TIGER	AHP 294 B	" B	"	5
4.	ROSEMARY SMITH/SHEILA TAYLOR.	HILLMAN IMP	EDU 710 C	" B	"	1

SERVICE CARS.

1. I.J. HALL/E. SCHOFIELD/R. GUY.   HUMBER SUPER SNIPE ESTATE   6111 VC
2. D. O'DELL/J. WALTON.   HILLMAN SUPER MINX ESTATE   974 CRW
3. G. SPENCER./E. BECK.   HILLMAN SUPER MINX ESTATE   505 CHP
4. G. COLES/T. SHARMAN.   COMMER VAN 15 CWT   975 CRW
5. M. CHAMBERS.   EX-RECCE TIGER.   -

-o-o-o-o-o-o-O-o-o-o-o-o-o-

WEDNESDAY 14th JULY.   SERVICE CARS.

The following personnel to leave COMPETITION DEPARTMENT with the Service Cars and make their way to the EAST CLIFF HOTEL, MARINE PARADE, EASTERN DOCKS, DOVER, where accommodation has been booked.

G. COLES / T. SHARMAN.   COMMER VAN.
E. SCHOFIELD / R. GUY.   HUMBER SUPER SNIPE ESTATE
E. BECK / J. WALTON.   HILLMAN SUPER MINX ESTATE 505 CHP.

THURSDAY 15th JULY.

The above personnel to report to DOVER EASTERN DOCKS to catch DOVER-BOULOGNE boat:-

Reporting time.   10.30 hours.
Depart Dover.   11.15 hours.
Arrive Boulogne.   12.45 hours.

On disembarking all three crews should proceed to the Hotel, LE RELAIS DE LA MAGDELEINE, GEMENOS, BOUCHES-DU-RHONE, FRANCE. (Telephone GEMENOS 5.)

The van should make its own way down to arrive by Saturday mid-day if possible. The SUPER SNIPE and SUPER MINX should travel together to enable the driving of both vehicles to be shared by Messrs. BECK, WALTON and SCHOFIELD. They should endeavour to reach GEMENOS by Friday night if possible, or alternatively early Saturday morning. Any delay should be notified by telephone to IAN HALL at the Hotel LE RELAIS DE LA MAGDELEINE, GEMENOS, on Friday evening.

RALLY CARS.

The following personnel to leave COMPETITION DEPARTMENT by 11.00 hours at the latest with Rally cars for delivery to respective Drivers, and to report to DOVER EASTERN DOCK to catch DOVER-BOULOGNE boat.

MRS. SHEILA TAYLOR   HILLMAN IMP   EDU 710 C
I.J. HALL   SUNBEAM TIGER   ADU 312 B
D. O'DELL   SUNBEAM TIGER   ADU 311 B
G. SPENCER   SUNBEAM TIGER   AHP 294 B
M. CHAMBERS   HILLMAN SUPER MINX ESTATE   974 CRW

Alpine Rally 1965

                Reporting time   16.30 hours.
                Depart Dover   17.15 hours.
                Arrive Boulogne 18.45 hours.

On arrival at BOULOGNE drivers to take the cars to the loading point at the GARE MARITIME before 19.45 hours to change to LYON CAR SLEEPER EXPRESS.

                Depart Boulogne 20.42 hours.

FRIDAY 16th JULY.

Arrive LYON 07.58 hours, cars to be collected from PORT DIEU Station at LYON using Station bus. From Lyon proceed direct to GEMENOS.

Accommodation has been reserved at the Hotel LE RELAIS DE LA MAGDELEINE, GEMENOS, BOUCHES-DU-RHONE, for the following persons for the nights of 16th 17th and 18th July.

        Single rooms   MR. M. CHAMBERS.
                           MR. I.J. HALL.
        Twin bedded rooms MISS R. SMITH /MRS. S. TAYLOR.
                           MR. P. HARPER/MR. D. POLLARD.
                           MR. I. LEWIS/MR. B. HUGHES.
                           MR. P. RILEY/MR. M. HUGHES.
                           MR. D. O'DELL/MR. J. WALTON.
                           MR. G. COLES/MR. T. SHARMAN.
                           MR. E. SCHOFIELD/MR. R. GUY.
                           MR. G. SPENCER/MR. E. BECK.

SATURDAY 17th JULY.

Preparation.

SUNDAY 18th JULY.

Preparation, SCRUTINEERING from 10.00 hours to 19.00 hours at MARSEILLE, QUAI DU PORT. All Rally Crews to attend SCRUTINEERING with Crash Hats Licences etc. Cars will be held in PARC FERME after SCRUTINEERING until the start.

MONDAY 19th JULY.

Extra SCRUTINEERING period for those cars not scrutineered on Sunday from 9.00 hours to 14.00 hours at the QUAI DU PORT.

Some Crews will probably have to use Taxis to go to the start as 2 Service Cars will have left to take up positions. Two spare Recce cars can be used as transport and will be left in the care of Rome Garage, 114 Rue de Rome, MARSEILLE.

21.30 hours, Rally Starts, TOWN HALL - MARSEILLE.

First Stage of rally MARSEILLE - GRENOBLE 879 Kms.

TUESDAY 20th JULY.

Arrive GRENOBLE from 13.00 hours onwards approximately.

Accommodation reserved for all rally crews at Hotel LESDIQUIERES, 122, COURS LIBERATION, GRENOBLE. (Telephone GRENOBLE 44.80.11).

WEDNESDAY 21st JULY.

Second Stage GRENOBLE - GRENOBLE 12.88 Kms. Depart GRENOBLE from 05.00 hours.

THURSDAY 22nd JULY.

Arrive GRENOBLE from 06.32 hours approximately.

Accommodation reserved at Hotel LESDIQUIERES as previously.

Alpine Rally 1965

FRIDAY 23rd JULY.

Third stage GRENOBLE - MONTE CARLO 1433 Kms.

Depart GRENOBLE approximately 05.00 hours.

There is a 4 hour NEUTRALISATION PERIOD at CHAMONIX which rally cars will reach at approximately 12.18 hours. 4 Twin bedded rooms have been reserved for drivers use in the names of HARPER, RILEY, LEWIS and MISS SMITH, at the HOTEL DE LA CROIX BLANCHE (telephone Chamonix 11 et 571.) Lunch has also been booked at the same hotel.

SATURDAY 24th JULY.

Arrive MONTE CARLO approximately 11.00 hours. Accommodation reserved at the HOTEL SPLENDID, 4 AVENUE ROQUEVILLE, MONTE CARLO. (Telephone Monte Carlo 30.65.93). for the following personnel.

      Single Rooms   MR. M. CHAMBERS.
                           MR. I.J. HALL.
      Twin bedded rooms MISS R. SMITH/MRS. S. TAYLOR.
                           MR. P. HARPER/MR. D. POLLARD.
                           MR. I. LEWIS/MR. B. HUGHES.
                           MR. P. RILEY/MR. M. HUGHES.
                           MR. D. O'DELL/MR. J. WALTON.
                           MR. G. COLES/MR. T. SHARMAN.
                           MR. E. SCHOFIELD/MR. R. GUY.
                           MR. G. SPENCER/MR. E. BECK.

SUNDAY 25th JULY.

PROVISIONAL RESULTS will be posted up at 10.00 hours. PRIZE-GIVING at 22.00 hours at a place to be announced.

MONDAY 26th JULY.

PETER HARPER to fly NICE - GENEVA - LONDON open dated ticket.

MISS ROSEMARY SMITH to fly NICE - LONDON.

The following vehicles are booked with open dated return tickets on the BOULOGNE - DOVER boat.

    COMMER VAN   G. COLES / T. SHARMAN.
    HUMBER SUPER SNIPE ESTATE   E. SCHOFIELD / R. GUY.
    HILLMAN SUPER MINX ESTATE   505 CHP E. BECK / J. WALTON.
    HILLMAN SUPER MINX ESTATE   974 CRW G. SPENCER / + 1.

I.J. HALL to travel in SUPER SNIPE as far as MARSEILLE.
D. O'DELL to travel with D.E. POLLARD as far as MARSEILLE.

The following vehicles are booked with open dated return tickets to fly Le-TOUQUET - LYDD.

    SUNBEAM TIGER   D.E. POLLARD + 1
    SUNBEAM TIGER   I.D. LEWIS / B. HUGHES.
    SUNBEAM TIGER   P. RILEY / M. HUGHES.
    SUNBEAM TIGER (RECCE)   D. O'DELL - to be collected from Marseille.
    SUNBEAM TIGER (RECCE)   M. CHAMBERS.
    SUNBEAM TIGER (RECCE)   I.J. HALL - to be collected from Marseille.
    HILLMAN IMP   MRS. S. TAYLOR.

-o-o-o-o-o-o-o-o-O-o-o-o-o-o-o-o-o-

Alpine Rally 1965

Des O'Dell

Des's early engineering experience came from the armed forces, where he trained as an engineer working on a wide range of Army vehicles. In the 1950's he joined Aston Martin as a test driver/ engineer and during part of his career there he spent a period away from the factory - in Italy - working on the early Astons and acting as a liaison engineer between Italy and England. This was in the country of Ferrari and Maserati - where Aston Martin was competing head-on with the Italian manufacturers in that class of sports car. He later joined John Wyer and became part of the racing team, staying with them until the days of the GT 40. Des joined Rootes Competition department as Workshop Manager at the beginning of the Tiger era. His engineering skills, extensive knowledge of V8's and practical experience gained in competition helped provide solutions to the problems - some minor and some not so minor - on the rally Tigers. Strong application of this experience, both in the workshops and during rallies, helped the Tiger to develop as a competition car to a state where it became a very effective tool, particularly on tarmac rallies.

Des went on to lead the engineering effort on the London to Sydney Marathon win in the Hillman Hunter and to become the Competition Manager during the highly successful Chrysler and Peugeot era.

Don Barrow

One of a breed of high quality British navigators, Don started road rallying in 1956, and his subsequent successes included winning the Motoring News Championships in 1963, 64, 67 and 70; the RAC Rally Championship in 1967, BTRDA Gold Star Championship in 1970 and the BTRDA Silver Star Championship in 1962, 63 and 67.

Having competed abroad on the 1963 Tulip (with Roy Fidler in a TR4 [6VC]), Alpine, 1964 Spa-Sofia-Liege (with Timo Makinen in the Healey 3000 [ARX92B]), Scottish, RAC, Welsh (almost abroad) and Irish Rallies (including the '65 Circuit with Roy Fidler in a works Triumph 2000), he was invited in 1965 by Ian Hall to join the Rootes works team. They made a few pre-event road books together before co-driving Ian on the 1965 Alpine. Later in the year he was paired up with Peter Harper on the RAC, the Tiger retiring early with a blown head gasket.

Targa Florio 1965

'The last remaining true road race in the old tradition..........'.

Targa Florio 1965

"The last remaining true road race in the old tradition, a test of man and machine against natural hazards of the road....", so wrote Denis Jenkinson in Motor Sport about the Targa Florio and, as a man who won the gruelling Mille Miglia with Stirling Moss in a Mercedes 300SLR, his opinion is not to be taken lightly. The classic Targa Florio is not just another motor race but more an exultation of the Italian approach to motor racing and, in particular, appears to be an essential part of Sicilian life, since spectators of this event are not naturally of passive nature and spectating takes on virtually active participation in the event, groups of spectators vociferously providing support for their particular hero. Whilst most of the most popular Italian support is saved for Ferrari, the Sicilian support is naturally preserved for a Sicilian driver, Nino Vacarella, driving, of course, a prototype Ferrari. The level of support is made clear when locals appear with buckets of whitewash and brushes to adorn the roads and walls with "FORZA FERRARI" or "VIVA VACARELLA" or "VIVA FERRARI", whilst in the village of Collesano properly constructed banners were strung across the road proclaiming similar messages. Similar enthusiasm is shown in the same way for other drivers, Bandini, Baghetti or constructors such as Abarth and Alfa Romeo.

The competition is around a 72km road circuit which the cars must complete ten times, with the circuit running around the island, winding its tortuous way through the hills and mountains, plains and in and out of numerous villages. Official practice is for one day only and, at 72km per lap, usually allowed each driver - there are two per car - to get in at least one lap, although the keener drivers or those who have the least car trouble can often manage three laps. There is, however, unofficial practice in the week preceding the event and an integral part of the Targa Florio allure is the sight of Ferraris, Porsches, Alfas, Alpine Renaults etc. weaving in and out of the traffic whilst the driver tries to commit to memory every little bump and bend, and the locals in their Fiat 500's and Lambretta scooters attempt to outrun the practising Ferraris. This generally means that unofficial practice is considerably more memorable than the official practice day - both for competitors and spectators alike!

After his foray on the RAC Rally in AHP483B under the Vitafoam banner, Rupert Jones and his associates decided to enter the Targa Florio in the same car in the Grand Touring class. In the previous year he and Harry Ratcliffe had competed in a Mini Cooper, but with Harry driving a wheel had come off, fortunately without too much damage to either car or driver. This time they hoped for greater things! Advice and parts were gladly accepted from Rootes and since AHP483B was still at Vitafoam's premises, it was decided to use that particular car. It was thought advisable to fit an engine with more power, so a Shelby Cobra 4.7 unit was installed along with a standard 4-speed gearbox, even though the car could have done with a fifth gear along the only straight on the circuit - a full 6km. Also, as the event was run in the hot Italian sun, some modification was obviously going to be necessary to the engine cooling system and also to the rear brakes. Since these were still drums and susceptible to fade under heavy useage, air ducts were constructed which fed cooling air to the rear brakes and exhausted through the boot. As these modifications now put the car into the prototype class, the front bumper was left off and the lower valence cut away to allow more air to pass through the radiator and oil cooler, with perhaps a little more cool air into the engine compartment.

To cope with the extra through-flow of air, the bonnet was propped open in the usual manner and secured with leather straps. In addition, to allow direct access of air to the discs, the front valence was extensively cut away on both sides just below the side light/indicator cluster. Apart from the reshaped front end, the most noticeable additional modification was the large bonnet bulge that fed ambient temperature air direct to the 4 barrel Holley carburettor. Open exhaust pipes were used which fed out under either side of the car just at the rear of the doors.

Targa Florio 1965

Peter Harper awaits the start in true Italian style – enthusiasts everywhere. (via D.McDermott)

The much-modified front apron of the Tiger shows clearly the Rootes two-tiered 'hedgehog' oil cooler. (via D.McDermott)

Targa Florio 1965

Servicing was simple in the 1960's – one Ford Zephyr Estate service car and a few tyres – and magnificent countryside. (Geoffrey Goddard)

Another good view of the modification to the bodywork that was allowed in the prototype category of the Targa Florio. (Geoffrey Goddard)

Targa Florio 1965

The Vitafoam Targa Tiger at Oulton Park on its pre-Targa testing session. Brian Gillibrand looks after the car, which is in its pre-modification standard bodywork state. (Alan Clegg)

As benefits an event of this type, wider Minilite wheels and racing tyres were used with the larger section tyre at the front, in order to combat the inherent understeer and to try to provide the more neutral characteristics necessary on tarmac, necessitating some flaring to the wings. The rear arches were left standard. Although the Tiger was in the over 3000cc prototype class and amongst the faster entries, a last minute entry in the same class was made by Scuderia Ferrari of four works cars - three 275P/2 4 camshaft 3.3 litre V12 cars and a single competition GTB - along with the lone Ford GT 4.7 litre prototype. As these entries meant that there was liable to be some quicker traffic, a single wing mirror was fitted on the driver's side to assist with the rear view. The modifications to the boot and bonnet had been carried out on a different set of panels and so the car started the event in an impressive set of colours. The body remained in Carnival red, as it always had been, the hardtop was black whilst the bonnet and boot were in Midnight blue. Along with the bonnet bulge, it gave the car a very distinctive look. Before the car was finally modified, however, the original AHP483B was tested around Oulton Park racing circuit after Geoff Goodliffe had worked on the suspension, altering the springing and damping rates and Harry Ratcliffe had found more power and torque from the engine. Peter Harper was to be the number one driver and had come to try the car.

The car ran well, and apart from fuel surge on the right hand corners, which was temporarily solved by running the car the 'wrong' way round the circuit, the car was taken away, prepared for the event, towed on a trailer by the Ford Zephyr service car to Naples and thence by ferry to Palermo.

Targa Florio 1965

Traversing a village in central Sicily, the Harper/Jones 289 Tiger. (LAT)

Practice had gone well, with both drivers learning the route in sections, although Rupert Jones had an advantage from competing, at least in practice, the previous year.

The Vitafoam entry was for Peter Harper and Rupert Jones as the drivers, but the Italians, or more strictly Sicilians, perhaps have as much trouble with "foreign" names as the English do with some Italian names. The Motoring News reported it as such: "A Tiger was entered by Vitafoam for Peter Harper and a mysterious gentleman called 'Ruper' to drive. With the suspension screwed down so hard that it practically bounced from corner to corner, it impressed the timekeepers so much that they awarded 'Ruper' a very impressive practice time, which even he sadly disbelieved."

With the Friday practice behind them the crew rose early on Sunday morning and set out from the Palermo Hotel to the pit area and the start. The roads had been closed to the public since 4am but by that time thousands of vehicles had taken the spectators up into the mountains to their vantage points on hillsides, bridges and walls, but by 6.30am even the competitors and officials had to clear the circuit in readiness for the start at 8am. In the pits the largish British contingent chatted as the seconds ticked away to the start. As the starting order for the event was based on capacity rather than practice time, of the British entries the Dick Jacobs MG Midget coupe driven by Andrew Hedges and Paddy Hopkirk would be the first away followed in the 3-litre GT class by the Healey 3000 of Timo Makinen/Paul Hawkins. The third British entry, in the 1000-1600cc prototype class, was the Rauno Aaltonen/Clive Baker works Austin Healey Sprite, painted in an unusual 'dayglo' green, followed by the Tiger in the

Targa Florio 1965

over 3-litre prototype class. The 8.00am start was delayed by a few minutes by the late return of the course car, but finally the first car was flagged away followed at thirty-second intervals by the remaining 59 cars and the 49th Targa Florio was underway. Peter Harper was to take the first stint and shortly after he was flagged away, the leading car on the road, a yellow Abarth Simca, was round again starting its second lap.

Seven km from the start, in the village of Cerda, Denis Jenkinson was spectating and reporting for Motor Sport and observed that "Harper came bouncing and wallowing through in the ungainly Sunbeam Tiger" followed closely by Bondurant in the Ford GT Prototype. The Tiger was running well although leaking some oil from the engine compartment and shortly Peter was pulling into the pits at the end of his first stint. Ruper(t) Jones, writing in Collectors Car, describes his turn thus: "As I took over he (Peter Harper) told me the brakes were unpredictable, pulling first one way and then the other, and indeed this was the case. It didn't affect my drive a lot until I came to the pit area at the end of my stint. Arriving perhaps a little hastily I braked hard, went sideways and cleared the area. My team manager and Peter didn't seem amused, but I hadn't hit anything.

The Harper/Jones Tiger thunders through one of the more spectator controlled areas of the island route, crossing the exhortations for the Italian heroes, Bandini and Vacarella, to uphold Italian honour. (LAT)

Targa Florio 1965

Apart from the naturally hazardous nature of the circuit and the local dog and goat population, people also carry crates of ale across the road as you approach and stand totally unprotected two and three deep in the villages. No wonder the Mille Miglia was stopped."

Having survived potential annihilation in the pits area, the refuelled Tiger was driven away by Peter on his second stint, which, apart from the physical exhaustion of the driving effort combined with the heat and stiff suspension, went by without further trouble. Peter had put in the Tiger's fastest lap at 45mins 41secs for the 72km circuit, only 10secs slower than the Healey 3000 time of 45.31 (although this was in a different class), but both of these were understandably below the 39.21 of Nino Vacarella, the Sicilian lawyer/professor who put in the fastest lap, breaking the previous record set in 1962 by 39secs and who brought home the sole remaining prototype Ferrari 275/P2 in first place overall.

All four British cars finished, with only the second-in-class Hedges/Hopkirk Midget finishing on the same lap as the winning vehicle, some 47mins in arrears, the remaining cars being one lap behind. With the demise of the over 3-litre prototype class the reliability of the Tiger, combined with the ability of the crew to keep the vehicle on the island, had netted them second place in class to the winning Ferrari.

Trying hard, the Harper/Jones Tiger powers away from a corner on the Targa Florio Circuit maintaining the polite interest of the spectators. Only when the Ferraris arrived is there a release of the true Italian devotional fervour for motorsport - particularly Italian motorsport! (LAT)

Targa Florio 1965

The organisers, however, felt otherwise and as the car had not finished within 15% of the class-winner's time, the Tiger was not to be classified as a finisher. Three weeks after the event, however, the organisers published the final results and confirmed the Tiger in second place in class, but as the Reverend Rupert Jones noted in 1981 "We are still waiting for our prize money."

In retrospect the Tiger was not particularly suited to such a circuit and it is to the credit of the car, crew and support crews that the car not only finished, but finished well in its class, as, of the 59 starters, 29 finished, only 14 on the same lap with 5 more outside of the time limit.

A brief chance of some cool air from the shade of an olive tree during the frantic chase through the mountains in the scorching Sicilian countryside. (via D.McDermott)

Targa Florio 1965

Watched by the Carabinieri and the local villagers, the Harper/Jones Tiger presses on and shows the propped open boot lid, with bonnet pins inserted, intended to help with the through-flow of cooling air. (via D.McDermott)

This photo, taken after the Targa Florio, on the Tholt-y-Will Hill Climb on the Isle of Man, shows the extent to which the front bodywork was, and allowed to be, modified. Most of the effort was to try and get the right amounts of cooling air to both the radiator and the hard used front disc. (LAT)

RAC Rally 1965

One of the briefer rallies for Humber Road.

RAC Rally 1965

Destined to be one of the shorter rallies for a works entered Tiger, Humber Road entered a single Tiger (ADU311B) in the 1965 RAC Rally for Peter Harper with Don Barrow taking over the co-driver's right hand seat, after the run with Ian Hall on the previous event, the Alpine Rally.

The rally itself was a usual RAC route of around 2350 miles in total, taking in 57 special stages on forest tracks on which the rally was won or lost. The route ran around England, Wales and Scotland, starting in London, driving into the West Country, up through Wales and across the country to the Yorkshire and Northumbria stages; cutting across Scotland as far north as Perth and back down through the Lake District before a mirror image of the route back through Wales to the finish in London.

ADU311B was a fairly standard works car with the normal 4260cc engine, but with the obligatory large sump shield to protect the engine and gearbox as well as the underside of the car from the constant pounding of the rough forest tracks. Since much of the rally was in darkness - around 16 hours per day in November - Peter Harper had fitted an array of lights which would take into account virtually all the weather conditions expected - fog, snow, rain, frost and ice - that is normal RAC Rally weather! Stone guards were fitted to the headlamps to provide some protection against flying stones when catching another competitor on the stages. The car still sported a shortened version of the Alpine rally air scoop, which again led the cooler outside air directly to the carburettor.

Scrutineering was on the Saturday at the Airport Hotel at London Heathrow, and took place in the open air under leaden skies that had drizzled sporadically all day. Checks were made for safety and compliance with the law, including an exhaust noise check, and special paints were daubed on vital parts of the car (e.g. engine block) to prevent unauthorised substitution during the rally proper. The Tiger glided through scrutineering, was put into the parc fermé and the crews retired to their hotel for the last good night's sleep they were to have for some time.

The drizzle had ceased on the Sunday morning, and at 2pm precisely, Graham Hill, as the official starter, flagged away the first of the 162 starters - the Timo Makinen/Paul Easter works red Healey 3000. Nineteen minutes later, at number 20, Peter Harper eased in the clutch, drove carefully down the ramp and headed down the B379 towards the A30 and the first special stages.

The Tiger had been entered in Class 13 along with its main rivals, the Healey 3000 of Makinen/Easter (No.2) and the similar car of the Morley brothers (No.14). Whilst the weather was improving marginally, it had been raining enough in the previous two days - three inches falling on Saturday alone - to wash out the first of the 57 stages in the sandy depths of Bramshill forest near Camberley. So the crews had an uneventful 50 mile run down the A30/A303 to Salisbury Plain where the next two stages were set. The first was a five mile at Milston Down, consisting mainly of open grassland, whilst the second was at Rolleston Camp and was deeply rutted and muddy. A further difficulty was that this second stage was taken in total darkness and the route on the stage was ill defined and caused the crews considerable problems in picking out the correct route through the stage. It was on one of these stages that Peter Harper's rally began to draw to a close.

On one of the bigger bumps the engine of the Tiger moved forward on its mountings allowing the fan to make contact with the radiator with the predictable results. The car roared through the third stage with clouds of steam issuing from every slot, and losing quantities of water with every mile. Peter coaxed the car away from Salisbury Plain and had the radiator changed by the service crews at the second time control on the A303 at Camel Hill Cafe, the crew keeping their fingers crossed that the head gaskets had not been damaged. After this brief halt and the stage at King Alfred's Tower the rally headed towards the Brendon Hills and the first real forestry stages. The bogey time for this stage was 4mins 52secs and whilst Makinen took fastest time at 5.07, Peter Harper's luck didn't hold and he finished the stage with the front right tyre punctured and flat.

RAC Rally 1965

The Peter Harper/Don Barrow Tiger hustles through one of the early special stages on the 65 RAC Rally. The car is running on steel wheels in preference to the more usual magnesium Minilites. (Foster & Skeffington)

A tell-tale continuous wisp of steam signals trouble for the Harper/Barrow Tiger on one of the Salisbury Plain stages during the 65 RAC Rally. Usually it signified some contact between the fan and radiator after a heavy landing or contact with a significant bump on the stage. (Classic Cars/Autocar)

RAC Rally 1965

By this time the engine was distinctly off song and although on the next stage, the Old Porlock Toll Road, the crew were still returning respectable stage times - reputedly on one bank of cylinders only - by the next stage in the Quantock Hills the car had given up the ghost and the crew and car were towed into the time control at Bristol Airport - and official retirement.

Accelerating hard, Peter Harper sweeps past a Ford Anglia out of the Camberley round about on the A30, prior to the cancelled first stage at Bramshill. (Author)

Monte Carlo Rally 1966

The first International Rally run under the new Appendix J and the Automobile Club de Monaco's regulations favour the unmodified 'showroom' Group 1 cars.

The 1966 Monte Carlo Rally was the first of the international rallies run under the new Appendix J regulations. Under these new rules the Tiger was classified as a category 'A' car - production cars meant for road use - and sub-classified as a Group 3 Grand Touring car, the annual production rate of which must exceed 500 units. This put them in the same category as the Porsche 911, and, having beaten such cars before, the Tiger was expected to be very competitive in this Grand Touring category.

The chances of outright victory, however, had diminished, as not only were the penalties on the run-in into Monte three times those of the Group 1 (unmodified) saloons, but on the tests after the Monte run-in, the penalties were still three times the Group 1 cars, but with an addition of 18% added to the actual stage times. Such a heavy handicap meant that only a class win was possible, the outright win would undoubtedly go to a Group 1 vehicle - a pity in many ways, since the Monte was a Peter Harper speciality and after his fine fourth place in the previous year, there had always been an outside chance of an outright win.

With the new regulations in force, the factory carefully prepared the two Tigers to a slightly different specification. The car for Andrew Cowan

Monte Carlo Rally 1966

and Brian Coyle (FRW667C) was a totally new car whilst the car for Peter Harper and Robin Turvey (AHP294B) was a rebuild of the car last used by 'Tiny' Lewis on the Alpine rally. Engine preparation for the cars was close to the usual build with a high lift cam, polished ports etc., but the major change was the fitting of a two-choke Ford (modified) carburettor and a cast iron 289 inlet manifold, which replaced the 4-barrel carburettor and alloy manifold. This was a consequence of the new regulations and reduced engine power output to around 200bhp. In terms of road performance Rootes Engineering Development had carried out some tests at the Motor Industries Research Association (MIRA) test track and had found that the current build of car - AHP295B tested on 19.8.65 and built to the same standard as FRW667C (and later FRW668C) - was only 0.5secs slower than the 1965 Monte car (ADU312B) up to 60 mph - tested on 11.2.65 - and some 1.5secs slower from 60 to 80 mph in top gear. Where the alterations really showed, however, was in the breathing at higher revs. In the 0 to 90 mph time the car was some 4secs slower, although what was lost in terms of acceleration appeared to be balanced to some extent by flexibility as the 60 to 70 mph time in third gear was similar. For the transmission and suspension, the usual 3.77 differential was fitted with a limited slip, and both the front and rear spring rates were revised, along with the damper settings. As in the previous years Monte, the promise of cold and snowy conditions prompted the fitting of an electrically heated windscreen, and an alternator to help with the extra power loads - which also included the four extra forward facing lamps. The tyre contract with Dunlop had been renewed and the car ran exclusively with either partly studded or fully studded SP44's or SP41 for the less icy sections.

The route for this 35th 'Rallye Monte Carlo' was similar to the previous years, with its multitude of starting points, but, in contrast, the layout was altered. For the first time for many years, there was to be no common route before Monte Carlo, where, previously, all the surviving competitors competed on six or so special stages before they reached the Principality, in order to align themselves for the mountain circuit. This year the competitors would meet in Monte Carlo, after an 1800 mile run-in, before tackling the 888 mile Route Commune with six special stages in and around the Alps between Chambery, Avignon and Nice. With the road penalties and special stage penalties, calculated including the "factor of comparison", the top 60 entrants would leave the parc fermé on the night of Wednesday 19th January for the final 380 mile Mountain Circuit in the mountains behind Monaco - fast road sections and six special stages, which included three runs over the demanding Col de Turini - and from this the winner would emerge.

This year, Rootes had decided to split their entries with regard to starting points, no doubt with the 1964 Monte weather in mind. Peter Harper and Robin Turvey (No.150) were to start from Reims, the French starting point, and the Andrew Cowan/Brian Coyle Tiger was to start from London. By splitting the entry, there was obviously a greater chance of getting one of the cars to the finish if some catastrophe struck on the run into Monte and the route became totally blocked - an occurrence that was not out of the question in mid-winter in the mountains - or the English Channel ferries were cancelled due to bad weather (an even greater chance). Also two starting points generally attracted at least twice the publicity and one of the major aspects of rallying is, of course, the publicity it attracts for the manufacturer.

In the event, both cars met up at Liege to carry out a northern loop through Arnhem, Den Haag, Antwerp, Ostende and Boulogne (again for the London starters) before striking out across the Massif Central towards the southern-most part of the common route at Avignon, Digne and finally Monte Carlo. Almost two and one half days of relatively leisurely motoring, in distinct contrast to that which was to follow!

Monte Carlo Rally 1966

Andrew Cowan and Brian Coyle leave the London Airport start of the 1966 Monte Carlo rally. The car is already running on studs and interestingly the Tiger sports an Alpine wing motif. (Rootes)

Andrew Cowan and Brian Coyle leave the starting ramp at the Excelsior Hotel at London Airport. (Rootes)

Monte Carlo Rally 1966

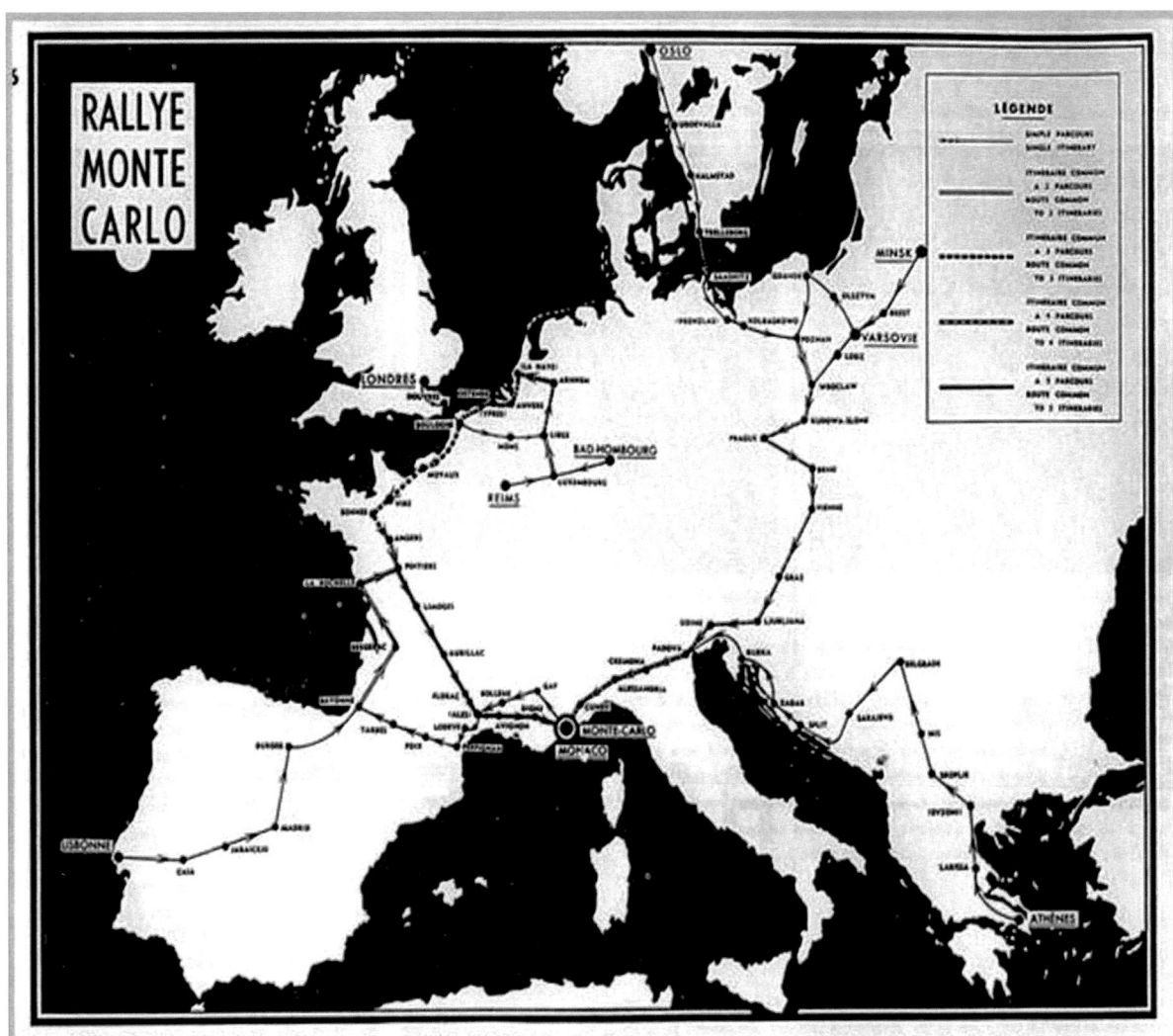

OU LES VOIR PASSER (France et Belgique)

Itinéraires de concentration

Vendredi 14 Janvier
Boulogne s/Mer : 19 h 41 à 20 h 35
Monte-Carlo (départ) : 20 h 16 à 20 h 54
Reims (départ) : 20 h 36 à 21 h 20
Mons : 22 h 58 à 23 h 42
Luxembourg : 23 h 25 à 0 h 35

Samedi 15 janvier
Gap : 0 h 45 à 1 h 23
Liège : 1 h 41 à 3 h 35
Bollène : 3 h 08 à 3 h 46
Lodève : 6 h 0 à 6 h 38
Perpignan : 8 h 34 à 9 h 12
Anvers : 9 h 56 à 11 h 50
Foix : 10 h 46 à 11 h 24
Ostende : 12 h 18 à 14 h 12
Tarbes : 13 h 30 à 14 h 08
Boulogne s/Mer : 14 h 52 à 16 h 46
Bayonne : 15 h 23 à 16 h 36
Moyaux : 19 h 07 à 21 h 01
Bergerac : 19 h 43 à 20 h 56
Vire : 21 h 05 à 22 h 59
Rennes : 23 h 01 à 0 h 55
La Rochelle : 23 h 51 à 1 h 14

Dimanche 16 janvier
Angers : 1 h 09 à 3 h 03
Poitiers : 2 h 09 à 5 h 16
Limoges : 4 h 09 à 6 h 16
Aurillac : 7 h 05 à 10 h 12
Florac : 10 h 19 à 13 h 26
Avignon : 12 h 44 à 15 h 51
Digne : 15 h 13 à 18 h 20
Cuneo (Italie) : 19 h 27 à 20 h 24
Monaco (jardins) : 18 h 45 à 22 h 49
Monaco (Parc fermé) : 18 h 55 à 22 h 59

L'horaire figurant ci-dessus représente l'heure de départ du premier au dernier concurrent devant passer au contrôle. Il va sans dire que l'on peut s'attendre, surtout sur certains parcours, à ce que les plus rapides prennent une assez large avance. Ces horaires sont susceptibles d'être modifiés à la dernière minute. Pour tous renseignements complémentaires, il est recommandé de consulter son automobile-club local ou le Comité d'Organisation du Rallye : 23 Boulevard Albert-1er, Monaco, tél. : 30-32-20.

The route and timings of the 1966 Monte Concentration Run (en Francais). Andrew Cowan and Brian Coyle started from London at No.105, whilst the Peter Harper/Robin Turvey Tiger ran at No.150 from Reims. 'Tiny' Lewis and Tim Bosence also started from Reims in a works Imp at No.146. This was the first year that the entrants had not competed on any stages prior to reaching Monaco. Under the new regulations the cars converged from their individual starting towns on the Principality for the 24 hour Monaco – Chambery – Monaco loop followed by the 500 km dash through the Maritime Alpes and back to Monaco through Nice. (Sport Auto)

Monte Carlo Rally 1966

The Cowan/Coyle Tiger turns onto the M2 heading for Dover.

On Friday morning, the 14th January, 39 cars lined up at the Excelsior Hotel at London Airport, having been scrutineered the previous evening at Henley's Garage on the Great West Road, and at 10.38am precisely, A K Stevenson - now nearing 80 years old and doing his 36th starting stint since 1924 - flagged away the first car, the Lotus Cortina (NVW243C) of Roger Clark and Brian Melia (No.75). Shortly after, the Tiger of Cowan and Coyle rolled off the ramp and headed towards the control at Dover, the due arrival time being three hours and twenty minutes later. It was a fairly hectic time for Brian Coyle as he had taken some of his exams at Glasgow University on the Wednesday evening and then had flown south to join the start and the general hassle of co-driving and navigating a car on a major international rally.

It was bitterly cold in London and as there were reports of snow en-route in Kent, the crew had chosen to fit lightly studded Dunlop Weathermasters for the run to the first control. Rather surprisingly, the London starters had some of the worst weather, and snow was indeed apparent in Kent, with poor visibility at times, and, having crossed the channel the competitors still faced snowy roads when they arrived in Boulogne. As Andrew Cowan arrived in Boulogne, Peter Harper and Robin Turvey were readying themselves for the start in Reims with the weather not much of an improvement on the English start, a cold dark night with slush frozen to the ground. At 8.36pm the starter dropped his flag and the first car left the ramp. One minute later 'Tiny' Lewis and Tim Bosence started, this time in an Imp, and four minutes after them the Harper Tiger burbled away from the start heading towards Luxembourg and on to Liege where they were to meet up with the London starters and slot in 70mins behind Andrew Cowan.

That meeting of Tigers, however, was not to be, as very soon after leaving the Boulogne control, Andrew Cowan inverted his car on the snow and ice and withdrew from the rally. In his book "Why Finish Last" Andrew sets out the circumstances - "We were on a simple road section of the rally when you go stooging around Northern France and were in no great hurry, when, as we crossed a ridge into a corner, the car started to slide towards the verge. There must have been something under the snow at the edge and we hit this with the front cross member and the next thing we knew the car somersaulted end over end. If I had thought that the car was going to roll I would never have let it slide anywhere near the verge, but, a little mistake like that ended with a badly bent motor car and some rather tricky explaining to Marcus Chambers, the team manager." An unfortunate consequence of running studded tyres on dryish tarmac at this point, a kilometre stone to help the car over corner-to-corner and a lot of bad luck. The car had slid down the road on its

Monte Carlo Rally 1966

roof, which had been completely flattened. Both crew were unhurt but understandably annoyed as they packed up to return to Scotland for an "early bath". Ian Hall noted later that it was "...not a Cowan-like thing to do..."

Spread out across France in front of the competitors, Marcus Chambers had strategically placed his three Hillman Minx Estate service cars, whilst he, along with Gerry Sloniger was supporting in a Tiger (ERW729C) complete with a trailer of parts, tyres and fuel bags. Additionally, travelling just in front of the rally, was Peter Riley driving the Andrew Cowan recce car (ADU312B) and acting as a 'pathfinder' vehicle.

With this assistance, the Harper/Turvey Tiger arrived at the Quai Albert Premier early on Sunday evening and both the car's crew and support crews, having seen the cars safely into the parc fermé, retired for a good night's sleep.

Andrew Cowan and Brian Coyle, fresh from his exams at Glasgow University, prepare for the start of the Monte in London. Des O'Dell recalls that FRW667C was "the best Tiger we ever built". (Rootes)

Monte Carlo Rally 1966

Andrew Cowan and Brian Coyle top up with fuel at Dover prior to the Channel crossing. The run down from the start at London Heathrow has been through the snow in East Kent and the Tiger is already on lightly studded Dunlops. (UnitedPress)

The restart was at 9am the following morning, when the crews would tackle the 'Route Commun', almost 900 miles from Monaco to Chambery and back, divided into 14 road sections with six special stages varying in length from 7km (La Roquette - which would almost certainly be dry) to the 47km of the Cols du Granier, Cucheron and Porte – three distinct cols which were generally under deep packed snow.

The weather was sunny, but bitterly cold, as the sole remaining Tiger set out on the Route Commun. The first stage came soon after the start and ran from Pont de Miolans to St.Auban, a very twisty road which clings to the side of the mountain, but which was relatively free from snow. The service crews had gone ahead and set up in Les Grillons, and Peter passed through without trouble. The next special stage from Thoard to St.Geniez, over the Col de Fontbelle, had been cancelled, but even then the crews were hard pushed to keep up the required 60kph average on the icy roads. One of the main hazards was that the sun had begun to melt some of the ice, but left ice patches hidden in the shadows. Having completed the third special stage from Remollon to Gap, mainly on dry roads, the crew started the fourth road section from Gap to St.Sebastian and then onto the fifth road section to Uriage, near Grenoble, and it was on this section that the rally was to finish for the Harper/Turvey Tiger.

Whilst traversing the Col d' Ornon, with plenty of polished ice, packed snow and waist high snow drifts, Robin called a caution which was a triple caution in his road notes, and as Peter answered that he remembered the spot, the car hit this notorious bump – a snow covered gulley - the engine moved forward, putting the fan into the radiator, and, as in the previous RAC Rally, the event was over.

Monte Carlo Rally 1966

In a Reims garage, before the start, Peter Harper and the Rootes team run through the last loading of all of the emergency paraphernalia needed to reach Monte Carlo should the service cars be absent or late on the route – a very rare occurence. The spare tyre is a fully studded Dunlop SP44 Weathermaster. (via Ian Hall)

Monte Carlo Rally 1966

In the same Reims garage the works mechanics rapidly change the shock absorbers on the rear of the car, while the French mechanics look on with interest. The Monte Carlo Rally created great interest in Reims and the whole town, including the police, were enthusiastic participants. The Tiger wears its Alpine motif on the wing rather the Tiger pattern. The rear tyres are already studded. (via Ian Hall)

The end of the 'best Tiger we ever built'. (via Andrew Cowan)

Monte Carlo Rally 1966

Ian Hall notes that "Rosemary Smith and I had done the Road Book recce in one of the Super Minxes before Christmas and recorded this gulley very clearly so Messrs. Harper and Turvey didn't get much sympathy from me this time!"

The Rootes team packed up their service cars and vans and, with the Tiger, made their way back to Humber Road.

As a footnote, this was the rally in which the BMC team of Makinen, Aaltonen and Hopkirk in their Cooper S's in the first three places overall and the fourth placed Lotus Cortina of Roger Clark were disqualified for a "lighting infringement". Rootes too had also suffered, as the Rosemary Smith and Val Domleo had been disqualified and thus lost the prestigious Coupe des Dames in their Imp (FRW306C).

Not an outstanding rally for Rootes, but as compensation, Patrick Lier won the Group 1 Production Saloons up to 1000cc in his Imp, and 'Tiny' Lewis and Tim Bosence won the Group 2 modified saloons up to 1000cc, also in an Imp.

Monte Carlo Rally 1966

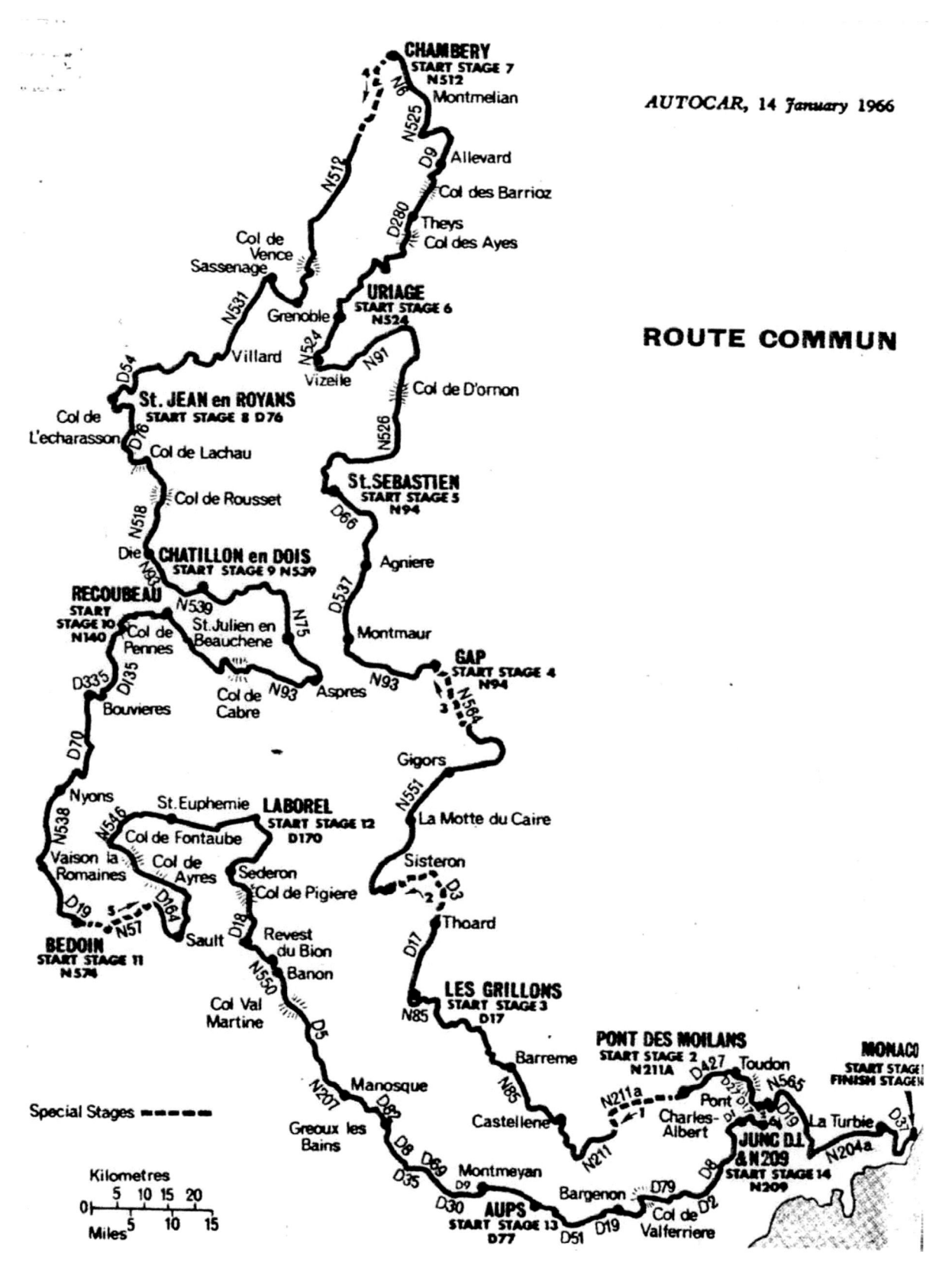

AUTOCAR, 14 January 1966

ROUTE COMMUN

The 900 mile anti-clockwise route from Monaco to Chambery and back, divided into 14 road sections and six special stages. The Harper/Turvey Tiger got through three special stages before coming to grief on a road section at the Col d'Ornon. (Autocar)

Monte Carlo Rally 1966

Peter Harper and Robin Turvey push-on on slippery roads with the Tiger showing some signs of wear & tear. The right hand front has obviously made contact with the scenery, perhaps with a snow bank, with the fog lamp and headlamp broken and the light surround missing. (Rootes)

The Harper/Turvey Tiger hustles along in the slush of the lower mountain slopes. (Rootes)

Monte Carlo Rally 1966

These two photographs taken, possibly during a publicity session, show the Tiger on one of the many snow covered ascents and descents on the route to Monte Carlo. (Rootes)

Monte Carlo Rally 1966

All routes on the Monte Carlo Rally are copiously policed by the Gendarmerie as part of the French national pride in the rally. (Rootes)

The Tiger is serviced at one of the many pre-arranged points around the route – normally for tyres and fuel. The well-stocked service car is parked behind the rally car. (via Ian Hall)

Monte Carlo Rally 1966

Peter Harper powers the Tiger over a Col shortly before retiring from mechanical maladies. (Rootes)

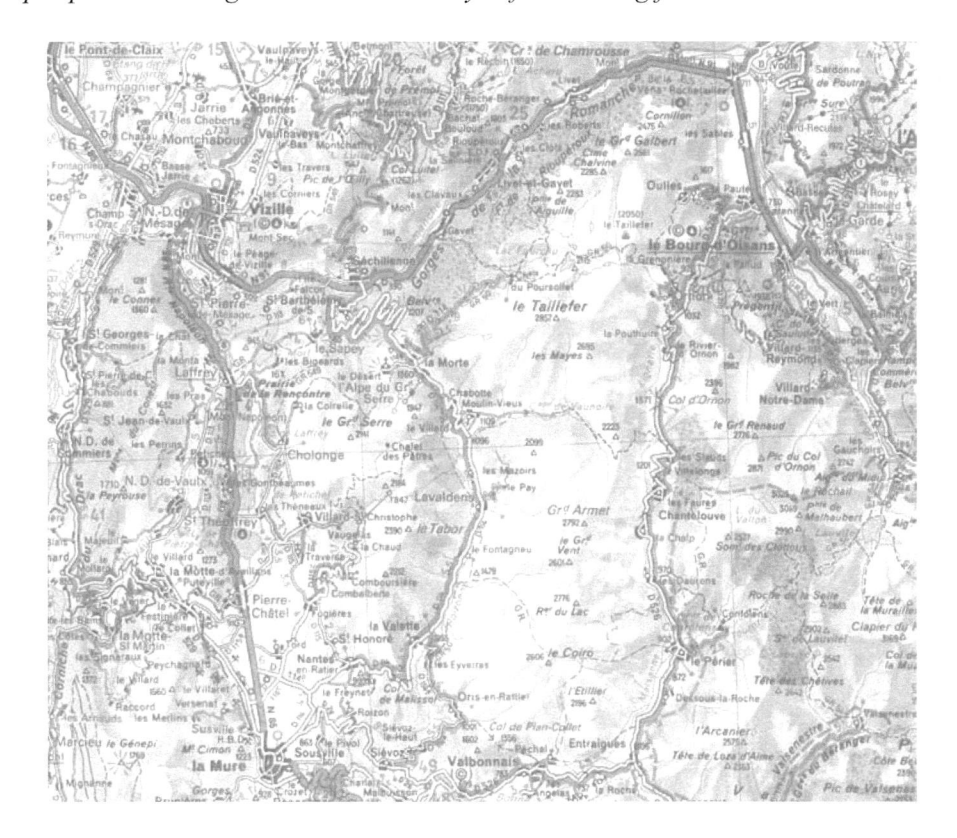

Monte Carlo Rally 1966

Marcus Chambers

The Competition Manager for BMC between 1954 and 1961, Marcus built and led the BMC team from its early beginnings – he started at the time that MG were just about to re-open its Competition Department and resume racing and rallying - and provided the leadership to become a fiercely competitive works team in International Rallying. He had been a competitor, a member of the BRDC team who came 10th at Le Mans in 1938 and post-war 1947 – 49 he was the chief mechanic in the BRMC HRG racing team. Known affectionately as the 'Poor Man's Neubauer' he had much in common with the great Mercedes Racing Manager and enjoyed good food and better wine, - his books expound the gastronomique tours that occurred on the way to, and back from, his wide range of International Rallies. He left BMC to become an Executive with the Appleyard Group in 1961 before succumbing to the lure of competiton to become Rootes Competiton Manager in 1964.

Andrew Cowan

Like the BMC works drivers – the Morley brothers – Andrew was a farmer in Duns - along with Jim Clark - and, like all farmers, his rallying year was controlled to a large extent by the seasonal timeline of seeding and harvesting. He was a regular competitor in Scotland and on the 1963 International Scottish Rally was out in his private Rapier and, for the second time, won the rally outright. Catching the eye of Lewis Garrad, he was pencilled in for a works drive on the Alpine Rally of that year, but this didn't materialize. For the following RAC Rally he was loaned a works engine, but this rally ended with a broken valve spring. Rootes then offered a works co-drive on the 1964 Monte in one of the first Group 3 Hillman Imps with Keith Ballisat, and, whilst the Imp had almost terminal engine problems, they managed to be classified as finishers in 133rd place. A potential outing in a Ford Falcon Sprint for the 1964 Alpine ended extra-early as all the Falcons were disqualified at scrutineering for fitting un-homologated aluminium bonnets. The 1964 RAC was driven in a works Rapier and Andrew and Brian Coyle finished 20th overall, having lost time in an ice-covered Dovey Forest after a multiple car accident. His works drive in the Tiger on the 1965 Monte and Scottish followed, before some time in works Group 3 Rover 2000 TCs before returning to Rootes and successfully competing in their then front-line rally car – the Imp – and ultimately winning the London – Sydney Rally in the Hunter with Brian Coyle and Colin Malkin.

Tulip Rally 1966

The Tulip 'class improvement' scheme is scrapped for this year's rally and the Tiger stands a good chance of an outright win.

After the ignominious result of the previous year, at least as far as the Tiger was concerned, Rootes entered a single Group 3 Tiger (FRW668C) for Peter Harper and Robin Turvey, backed up by a Group 3 Rally Imp for 'Tiny' Lewis and Tim Bosence.

In previous years, the powerful cars like the Tigers or Healeys did not necessarily hold the whip hand, as the overall results were calculated on a 'class improvement' scheme, which did not always favour the faster cars. In 1965, for instance, the Morley brothers in their Healey 3000 were fastest on scratch, but after the handicap was applied, were relegated to fourth position overall. This year the formula was very simple - the fastest car wins - which, of course, made the Tiger very competitive, especially as virtually all of the stages were on tarmac. As in prior years, the route comprised a series of long road sections, some of which were more demanding and called 'selectifs', connecting groups of short hill climbs - the special stages. One of the reasons for implementing such a change was that permission had been refused, by the police, to close some of the public roads used as special stages and eight stages had to be cancelled only two weeks before the rally. The itinerary was now 2700km in length, interspersed with 88km of hill climbs, split into 15 stages; 128km of selectives, two tests on Army land at Utrecht and a single lap around the Zandvoort circuit - a total of 18 stages and 9 selective sections.

The Group 3 Tiger (FRW668C) was a new car, built to the 1966 regulations and very similar to the Monte Carlo cars (AHP294B and FRW667C).

Tulip Rally 1966

Power output was around 200bhp, the increase over the standard output being obtained by using polished heads, a high lift cam, solid lifters and Hi-Po 289 valve springs to allow higher revs, the sparks for these revs being assisted by a twin-point competition distributor. The carburation was virtually standard, the car using a 289 cast-iron manifold and a 289 two-choke carburettor. As with all the later cars, and incidentally on ADU311B on the Acropolis Rally, braking was improved with a dual braking system and dual servos - the servo for the rear brakes sitting on the rear seat on the right hand side. Apart from a different set of spring rates and damper settings, the suspension was standard, albeit to the latest competition standard, although the rear axle used a 3.77 differential fitted with a Powr-Lok limited slip. Overall a car that was suprisingly close to 'standard' but very suited to the type of going on the Tulip.

Scrutineering took place on Monday in the grounds of the Huis ter Duin Hotel in Noordwijk aan Zee, a town described respectively by 'Motor' and 'Motor Sport' as 'a sort of Dutch Hastings' or a 'seaside town of Clacton proportions', which in spite of these mild invectives provided a friendly and helpful atmosphere, and the Tiger passed through without problems. The scrutineers, however, were insisting on the new rulings on body modifications - especially petrol filler cap locations - which didn't affect the Tiger but did the Group 2 Lotus Cortina.

On Tuesday at 6.15pm Jack Kemsley flagged away the first car, Peter Harper's Tiger, one of the favourites for a win along with the other powerful Ford Lotus-Cortinas, the Alfa Romeo GTAs, the Porsche 911s or the more nimble Group 2 Mini Cooper S's.

A leisurely three-hour section led the competitors south through Holland, past Rotterdam, over one of the cancelled stages at Brecht to Halle, the first time control.

On into Belgium and into the Ardennes, where, between Liege and Luxembourg, the first of the four tests was sited. This was behind Spa at La Reid, a short 2.5km stage but which was slippery and twisty, the first bend being a hairpin right that caught some crews out - Pat Moss being one of them in her Barracuda. The next test was La Roche-Samree, a long and very fast 7.8km up the main N28 out of La Roche with the conditions suiting the power and torque of the Tiger. Over this test the Tiger was third fastest and averaged a speed of over 72 mph (118 km/hr). Vic Elford, in his Group 2 Lotus-Cortina, was reputed to be lifting of at 7000 rpm in top at a few places on this stage!

Test 3 - Kautenbach - is a 3km twisty, tight little test, full of hairpins, that did not particularly suit the Tiger, but did the more nimble Alfa GTAs. However, the uphill start did suit the torque of the V-8 whilst the more highly tuned smaller engines had a few problems away from the start. A little further down the road lay the fourth of this group of tests, Bourscheid. This is a very fast stage and Peter Harper kept up his challenge behind the GTAs of Slotemaker and van Lennep and the Lotus Cortina of Vic Elford and John Davenport. Straight from the time control in Sarrebourg, the Tiger led the field to the Col de Charbonniere, a very fast 5km stage. Rauno Aaltonen in the Mini Cooper S put up the fastest time but Peter Harper provided the competition when he was only 4secs behind the Flying Finn. The stage led virtually directly onto the first of the selective sections, up and over the Col de Fouchy.

This was normally one of the special stages with a climb up the north side of the Col, as it had been in 1965, but this year it fell foul of the problems in closing the road to non-competing traffic and so the whole of the steep and narrow 8km was being used as a selective with the average speed set at an immoderate 70kph. Not suprisingly, only five crews managed to beat the bogey time; Aaltonen, Elford, Harper, Gass (Porsche 911) and Lampinen (Lotus Cortina) - so the Tiger was keeping good company!

Tulip Rally 1966

The Peter Harper and Robin Turvey Tiger, the last built of the works cars and with all of the latest competition suspension changes, power slides around a hairpin on the Ballon d'Alsace épreuve. In nicely balanced equilibrium on dry tarmac, the stage was well suited to the Tiger's driving characteristics. The crews were using an intercom to communicate the pace notes on this event. (Foster & Skeffington)

Meanwhile, at the main control of the evening at St.Maurice sur Moselle, the service crews had set up their pitches to provide relief and sustenance to the hard worked Tiger, and waited patiently, along with the Dunlop and Ferodo vans, for the first audible signs of the throaty burble of the Tiger. Peter Harper and Robin Turvey completed the selectives over the Col de Wettstein (18km) and Col de la Schlucht (18km), both set at 60kph, without problems. As midnight approached the cars started to arrive at the time control at St.Maurice and were delivered to the care of the service crews for mechanical refettling, a change of brake pads where necessary and a change of tyres before setting off for a climb of the Ballon d'Alsace.

Two selectives later, in the early hours of the morning, the weary crews pulled into Morez, near Geneva, at the most southerly control on the rally. On the following loop over 246km to the south and west of Geneva, the three leading crews of Aaltonen, Elford and Harper battled it out over three more stages, La Croisette, Le Saleve and La Faucille - with Robin Turvey keeping his fingers crossed this year- before returning to the half way halt, back at Morez.

Tulip Rally 1966

Klassementsproeven - Epreuves de Classement - Eliminating tests - Sonderprüfungen

1	La Reid	2.500 m
2	La Roche - Samrée	7.500 m
3	Kautenbach	3.000 m
4	Bourscheid	3.200 m
5	Col de la Charbonnière	5.000 m
6	Ballon d'Alsace	9.000 m
7	La Croisette	4.200 m
8	Le Salève	7.500 m
9	La Faucille	10.600 m
10	Ballon d'Alsace	5.900 m
11	Col du Bramont	4.200 m
12	Trois-Epis	4.900 m
13	Breitenbach	4.500 m
14	Bourscheid	3.200 m
15	Route de Mont	3.000 m
16	Vlasakkers	3.000 m
17	Soesterberg	3.000 m
18	Zandvoort	3.800 m
		88.000 m

Speciale Etappes - Etapes Spéciales - Special Stages Spezielle Etappen

1	Fouchy	7.900 m
2	Le Wettstein	18.000 m
3	La Schlucht	18.000 m
4	Route Joffre	14.000 m
5	Col Amic	10.000 m
6	Fouchy	7.900 m
7	Beaufort	15.000 m
8	Reisdorf	14.000 m
9	Huldange	24.000 m
		128.800 m

A page from the 1966 Tulip results showing the Eliminating speed tests, to be traversed at maximum speed, the special stages, which had to be completed under the time shown to be road penalty free, and the Time Controls to be visited - usually in restaurants or hostelries!

Tulip Rally 1966

locality	route no.	average speed	time-schedule No. 0 No. 210	date
Le Bonhomme	N415			
Col du Bonhomme	D48II			
D48II/D48IV	D48IV			
D48IV/D48	D48			
D48/N417	N417			
Col de la Schlucht	N417			
Le Collet	D34d			
D34d/D34	D34			
D34/D13b	D13b			
Col de Bramont	D13b			
Wildenstein	D13b			
Wesserling	N66			
St. Maurice-sur-Moselle	—			

ST. MAURICE-sur-MOSELLE — CHAMPAGNOLE (278 km)

locality	route no.	average speed	time-schedule	date
St. Maurice-s.M.	N465	60 km/h	2316-0246	26-27/4-'66
Ballon d'Alsace	N465			
N465/N466	N466			
Masevaux	D14bIV			
Bitschwiller	N66			
Willer-sur-Thur	D13bVI			
Col Amic	N431			
Col de Herrenfluh	N431			
Uffholtz	D5			
Cernay	N83			
Pont d'Aspach	N466			
Burnhaupt-le-Bas	D103			
Dannemarie	D103			
Chavannes	D3			
Delle	N463			
Badevel	D210			
Beaucourt	D39			
Montbouton	D39			
Hérimoncourt	D121			
St. Hypolite	N437			
Maiche	N437			
Morteau	N437			
Pontarlier	N471			
Champagnole	—			

CHAMPAGNOLE — CHAMPAGNOLE (301 km)

locality	route no.	average speed	time-schedule	date
Champagnole	N5	55 km/h	0354-0724	27/4-'66
St. Laurent	N437			
St. Claude	D124/D33			
St. Germain-des-Joux	N84			

28

The route as defined in the regulations that allows the route to be transferred to map prior to the rally.

Tulip Rally 1966

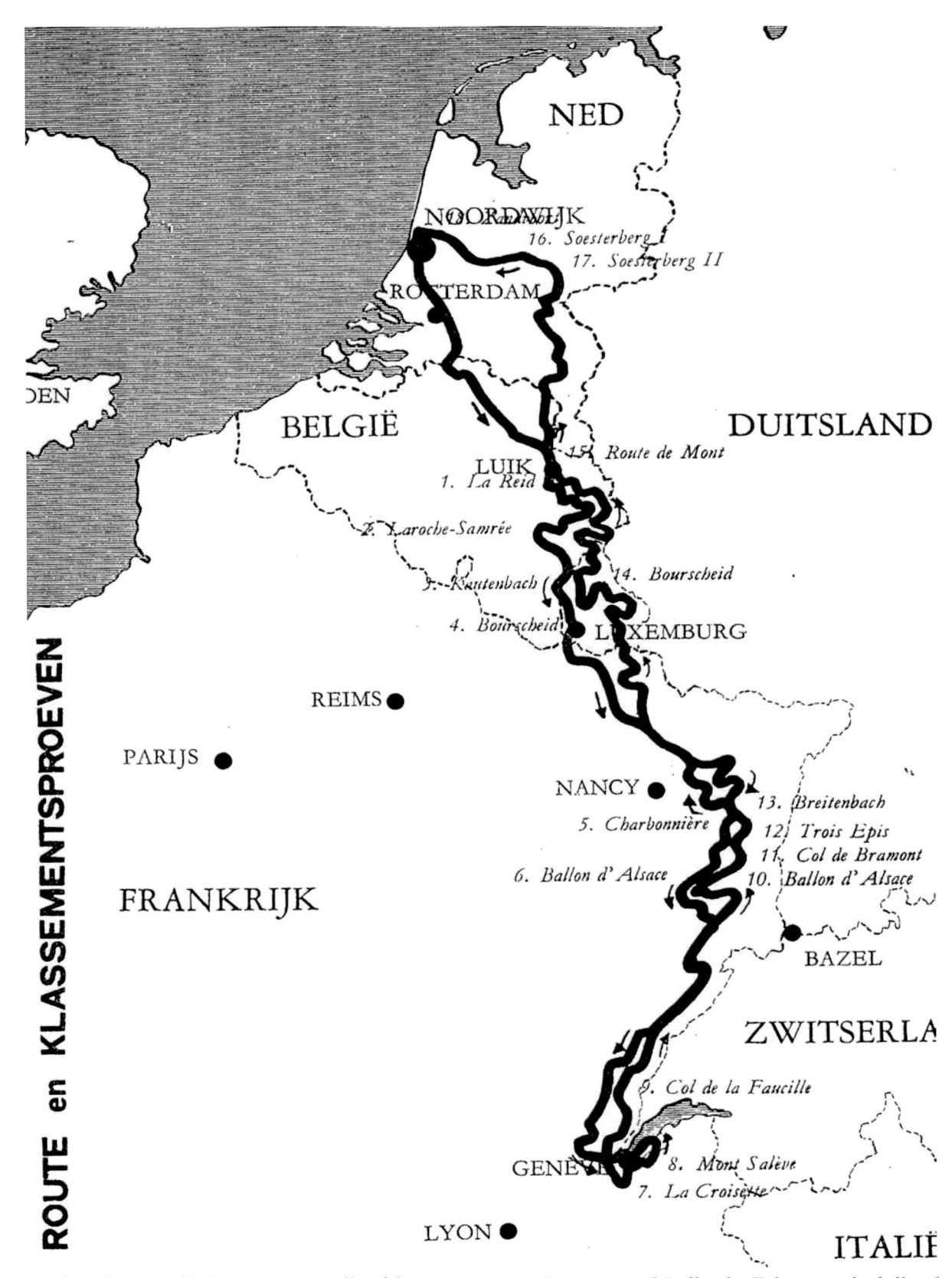

ROUTE en KLASSEMENTSPROEVEN

- 1. La Reid
- 2. Laroche-Samrée
- 3. Rautenbach
- 4. Bourscheid
- 5. Charbonnière
- 6. Ballon d'Alsace
- 7. La Croisette
- 8. Mont Salève
- 9. Col de la Faucille
- 10. Ballon d'Alsace
- 11. Col de Bramont
- 12. Trois Epis
- 13. Breitenbach
- 14. Bourscheid
- 15. Route de Mont
- 16. Soesterberg I
- 17. Soesterberg II

With so few suitable locations in Holland for a competitive International Rally, the Tulip uses the hills of the Ardennes, the hilly parts of the Vosges and the Haute-Alpes - north of Geneva - for the more keenly contested 'épreuves de classement' and 'étapes speciales'. (via Robert Clayson)

Tulip Rally 1966

```
ST.MAURICE-sur-MOSELLE  -  MOREZ  -  301 km
```

kilometers km	tot	plaats/locality		route no:	richting direction
0.0	0.0	ST.MAURICE-sur-MOSELLE	—	N66	TC4
0.1	0.1	St.Maurice-s/Moselle	⊣	N465	BELFORT
0.2	0.3	START KP6 BALLON d'ALSACE			Open: 23.15 - 02.45
9.0	9.3	FINISH KP6			
2.3	11.6	-	Y	-	-
1.1	12.7	-	⊤	(N464)	(ALTKIRCH) (MASEVAUX)
18.5	31.2	MASEVAUX	Y	-	ROUTE JOFFRE
0.6	31.8	Masevaux	+	D14^{BIV}	BITSCHWILLER
0.2	32.0	START SE4 "ROUTE JOFFRE" 14 km = 14 min			
4.9	36.9	BOURBACH-LE-HAUT		D14^{BIV}	BITSCHWILLER
9.1	46.0	FINISH SE4			
0.8	46.8	BITSCHWILLER	⊤	N66	COL DE BUSSANG
1.5	48.3	WILLER-s/THUR		D13^{BISVI}	GD.BALLON

A page from the 1966 Roadbook using the 'Tulips' notation of road direction that was first used by the Dutch (hence Tulips). The Time Control in St. Maurice-sur-Moselle is immediately followed by the start of 9 km KP6 (Épreuve No 6) - Ballon d'Alsace. This is followed by a 22.7 km road section to the start of a 14 km Étapes special to be completed in 14 minutes to be without penalty. The whole rally route is defined in this manner on 49 pages. (via Robert Clayson)

Tulip Rally 1966

Here the 1275 Cooper S of Rauno Aaltonen / Henry Lidden was in the lead with 2219.6 penalties, followed just under 30secs later by the Vic Elford/ John Davenport Lotus Cortina on 2249.1 penalties with the Tiger snapping on their heels with a penalty total of 2263.0 - a mere 14 seconds behind. Following behind were the three remaining chief protagonists, two Porsche 911s and an Alfa Romeo GTA.

Positions at the half way halt:

1	Aaltonen/Lidden	BMC Cooper S	2219.6
2	Elford/Davenport	Lotus Cortina	2249.1
3	Harper/Turvey	Sunbeam Tiger	2263.0
4	Gass/Bretthauer	Porsche 911	2281.6
5	Gijs/David van Lennep	Porsche 911	2294.0
6	Cavallari/Salvay	Alfa Romeo GTA	2297.2
7	Trana/Berggren	Volvo 122	2339.2
8	Pizzmato/Mathay	Alfa Romeo GTA	2369.5
9	Koob/Wies	BMW 1800	2375.4
10	Gray/Needham	Jaguar E Type	2394.7

Peter Harper and Robin Turvey leave the La Roche eliminating test on the 1966 Tulip Rally holding third place overall and first in class. Communication between the crew is by intercom. (Classic Cars)

Tulip Rally 1966

With the power full on, Peter Harper forces his Tiger through the bends on the Zandvoort Circuit stage at the end of the 1966 Tulip Rally. Over this 3.8 km stage Peter averaged just over 70 mph (116 km/hr), and was third fastest to Gijs van Lennep and Vic Elford. (Rootes)

Harper had been complaining of a fluffing engine during the event, and although the service crews hunted high and low, no cure could be found. However the lack of power was not an obvious impairment, for as the route retraced its steps to St.Maurice, the cars tackled the Ballon d'Alsace again, but this time from the Sewen side and only three seconds covered the four fastest cars - those of Gass, van Lennep, Harper and Aaltonen - in that order. A compulsory 25 minute halt ensued at St.Maurice, where the service crews again tended their charges and after this brief respite, the cars set off over the 224km return leg to Sarrebourg. Apart from the fluffing in the engine the Tiger had been utterly reliable and the only problem at this point was that the steering column adjuster refused to lock.

Over the next three stages, the Bramont, Trois Epis and Breitenbach, Peter Harper kept up the challenge and on the return run over the Col de Fouchy, this time from south to north, only three crews managed to clean this selective: Harper, Aaltonen and Elford. Over this section Peter had his statutory piece of luck - most crews get one piece of luck per rally amongst a veritable avalanche of bad luck, the most common form of which are punctures - when he had the good fortune to clear the Fouchy in the dry whilst a shower preceding a thunderstorm made the hill even more exciting for the remaining crews. By now night had fallen and the pace quickened as the rally sped through the lanes of Luxembourg towards the control in Liege, where most of the hard work was over, although many crews had little time in hand. The Tiger had held its third place and only two more speed tests and a lap of the Zandvoort circuit remained before the finish.

Tulip Rally 1966

The first two tests were on Army land near Utrecht, the first being a 3km slalom through straw bales - hardly international rallying. Peter Harper was not amused and considered the tests "All right for kids in go-karts" - but not for much else - although it was more suited to Aaltonen's nimble Cooper S. The second test at Soesterberg was run on narrow concrete paths constructed between great tank dips, an 'off' at this point would not be particularly wise and as the Tiger had some 30 seconds lead over the fourth placed man, Peter took it carefully. From the final stage, a lap around the Zandvoort circuit with the Porsche of the home driver Gijs van Lennep fastest, the competitors headed for the finish in bright sunshine in Noordwijk to finally complete the loop.

When the results were made final, Peter Harper and Robin Turvey had secured not only third place overall ahead of two rapid Porsche 911s and a Jolly Club Alfa Romeo GTA, but also won the Group 3 Grand Touring class ahead of the two same Porsches.

But this excellent result was not the only victory for Rootes to celebrate, for as a significant bonus, they had gained a clean 1,2,3 sweep in the one litre GT category with the Rally Imps, led by the Tiger "expatriate" 'Tiny' Lewis.

Final Results:

1	Rauno Aaltonen/Henry Lidden	BMC Cooper S	3880.5	Overall and Group 2
2	Vic Elford/John Davenport	Ford Lotus Cortina	3925.4	2nd Group 2
3	Peter Harper/Robin Turvey	Sunbeam Tiger	3962.5	1st Group 3
4	Wilfried Gass/W.Bretthauer	Porsche 911	3994.1	2nd Group 3
5	Arnaldo Cavallari/Dante Salvay	Alfa Romeo GTA	4003.0	3rd Group 2
6	Gijs/David van Lennep	Porsche 911	4027.5	3rd Group 3
7	Tom Trana/Lennart Berggren	Volvo 122	4116.4	
8	Nicolas Koob/Armand Wies	BMW 1800	4147.2	
9	Timo Makinen/Paul Easter	BMC Cooper S	4171.4	1st Group 1
10	John Kennerley/Digby Martland	Shelby Mustang	4176.8	

One of the easier stages for the navigator, Robin Turvey has time to survey the scenery while Peter Harper works hard to put up the third fastest time on the last Zandvoort stage. (Rootes)

Tulip Rally 1966

Tulip Rally 1966			1	60	89	42	59	43	100	113
Epreuve			Harper	Elford	Aaltonen	Gass	Cavallieri	van Lennep	Makinen	Lewis
			Tiger	Lotus Cort	Cooper S	911	Alfa GTA	911	Cooper S	998 Imp
			Group 3	Group 2	Group 2	Group 3	Group 2	Group 3	Group 1	Group 3
		Dist: km								
La Reid		2.50	1.48	1.44	1.43	1.44	1.45	1.42	1.50	1.57
La Roche-Samree		7.50	3.48	3.46	3.50	3.54	3.45	3.46	4.12	4.27
Kautenbach		3.00	2.44	2.41	2.41	2.43	2.43	2.40	2.51	3.02
Bourscheid		3.20	2.09	2.06	2.07	2.07	2.09	2.05	2.20	2.32
Col de la Charbonniere		5.00	3.45	3.46	3.41	3.48	3.54	3.53	4.01	4.19
Ballon d'Alsace		9.00	6.25	6.22	6.22	6.28	6.27	6.27	6.55	7.27
La Croisette		4.20	4.04	4.10	4.00	4.05	4.10	4.07	4.21	4.41
La Saleve		7.50	5.47	5.49	5.41	5.45	5.54	5.57	6.05	6.27
La Faucille		10.60	7.10	7.04	6.51	7.14	7.10	7.30	7.25	7.54
Ballon d'Alsace		5.90	4.42	4.46	4.43	4.41	4.43	4.42	4.51	5.07
Col du Bramont		4.20	3.31	3.24	3.26	3.26	3.23	3.25	3.42	3.50
Trois-Epis		4.90	3.29	3.23	3.26	3.26	3.25	3.29	3.43	3.55
Breitenbach		4.50	3.15	3.14	3.17	3.23	3.20	3.26	3.29	3.43
Bourscheid		3.20	2.11	2.02	2.06	2.06	2.13	2.13	2.15	2.29
Route de Mont		3.00	3.02	2.52	2.50	3.06	3.16	3.20	3.02	3.15
Vlasakkers		3.00	2.50	2.50	2.44	2.50	2.44	2.54	2.51	3.05
Soesterberg		3.00	3.23	3.30	3.13	3.24	3.21	3.20	3.21	3.26
Zandvoort		3.80	1.58	1.55	1.58	2.00	1.59	1.53	2.04	2.16
Etappe	Target	Dist:km								
Fouchy	6.46	7.90	6.33	6.28	6.40	6.59	7.06	6.52	6.53	7.09
Le Wettstein	18.00	18.00	14.05	14.44	14.18	15.03	14.51	13.58	14.22	14.36
La Schlucht	18.00	18.00	13.34	14.27	14.08	15.09	14.46	13.59	13.59	14.12
Route Joffre	14.00	14.00	11.54	12.20	11.43	12.16	12.37	12.11	11.58	12.44
Col Amic	10.00	10.00	8.24	8.26	8.25	8.38	8.56	8.43	8.20	8.54
Fouchy	6.46	7.90	6.25	6.32	6.42	6.55	6.47	6.57	6.52	7.16
Beaufort	15.00	15.00	12.07	11.50	10.58	12.01	12.25	11.25	11.11	11.49
Reisdorf	14.00	14.00	12.07	12.09	11.20	12.34	13.12	11.46	11.43	12.01
Huldange	24.00	24.00	20.00	19.15	18.29	19.11	23.59	21.23	17.30	19.22

The épreuve and étappe times of the top six runners and the leading Group 1 times as well as 'Tiny' Lewis's 998 Group 3 Imp times, all for the 1966 Tulip Rally.

Tulip Rally 1966

722
AUTOSPORT, MAY 6, 1966

1966 International Tulip Rally

Toe down through the Tulips!

SUNBEAM
1ST Grand Touring Category
1st over 2,500 c.c. G.T. class
Sunbeam Tiger driven by Peter Harper/Robin Turvey

HILLMAN IMP AGAIN!
1st, 2nd, 3rd up to 1,150 c.c. G.T. class
Drivers: Tiny Lewis/Tim Bosence, Nicholas Rowe/Stuart Turner, Simon Heijndijk/Nol Martini

Yet again Rootes cars win places of honour in the International Tulip Rally — 1,750 miles of tough, hard Continental driving with 23 timed tests on racing circuits and mountain climbs. The Tiger, from the Rally-proved range of Sunbeam cars, is supreme in the G.T. category, and the successful Hillman Imp again dominates its class.

(Results subject to official confirmation)

ROOTES MOTORS LIMITED
LONDON SHOWROOMS AND OVERSEAS DIVISION
DEVONSHIRE HOUSE, PICCADILLY LONDON W 1

Rootes considered advertising of rally successes an effective tool in encouraging interest in the strength and quality of their car range. (Autosport)

Acropolis Rally 1966

The Greek Gods look favourably on the Tiger on this traditionally hot, rough and demanding rally.

Known, quite correctly, as one of the toughest rallies in the world, the Acropolis Rally is a 50 hour 3000km thrash around the lesser known parts of Greece on roads which are normally used mainly for horse drawn transport, from which only the strongest cars and crews survive - a kind of small time evolution of mankind!

This year only 40 returned to the finish in Athens out of an original 105 starters, and even this was considered an excessive number by the organisers. The FIA ruling for 1966 was that only two of the permitted group variations of eligible cars were allowed to count for each championship rally, which meant that the Acropolis Rally was restricted to Group 2 (Improved Touring Cars) and Group 3 (Grand Touring Cars).

Acropolis Rally 1966

Peter Harper waits for the start of the 1966 Acropolis Rally whilst Ian Hall contemplates the tortuous route. The Rosemary Smith Imp follows on. (Autosport)

A single Tiger (ADU311B) was entered by the factory for Peter Harper and Ian Hall, and represented, in effect, the final state-of-the-art of the rally Tiger. The braking system had been brought up to date and to the state of the 1966 Tiger build (FRW667C and 668C) by the inclusion of a dual brake master cylinder and brake servos, whilst at the front two large electrically operated fans added extra cooling to the radiator. The fans were manually controlled by the driver and a single white indicator light denoted the operation of the fans. A fan was also fitted inside the car, behind the seats, to provide a modicum of crew cooling, and also the interior was lined with silver foil, under the carpeting, to try and keep the heat from the engine and transmission away from the crew.

To cope with the atrocious, but exciting, roads, an enormous sumpguard was fitted which protected a substantial part of the underside of the car. The allowed six forward facing lights comprised the two headlights supplemented by two Lucas 7 inch 'Flamethrowers' and the two 5 inch fog lamps mounted, as usual, on the outer extremities of the front bumper. As was usual in the rougher rallies two spare wheels were carried, one inside the boot, the other being mounted on the boot lid. A combination of Minilite and steel wheels were used with Dunlop 'Weathermaster' tyres and in some cases Minilites were fitted to the rear, whilst steel wheels adorned the front end.

The route ran in the opposite direction to the 1965 event and comprised 11 groups of special stages (17 in total), 3 with hill climbs and a half hour race around Tatoi airfield. Each special stage had a set time, different for each class; the hill climb penalties were based upon the fastest car, which took a zero penalty, whilst the penalties for the Tatoi race were based on one-tenth of a mark penalty per kilometre slower than the fastest over the 30 minute period of the race.

Acropolis Rally 1966

The Acropolis Rally route uses nearly all of the Greek 'roads'. (Foulis)

The practice for the rally, in order to pace note the stages, had been carried out in the rain and inevitable mud, but to the relief of the more powerful cars the weather changed for the event proper and it was sunny, hot, dry and dusty for the whole period. For Ian Hall, the Acropolis was one of his favourite events. However, he notes that "...for budget reasons the recce was done by two drivers with no co-driver brains present. This was Peter Harper and Andrew Cowan, the latter being entered in an Imp. I don't remember what sort of car they used but one thing's for sure, its odometer didn't read the same as the rally Tiger which I co-drove with Peter for our last rally together..."

At 5.17 on Thursday afternoon, Peter Harper eased the car onto the podium below the Acropolis, in sight of the Parthenon, to lead the cars away for the first loop through the Peloponnese.

Whilst running number one there is the major advantage of not having to run in someone's dust, but there is also a corresponding disadvantage in that the Tiger now had to 'open' the course and many times Peter met lurking traffic on special stages that were meant to be clear - a problem that still bedevils rally leaders and not only on the Acropolis rally. The route ran first along the new main road to Korinth to the first of the 17 special stages, Kiaton to Soulton, a 12km stage situated in the hills east of Korinth. The order was quickly established with Timo Makinen's Cooper S setting the fastest time of 8mins 54secs, followed

Acropolis Rally 1966

closely by the similar car of Paddy Hopkirk (ex-Rootes!) on 9mins dead. Peter Harper, however, put in a time only 19secs slower than Makinen to record a 9.13 and make fifth fastest.

The route continued south through the hot and dusty Lacedaemonian countryside towards Sparta. A very difficult road section followed from Sparta to Kalamata with mile upon mile of rough roads and roadworks. The first 8km from Sparta to Trypi are reasonable but at this point the road climbs rapidly across the Langhada Pass, which crosses the spine of the Taygetus mountain range following the route, well noted in Greek history, taken by Telemachus on his way from the capital of Nestor to the court of Menelaus. The 'road' is winding, precipitous and, in places, extremely narrow, the mountain-sides bare of vegetation. Already 'Tiny' Lewis, who was driving an Imp, was out. Having lost reverse gear and whilst being pushed out of an overshoot, the car unfortunately fell over the edge of the road and remained permanently hors-de-combat.

Negotiating a hairpin on one of the few tarmac special stage roads on this event, the Tiger is luckier than a previous traveller who has come into contact with the outer wall. (Rootes)

Acropolis Rally 1966

A brief stop for service from the Super Minx service car and a discussion with Marcus Chambers and Des O'Dell on the Acropolis rally for the Peter Harper/Ian Hall Tiger. The car is on a mixture of steel and magnesium Minilite wheels. (Rootes)

Pushing north from Kalamata, the second group of stages at Ladon (23km) and Vytina (27km) were tackled and whilst the Tiger crew maintained the pressure in the Grand Touring category, they did not figure in the top five times, although remaining in the top ten. This was until the Kataraktis stage, however, when the throttle on the Tiger broke and had to be wired fully open as a temporary repair by the crew on the stage, the final 10km being finished on the ignition key and brakes, about 4 mins of stage time being lost in effecting the repairs. In this Peloponese leg the rough roads had also caused the Tiger to have two punctures in one stage and to cap it all, the Halda had packed up.

Dawn had broken by the time that the cars reached Patras to catch the 15 min ferry trip across to the mainland at Antirrion - although 22 cars did not reach this point. The pleasant 15 min sojourn was soon over and the route led rapidly northwards towards the Albanian border near Igoumenitsa, then swung east through the hot and dusty foothills of the rugged central mountains to Hani Mourgani and the fourth special stage. Although 30 cars finished the stage without penalty, Peter Harper pulled out all the stops and was second fastest to Roger Clark. Roger repeated this performance on Stage 5, where the only two Group Three cars to achieve their target time were Harper's Tiger and Ove Andersson's Lancia Fulvia. The itinerary continued inland and over the barren scrub mountains following the Albanian border. The longest and roughest stage followed, 56.5km of loose mountain road in 42mins! The special stages were all against the clock and the set times, and were placed at regular intervals along the road section, but on the

Acropolis Rally 1966

The Tiger gets a well-earned service beside the road surrounded by interested Greeks. (via Ian Hall)

whole the stages were smoother than the road sections! Only Timo Makinen in his works Cooper S remained un-penalised on both road and stage performance, and only seven cars remained free of all road penalties. Much to their and the Tiger's credit, Peter Harper and Ian Hall were alone with the three factory Fords and three works Mini Cooper S's who remained penalty free on the road.

The sixth group of stages were on an anti-clockwise loop east of Thessaloniki with the seventh group of two stages following this group. The first was 9.7km in length and the second 13km, and over both of these groups the Tiger crew held their place in the top ten stage times. Continuing south, the rally took in the first hill climb at Portaria, incorporated in the loop centred on the small town of Volos. There was service for the Tiger before and after the loop. Ian Hall remembers "All day we had refrained from drinking water from dubious sources. At Volos for the first service Marcus offered us water. We drank the lot. At the second service we asked for more - Marcus had run out, but "not to worry, it came from the village pumps over there!"

At 10.26 in the morning, the Tiger arrived at the Kedros control, with a little time in hand for a quick wipe of the car before crossing the bridge south of the control, and on towards Lamia, down the mountainside and through the pine forests. About 2km out of Lamia, SS10 started and the Tiger crew lost only 43 secs against the bogey time with Elford, Hopkirk and Makinen cleaning the stage. Then onto the Distomon hillclimb, where the rally of Rauno Aaltonen in his works Cooper S came to and end with a broken timing chain. The hill however, suited the Tiger. Peter managed a 7min 13.1 sec, just 14 secs slower than Vic Elford and only 8 secs slower than the Cooper S of Paddy Hopkirk. After this hillclimb the road ran around Mount Parnassus to the National highway and on to the last two stages – both rough – before

Acropolis Rally 1966

the Saturday evening finish in Athens. The first stage finished in a village with the second starting immediately after. Peter lost only 20 secs on them both, whilst Andersson in the Lancia Fulvia lost 31 secs on the first, but cleaned the second – Hopkirk being the fastest. The 40 remaining cars, of the 105 starters, motored back to a floodlit finish in Athens, the Tiger heading the dusty arrivals. The 40 cars that returned to the Athens control was a higher proportion than usual which was probably due to the lack of rain during the event.

As the weary crews headed for a well earned night in bed, the results team sorted out the times and the usual speculation, argument and rumour that normally surrounding the rally continued. It finally emerged that Hopkirk was leading with 232 penalties followed by Soderstrom (Lotus Cortina) with 281, Roger Clark (Lotus Cortina) on 367, Ove Andersson (Lancia Fulvia) with 710 and Peter Harper/Ian Hall in fifth place on 1059. There remained only the Parnis hillclimb and the half-hour Tatoi race, which took place early on Sunday morning. Makinen provided the fireworks with fastest time on the hillclimb at 7mins 14.5sec with Harper showing the Tiger's claws on tarmac by returning the third fastest time, 7 mins 25 sec, behind Bengt Soderdtrom on 7 min 15.5 sec but in front of Roger Clark and the leader, Paddy Hopkirk.

The final race around Tatoi Airfield took place without any further drama, apart from Timo Makinen who blew a head gasket on the car, but finished. The Peter Harper/Ian Hall Tiger finished in a fine seventh position overall and would have led home the other over 2 litre class cars, had there been any, but the attrition had been high and they comfortably won their Group 3 class.

The travel stained and well-used Harper & Hall Tiger is guided towards the Time Control towards the end of the event. (via Ian Hall)

Acropolis Rally 1966

The final race around Tatoi airfield makes a good spectacle for the many enthusiastic spectators. In the lower picture the works Cortina oversteers while the Tiger looks surprisingly neutral. (Rootes)

Acropolis Rally 1966

Overall it was a very fine effort as the car had not been outclassed by the more nimble Group 2 works Lotus Cortinas and Mini Cooper S's and had matched them second for second on both the roads and stages. Under Acropolis Rally conditions - and it still applies today - only the strongest and robust cars (and crews) survive, and the Tiger and crew had adequately proved their class.

As a postscript, the rally is better known for the penalisation of Paddy Hopkirk by some 420 marks for booking-in early at a control (which was later rescinded) and 120 for working on the car in the control (which wasn't), thus demoting them to third place overall. On a more upbeat note, Rosemary Smith and Val Domleo also upheld the Rootes banner and were well-deserved winners of the Coupe Des Dames in their Imp.

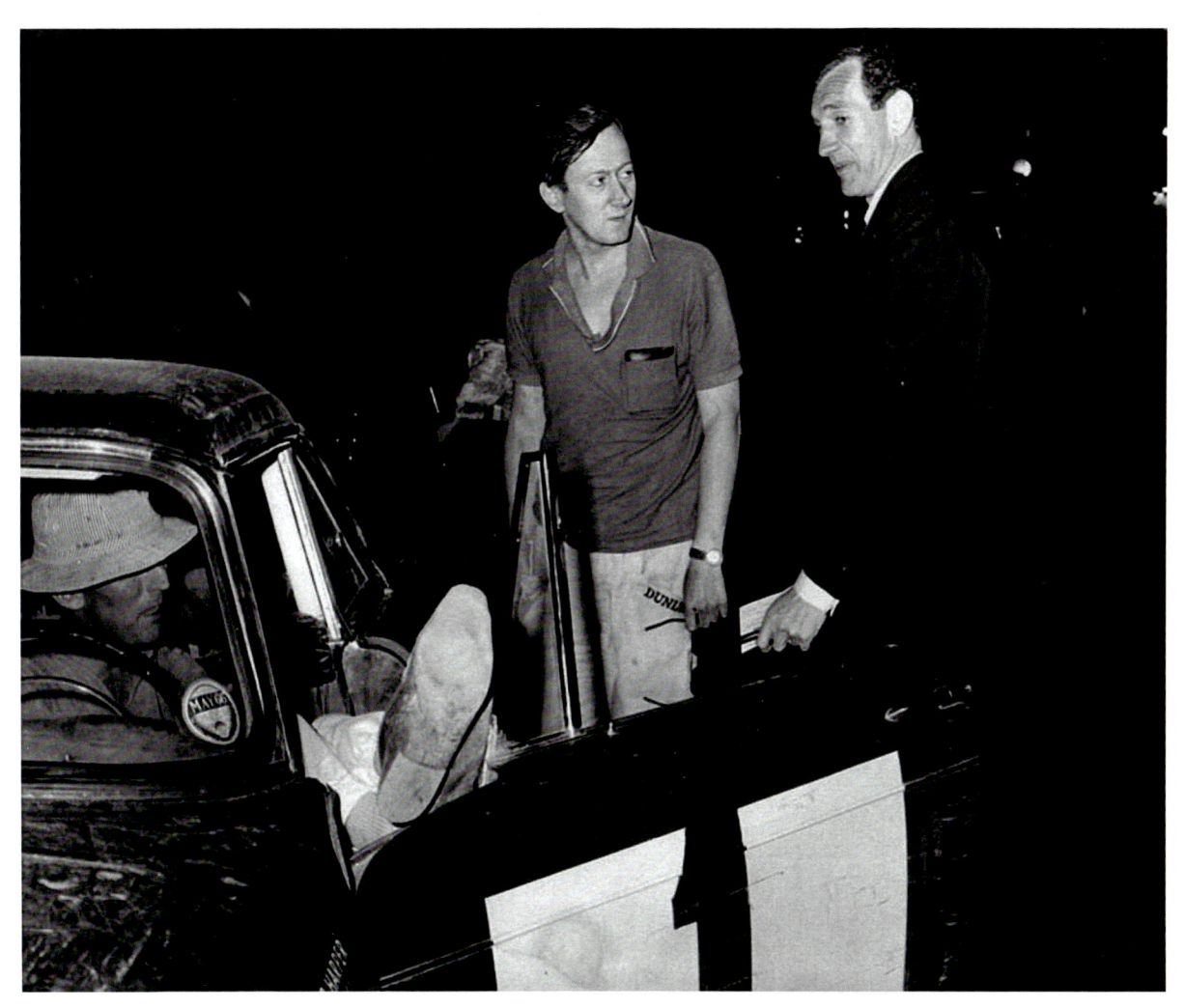

Ian chats to an official while Peter rests and cools weary feet. (Rootes)

Acropolis Rally 1966

Gulf London Rally 1966

The final rally for the works Tigers.

Before the start of the Gulf London Rally for the Peter Harper and Robin Turvey Tiger, freshly returned from their success on the Acropolis rally. The Tiger retains its well-proportioned sump guard to protect against the equally damaging British forests. (Rootes)

Immediately following the Acropolis success, the Tiger (ADU311B) was returned rapidly to Humber Road to be refurbished to take place in the Gulf London Rally which was due to start in London in the evening of Thursday 23rd June. The Acropolis had not finished until the afternoon of Sunday 29th May, which, by the time the car had been brought back to the UK, left precious little time to re-prepare the car.

The Gulf London Rally was one of the more classic rallies involving a hard rally with very little time allowed to replenish man or machine. It was very efficiently organised by the London Motor Club and sponsored by the Gulf Oil Company who generously supplied both fuel and oil as required.

This year's event started in London and ran directly north to the classic Yorkshire forest stages of Wykeham, Allerston, Pickering and Cropton, after which the rally continued further north to the forests of Newcastleton and Kershope on the Scottish border. From these border areas the event led to Penrith and then direct to Chester for one of the refuelling stops. The Welsh stages were next, running north to south followed very closely by the Forest of Dean forest complex around Symonds Yat, Serridge and Speech House. Another refuelling stop preceded the run back into the finish in London tackling two stages in

Gulf London Rally 1966

Bramshill Forest near Camberley on the way. All in all, 34 stages were to be attempted in a very short time.

The Tiger (ADU311B) was left virtually in the same form as the Acropolis build, but running for this rally on steel wheels fitted with Dunlop SP44 tyres. The massive and accustomed sump guard used on the Acropolis was left in position to combat the roughness of the forest stages, some of which were as rough as those experienced on the Greek mainland.

On Thursday evening at 6.01, the first car set off for the run out of London and the long drag up the M1 motorway to the first stage in Bishopswood some 5 hours later. As his turn to start approached, the car was at number 9, Peter Harper strapped himself in, turned the key and the same thing occurred that had happened on the Scottish - incidentally in the same car - the engine steadfastly refused to fire. After an embarrassing tow around the car park, the engine eventually started and the Tiger sped away towards the M1 and the north, much to the relief of both Peter and Robin Turvey, his navigator.

The first stage was situated just south of the City of York in Bishopswood forest and it was approaching midnight before Peter Harper let in the clutch of the Tiger at the start of the stage. The stage was relatively short, some 2.35 miles, with a bogey time of 2mins 49secs. Peter put the power and torque of the Tiger to its best effect and returned a time only 4secs behind the quickest time, those 4secs putting him equal fourth fastest. On the stage the gravel road had passed over a forest tarmac road and a tricky straw bale chicane had been put in to slow the crews down before the yump caused by the camber of the road.

This could well have been profitable for the Tiger since hard yumps had invariably put the fan through the radiator in previous rallies, although by this time the engine mountings had been modified to prevent the engine moving too far forward and no difficulties had been found on the Acropolis Rally.

The Harper/Turvey Tiger waits for the start of its final works rally, the Gulf London Rally of 1966. (Author)

Gulf London Rally 1966

The Harper/Turvey Tiger pulls away from the start of the '66 Gulf London Rally after its somewhat involved engine start. (Rootes)

Special Stage 1 Bishopswood

1	Anderson/Svedberg	Saab	3.06
2	Clark/Porter	Lotus Cortina	3.08
3	Lemmstom/Dahlgren	Cooper S	3.09
4	Harper/Turvey	Sunbeam Tiger	3.10
5	Lindberg/Wallin	R8 Gordini	3.10

Gulf London Rally 1966

After this encouraging start, the Tiger travelled direct to the time control at the Hazlebush Cafe just north of York where a welcome meal was in store, before setting out into the Yorkshire forest complex to take on some fairly fierce rallying in the next three hours or so, with four stages set out in a group. The first pair of these stages were in Wykeham Forest and it was in this forest, on a nasty downhill adverse-camber right hand corner, that the Tiger went off into the bushes, followed very closely by Vic Elford in his Lotus Cortina and then almost immediately by the Lotus Elan of Terry Hunter. Luckily none of the cars were damaged and between the crews and willing spectators the cars were heaved out and sent on their way. The next stage was a giant 40 miler in Allerston Forest and the service crews gathered in strength at the end to fettle their cars as they reached the end of the stage in various states of repair. The Tiger came through with no problems and after a good check over and refuel the car sped off to the last two stages before the time control at Ferryhill, due to be reached just as dawn was breaking.

The first of the stages was in Pickering Forest and this passed without event but it was on the second of the stages, in Cropton Forest, just north west of the village of Pickering, that the Tiger first had a puncture on the rear and the wheel was rapidly replaced on the stage, but later in the stage the wheel came completely off and the Tiger was parked beside the forest track on three wheels. The stage was not particularly long, 6.75 miles in 8mins 6secs, but by the time that Robin Turvey had walked out of the forest to get help and found the service crew, the car was out of its time allowance.

An unfortunate end to a promising start.

This was the last time that a Tiger appeared in a rally under the auspices of the works team, since by this time the more nimble Imps were beginning to make their mark and the days of the Tiger were drawing to a close.

A rapid exit from the eventual start with some road time to make up. The Peter Harper Tiger carries a spare tyre cover without a wheel – perhaps all the Minilites were still on their way back from the Acropolis? (Author)

Gulf London Rally 1966

1,400 GULF LONDON RALLY - 40 HOURS' NON-STOP MOTORING

JUNE 23/25th, 1966

Europe's top international rally drivers set off from London last night (June 23rd) on the first stage of the 1,400 Gulf London Rally which calls for 40 hours non stop motoring. Competitors headed north for the first special stage near York, on to Plashets and Carlisle returning through the Lake district, the mountains of Wales, the Cotswold and finally to rally control at London Airport Hotel.

PICTURE SHOWS:- Peter Harper of Stevenage, Herts (left) and his Sunbeam Tiger co-driver Robin Turvey from Weston-Super-Mare make a final check of the route before leaving on the first stage.

R.56992.

Gulf London Rally 1966

The Build of the Works Rally Cars

The build of any car used in International competition is guided by the construction regulations of the FIA (Federation International de l'Automobile) and is enforced by scrutineers appointed by the FIA and the National Automobile Clubs who inspect the cars before, sometimes during, and frequently after, the competition to confirm that the cars comply with the regulations, sometimes down to the minutest detail. Each type of car has a Homologation Form on which all the details of the car are entered, and it is against this form that the dimensions, weights etc of the car and its components are checked where and when necessary. Thus if limited slip differentials are allowed in the regulations, then the type and construction details must be entered in the homologation form, as must be any change in dimension of, say, poppet valve diameters.

The final touches are put to one of the Tigers, most probably ADU312B, during preparation for the 1965 Monte Carlo Rally at the Rootes Competition Department. (Rootes)

Build of the Works Rally Cars

The final touches are put to one of the Tigers, most probably ADU312B, during preparation for the 1965 Monte Carlo Rally at the Rootes Competition Department. (Rootes)

For the Tiger, Appendix J to the FIA International Sporting Code contained the details of the allowable modifications. The specification changed in 1966, half way through the rallying life of the Tiger, and for the 1966 year, the car ran under Category A - recognised production cars - and under Group 3 Grand Touring Cars for which a minimum production in 12 consecutive months of 500 was required. Amongst the many authorised modifications and additions, a limited slip axle, for instance, could be fitted, only six forward facing lights were allowed, an alternator could be fitted, complete freedom was allowed for pistons and camshafts and many other modifications - shown in detail in Appendices 6 & 7.

For the engine capacity, the engine could be re-bored to a maximum tolerance of 1.2mm (0.048 inch), providing that the resulting increase in cylinder capacity did not take the car into the next capacity class. Hence all Tigers in all International rallies entered by Humber Road only ran in 4.2 litre form - never 4.7 litre. The only time a "works" car ran in 4.7 litre form was in the Targa Florio when the car (AHP483B) ran in the prototype class. Cars for recces may well have had 4.7 litre engines fitted, but they were not allowed to compete in the competition proper.

However, within the regulations many modifications were made to make them more suitable for competition, some of which were to last the life of the rally cars.

Build of the Works Rally Cars

The Engine.

Since the engine is innately the heart of a rally car, there are very few successful rally cars that have a poor engine, and the Tiger was no exception.

The engine in the standard US Ford road car was a development of the 221 cu. inch (3621cc) small block engine used in the 1962 Ford Fairlane, which had a 3.5 inch bore and 2.87 inch stroke. The original conception had been in 1958 when Ford had wished to produce a cast iron engine which would compare favourably in weight with an equivalent engine made of alloy. Apart from the high cost of producing alloy engines, about which Ford had some experience, cast iron had some distinct advantages. It has a high graphite content inherent in its structure, which allows it to act as a lubricant whilst its thermal expansion properties are ideal over a wide operating temperature range and in addition it has good sound and vibration damping properties, both of which are important in production engines. Thus in conjunction with the thin wall casting techniques, which, amongst other advantages, allowed almost equal cooling of each cylinder, an engine was produced which was down to 204kg (450lb) in weight and extremely compact. The block measured only 226.8mm (8.93in) in height by 415.5mm (16.36in) wide by 529.3mm (20.48in) long. By increasing the bore by 0.30in to 3.80in, the capacity was increased to 260 cu.in. (4261cc) and the engine that was to be used in the Tiger was born.

Even in its standard form the 4.2 engine produced a healthy 136bhp nett at 4200 rev/min and an even more robust 225lb.ft of nett torque at only 2400 rev/min. These figures represent the engine tested with air cleaner, fan, dynamo and a test bed exhaust system, but without the losses incurred through a gearbox.

The corresponding gross figures were 164bhp at 4400 rev/min and 258lb.ft of torque at 2200 rev/min. In early March 1964 two engines were bench tested by the works straight from delivery from the USA and they produced 135.5bhp at 4200 rev/min and 135.8bhp at the same rpm - these figures being complete with gearbox this time.

The 260 standard Tiger engine Power and Torque curves.

Build of the Works Rally Cars

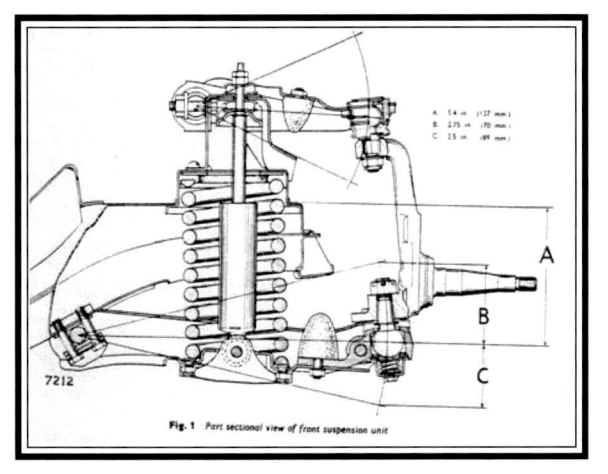

The sturdy front cross member of the Tiger, which, for the cut and thrust of rallying, still needed strengthening.

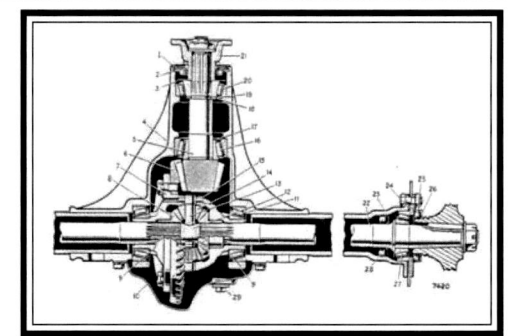

The Salisbury HA axle of the Tiger.

Build of the Works Rally Cars

In order to obtain higher outputs from the 4.2 unit - to allow the car to be more competitive with the Healey 3000 in rally form - the engine had to be made to attain higher engine speeds, since this was the primary way of producing the necessary power outputs. To produce the correct breathing at higher revs, both the induction and the valve timing, via the camshaft, had to be improved.

To improve the flow of air into the cylinders, the cylinder heads were polished without increasing their size which, in conjunction with a 4-barrel carburettor, either a Holley or Autolite depending on the car build, and a well fitted manifold - alloy in some cases - provided an increase in power of some 55bhp. Not all cars, however, were fitted with 4-barrel carburettors. In the 1966 Appendix J Group 3 regulations "the carburettor may be replaced by another of different diameter providing the number was the same as that provided by the manufacturer and that it could be mounted on the inlet manifold of the engine without need of an intermediary device and by using original attachment parts". This effectively restricted the Tiger to a 2-barrel carburettor although the 289 manifold and carburettor could be used. This type of carburation was fitted to both FRW667C and FRW668C and whilst it did not produce quite as much power, it was healthy enough as the 1966 Tulip Rally result showed. For the 4-barrel Holley carburettor, allowed in the pre '66 regulations, minor modifications were necessary in the form of a cutaway in the bulkhead to provide the necessary space. Valve size remained the same as the production vehicle both for the exhaust and inlet valves.

By suitable strengthening of the bottom end of the engine, principally by use of the HiPo 289 crankshaft, the rev. limit was raised to 6500 rev/min, enough to give a useful output in power in conjunction with the other modifications. To allow the engine to breath correctly at these revs a HiPo 289 camshaft was installed (C30Z-6250-C) which had a cam lift of 0.298 inch compared to the lift on the standard cam (C30Z-6250-B) of 0.2375 inch. The valve duration was increased to 306 degrees with an 82-degree overlap. This cam, in conjunction with a rocker arm with a ratio of 1:1.6 allowed a valve lift of 0.477 inch which, when all combined, raised the power by some

A shot of the empty engine compartment of ADU311B during renovation, showing the 'hedgehog' oil cooler and the two large Kenlowe cooling fans on this Tiger. (Author)

Build of the Works Rally Cars

20bhp. Solid cam followers (lifters) were incorporated, usually the early Shelby type and, due to the higher loads imposed on the rocker arms and valves at these higher revs, the rocker posts were screwed into the heads as distinct to the normal interference fit and the HiPo valve springs were fitted (red springs).

Pistons were allowed to be replaced by any type or manufacturer and weight was free. In some cases (ADU311B at least) flat top pistons were used with valve cut-outs machined to allow greater valve-piston crown clearances. It goes without emphasis that all the rotating engine components were fully balanced.

The lubrication system was left essentially the same. The only change that had to be incorporated during engine build, apart from a strengthened oil pick-up pipe in the sump, was that the oil gallery blanking plugs at the front of the engine block, instead of being a pressed-in blank disc, were tapped and a screw-in plug substituted to safeguard against leakage and possible catastrophic loss of oil pressure if the disc should work loose. Three plugs were used, one at the end of each horizontal feed gallery, each one being of the allen-screw type.

The engine oil was cooled by taking the feed from the oil pump and passing it directly through a two row "hedgehog" type oil cooler fitted in front of the engine with cooling air passing through the front valance. The cooled oil was then passed directly back into the main oil gallery feed via the normal canister type oil filter. Aeroquip type reinforced oil pipes were used to feed to and from the filter.

ADU311B in the Competition Dept. after the 1965 Alpine and with a new wing. The Tiger has sprouted a 5 inch Lucas lamp on the front bumper since the Alpine, but still has the long air-scoop on the bonnet (shortened for the RAC). The photograph was probably taken before the RAC Rally and the car is also on its forest wear of Dunlop SP44s. Gerry Spencer applies some TLC. (Autosport)

Build of the Works Rally Cars

'Super Shell' oil was used exclusively in the engine and since, at that time, mineral engine oils were not as advanced in terms of film strengths with respect to temperature and bearing loads, vegetable oils were used when required, having improved lubrication characteristics under rally conditions. The only problem was that, being a specialist vegetable-based oil, it could not be mixed with the more common mineral-based oils - as the 1965 Scottish Rally showed.

At 6000 rev/min, some 24000 sparks are required from the distributor per minute, or alternatively 400 per second, which is towards the upper limit for a standard single contact point distributor. A standard fitting on the factory Tigers from 1965 was the dual-point distributor (C50F-12127-E or C5GF-12131-B), which provided the necessary reliable energy to the spark plugs (BF601's).

One of the major problems encountered on the rougher rallies was the forward movement of the engine that usually damaged the radiator with catastrophic consequences (RAC1965, Monte Carlo 1966), and the later Tigers had modified engine mountings which restricted the forward movement of the engine and prevented such damage.

Cooling System

The cooling system for the Tiger was a conventional system, but with the heat sink of the V8 engine it was a bit marginal. The early rally cars maximised the cooling by keeping airways clear and fitting twin fans, used when the car was in slow traffic or stationary. The later rally car cooling system was simply re-engineered by Des O'Dell. In his words – from Marcus Chamber's book 'Works Wonders'- "But, initially, cooling was a problem. When I first came I had several discussions with the slide-rule boffins, chaps who had never sat inside a rally car in their lives. They told me that I should raise the engine by an inch and move it back in the frame by an inch and use a larger fan. Well, I would have preferred not to use a fan at all, and as for raising the centre of gravity....The problem was that the car overheated even on early morning runs down the motorway, so it was certainly going to overheat on something like the Acropolis Rally. Using one of the development cars, I would go for a run down the motorway and open it up to 120 mph, but within six miles it would boil. Anyway, I did some checks and found that the air was passing through everywhere but the radiator, so I instructed the engineers to put in more air ducts. Then I remembered that Aston Martin and Mercedes had suffered from similar problems, and they had cured them by altering the header tank arrangement, so I re-piped the Tiger to match the Mercedes layout. I took a pipe from the header tank to the bottom hose, a modification that the boffins said would never work, and tried again. I took it onto the motorway, tucking in behind a lorry until it boiled, and then broke free and went like hell, and the temperature went down. I had cured the problem in three weeks." The rally cars retained their electrically operated fans for slow speed extra cooling but one of the major problem areas had been solved.

Fuel System

The fuel system on the factory Tigers was not drastically different to the normal system fitted to the production car. At the rear, the tank capacity was increased from the usual 11.25 Imperial gallons (13.5 US or 51.1 litres) contained in the two rear wing tanks, by the fitting of a rectangular saddle tank across the boot between the wing tanks. This tank provided a further 8.5 Imp. gallons (10.2 US or 36.5 litres) giving a total capacity of 19.75 Imp.gallons (23.7 US or 87.6 litres.). The fuel fed, without any form of inter-tank restriction, to the fuel pump and thence to the carburettor. This supplementary fuel tank was an available option under the English Part Number 1219175A. One of the homologation sheets notes an additional fuel tank to bring the total capacity to 140 litres.

The standard fuel pump (AUF301 type) was replaced by a double pump of the AUF400 type fitted behind the seats just forward of the supplementary fuel tank and shielded from the

Build of the Works Rally Cars

driver's compartment by the panel separating the boot from the rear seat space. Electrical feed to the pump(s) was through a line fuse, with both sides of the pump being electrically connected in parallel. A detail, which shows the length to which it is necessary to go to make a rally car reliable, is the replacement of the push-on Lucar clip, which feeds power to the pump on the standard car, by a ring connector, which cannot vibrate free, with the ring connector held in position by a 'Nyloc' lock nut. Such are the details that win rallies or, more likely, lack of detailed preparation that loses them.

From the fuel pump the fuel fed through a sintered bronze filter and thence through the car on the right hand side of the co-driver's compartment to feed the carburettor.

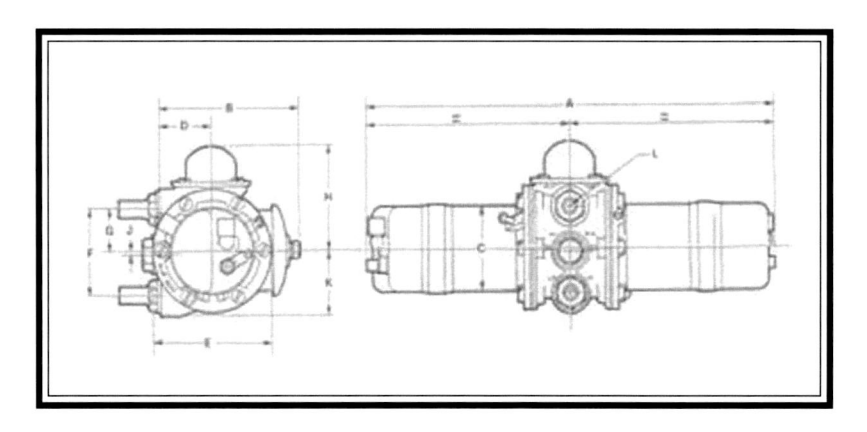

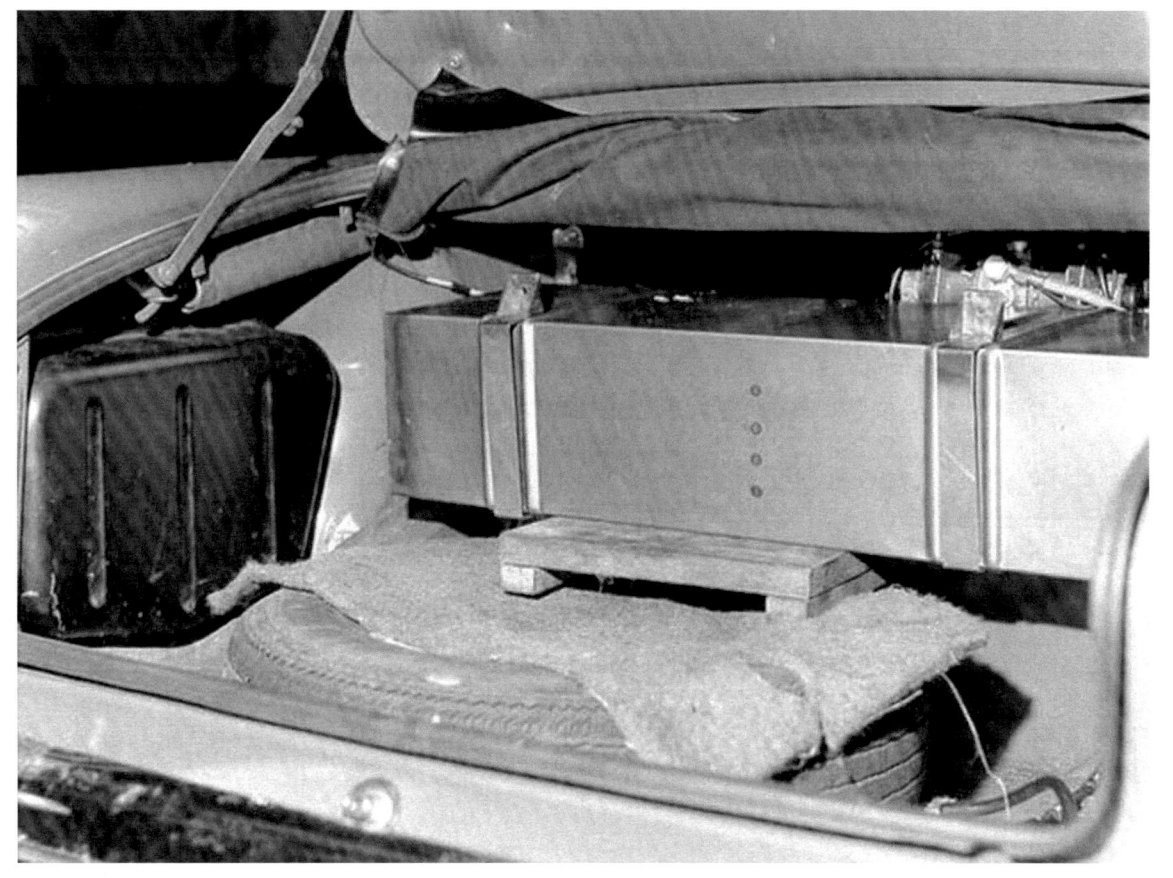

Fitting of the auxiliary 8.5 gallon saddle tank (English Part Number 1219175A), which enlarged the total of all three tanks to a capacity of 19.75 Imperial gallons. The car is most probably AHP294B and the rear view of the fuel pump can be clearly seen. (Rootes)

Build of the Works Rally Cars

Gearbox

The Tiger used a Ford designed four-speed gearbox of the fully synchronised type, with all the gears, except the reverse sliding gear, being in constant mesh.

Generally the box was considered to be strong enough to survive the rigours of rallying without major modification. The early cars used the T10 box, but later cars fitted the standard HEH-E or the HEH-B, which had an alternative set of gear ratios. The homologation papers noted only the HEH-E gearbox, but included both sets of ratios.

On the HEH-E box, the standard Mk 1 Tiger box, the ratios were 2.32, 1.69, 1.29 and 1.00 for first to top gear respectively, whilst the corresponding ratios for the alternative B box were 2.78, 1.93, 1.36 and 1.00. The corresponding number of teeth on each gear cog for both boxes is shown in the Appendices. The reverse gear ratio in both types of gearbox was the same as the first gear ratio i.e. 2.32 and 2.78 - although in the homologation papers no reverse ratio is given for the HEH-E box and 2.32 for the HEH-B box - an oversight perhaps? The gear lever remained standard with its distinctive finger operated release lever for the selection of reverse.

Adjustment of the gear lever linkage was as in the normal cars, but, in the rally cars, having adjusted the three linkage adjustment nuts and checked the operation of the gearbox, the three nuts were brazed in position to prevent slippage.

Preparation of a Tiger, probably AHP294B, in the Competition Department, showing the fitting of the rear brake servo for the rear brakes off the dual brake master cylinder, the dual SU AUF400 type fuel pump and fuel filter. Also shown are one of the lugs for the seat belts and the pads that the works cars had fitted to prevent their crews from damaging themselves during hard cornering. (Rootes)

Build of the Works Rally Cars

Clutch

The clutch remained a ten-inch single dry plate unit as on the standard Tiger, although a competition plate and unit were fitted, the linings of which had outside and inside diameters of 10 inches and 6.75 inches respectively. Clutch operation was by hydraulic actuation, with centrifugal assistance. However, whilst the standard master and slave cylinder assemblies were retained, the connecting pipe was changed from a solid to a flexible pipe, which was suitably encased in asbestos tape to prevent too much heat from the engine affecting both pipe and contents.

Rear Axle

Like the gearbox, the axle was considered to have enough strength to be used without structural modification. A limited slip differential and a change of final drive ratio were, however, incorporated. The standard unit was manufactured by Salisbury and was the 4HA model with a 49 tooth gear wheel and 17 tooth pinion, giving an axle ratio of 2.88. Since this ratio was too high (or long) for the cut and thrust of rallying, a 3.77 differential was utilised and sold under part number 5221008. This gave a road speed of 18.3 mph (29.2 kph) per 1000 revs in top gear, which, with a rev limit of 6500 rpm, gave a high enough top speed under virtually all circumstances. In conjunction with this differential, a Salisbury Powr-Lok limited slip differential (Part Number 1229810) was fitted which made sure that the power was transmitted to the road as efficiently as possible. Both the 2.88 and the 3.77 final drives and the limited slip were homologated, and in addition Rootes offered two more alternative ratios, 3.31 and 3.54, although these were not noted in the homologation sheet and thus could not be used in International competition. They were, however, offered at what would nowadays appear to be a give-away price of £24 per set!

Steering

The early rally cars retained both the normal steering linkages and the standard ratio rack and pinion drive of 3.1 turns lock-to-lock. Later in the life of the Tiger a 'quick' rack was produced (Part No 5221021), which required only 2.33 turns and after being added to the homologation forms as a supplement was fitted to the works cars allowing the back of the car to be caught and controlled with considerably less arm flailing.

Suspension

Yet again no changes were made to the basic suspension, the competition department being satisfied with uprating both ends of the car.

At the front heavier coil springs from the export Hillman Husky were fitted and along with a thicker 5/8 inch roll (stabiliser) bar to increase the front roll stiffness which, with the Armstrong adjustable shock absorbers provided a stiff enough front end. Adjustment of the shock absorber rates was by turning a small screw to one of the seven different positions, each one providing a different rate.

The rear suspension was set up in a similar way to other cart-sprung rally cars of the period, with the export Husky nine leaf rear springs stiffening the suspension considerably and the solid rear spring bushes limiting unwanted axle movement and the subsequent rear axle steering caused, in the standard bush, by the rubber movement. As with the front suspension, adjustable shock absorbers provided good damping of the axle over the rough terrain and limited axle hop. Lateral axle movement was taken care of by the standard Panhard rod.

Braking System

The braking system on a rally car is of primary importance and, as in the life of most successful

Build of the Works Rally Cars

rally cars, evolution of the braking systems within the confines of the regulations provided progressively more efficient brakes.

In 1964 the Appendix J regulations specified that, on Group 3 (Grand Touring) cars, "the braking power may be increased subject to the system of operation provided by the manufacturer (drum brakes or disc brakes) being maintained as well as the original supports." Additionally "the fitting of a dual pump or any type of device providing both a simultaneous action on the four wheels and a divided action on the front and rear wheels is authorised." But whilst the regulations allowed complete freedom on the make and attachment of brake linings, it was very specific in forbidding any change in the dimensions of the friction surfaces.

Thus, in practice, very little change could be made to the Tigers braking system and virtually the standard system was kept in use. The standard front discs, 9.85 inches in diameter and 0.5 inches in thickness, were kept and these gave a total front brake area of 210.4 sq.inches. The type 16P callipers were retained with their 2.125 inch (54mm) piston. At the rear the whole set up was virtually standard with the 9 inch rear drum and a brake lining 1.75 inches in width, giving a brake area of 230.2 sq.inches per brake. Also the standard 0.75 inch (19mm) brake cylinder was retained.

Essentially the only change in the early build rally cars was the use of the standard Ferodo competition brake pads and rear linings. DS11 pads replaced the standard front pads whilst at the rear VG95/1 linings were brought into use. With the use of competition brake fluid, in this case Castrol amber fluid, and the improved high temperature performance of the brake materials, both of which substantially reduced brake fade during hard and prolonged use of the brakes - which with the front end weight of the Tiger was substantial - the braking performance was considered adequate if not always ideal, especially on tarmac events like the Alpine Rally.

The DS11 pad was standard fit for rallies not only on the Tiger but also on virtually all British rally cars of the period and many continental teams also used the Ferodo pads - including every Formula 1 team of the period.

The major reason for its widespread use was that the DS11 pad had a friction/temperature curve that was, in the mid-60's, little short of miraculous. The coefficient of friction at around 30deg.C was 0.30 rising only to 0.31 at over 900deg.C, with the curve being totally devoid of peaks, troughs and declivities over the whole of that temperature range, providing stable braking for the front of the car over this whole range. This was important for the Tiger which, having a heavy front end, relied for much of its braking power on the front discs.

The rear drum brakes were fitted with the VG95 type lining which had been first developed for the land speed record cars of the 1930's when Sir George Eyston's Thunderbolt was crossing the Utah Salt Flats at 6 miles per minute. The lining used on the Tiger was a development of this material, the VG95/1, and had a friction/temperature curve compatible with the DS11 pad, although only maintaining its performance up to around 500deg.C. Over this range, 30 to 500deg.C, the coefficient of friction varied from 0.28 at lower temperatures to a maximum of 0.33 at 250deg.C and falling to around 0.26 at 500deg.C. The curve was, however, very smooth and over the temperature range 90 to 410deg.C maintained a coefficient of fiction above 0.30.

Thus both friction materials were compatible for front/rear balance of braking and provided an almost ideal temperature stability whilst the compensation for the relatively low friction coefficient was provided by the servo-powered braking system allowing low brake pedal pressures with no loss of the required high pad pressures.

For the 1966 season, new Appendix J regulations were enforced which, whilst still preventing any increase in brake friction areas,

Build of the Works Rally Cars

still allowed a dual braking system but authorised for both Group 2 and 3 cars servo assistance for the braking system, even if the car in its standard production form did not fit such a braking assistance system. A further specific paragraph [260(t)] allowed all the lines providing the "passage of fluid elements" to be entirely modified - thus allowing brake lines, amongst others, to be run inside the car for protection.

The later build rally cars, notably FRW667C and FRW668C - and at least one of the earliest cars during rebuild (ADU311B) were fitted with an Aston Martin DB6 type brake master cylinder which allowed the front and rear brake systems to be independently operated. The master cylinder was fed by two independent Girling brake fluid reservoirs and each of the independent brake systems had its own brake servo. The front servo was fitted in its usual place in the rear corner of the engine compartment, whilst the servo providing assistance to the rear brakes was positioned on the rear seat behind the passenger (the right-hand side or nearside on a left-hand drive car - which all the rally cars were) and tucked into the corner. The necessary vacuum was bled in series with the front servo with the solid vacuum pipe running inside the car alongside the other supply lines (fuel, electrics and brakes).

FRW 668C: This figure shows the painting on the bell-housing tunnel to minimise heat flow to inside the car (left) and modified front engine mounts to restrict forward engine movement (right).

Build of the Works Rally Cars

FRW 668C works and standard rear gearbox mounts showing modifications and stiffening flanges.

FRW 668C strengthened front cross member and tow hook. (Below)

These images show some of the works chassis and engine modifications on FRW 668C.

Build of the Works Rally Cars

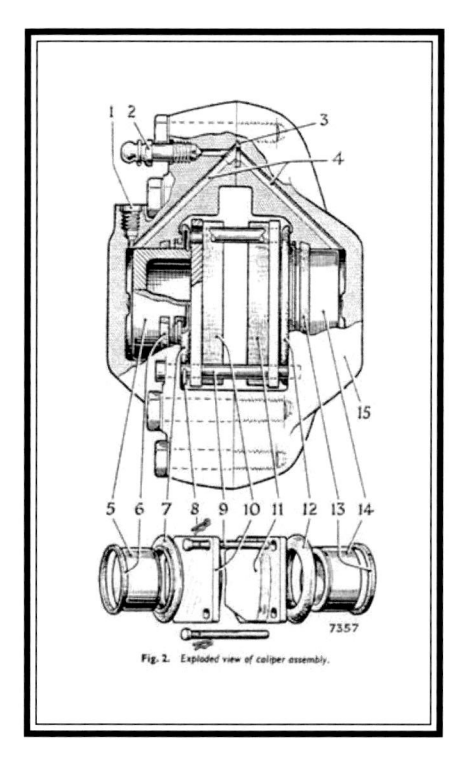

The engine compartment of ADU311B showing the dual master-cylinder, also fitted to the Aston Martin DB6, feeding the front and rear brake servos. (Author)

Andrew Cowan's Monte en-route pin mod to make the handbrake effectively a 'fly-off'- or at least a 'stay-off' type (from FRW 668C). (Author)

A standard handbrake system was retained, the only significant modification being the drilling of a hole in the release button and its surround, in which a split-pin could be inserted to prevent the latch from locking the brake lever in the 'on' position - providing essentially a fly-off handbrake - which wouldn't, of course, lock 'on'. The split-pin was retained on the handbrake shaft by a small chain, suitably covered by a plastic sleeve. This was a modification that was attributed to Andrew Cowan on the 1965 Monte Carlo Rally who had it fitted in a small French roadside garage on the run-in to Monaco.

Build of the Works Rally Cars

Wheels and Tyres

Throughout the rally lifetime of the Tiger, starting with the Geneva Rally in 1964 and finishing essentially with the Acropolis Rally in 1966, all of the cars used the ventilated magnesium the track provided and stated by the manufacturer. Rootes Competition Department took advantage of this to be the first works team to use Minilite wheels, later to be used by many other works teams. In the homologation forms the front track was stated as 1331mm (52.4in.) and the rear

Preparation for the 1966 Monte Carlo Rally at the Rootes Competition Department. The Tiger on the stands is AHP294B with its distinctive Alpine wing motif and 260 badge, ahead of its start from Paris in the hands of Gatsonides. This is believed to be a new shell. FRW667C, the Cowan/Coyle Monte car, stands in the background. Both cars comply with the new 1966 Appendix J regulations in their lighting set-up. (Rootes)

Minilite 8-spoked wheel in place of the standard steel wheel, some of which had been losing wheel centres during testing.

The regulations allowed the wheel to be of a different type provided that the hub remained unchanged, as well as the dimensions of the rim and track as 1229.3mm (48.4in.); this with the standard 13 inch steel wheel of rim width 114.2mm (4.5in.) i.e. the standard 4Jx13 wheel with the 4-stud fixing. For the Minilite wheel (Part No.5221007), with a 139.7mm (5.5in.) rim width, the front wheels were fitted with a single spacer with no increase in track, this anomaly being caused by a difference in

Build of the Works Rally Cars

At Rootes Competition department rally engine has its post-rally check and rebuild by Ernie Beck. The valve cover sticker (EEY-MG5-2) and large damper indicate that the engine was probably one of those supplied by the Shelby organisation. (Rootes)

offset between the magnesium and steel wheels, whilst at the rear two spacers per wheel were used (0.125in.each) which in conjunction with the rim offset resulted in a track of 1254.1mm (49.375in.)

Further assets of using magnesium wheels, in addition to the substantially increased heat sink provided for the brakes and the extra cooling to the discs provided by the wheel design in sucking the air through the wheel spokes and over the brake disc, was the significant decrease in weight, and significant increase in strength, over the standard wheel. They were, however - for the time - expensive. The Minilites weighed in at 4.08kg (9lb) against the steel wheel's 5.76kg (12.7lb). This decrease in unsprung weight helped to improve handling in addition to the rim being virtually indestructible - a salient feature when it was necessary to reach the end of a special stage on a punctured tyre.

In some cases, longer wheel studs were fitted to take the special Minilite wheel nut and in virtually all cases the wheel arches at both ends were modified, by cutting and flattening the inner wheel well panel to provide a greater clearance for use with the wide range of tyres used.

For the whole of its rally career, Dunlop tyres were exclusively and successfully used on the works Tigers. For the many forest events (RAC, Scottish etc.) and events where poor road conditions prevailed (Monte Carlo, Acropolis etc.) Dunlop SP44 Weathermasters were used, with or without a variety of studded patterns - depending upon the regulations in force. For the smoother events which ran predominantly on tarmac (Alpine, Tulip etc.) the current Dunlop racing tyres were used in a variety of rubber compounds for different road conditions, whilst for the in-between road surfaces the SP3 tread pattern and compounds were utilised.

Build of the Works Rally Cars

Electrical System

In both 1964 and 1965, and also with the change of Appendix J regulations in 1966, fair latitude was allowed with regard to the electrical system. Whilst the voltage of the electrical devices could not be changed (i.e. a 12 volt system was mandatory on the Tiger), the dynamo could be changed for an alternator, with all its advantages for rallying, providing the original attachment to the engine was retained. Similarly the make, type and capacity of the battery were free provided the battery was retained at its original location.

For the works cars, Lucas wired the cars from scratch, building up the electrical looms in the cars by laying out all the wire runs and looming at the completion of the layout. Line fuses were incorporated in all of the forward facing lights, with the fuses, both nearside and offside lighting, under the bonnet just before the looms passed through the body wing plate. The tail lamps were line-fused at the top of the nearside scuttle kick, whilst the windscreen wiper was fused on its power input lead.

The navigator's plug and socket, used mainly for the Poti or Eolite map magnifier and mounted at the top of the scuttle at the door, was fitted with a line fuse situated on the top side of the offside scuttle kick. An extra Lucas 7EJ fuse-box was incorporated above the driver's knee fitted with four fuses.

The top fuse controlled the Halda light and the airhorns, the second the roof light, map light and cigar lighter, the third the fuel gauge and the direction indicators whilst the last fuse was used on the reverse light and the heater two-speed blower. On FRW668C, an extra three-way switch was fitted next to the Halda, allowing the navigator/co-driver to select either the map light and Halda light together, the Halda light alone or both off. Also fitted was a rotary rheostat switch mounted centrally just below the dash which allowed the light on the additional rev-counter to be either varied continuously, varied in brilliance or switched off completely. Both of these switches were powered independently of the lights, as was the light socket for the map magnifier.

In an attempt to combat the constant problem of overheating, ADU311B was fitted with a pair of electrically operated cooling fans behind the radiator, switched manually from the driver's side with a white warning light illuminating when the fans were running. Electrical feed was through a Lucas double fuse box, each fan fed from a separate 35amp fuse.

A view of the driving compartment of the 1966 Tulip Tiger, FRW668C. (Author)

Build of the Works Rally Cars

Generally the switches for lights etc. were mounted on the dashboard, but later cars, FRW668C at least and ADU311B during rebuild, had the two-speed windscreen wiper switch and the switch for the two fog lamps (two position Lucas switch) fitted on the front of the centre arm rest and operated by the driver's right hand. All the main auxiliary lights were wired through relays fitted under the bonnet on top of the left hand wheel arch. Wiring for the spot and fog lamps depended upon the particular lamp set up for the particular rally and driver choice, although all wiring was routed through relays. In 1964 and 1965, the additional number of lights was free, provided they complied with the International Convention on Road Traffic.

The 1966 regulations restricted forward facing lamps to six, which included the two headlights. Thus in some cases (the 1965 Monte for example) the cars were allowed, and fitted, seven lights, whilst on others (1965 Tulip) ADU311B still ran on seven lights with AHP294B on only six lights. The record must be on the 1965 RAC Rally when ADU311B ran a total of eight forward facing lights. In the 1966 season all cars ran six lights only.

The lamps were always Lucas, the main auxiliary lights being the 7-inch SLR/CLR700 Spot or the equivalent Driving Lamp and the smaller, rear-mounted, WFT576 fog-lamps on the outer reaches of the front bumper to illuminate the verges and see round the more acute bends.

A reverse light was always fitted and operated from the reverse gear selector. Generally it was of the Lucas WFT576 5.75-inch round centre fixing type (ADU311B for example) or the equivalent rectangular fog lamp in later years (FRW668C).

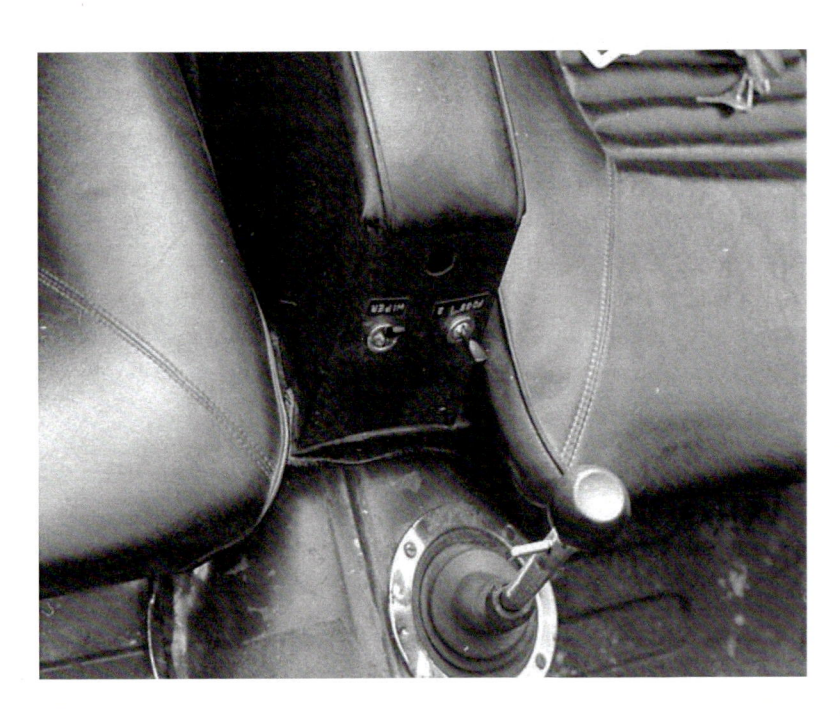

The central console of FRW668C showing the three-position switches for the fog lights and the two-speed windscreen wiper. Also the original fuses card from ADU311B is shown. (Author)

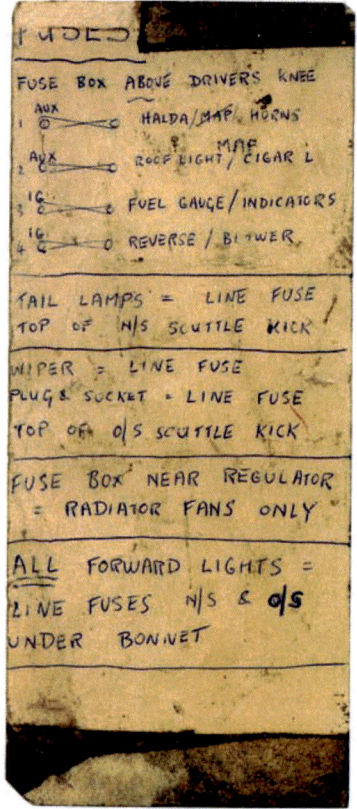

Build of the Works Rally Cars

The heated screens on the 1966 Monte Carlo Rally Tigers.

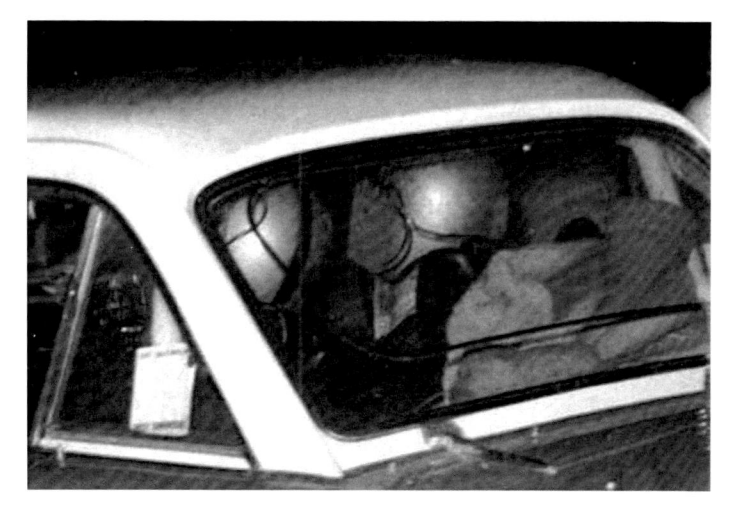

The intercom in use on the last night of the 1965 Monte Carlo Rally with the control box fitted on the crew's crash helmets.

Build of the Works Rally Cars

For the 1966 Monte Carlo Rally, due to the potential interference with visibility by ice and snow in the mountains, both FRW668C and AHP 294B were fitted with heated windscreens. The heating elements cleared directly a vertical space approximately 60 to 70% of the screen depth, but the remainder was, of course, cleared by the usual conduction of the heat to the upper and lower edges of the screen. Similarly for the width, the main part of the screen was directly cleared with the sides using the conducted heat-flow.

In the early and mid '60s, a number of teams were experimenting, and using, intercom systems to enhance communications between driver and co-driver. This was particularly necessary when the crew were using crash helmets on the more competitive sections, such as special stages or épreuves. As the use of route notes - or pace notes - became more necessary as competition increased between the teams and manufacturers, better communication became a necessity, as the missing of a note could become terminal for the car and dangerous for the crew.

Rootes Competition department were in the forefront of using such systems, and this was essentially first used in anger on the 1965 Monte Carlo Rally. In the Stanley Schofield film for the Rootes Group -'Special Section'- Raymond Baxter commentates that Peter Harper and Ian Hall used an aircraft system intercom for communication, and the film shows its use on the La Roquette (Levens) Special Stage of that year.

The helmets of the intercom system fitted on the 65 Alpine, the 1966 Monte Carlo and Tulip Rallies.

Build of the Works Rally Cars

From the pictures taken during the event, and from a later Rootes film, the system was a type that was used in military transport and some civil aircraft that allowed communication between the two crew. The type was, in all probability from identification in the photos and film, an Amplivox Ampliphone, which was in production for aircraft at the time, had a single volume control and was powered by internal batteries. For the 65 Monte the electronics box of the Ampliphone was attached to the side of both crew's helmet. At this time, the author was building a similar system for use in his Cooper S.

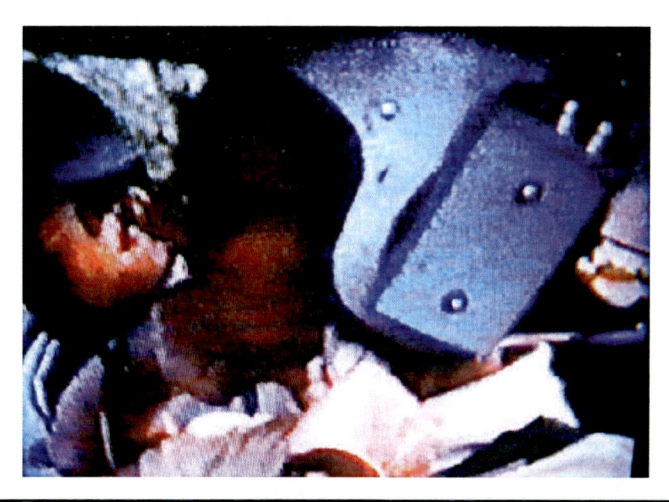

These two upper images are taken from the Rootes film and show in better detail the intercom units used on the Alpine 1965 rally.

The Amplivox units are strapped to the side of both crew's helmets with the leads connecting both units, allowing the crew to communicate with each other.

The images show Peter Harper (upper) and Mike Hughes (lower).

The image (left) shows a recent picture of the same Amplivox Ampliphone Intercom with the on/off and volume knob next to the two connecting plugs.

Build of the Works Rally Cars

The photographic evidence points to continued use of the intercom system on later rallies in that year – the Alpine and RAC rallies at least – and in the Rootes film 'Miss Smith and her Imp', covering the 1965 Alpine rally, the intercom units can be clearly seen strapped to the side of the crash helmets of both Peter Harper and Mike Hughes. By the Monte Carlo and Tulip rallies of 1966 the electronic box had been removed from the helmet and probably attached to the roof of the hard top. The Tulip rally Tiger, FRW 668C, has a drill hole in the roof that could have held the control box.

Body and Coachwork.

Construction of the works rally cars usually began with either a fully completed car, stripped and rebuilt as a rally car or a bare body shell, obtained from the production body line, being transferred to the competition department and being built up from that state.

Firstly, many of the body seams, spot welded in production at Pressed Steel and Jensen, were seam welded or brazed, generally in short lengths along the seams to retain some of the flexing of the shell, whilst strengthening it against the shock loads expected during the rougher rallies. In places, gussets were added to provide extra strength and in some cars (ADU311B for instance) plates were welded across the front chassis cross members to prevent stone or rock damage to the chassis boxes - especially on cars where gravelled roads were to be used (e.g. Acropolis, Scottish, RAC rallies etc). Additional support was given to the steering column brackets by welding strengthening plates between the bracket and body - but not on all cars.

On the later cars, the front suspension crossmember was reinforced by an intricate series of plates welded inside the cross member itself.

Generally, though, the Rootes design was found to be strong enough in its original form to survive without serious modification and apart from the general seam welding only a few points needed further strengthening.

Access to the mechanical parts was never a strong point on the production Tiger, especially in the engine compartment, and in the heat of rallying access had to be made considerably easier. This was facilitated by cutting extra holes in the bodywork at the salient points. On the production Tiger, the changing of the spark plugs, especially those at the rear of the cylinder head, was an intricate and time consuming business and to speed up the process for rallying, a four inch hole was cut in the front wheel arch on the left hand side of the car to allow the plug change to be more rapidly facilitated. This access hole was normally sealed by a round metal plate held in position by Phillips type screws. A similar panel on the gearbox tunnel allowed access to the gearbox linkages.

Later in its life ADU311B had a peculiar venting arrangement, which fed from a slot cut in the gearbox tunnel and led between the front seats to a bifurcated duct that exhausted out onto the backseat panel either side of the rear axle casing – perhaps to allow better airflows around the gearbox.

In order to help reduce under-bonnet temperatures and consequently engine coolant temperature, several cars had wing vents to help the flow of air out of the engine compartment, in the same way as the rally Healey 3000s - in addition to running with the bonnet propped open at the rear. The June 1964 build Tigers - AHP294B, AHP295B, ADU311B and ADU312B - all had wing vents.

Of these four Tigers, the only two cars that changed from vented to non-vented wings in their rally history were ADU311B and AHP294B suggesting a change of body. The remaining five works Tigers were built un-vented.

Looking chronologically at the rally record photographs, ADU311B had vents for its first three events - immediately after the original

Build of the Works Rally Cars

Two views of the venting arrangement on ADU311B feeding from the gearbox tunnel to a bifurcated feed at the rear axle. (Author)

build for the San Martino, the Tulip and finally the Scottish Rally. On its next rally, the 1965 Alpine in July, it appeared without vents.

AHP294B did four events with vents, the last being the 1965 Alpine in July and by the time of its next event, the Monte Carlo of January 1966, it also appeared without wing vents.

The history of AHP294B has been researched in detail by Norman Miller and Graham Vickery. It started out in June 64 as B9470014 with body number 550005 and engine number 1056 E7KL – a standard production 260 Tiger. It now carries the body number 563254 – a JAL number first attached to B9473740 HRO, a car built with a Jensen date of 3 August 1965. The photos also show that the rear edges of the bonnet and doors were of the squared off type rather than the earlier rounded form – indicative of a later body. The STOC Register and the NCM's International Register of known Tigers shows this car to remain unclaimed – more circumstantial evidence of a rebody. The dates also fit.

With both the evidence of the written records combined with the photographic records of the rallies – and the date that the vents disappeared – there must be a strong probability that AHP294B was rebodied after the Alpine in the five months or so before its next rally – the 1966 Monte Carlo.

The case for ADU311B, however, is slightly different. The wing vents disappeared after the Scottish in June 1965 and it appeared on the Alpine in July – some 9 weeks later - with no vents. However, both the doors and bonnet remained with rounded rear edges of the first build and the early production cars. It may well be that after the pounding it took on the Scottish in June 1965 the whole front end was quickly rebuilt, including the front wings. AHP295B, AHP293B and ERW729C were all out on Alpine Rally recces in late June and early July and not available to rebuild as the Alpine rally cars in the time left before the rally – at least not without much overtime. Certainly ADU311B on the Alpine had the same bonnet fixings as used on the car on the previous Tulip, with ADU312B having identical bonnet fixings. It would have been easier to change the wings and inner panels without changing the scuttle panels – hence the same bonnet fixings.

So the current evidence suggests that AHP294B was rebodied, but unlikely for ADU311B. However, the whole issue – apart from AHP294B - would become more complicated if the Competition Department had indulged in swopping registrations on the rally cars – perhaps unlikely, but not unheard of in all the other works teams of the period.

Because under-bonnet air temperatures still remained on the high side, the full power potential of the engine, running with a cooler air temperature, was rarely fully exploited. An attempt was made on the Alpine Rally of 1965,

Build of the Works Rally Cars

when all three cars, ADU311B, ADU312B and AHP294B were fitted with bonnet scoops which ran the full length of the bonnet and fed outside air direct into the carburettor, as distinct from just feeding cool air under the bonnet. At the front of the scoop, and over the carburettor intake, a wire mesh was fitted to prevent ingress of debris.

Whether the scoops were successful or not was not published, but a shortened variant was used on the 1965 RAC Rally on ADU311B, and after this the cars returned to the standard bonnet.

On looking through the photographs an interesting conundrum is in the fixing of the bonnet. Generally the bonnet was propped open at the rear, secured by two bonnet pins and held open by a strip of foam fitted in the drain gully for the bonnet lid. Air from the engine compartment then escaped directly from around the bonnet aperture. In place of the bonnet-locking pin, a spring had been secured which sprung the bonnet open when the bonnet pins were released. On virtually every rally, however, even with the same rally car on both rallies, the cars were fitted with a different type of bonnet pin.

On the 1964 RAC Rally, Rupert Jones (AHP483B) had currently "traditional" leather straps, one on each side of the bonnet lid and fixed to the scuttle in front of the windscreen. This allowed the bonnet to remain partially open to allow engine compartment air to escape.

For the 1965 Monte both Peter Harper's car (ADU312B) and that of Andrew Cowan (AHP295B) had a metallic spring-loaded clip that was angled at 45 degrees across the rear corners of the bonnet (the rounded edge bonnet). Interestingly, the car of Maurice Gatsonides (AHP294B) still retained non-metallic straps across the back of the bonnet as on the 1964 RAC car. Again, all three cars had the bonnet partially open.

For the next rally, the 1965 Tulip, both the cars of Harper and Riley (ADU311B and AHP295B respectively) retained the spring-loaded clips but they had moved from the corners of the bonnet inboard and now in the fore and aft line of the car, about six inches in front of the side of the bonnet, in the same position as the 1964 RAC car (AHP483B). John Gott, in the Police Rally of 1965 (AHP295B) used the new in-line clip of the Tulip Rally, of the same construction and in the same position but had a large rubber grommet or ring holding the bonnet-mounted clip off the bonnet.

For the next major onslaught, the 1965 Alpine Rally, all three cars (ADU311B, ADU312B and AHP294B) had the same types as on the Police Rally.

Interestingly, again, ADU312B still retained the fixing holes from the 1965 Monte - which shows the same car - or at least bonnet - was being used. Both of the other cars, which, of course, had not had the angled clips fitted, showed no old clip holes.

In the last rally of 1965, the RAC car (ADU311B) still retained the in-line clips but without the grommet.

AHP483B, meanwhile, had not changed the bonnet fixings at all and retained the traditional leather straps for the 1965 Targa Florio, even though the bonnet was extensively modified with a large power bulge which fed the cold air to the four-barrel Holley carburettor.

Bonnet fixings on ADU312B on the Alpine 65 (left) and Monte Carlo 65 (right).

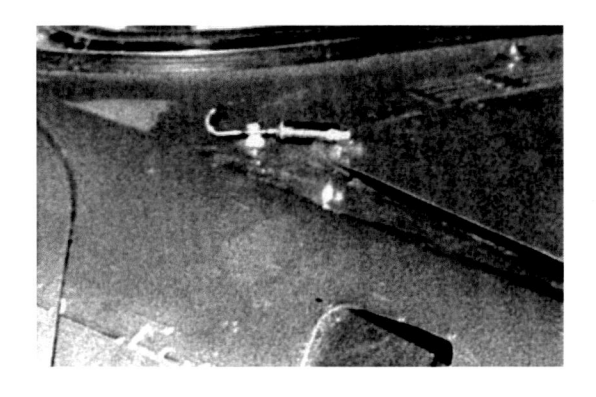

Build of the Works Rally Cars

Peter Harper on the shell of an inverted Tiger

Shell in the Tiger's tank

Peter Harper visits the Rootes Competition Department at Humber Road. A close inspection shows the body seam welding to add strength. This body may well the shell for ADU311B – however, the probable date of the photograph could indicate that this is a new body for AHP294B. (Motor)

Build of the Works Rally Cars

A close view of the cooling fans on ADU311B. The cooling problems were sorted for the later Tigers and no fans were necessary. (Author)

For the first rally of the 1966 season - the Monte Carlo - AHP294B, was used by Peter Harper and a new car constructed for Andrew Cowan and Brian Coyle (FRW667C). With the new Appendix J Regulations and these new cars, the bonnet clips disappeared completely, the bonnet being secured by the production system. Similarly for the Tulip Rally of 1966, another new car (FRW668C) used the standard production system. From then onwards, until the end of its rally life the car (ADU311B on both the Acropolis and Gulf London Rallies) used a standard system.

The placing of the bonnet clips showed interesting, and no doubt logical, sitings, and as a postscript both the Le Mans cars (ADU179B and ADU180B) used a post and clip system, with the hole drilled in the bonnet rear corners, the post being fitted through the hole and secured with a clip.

Turning to the inside of the cars, the most obvious feature was that all the cars were left-hand drive, even the later FRW cars, when right-hand drive shells were freely available. The primary reason for this was that the majority of the rallies took place over the pond, on the continent. Of the 13 rallies in which the works cars competed, nine were outside of the United Kingdom, which made left-hand drive virtually mandatory, especially since the rallies in the UK (RAC, Scottish and Gulf London) all had the competitive sections in the many forests and the road sections, where left-hand drive could be a disadvantage, were relatively relaxed (except perhaps for the Reverend Rupert Jones). In contrast, continental rallies like the Alpine Rally had three types of road section, the liaison sections which were comparatively relaxed and linked the more frantic "selectifs", which had to be attempted at a particularly high average speed. Finally were the "épreuves" which were timed to the nearest one-tenth of a second and required herculean efforts to clean and where the extra vision provided by left-hand drive was an advantage.

The driver sat in the standard production seat but secured from minor, and sometimes more than

Build of the Works Rally Cars

minor, fracas with the scenery, by a full harness seat belt. The belts were secured with eye-bolts bolted through the body floor, one on either side of, and to the rear of, the seat, with the bolt for the shoulder straps fitted centrally behind the seat and back as far as it would go in the "rear seat" area. In the event of a mishap a large un-braced one-inch single loop roll bar provided a modicum of protection for both occupants.

To help brace the driver over the rougher bits of the rally and during the inevitable enthusiastic cornering, a large footrest was provided for the left foot, on top of which was mounted the main-beam dip switch.

As far as crew comfort was concerned Ian Hall, who spent many hours under rallying conditions – both in the cold (Monte 65) and heat (Acropolis 66) – noted that "all rally cars are stiffened up a lot, obviously, and I wouldn't describe it as comfortable, and there were good seats."

Dominating the instrument area and invariably just to the right of the driver at eye level on the dash was the rev counter. Manufactured by Smiths, the counter read up to 8000 rev/min and was not red-lined, although the rev limit was around 6500 rev/min. The position varied marginally from rally to rally, even within the same car. For instance in ADU311B for the Alpine Rally of 1965, the counter was buried in the dash and set virtually centrally in front of the driver whilst in the same car on the Acropolis of 1966 it was mounted forward and above the dash, slightly higher and to the right of the driver. Wherever the position, however, it remained in the primary sightline of the driver. Individual drivers have their own preferences (as do navigators) and Peter Harper had a dislike of the rev counter being in his direct line of vision, for obvious reasons. The mechanics mischievously suggested that it might fit on the end of the bonnet! The standard instrument remained in position in the dashboard but was disconnected. In FRW668C, a rheostat (variable resistance) was fitted centrally on the bottom of the dash and the instrument lighting for the rev-counter routed through it. The wiring was independent of the normal panel lighting allowing the normal instrument lighting to be off and the rev-counter to be illuminated to whatever degree of lighting level required - obviously depending on the prevailing rally conditions. An 'off' position was incorporated in the rheostat.

FRW668C was fitted with an electrical rheostat fitted just below the dashboard to control the illumination of the Rev Counter under the control of the driver. (Author)

Build of the Works Rally Cars

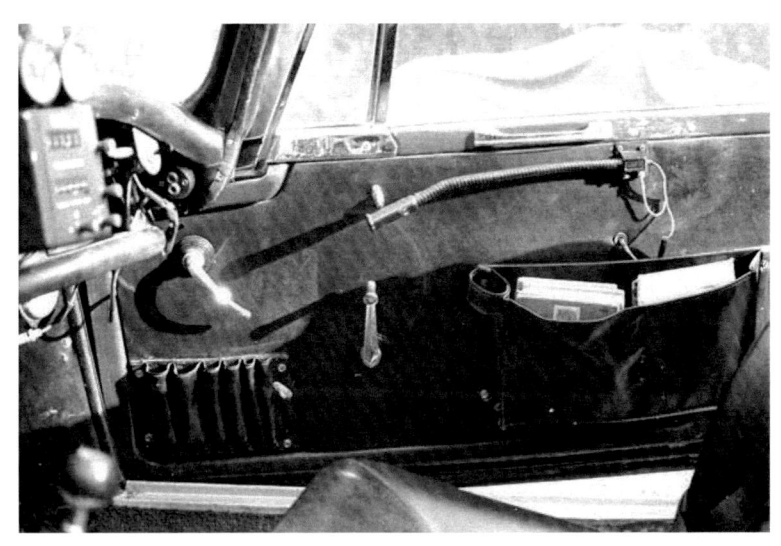

Door pockets on both sides of Tiger FRW668C carried a variety of contents. The driver's side was used mainly for essential tools, whilst the navigator's side carried maps and associated paperwork. (Author)

The two pin Poti plug used to power the illuminating map magnifier. (Author)

Build of the Works Rally Cars

A shot of the navigator's side of FRW668C, with the Halda Twinmaster and Heuer clocks in place and the Poti socket and Halda/Heuer/Map Light switch at the top right. (Author)

On the insides of both doors supplementary pockets were fitted which, on the driver's side, held a variety of tools in four individual pockets incorporated in a single large pocket whilst on the co-driver's/navigator's side a similar pocket held six tools, both pockets being positioned forward of the window winder. For the navigator an additional pocket was fitted, sub-divided into two sections, which held maps in both pockets, whilst at the front of the pocket a loop held a torch.

An Avanti map-light was fitted to the top edge of the door and curled around the navigator's shoulder to illuminate the maps, road book and sundry other instructions. On FRW668C the light was switched from a three way switch fitted in front of the co-driver on the dash, the switch controlling both map-light and tripmeter, allowing all lights to be off, both Halda and map light on or just providing illumination to the Halda.

For the more intricate map reading activities a Poti map magnifier was normally used and its internal illumination was provided from a two-pin plug situated at the right hand corner of the dash, and which was permanently live.

As with the driver, whose most important instrument was probably the rev-counter, which was fitted directly in front of him, so it was with the co-driver. Mounted clearly in front of him was a twin Halda Trip-master and a set of Heuer clocks, one of which was set to the normal or rally time, whilst the other was a stop-watch used to time the selectives or stages. The Trip-master was driven off a T-piece fitted to the back of the speedometer, with gearing, appropriate to the back axle ratio and tyre type and aspect ratio, being changed in the Trip-meter itself. The speedometer was geared to suit the back axle in use - normally the 3.7 differential unit. Ian Hall noted that "I think that I was one of the first co-drivers to insist on clocks and map-reading lights where I wanted them – up until then Rootes used to be horrified if you actually asked them to drill a hole in the trim!"

255

Build of the Works Rally Cars

As a final refinement, a small pad was fitted on the door trim above the window winder to prevent the crew and car coming painfully into contact with the sharper parts of the bodywork during the frequent fervid cornering. As with most rally cars of this period the bodywork was not modified to any great extent, and was easily identifiable with their corresponding road versions, but each car was modified enough to make it an individual item.

The left hand inner wing of FRW668C showing the in-line fuses for the front lights (at the front end of the water header tank), the Lucas relays for the spot lights and the brake reservoirs for the dual master cylinder and clutch fluid reservoir. (Author)

The driver's footrest and dip-switch on FRW668C. (Author)

Obituary and Reflections

The Gulf London and the Acropolis were the last two rallies in which the Tiger competed under the works banner. By that time, the lighter, smaller and nimbler Rallye Imps were beginning to take some honours in their classes, and the publicity generated for the Imp was needed to aid sales in a very competitive end of the sales market.

Other manufacturers, notably BMC, were turning to the Cooper S to front their Competition Department and to provide good overall and class wins. Likewise Ford Competition department at Boreham were pushing for success with their Cortina GTs and Lotus Cortinas. All of these potential and actual rally successes were with the newer generations of automobile - moving away from the bigger (and heavier) Healeys and Tigers. The Lotus Cortinas of the period were producing around 150 to 160bhp, and the Cooper S's between 110 and 130bhp, and with their considerably lighter weight were generally quicker through the lanes than the Tiger or Healey - and with their considerably better handling were certainly less of a handful.

At this point it might be a sensible question to ask if the Tiger was that good as a rally car? One answer would be "what is meant by 'good'?" As a rally car it bought much needed competition to the BMC Healey 3000, which, at that time had a relatively free run in the big-engined class, and it was a charismatic car in the 'macho' sense - perhaps analogous to heavyweights in boxing.

As, hopefully, a part of Tiger history, this book should aim to paint an accurate picture of the Tiger as a rally car of the mid 60's. There is always a risk that with a nostalgic backwards look, the car may be seen to be better than it was - particularly now, as historic rallying is on the rise. In his excellent book "Tiger, Alpine and Rapier", Richard Langworth quotes Wilson McCoomb, who wrote..."we may sometimes have to challenge a few statements that other people accept without question. We must not get too misty eyed or sentimental about the girls or the cars. We must ask ourselves if they were really that good?"

Similar questions are often asked about 'charismatic' cars, which are often 'legends' of their time. In many ways it depends upon the critic or the driver - read any classic car magazine letters column for support of almost any car manufactured (including the Austin Allegro). The 1930's Bentley and its later derivatives may be either looked upon as a landmark, as undoubtedly its engineering heritage allowed, or as a small lorry with commensurate handling - Ettore Bugatti's well disseminated remark on the lines that that 'Mr Bentley builds the best lorries in the world', may, or may not, be wide of the mark. Certainly more modern competent and professional drivers, who lack no enthusiasm for automotive history, such as Sir John Whitmore, often found driving such legends to be disappointing in many ways. Again, in one of the more holier institutions, Ferrari, some discerning drivers have been less than enthusiastic about the earlier V-12's, up to and including the 365 GTB/4 Daytona. The out-and-out performance may be outstanding - even by some modern standards - but in other areas, that, when combined with performance, make a 'good' car - such as handling, agility and braking - may not be up-to-scratch.

The notion of up-to-scratch, of course, also changes with time, and, the giant killer of the 60's, the 1275 Cooper S, which had essentially all the right attributes, power, handling, agility, brakes, will now be easily outrun, outhandled and outbraked by virtually any of the standard hot hatchbacks, all with the same attributes but better developed - and better tyres! And quite rightly so, that is called progress. Even within rallying itself progress is rapid. The stage times

Obituary and Reflections

that the 1980 Group B cars were returning with around 550 to 600bhp, just before the FIA banned the cars on safety grounds, were quickly equalled by the heavier and lower power (350 to 400bhp) cars that replaced the Group B cars. All essentially down to tyres, brakes and suspension. One driver with a impeccable history of success from the earlier Saab V4's right through the Audi Quattro Group B days to driving the latest 1994 Ford Escort Cosworth - Stig Blomquist - noted quite clearly that driving the older Group B cars, compared to the latest cars, was a bit like 'driving a tractor' - (even a 600bhp tractor!)

In this context the Tiger (and the Healey 3000) fit clearly into the 'good at the time' bracket - but at the end of an era and shortly to be superseded. They were both cars which had a good power-to-weight ratio but generally lacked the handling and braking refinements with which the later small cars, such as the Cooper S, Rallye Imp, Lotus Cortina and Cortina GTs, were endowed.

The Tiger was not necessarily an easy car to drive in its rally form. It certainly was quick, making use of its superb torque curve to return a 0 - 60 mph time in the region of 6.5 to 7secs (Competition Dept MIRA tests - ADU311B Ex Monte: 11.2.65: 7.5secs; AHP295B: Alpine Recce: 11.8.65: 6.8secs; 17.8.65: 6.45secs). The later two-barrelled carb engined cars (AHP295B tested at MIRA on 19.8.65 turned in 8.0secs. This was against around 8.2secs for the rally Healey 3000 (Autocar 3 Sept 1965 Alpine Healey 3000 DRX 258C). This was only equalled by the Healey in the 60 to 80 mph in top and 50 to 70 mph in 3rd gear. But with a weight some 150lb heavier than the Healey and its weight distribution predominantly nose heavy, with a subsequent tendency to understeer, and with its Alpine brakes, the downhill performance, in particular, left much to be desired - particularly in tarmac rallies with a lot of downhill motoring - the Coupe des Alpes for instance.

Also the Tiger had a short wheelbase in relation to its track. It had started life as the Alpine in 1959, which had used the Hillman Husky's short wheelbase floor-pan. At 7ft 2 inches it was some 6 inches shorter than the Healey (7ft 8in) but with virtually the same track. The then current MGA (7ft 10in) and MGB (7ft 7in) were both contemporary cars with a wheelbase similar to the Healey and with similar tracks. A short wheelbase to track ratio (like the later Triumph TR8s), makes the car less stable longitudinally (i.e. twitchy) and whilst this as not seen as a major disadvantage on tarmac, it was more of a problem in the forests. As Des O'Dell noted "on the tarmac it was impressive, but it was never any good in forest rallies!"

So, in reality, a number of associated items killed off the Tiger in rallying, perhaps, paradoxically, at a point where it was developing well. With the Mk2 4.7 litre (289 cu inch) engine and 200 to 300lb less weight it would have undoubtedly been more successful, but probably not to the extent of challenging the BMC and Ford works teams. Robin Turvey relates a story of using a recce Tiger with a 4.7 engine on the Tulip 66 recce, and climbing the same hills as Peter Harper in the 4.2 rally version and regularly beating Peter's times. He noted that the car must be considerably quicker and better, as his driving wasn't even in the same league as Peter's.

After the Acropolis Rally of 66, which was hard by any standards, Ian Hall noted..."It was this rally that convinced me, at least, that the Tiger had had its day. Ove Andersson's little Lancia Fulvia was the pointer. I felt that the factory should be concentrating all of its limited resources on the Imp, which was the car it wanted to sell. Absolutely no part of the Imp or Tiger was common, so the mechanics were really being asked to do too much in my view. This view eventually prevailed....."

Even Peter Harper, with his experience of the Tiger and later the Imp (as well as most other Rootes cars) thought likewise. In an interview for a rally video he noted "If you compared it with the Tiger, the Imp was far, far quicker than the Tiger – in a forest – for two reasons. First of

258

Obituary and Reflections

all, it was a lot smaller – you could get it sideways-on and still stay on the road, whereas if you got a Tiger sideways-on you probably lost the back-end. Secondly, it had terrific traction – out of a hairpin, for example, an Imp would leave a Tiger miles behind."

So, in summary, a combination of events bought the Tiger's demise - company politics were pushing for the Imp to be used in competition, to enhance sales; the company had been taken over by Chrysler, who were not happy to see a Ford engine in one of their range of cars - let alone in well publicised motorsport and the 1966 Motorsport rules left the Tiger with less power and less flexibility to loose weight (which was also a major problem with the Healey) which would have made it considerably less competitive. The tide was turning against the Tiger and the smaller, lighter, nimble and less physically demanding cars were in the ascendancy and its time finally came - as it does, inevitably, with all rally cars – however good their record.

A good record in its class, competitive against the contemporary winners on tarmac, a charismatic car, one of the last of the "big bangers" and a rewarding car if driven well. It has a definite place in the annals of motorsport, having made its mark, and it is more than interesting to see the competitive revival of the Tiger in Historic Rallying and to see the new comparisons with the Healey 3000 and the Imps and the Cooper S's...............

(Autosport)

Obituary and Reflections

Appendix 1: Le Mans Tiger Wind Tunnel Tests 1964

Prior to the building of the bodies for the Le Mans Tigers, Rootes Experimental Department carried out a sequence of tests on a ¼ scale model of the proposed shape, and formulated a number of modifications to ensure that the car was aerodynamically stable in lift and pitch, directionally stable in a cross wind, had adequate cooling for the engine, brakes and rear axle and the car was shaped, within its original design constraints, to minimize form drag.

In the early 1960's not a lot was understood, or known, about high-speed road vehicle aerodynamics. Apart from some academic research and the work that the main motor manufacturers were carrying out – mainly into reducing the aerodynamic drag of their models – there was very little progress in motorsport to a higher understanding of aerodynamic effects on a cars overall performance (i.e. speed, stability etc).

Ferrari had installed, early in the 1960's, a small wind-tunnel at Maranello to study body shapes for both its racing cars and sports cars. Carlo Chiti had been one of the main instigators and the initial work was on studies to reduce aerodynamic drag. Reduction of drag leads, obviously, to higher speeds, but the pathways to such reduction are not always obvious. At Ferrari these studies had led to, amongst other innovations, twin nostrils at the front of the cars and higher windscreens and tails at the rear appearing on their sports racing cars of the 1961 season.

The 1961 Ferrari 246SP – Sports Prototype – had been found, by test driver Richie Ginther, to be quick on the straights but somewhat unstable in the high-speed corners at Monza – which was not unusual in low-drag body shapes and this was due to two major parameters. Firstly, the aerodynamic lift on the rear body reduced the downforce on the rear suspension and un-loaded the rear tyres. Secondly, the aerodynamic Centre of Pressure (CoP) was too far forward of the Centre of Gravity (CoG) of the car – and this is particularly important on rear-engined cars where the CoG is situated towards the rear – which resulted in aerodynamic instability. Ideally the CoG should always be forward of the CoP.

By adding a rear fin to the 246SP, behind the drivers head and thus more rear surface area, the CoP was moved rearwards, but, for the Ferrari, not far enough to provide the necessary high speed stability, as the rear body lift was also still present, particularly in a cross-wind.

However, in testing, the long serving engineer, Jano, had suggested that a spoiler fitted across the upper surface of the tail of the car would reduce rear-body lift and this was found to be effective and to provide a significant reduction in the lightening of the rear of the car at speed – and consequently the instability of the car under high-speed cornering. While this is well understood today, in 1961 it was a significant advance.

These 'Ferrari spoilers' resulted in two main effects. One was to reduce the lift on the rear of the car by forming a higher pressure area on the rear bodywork (i.e. less negative pressure and thus less lift) and the other was to smooth out the turbulent flow over the rear body by use of this higher pressure area – resulting in a reduced drag coefficient.

This is clearly corroborated from both the early 1963/64 Rootes Tiger data and from later Porsche tests on their 1972 911 Carrera RS with the 'duck's tail' spoiler.

For Porsche, with the standard front air dam

Appendix 1

and the duck's tail spoiler, the drag co-efficient was reduced from 0.409 without the spoiler to 0.397 with – not a significant amount, but enough to increase top speed by 3 km/hr. But the primary effect had been achieved in reducing the Coefficient of Lift on the rear of the car at 150 mph from 0.290 to 0.084. In practical terms this reduced the rear end lift from 139 kg (307 lb) to 40 kg (88lb) whilst only increasing the lift on the front of the car by 3 kg (6.6lb) – (from 30 kg to 33 kg).

For the Le Mans Tiger the comparisons of Tests 19 & 20 in this Appendix (essentially the Le Mans shape with & without the spoiler) show that the use of a 4 inch high 'Ferrrari type' spoiler both reduced the drag – resulting in an estimated 3 mph increase in top speed - with little effect on side force and yawing effect and significantly reduced the lift on the rear of the car at 170 mph. The spoiler increased the load on the rear end, at 170 mph, by 135lb whilst only un-loading the front end by 8 lb – an insignificant amount. More significantly, at 170 mph in a 30 mph crosswind, the load on the rear end went from 131 lb lift to 26 lb down-force. In addition, the Centre of Pressure moved backwards by 1.4% resulting in a greater margin of stability in cross winds.

From reading the following report, it can be seen that the engineers carried out a thorough series of tests and ended with a practical solution. No doubt a lower drag co-efficient could have been reached, but the publicity requirement to keep it looking as close to a production Tiger as possible, particularly from the front view, clashed with the aerodynamic needs.

Clearly, the Experimental Department had succeeded in understanding the speed-based dynamics of the Tiger and provided a good basis for further testing, suggesting in this report that the spoiler be detachable so that, in the pre-Le Mans testing sessions, the handling could be explored with and without the spoiler fitted. It would appear that no time was available for such tests.

The records come from the archives of the Sunbeam Tigers Owners Club (STOC) and are used with their permission.

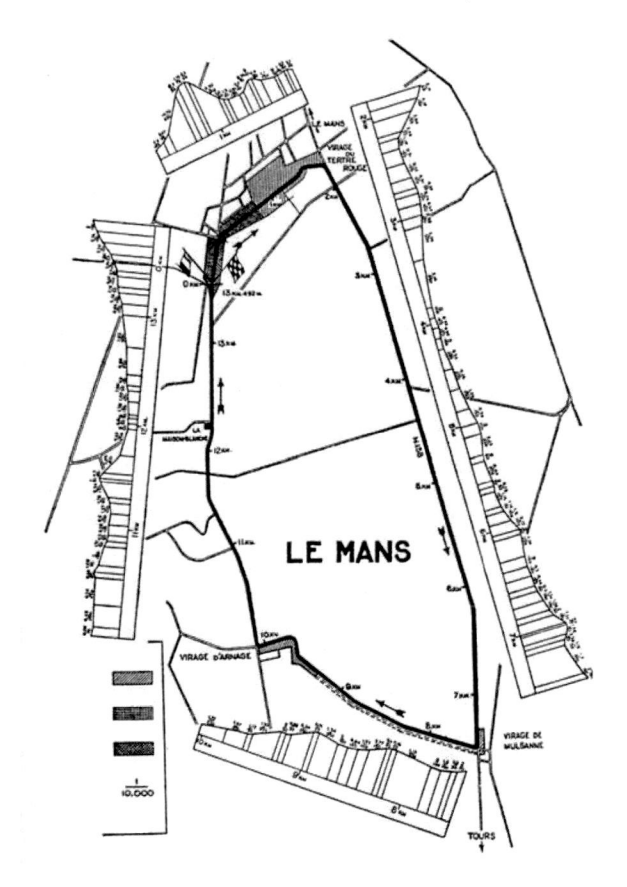

Appendix 1

CONFIDENTIAL

EXPERIMENTAL DEPT. REPORT

File: B.2, Sunbeam

TO: Mr. F.A. Caine (2)

Report No.	2416
Date	4.2.64
Model Project No.	3011
Sub-Project No.	
Phase	
T.R. No.	40358

MODEL: Competition Le Mans V.8 Alpine   VEHICLE   MILEAGE

SECTION I

SUBJECT:

Wind Tunnel testing of ¼ scale model V.8 Alpine Le Mans.

AIM:

To develop a satisfactory Body Envelope with reference to:-

1. Minimum drag
2. Directional stability up to $10°$ yaw
3. Lift and pitching aerodynamic stability
4. Engine water and oil cooling
5. Rear axle and brake cooling
6. Engine compartment ventilation
7. Interior ventilation and buffeting
8. Windscreen wiping

Frontal aspect to be interfered with as little as possible.

CONCLUSIONS:

1. The lowest Cd obtained with the ¼ scale model was .312. This was with flush wheel discs, but as it will possibly be difficult to cool the brakes with wheel discs on, then, it is thought that the accepted condition of the model will be without wheel discs and will therefore have a C_d of .346 (test 20). This is estimated to be .369 when cooling drag and drag of small underbody projections are added on the final full size vehicle.

   It can be seen from the total drag HP graph that with the 260 HP engine installed the car with this body form should have a max. speed of 170 m.p.h.

2. The above condition of the model had a CY of .107 and CS of .322 giving a centre of pressure location 16.9% of the wheelbase aft of front wheel centre line.

   This estimated for the full size vehicle would be a CY of .067 and a CS of .286. These results are better than average and as this is a front engined car with a heavy engine, then this vehicle should be quite stable in cross winds.

Appendix 1

Report No. 2416
4.3.64
TR.40358

Cont'd......

3. The lift coefficient at 0° yaw angle for the model in the probable final condition is -.051 and the pitching moment coefficient is .098. This condition is with a Ferrari type spoiler on the rear end of the fastback.

   In this condition there is negative lift but positive pitching moment therefore the rear end is held down and the front end has a slight tendency to lift. It is felt that this condition is desirable since better rear end traction will occur at high speed and the lift force acting at the front is relatively small and is virtually the same with and without spoiler, and should have little effect on the vehicle handling. The spoiler is to be made detachable so that the effect on vehicle handling can be assessed in the Le Mans practise and the drivers can then choose whether to have the spoiler fitted or not, although the Cd is increased by .010 when the spoiler is left off, which will reduce maximum speed by approximately 3 m.p.h. and slightly reduce acceleration.

4 & 5 The model was made with the front apron extended downwards to allow room for incorporating extra ducting for air to radiator and front brakes. Actual ducting will have to be developed on full size vehicle when available.

   There is no rear undertray so that air can circulate round rear axle and rear wheels. Scoops for extra air to rear axle and brakes will have to be developed on full size vehicle if required.

6. Louvers in the bonnet top could be developed on the V.8 production Alpine, also, ducting panels to the radiator for optimum cooling with low intake drag.

7. From the results of pressures taken on the model surface it is found to be satisfactory to take air in at the normal heater air intake at the front scuttle and can be either extracted at the top of the roof above the windscreen or at the rear quarter light panels.

8. The airflow all over the windscreen is parallel to car centre line, therefore it is desirable to have the windscreen wiper blades as upright as possible for most of the wiping arc to avoid wiper blade windlift.

STATE OF TR:

TR.40358 is now closed.

REPORTED BY... R.K. Justin
AIRFLOW ENGINEER

DEVELOPMENT ENGINEER

CIRCULATION:

Mr. P.G.Ware   Mr. S.Grierson
Mr. T.L.Jump   Mr. D.G.Tarbun
Mr. D.Hodkin   Mr. L.Kuzmicki
Mr. P.S.Wilson   Mr. E.S.White
Mr. D.R.Welbourne Mr. R.Wisdom   ) Studio
Mr. E.F.Litchfield Mr. T.G.R.Fleming)
Mr. V.J.Adrian   Mr. K.Sharpe   )
Mr. F.J.Smithyman Mr. C.W.Mann   ) Ryton

Report No. 2416
4.2.64
TR. 40358

SECTION II

DESCRIPTION OF TESTS:

The following table summarises the wind tunnel test results obtained in the M.I.R.A. model wind tunnel.

The model had an under tray right across the underbody below the car interior and a smaller undertray under the engine sump. Air intakes on the front of the model for radiator and engine cooling ducts were recessed on the model surface but were not cut right through to the engine compartment.

Tests 1 - 14 are based on a frontal area of 18.2 sq.ft. for full size vehicle and tests 15 - 20 are based on a frontal area of 17.7 sq.ft. full size.

TABLE 1

TEST NO.	CONDITION OF MODEL	Cd 0° yaw	CL 0° yaw	Cp 0° yaw	Cs 10° yaw	Cy 10° yaw	C of P % W.B. aft front wheel centreline @ 10° yaw
1	Original condition as received from Styling Studio made to instructions from Airflow Section.	.362	.015	.085	.347	.117	16.5
2	Height of fastback reduced 2" full size on rear end.	.353	.022	.088	.306	.122	10.2
3	Windscreen extended forward at base by 2" full size & blended into existing A posts to give more curvature to windscreen.	.358	.040	.089	.321	.121	12.5
4	Centre of windscreen back to original, more radius into 'A' posts.	.364	.073	.082	.333	.118	14.4
5	Windscreen back to original form. Peak between windscreen and roof slightly reduced.	.359	.041	.082	.334	.122	13.7

Appendix 1

4.2.64
TR.40358

Cont'd..........

TEST NO.	CONDITION OF MODEL	Cd 0° yaw	CL 0° yaw	Cp 0° yaw	Cs 10° yaw	Cy 10° yaw	C of P % W.B. aft front wheel centreline @ 10° yaw
6	Fast back narrowed in plan 2" full size each side at rear end.	.358	.043	.081	.321	.117	14.0
7	Tops of rear wings narrowed in plan 1" full size at each side on rear end.	.355	.055	.081	.323	.119	13.1
8	Radius running along rear end of under body replaced by sharp edge	.357	.056	.078	.326	.118	13.7
9	Fast back narrowed in plan a further 2" full size each side at rear end.	.358	.055	.071	.321	.118	13.2
10	Flush wheel discs	.329	.055	.071	.321	.118	13.2
11	Tops of rear wings narrowed in plan 2" further full size each side.	.323	.029	.071	.348	.130	12.7
12	Cooling ducts blanked flush to surrounding profile, instead of being recessed.	.312	-.001	.049	.344	.127	12.9
13	Wheel discs removed wheels repositioned with stronger mounting brackets, as original brackets had been bent under model weight.	.334	.067	.059	.317	.119	12.4
14	4" long full size Ferrari type spoiler on rear end of fast back.	.326	-.009	.094	.320	.118	13.1
15	Max. height of roof reduced by 2" full size	.329	-.021	.108	.320	.117	13.8

Cont'd...

Report No. 2416
4.2.64
TR. 40358

Cont'd....

TEST NO.	CONDITION OF MODEL	Cd 0° yaw	CL 0° yaw	Cp 0° yaw	Cs 10° yaw	Cy 10° yaw	C of P % W.B. after front wheel centreline @ 10° yaw
16	Fast back extended to top rear edge of boot, spoiler removed.	.342	.066	.054	.307	.116	12.2
17	Spoiler added 3" long full size from extended fast back.	.332	⁻.011	.101	.320	.118	13.0
18	Spoiler extended to 5" full size from extended fast back.	.332	⁻.047	.128	.315	.119	12.2
19	Model checked in styling Studio for symmetry etc., and form adjusted to suit, spoiler removed.	.356	.047	.044	.313	.108	15.5
20	4" long spoiler added.	.346	⁻.051	.098	.322	.107	16.9

NOTE: In the above table each model condition is relative to the previous test condition.

GRAPH 5989 Shows the estimated total drag HP of the actual full size car.

GRAPHS 5986) Show the ¼ scale model aerodynamic coefficients for
       5987) tests 19 and 20.
       5988)

It can be seen that the spoiler reduces drag with little effect on side force and yawing moment. The centre of pressure is more rearward with the spoiler attached, lift forces are reduced and pitching and rolling moments are increased with the spoiler, although they are relatively small.

The following summary of tests 19 and 20 show the estimated full size car aerodynamic coefficients. This has been possible by comparing full size and ¼ scale model results of the Swallow.

Test No. 19 Condition: No spoiler

TABLE 2

	0° yaw angle			10° yaw angle					
	Cd	CL	CP	Cd	CL	Cp	Cs	Cy	Cr
¼ scale model	.356	.047	.044	.384	.297	.048	.313	.108	.154
Full size car esti-	.379	.047	.044	.448	.297	.048	.278	.068	.154

Appendix 1

```
                                              4.2.64
                                              TR. 40358
```

Cont'd..........

For test 19   Condition: no spoiler

@ 170 mph   Estimated forces on full size vehicle are:

@ <u>0° yaw</u>

    Drag force = 496 lbs.
    Vertical force @ front axle = +88.5 lbs
    Vertical force @ rear axle = -26.8 lbs

@ <u>10° yaw</u>

    i.e. @ 170 mph car speed and 30 mph side wind
    Drag force = 586 lbs
    Vertical force @ front axle = +258 lbs
    Vertical force @ rear axle = +131 lbs
    Side force @ front axle = +271 lbs
    Side force @ rear axle = +93 lbs

For test 20   Condition: with spoiler:

Table 3	0° yaw angle			10° yaw angle					
	CD	CL	CP	CD	CL	CP	CS	CY	CR
¼ scale model	.346	-.051	.098	.381	.159	.099	.322	.107	.165
Full size car estimate	.369	-.051	.098	.444	.159	.099	.236	.067	.165

For test 20   condition with spoiler:

@ 170 mph estimated forces on full size vehicle are:

@ <u>0° yaw</u>

    Drag force = 484 lbs
    Vertical force @ front axle = +95 lbs
    Vertical force @ rear axle = -162 lbs

@ <u>10° yaw</u>

    i.e. @ 170 mph car speed and 30 mph side wind
    Drag force = 580 lbs
    Vertical force @ front axle = +233 lbs
    Vertical force @ rear axle = -26.2 lbs
    Side force @ front axle = +275 lbs
    Side force @ rear axle = +99.5 lbs

<u>Effect of Aerodynamic forces on vehicle weight distribution:</u>

	Front	Rear	Total
Estimated static weight distribution of finished car	1348	1256	2604

Appendix 1

Report No. 2416
4.2.64
TR.40358

Cont'd........

	Front	Rear	Total
Without Spoiler:			
Estimated weight distribution @ 170 mph 0° yaw	1260	1283	2543
Estimated weight distribution @ 170 mph 10° yaw	1090	1125	2215
With an estimated side force @ 170 mph 10° yaw	271	93	364
With spoiler fitted:			
Estimated weight distribution @ 170 mph 0° yaw	1253	1418	2671
Estimated weight distribution @ 170 mph 10° yaw	1115	1282	2397
With an estimated side force @ 170 mph 10° yaw	275	99	374

Note:

The above weight distribution estimates are taken for the worst conditions likely to be encountered, i.e. max. speed of car, and max. speed of car and a side wind of 30 mph giving a resultant wind angle (or yaw angle) of 10°.

Appendix 1

Appendix 2: Pre Le Mans development on the 'mule' Tiger 7743KV

To take a road car and persuade it to run effectively and competitively on a racetrack, sometimes against serious opposition, normally requires considerable time and effort. Suspension, brakes, engine, transmission, steering etc.... all need testing to ensure that they will meet the strains of continuous high speeds and the additional manoeuvring and braking loads that are unlikely to be experienced on the public road. As well as the safety issues, aspects such as handling and road-holding generally need substantial improvement.

In this respect the Le Mans Tigers were no different to any other competition car.

The one day – or less – 'shakedown' at Mallory Park can have been only that – a quick indication of the general suitability for Le Mans, and on a short circuit like this, very little indication of aerodynamic stability could have been accomplished.

However, this was obviously not the priority of this test and enough was found to allow minimal modifications to take place for the Le Mans weekend tests a few days later.

The Snetterton tests, with the long high-speed straight, allowed for more refined changes to the car's suspension settings and some playing with the weight distribution of the Tiger.

As well as developing the car, other aspects had to be finished at Humber Road - wiring, trim, body detailing etc – and the final tests at Silverstone - some 2 weeks after the Snetterton test on the 14th May – was essentially the last chance for final adjustments.

The report in this Appendix is the original summary of the development work carried out in that five-week period, and comes from the archives of the Sunbeam Tigers Owners Club (STOC).

Appendix 2

The development work was spread over a period of five weeks and consisted of a reconnaisance at Mallory Park and development tests at both Snetterton and Silverstone.

TEST 1   DEVELOPMENT CARRIED OUT ON LE MANS TIGER

Mallory Park   7743 KV

Date: 15-4-64

Weather Conditions: Initially dry and windy turning to rain.
Driver: K. Ballistat

Vehicle Suspension Specification

FRONT

Spring 1,206,310
    144 lb/in. wheel rate on rationalised suspension.

Anti-Roll Bar   13/16"

Dampers: GT.7
    290-65-65-190

Wishbone modifications.

    Top Link - Series III with screwed bushes, i.e. a shorter link to clear the wheel.
    Lower Link - Series IV (rubber bushed) and ball swivel.

REAR

Spring 1,206,585
    115 lb/in. rate, 2¼" wide, Metaxcentric bush - Alpine III

Dampers: GT.7
    300-60-50-160

     Wheels   -   Magnesium 6.50L
     Tyres   -   6.50L-15 Dunlop R.6
     Pressures   -   50 lb/sq.in. front and rear

Vehicle Assessment

Run	Suspension	Driver's Assessment
(1)	As above	Tyres too hard.
(2)	Tyre pressures reduced to 40 lb/sq.in. all round.	Rear end coming out on bends after going over bumps.
(3)	Rear pressures reduced to 35 lb/sq.in.	Driver still unsatisfied - Severe rear axle tramp during starts.

Here a natural halt was called as rain was interfering with the tests and it was evident that additional material was needed:

(a) Rear dampers with higher settings to eliminate axle tramp.

(b) Front dampers with higher settings to overcome front end float in the straight ahead.

(c) Increase spring rates all round to reduce roll and improve cornering.

(d) Fit rear roll bar to counter tramp.

TEST II

During the week ending 18/19th April, a practise was held at Le Mans.

Weather conditions: Heavy rain - wet track
Driver: K. Ballistat

Vehicle Suspension Specification at Start of Tests

FRONT

Spring 1,215,570
(Ex. Competition Rapier)
170 lb/in. on rationalised suspension.

Anti-Roll Bar   13/16"

Dampers: GT.7
290-65-65-190

REAR

Spring 1,206,585
115 lb/in. rate,
2¼" wide Metaxcentric bush - Alpine III

Dampers: GT.7
300-60-50-180

Wheels - Magnesium 6.50L

Tyres - 6.00L- 15   R.6   Front
6.50L- 15   R.6   Rear

Pressures 35 lb/sq.in. Front
40 lb/sq.in. Rear

Vehicle Assessment

Complaints of rear axle tramp, excessive roll in corners and front end float in straight ahead.

TEST III

Snetterton

Date: 29-4-64

Weather conditions: Dry, Sunny, windy
Driver: K. Ballistat

Vehicle Suspension Specification at Start of Tests

Appendix 2

FRONT

Springs 1,215,570
170 lb/in. with insulator rubber removed.

Anti-roll bar - 13/16" Super Snipe type (frame mounted)

Dampers: GT.7
290-65-65-190

REAR

Springs 187 lb/in., 1.0" lower than previous test. Metaxcentric eye with adaptors for 1.0" solid bush.

Anti-roll bar - 1.0" roll bar fitted between radius rods.

Dampers: OT.8 Orifice type

Wheels - Magnesium

Tyres - 6.00L-15 R.6 Front
6.50L-15 R.6 Rear

Pressures - 35 lb/sq.in. Front
40 lb/sq.in. Rear

Vehicle Assessment

Run	Suspension	Driver's Assessment
(1)	As above	Rear roll bar fouled propshaft.
(2)	Rear roll bar removed.	Excessive float at rear end coupled with some axle tramp.
(3)	OT.8 rear dampers replaced by Koni adjustables.	Tramp eliminated, some rear end float still present.
(4)	Koni rear dampers screwed right up and let off one revolution.	Float eliminated, handling better but rear inner wheel picking up.

Petrol tank emptied and sandbags put in boot to simulate revised petrol tank position. One jerry can of petrol in petrol tank.

Run	Suspension	Driver's Assessment
(5)	As (4) with loading modification above.	Handling still better, less tendency to pick up inner rear wheel.
(6)	Panhard rod fitted in lower position.	Handling reported to be even better.

Tests ceased at this stage as additional material was needed.

(a) Higher rate front springs to increase the front end roll stiffness and lessen the tendency to pick up the inner rear wheel during cornering.

(b) Obtain larger diameter front roll bars - 1.0" and 1.125" to assist (a).

(c) Obtain a set of front dampers either fixed setting or

Appendix 2

TEST IV

Silverstone

Date: 14-5-64

Weather Conditions: Dry, windy
Driver(s): W.Ballistat, W.B.Unett

Vehicle Suspension Specification at Start of Tests

FRONT

Spring X.90603
    200 lb/in. wheel rate

Anti-roll bar   13/16"
    (frame mounted)

Dampers   Armstrong GB.637
    348-78-78-228

REAR

Spring   187 lb/in. wheel rate

Anti-roll bar   -

Dampers   Armstrong GB.639

Panhard Rod fitted at lowest position (2.0" lower than standard)

Wheels   -   Magnesium   6.50L

Tyres   -   6.00L-15   R.6   Front
                6.50L-15   R.6   Rear

Pressures-   35 lb/sq.in. Front
                40 lb/sq.in. Rear

Petrol Tank - As built in 'forward' position.

Vehicle Assessment

Run	Suspension	Driver's Assessment
(1)	As above.	Front end float particularly disturbing in the corners.
(2)	Fit Koni shock absorbers (as received settings)	Whole car now floats and some patter at rear.
(3)	Adjust Koni dampers by two full turns.	Excessive roll in corner.
(4)	Replace 13/16" diameter front roll bar with 1.0".	Wheel lift at rear but more control in the corners.
(5)	Raise Panhard rod position by 1.0".	Inferior handling to previous run.
(6)	(a) Replace Armstrong rear dampers with Konis adjusted by two full turns. (b) Return Panhard bar	Wheel lift reduced but front end float still present.

Appendix 2

Run	Suspension	Driver's Assessment
(7)	Screw up front dampers to maximum setting.	Float eliminated, handling generally good.
(8)	Fit heavier front springs to tune suspension still further. X.90602 – Wheel rate 244 lb/in.	Handling characteristics good

With the suspension to the specification used in Run (8), numerous practise laps were completed by both K. Ballistat and W. B. Onett whose best lap times were 1 min. 54.6 seconds and 1 min. 52.2 seconds respectively.

Suspension Specification used at Le Mans

FRONT

Springs X.90602
    250 lb/in. wheel rate

Roll bar Super Snipe type
    (frame mounting)
    1.0" diameter

Dampers Koni
P.V. characteristics
Max. Vel. (ins)
  1 1.5 3 6 10 15
Rebound Resist. (lb)
  200 280 290 330 390 460
Bump Resist. (lb)
  10 15 30 70 130 160

Tyres: Dunlop 6.00Lx 15 R.6

Pressures: 35 lb/sq.in.

Wishbone Modifications
Top link – Series III with screwed bushes, i.e. shorter link to clear wheel.
Bottom link – Series IV (rubber bushed) and ball swivel.

REAR

Springs X.90620
    187 lb/in. wheel rate

Roll bar –

Dampers Koni
P.V. characteristics
Max. Vel. (ins)
  2 4 6 10 15
Rebound Resist. (lb)
  170 240 280 360 500
Bump Resist. (lb)
  70 150 160 180 210

Tyres: Dunlop 6.50Lx 15 R.6

Pressures: 40 lb/sq.in.

Panhard bar – Fitted at lowest position (2" below current production position)

Appendix 3: Details of the Rally Cars

This Appendix contains details of the rally cars originally collected and stored by Ian Hall and held in the Rootes Competition Department records and from the STOC records. The records detail the date of build – from the Jensen records, which may differ from the registration date - the chassis and engine numbers and a record of the events tackled. There is, perhaps a minor discrepancy in the case of AHP 483B, in that the RAC Rally of 1964 is not noted in the records - although this is probably due to the rally not being officially a "works" event, but was run by the Vitafoam Team.

All of the 'works' Tigers were either in Rootes Carnival Red with a white roof or in Rootes Midnight Blue with a black roof.

REGISTRATION	1st BUILT	CHASSIS	ENGINE	BODY NUMBER
ADU 311B	June 64	B9470011	1051 E7KL	550006
ADU 312B	June 64	B9470012	1054 E7KL	550004
AHP 294B	June 64	B9470014	1056 E7KL	550005 / 563254
AHP 295B	June 64	B9470015	1055 E7KL	550003
AHP 483B	June 64	B9470035 FE	1049 E7KL	550039
FRW 667C	July 65	B9473705 LRO FE	4635 F21KA	563199
FRW 668C	Mar 66	B382001929 LRO FE	4576 F21KA	NIL
RECCE TIGERS				
AHP 293B	June 64	B9470013	1057 E7KL	550002
ERW 729C	Mar 65	9472967 HRO FE	4164 F21KA	562480

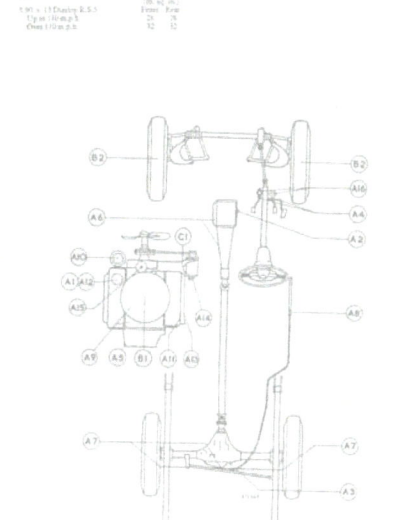

Appendix 3

```
SUNBEAM TIGER          REGISTRATION No. ADU 311 B.      June 1964.

Chassis No. 9470011
Engine No. 1051.E7.KL.FE.
Colour. Red.  -  Blue.
```

Monte Carlo Rally - Recce Car. 1965.	Drivers Peter Harper / Ian Hall.
Tulip Rally 1965.	Drivers Peter Harper / Ian Hall. Non-finisher.
Scottish Rally 1965.	Drivers Andrew Cowan / Allan Redpath. Retired.
Alpine Rally 1965.	Drivers Ian Hall / Don Barrow. Retired.
R.A.C. Rally. 1965.	Drivers Peter Harper / Don Barrow. Retired.
Monte Carlo Rally Recce. 1966.	Drivers Peter Harper / Robin Turvey.
Acropolis Rally 1966.	Drivers Peter Harper / Ian Hall. 7th Overall. 1st in Class.
London Rally 1966.	Drivers Peter Harper / Robin Turvey. Retired.

SOLD.

Appendix 3

SUNBEAM TIGER   REGISTRATION No. ADU 312 B.   June 1964.

Chassis No. 9470012.
Engine No. 1054.E7.KL.FE.
Colour. Red.

Geneva Rally 1964.	3rd in class. Drivers Rosemary Smith / Margaret McKenzie.
Monte Carlo Rally 1965.	4th in General Classification. 1st in Class. Drivers Peter Harper / Ian Hall.
Alpine Rally 1965.	Drivers Peter Harper / Michael Hughes. 1st in G.T. Category, 1st in Class. Coupe des Alpes winner. Disqualification.
Monte Carlo Rally Recce 1966.	Drivers Andrew Cowan / Brian Coyle.
Monte Carlo Rally 1966. (Pathfinder Car).	Drivers Peter Riley / Ann Riley.

SOLD.

N.B. MIRRA TEST   11. 2 65
J ASHWORTH   D. ODELL

Appendix 3

JAL.55 0002

SUNBEAM TIGER   REGISTRATION NO. AHP 293 B.   June 1964.

Chassis No. 9470013 LRX
Engine No. 1057.E7.KL.FE.
Colour. Red.

SOLD.

Alpine Reece

Appendix 3

SUNBEAM TIGER   REGISTRATION No.   AHP 294 B.   June 1964.

Chassis No. 9470014.
Engine No. 1056.E7.KL.FE.
Colour Red.

Geneva Rally 1964.   1st in Class.

                                          Drivers Tiny Lewis / Barry Hughes.

Monte Carlo Rally - Recce Car. 1965. Drivers Andrew Cowan / Robin Turvey.

Tulip Rally 1965.   **Drivers Peter Riley / Robin Turvey.**
                                      Non-finisher.

Alpine Rally 1965.   Drivers Tiny Lewis / Barry Hughes.
                                      Retired.

Monte Carlo Rally 1966.   Drivers Peter Harper / Robin Turvey.
                                      Retired.

Tulip Rally 1966 - Recce Car. Drivers Peter Harper / Robin Turvey.

                                    SOLD.

Appendix 3

SUNBEAM TIGER   REGISTRATION NO. AHP 295 B.   June 1964.

Chassis No. 9470015.
Engine No. 1055.E7.KL/FE.
Colour. Red/White.

Geneva Rally 1964.	2nd in class. Drivers Peter Riley / Robin Turvey.
Monte Carlo Rally 1965.	10th in general classification. 2nd in class. Drivers Andrew Cowan / Robin Turvey.
Tulip Recce Car 1965.	Drivers Peter Riley / Robin Turvey. Peter Harper / Ian Hall.
International Police Rally 1965.	Drivers John Gott / Sgt. Nicholson. Win, outright.
Alpine Rally Recce Car. 1965	Drivers Peter Harper / David Pollard.

SOLD - M. Coombe.

Appendix 3

SUNBEAM TIGER REGISTRATION No. AHP 483 B. August 1964.

Chassis No. 9470035 LRX.
Engine No. 1049.E7.KL.FE.
Colour. Red. (Vitafoam).

Targa Florio 1965. Drivers Peter Harper / Rupert Jones.
2nd in Class.

SOLD.

Appendix 3

SUNBEAM TIGER.   REGISTRATION No. ERW 729 C   First registered. 1.4.65

Chassis No. 9472967 HRO FE
Engine No.
Colour - Blue.

Brands Hatch Six Hour Race 1965.   Drivers M. Nunn / P. Brown.

Alpine Rally Recce Car 1965.   Drivers Tiny Lewis / Barry Hughes.

Service Car R.A.C. Rally 1965.   Drivers Marcus Chambers / Derek Hughes.

Service Car - Monte Carlo Rally.   Drivers Marcus Chambers / G. Sloniger.
    1966.

Sold - K. Ballisat (Shell.)

Appendix 3

SUNBEAM TIGER.　　　　REGISTRATION No.　FRW 667 C　　18 December 1965.

Chassis No.　B.9473705. LRO FE.
Engine No.　4635
Colour.　Blue - white.

Monte Carlo Rally 1966.　　　　Drivers - Andrew Cowan/Brian Coyle.

　　　　　　　　　　　　　　　　　　　　None finisher.

Sold - Tiny Lewis.

Appendix 3

SUNBEAM TIGER.   REGISTRATION No. FRW 668 C.   March 1966.

Chassis No. B.382001929.
Engine No.
Colour.   Blue.

Tulip Rally 1966.   Drivers - Peter Harper / Robin Turvey.
                         3rd Overall. 1st in G.T. Category.

SOLD.

Appendix 4: Summary of Results by Rally

This Appendix details the events entered by the Rootes Competition Department, with the identity of car and crew.

Additionally shown are the competition number with the results in both overall position (o/a) and class position (cl).

The Appendix also contains information on the recce cars and, in one case, where a Tiger was used as a service support vehicle - complete with high-speed trailer!

Appendix 4

DATE	EVENT	VEHICLE	CREW	NO.	O/A	CL
Sept. 64	San Martino di Castrozza	ADU 311B	'Tiny' Lewis/Ian Hall	101	DNF	-
Oct. 64	Geneva	AHP 294B	'Tiny' Lewis/Barry Hughes	1	11	1
		AHP 295B	Peter Riley/Robin Turvey	2	15	2
		ADU 312B	Ros. Smith/M Mackenzie	3	20	3
Nov. 64	RAC	AHP 483B	Rupert Jones/John Clegg	43	-	-
Jan. 65	Monte Carlo	ADU 312B	Peter Harper/Ian Hall	107	4	1
		AHP 295B	Andrew Cowan/Robin Turvey	103	11	2
		AHP 294B	M. Gatsonides/A.Ilken (AC/RT recce car)	186	DNF	-
		ADU 311B	(Harper/Hall recce car)	-	-	-
Apr. 65	Tulip	ADU 311B	Peter Harper/Ian Hall	1	DNF	-
		AHP 294B	Peter Riley/Robin Turvey	2	DNF	-
		AHP 295B	(PH/IH and PR/RT recce car)	-	-	-
June 65	Scottish	ADU 311B	Andrew Cowan/Alan Redpath	-	DNF	-
July 65	Alpine	ADU 311B	Ian Hall/Don Barrow	136	DNF	-
		ADU 312B	Peter Harper/Mike Hughes	134	DSQ	-
		AHP 294B	'Tiny' Lewis/Barry Hughes	138	DNF	-
		AHP 295B	(PH/David Pollard recce car)	-	-	-
		AHP 293B	recce car	-	-	-
		ERW 729C	(TL/BH recce car)	-	-	-
May 65	Int. Police	AHP 295B	John Gott/D. Nicholson	4	1	1
May 65	Targa Florio	AHP 483B	Peter Harper/Rupert Jones	192	-	2
Nov. 65	RAC	ADU 311B	Peter Harper/Don Barrow	20	DNF	-
		ERW 729C	(Marcus Chambers/Derek Hughes: service with trailer!)	-	-	-
Jan. 66	Monte Carlo	AHP 294B	Peter Harper/Robin Turvey	150	DNF	-
		FRW 667C	Andrew Cowan/Brian Coyle	105	DNF	-
		ADU 311B	(PH/RT recce car)	-	-	-
		ADU 312B	(AC/BC recce car and Peter Riley pathfinder car)	-	-	-
		ERW 729C	(Marcus Chambers/Gerry Sloniger (service))	-	-	-
Apr. 66	Tulip	FRW 668C	Peter Harper/Robin Turvey	1	3	1
		AHP 294B	(PH/RT recce car)	-	-	-
May 66	Acropolis	ADU 311B	Peter Harper/Ian Hall	1	7	1
June 66	Gulf London	ADU 311B	Peter Harper/Robin Turvey	-	DNF	-

Appendix 5: Events and Cars by Crews

This Appendix shows the events competed by each of the crews with the vehicle and result. It highlights the effort expended by Peter Harper, Robin Turvey and Ian Hall in the history of the works Tigers, these three crew-members putting in the major share of the effort over the times that the cars were in competition.

Crew	Event	Year	Car	Role	Position	Class
Peter Harper	Monte Carlo	1965	ADU 312B	Driver	4th	1st class
	Tulip	1965	ADU 311B	Driver	DNF	
	Alpine	1965	ADU 312B	Driver	DSQ	
	Targa Florio	1965	AHP 483B	Driver		2nd class
	RAC	1965	ADU 311B	Driver	DNF	
	Monte Carlo	1966	AHP 294B	Driver	DNF	
	Tulip	1966	FRW 668C	Driver	3rd	1st class
	Acropolis	1966	ADU 311B	Driver	7th	1st class
	Gulf London	1966	ADU 311B	Driver	DNF	
Robin Turvey	Geneva	1964	AHP 295B	Co-driver	15th	2nd class
	Monte Carlo	1966	AHP 295B	Co-driver	11th	2nd class
	Tulip	1965	AHP 294B	Co-driver	DNF	
	Monte Carlo	1966	AHP 294B	Co-driver	DNF	
	Tulip	1966	FRW 668C	Co-driver	3rd	1st class
	Gulf London	1966	ADU 311B	Co-driver	DNF	
Ian Hall	San Martino di Castrozza	1964	ADU 311B	Co-driver	DNF	
	Monte Carlo	1965	ADU 312B	Co-driver	4th	1st class
	Tulip	1965	ADU 311B	Co-driver	DNF	
	Alpine	1965	AHP 295B	Driver	DNF	
	Acropolis	1966	ADU 311B	Co-driver	7th	1st class
Andrew Cowan	Monte Carlo	1965	AHP 295B	Driver	11th	1st class
	Scottish	1965	ADU 311B	Driver	DNF	
	Monte Carlo	1966	FRW 667C	Driver	DNF	
'Tiny' Lewis	San Martino di Castrozza	1964	ADU 311B	Driver	DNF	
	Geneva	1964	AHP 294B	Driver	11th	1st class
	Alpine	1965	ADU 311B	Driver	DNF	
Peter Riley	Geneva	1964	AHP 295B	Driver	15th	2nd class
	Tulip	1965	AHP 294B	Driver	DNF	
Barry Hughes	Geneva	1964	AHP 294B	Co-driver	11th	1st class
	Alpine	1965	ADU 311B	Co-driver	DNF	
Don Barrow	Alpine	1965	AHP 295B	Co-driver	DNF	
	RAC	1965	ADU 311B	Co-driver	DNF	
Rupert Jones	RAC	1964	AHP 483B	Driver		
	Targa Florio	1965	AHP 483B	Driver		2nd class
Rosemary Smith	Geneva	1964	ADU 312B	Driver	20th	3rd class
Margaret Mackenzie	Geneva	1964	ADU 312B	Co-driver	20th	3rd class
Brian Coyle	Monte Carlo	1966	FRW 667C	Co-driver	DNF	
John Gott	Int. Police	1965	AHP 295B	Driver	1st	1st class
D. Nicholson	Int. Police	1965	AHP 295B	Co-driver	1st	1st class
Mike Hughes	Alpine	1965	ADU 312B	Co-driver	DSQ	
John Clegg	RAC	1964	AHP 483B	Co-driver		
Allan Redpath	Scottish	1965	ADU 311B	Co-driver	DNF	

Appendix 5

SUNBEAM UNLEASH THE TIGER

V8
4·2 litre engine
0-60 m.p.h. in 9·2 secs
top speed over 120 m.p.h.

At last! Powerful performance and placid personality in one car – the Sunbeam Tiger, now available to discerning drivers who appreciate ease of driving with fantastic acceleration, road holding and handling. 164 bhp project the Tiger from 0-60 mph in 9·2 seconds with a top speed above 120 mph. Spur this performance through 4 well-chosen gears; or pad along knowing there's power enough for top gear acceleration from 20 mph. Add firm suspension, extremely good fuel economy, rack-and-pinion steering, servo-assisted brakes with front discs, plus fully-adjustable seats, walnut facia and full instrumentation and you've got the supreme sports car for race track, rally circuit, motorway or town traffic. £1,445.10.5 inc £250.10.5 pt.

BY APPOINTMENT TO
HER MAJESTY THE QUEEN
MOTOR VEHICLE
MANUFACTURERS
ROOTES MOTORS LIMITED

ROOTES MOTORS LIMITED

LONDON SHOWROOMS AND EXPORT
DIVISION ROOTES LIMITED DEVONSHIRE
HOUSE PICCADILLY LONDON W1

SUNBEAM TIGER'S RECORD TO DATE...

1965 Monte Carlo Rally
1st and 2nd Over 2,500 cc GT Class   4th Overall

1964 Geneva Rally 1st 2nd 3rd   Over 2,500 cc GT Class.

1964 Pacific Divisional Championships
1st in Class 'B' production event.

1964 US 200-Mile National Sports Car Race
1st in Class   2nd overall

Also Dutch National 24-hour Speed Record   February 9th, 1965.

SUNBEAM TIGER

Appendix 6: FIA Homologation details (forms of Recognition) and USA 'homologation' notes

> **APPENDIX "J"** 235
>
> (h) *Recognition Forms.* All cars recognised by the F.I.A. shall be subject to a descriptive form called Recognition Form on which shall be entered all data required to identify the said model.
>
> To this effect only the standard recognition forms and standard additional form for "normal evolution of the type" and "variant" approved by the F.I.A. shall be used by all A.C.N's.
>
> The production of the forms at scrutineering and/or at the start may be required by the promoters who will be entitled to refuse the participation of the entrant in the event in case of non-production.
>
> In the case of any doubt remaining after the checking of a model of car against its homologation form, the scrutineers would have to refer themselves either to the maintenance booklet printed for the benefit of the make's distributors or to the general catalogue in which are listed all spare parts.
>
> It will rest with the competitor to obtain the recognition form and, if need be, the additional forms concerning his car, from the A.C.N. of the manufacturing country of the vehicle.
>
> **Forms of cars of British manufacture are obtainable only from the R.A.C. at a fee of £1.10.0. Money must be submitted with the order.**

The homologation forms laid out the full details of the dimensions, weights and detail of the production vehicle. This set out the exact specification to which the car could be built and the components that could be fitted. The accompanying FIA regulations set out the more general modifications that could be made to a vehicle when it fell within the categories specified (e.g. Touring Category: Group 1 - Series Touring Cars, Group 2 - Improved Touring Cars or Group 3 - Grand Touring Cars etc.)

The FIA regulations were set by the overall governing body, and the category was identified by the number of cars produced in that year. For instance, in 1964, Group 1 cars 'must have been manufactured in series at a minimum of 1000 units in 12 consecutive months and be identical as far as mechanism and coachwork are concerned'. In 1966 this was changed to 5000 units. The Tiger was classified under group 3 – Grand Touring Cars – for which, in 1964 and 65, 100 identical units had to be produced in the 12 consecutive months. In 1966, with the change in regulations, this became 500 units.

The FIA regulations categorised the group of car from its production figures and defined the modifications authorised in its own overall regulations (see Appendix 7). Specified modifications were allowed for each group, and changes could be made to lighting devices, fuel and oil tanks, cooling circuits, electrical equipment, spark plugs, transmission, brakes etc

Appendix 6

When the rally engineers had decided how they could best take advantage of the regulations, the details were entered in the Homologation Form and the Homologation Form forwarded and accepted, or rejected, by the FIA. From then on the Homologation Form was the document by which the vehicle was always judged at any form of scrutineering. Any discrepancy from the details entered on the Form, at any technical scrutineering, either pre or post rally, usually resulted in disqualification – even if it was not deliberate - as Rootes found in July 1965 at the post rally scrutineering of the Alpine Rally.

In its competition life the Tiger had three Homologation Forms. The first form of Recognition (FOR 176) was valid from 11 July 1964 and, being the first issue, would have been the one that Ian Hall and 'Tiny' Lewis used on the first rally for the Tiger – San Martino di Castrozza on the 12th to 14th of September 1964.

This form was used through until the Alpine Rally in mid July 1965, when post rally scrutineering found the poppet valve head diameter to be under that specified in FOR176.

A second Homologation Form was issued (FOR 211) and made valid by the FIA from 1 August 1965, which altered the valve sizes from the incorrect 49.25 mm inlet / 42.85 mm exhaust to the correct 42mm / 37mm diameters. The original valve diameters in the FOR 176 were the same as those entered in the Shelby Cobra ACC-US FIA recognition form of 30th November 1962.

The Tiger FOR changed for the last time due the change in FIA Regulations starting in the 1966 year. Amongst other changes, the Tiger had to run on a more standard carburettor and all of these changes were made in this final Form of Recognition 509.

All of the forms also contained pages that specified those items which could be used within the FIA authorised modifications, but were not part of the production vehicle. These were called 'Supplements to the Form of Recognition' and included items such as the Minilite magnesium wheels, Limited Slip differentials, Final drive ratios, the quick steering rack etc, etc. If alternative width wheels were used, then the associated changes to front and rear track had also to be accurately specified.

In this appendix, all three of the Homologation Forms are shown, partially because the history of the Tiger must have been exceptional - with three Forms in three years – but mainly for historical reasons. All three Homologation Forms were similar in the details apart from a few areas. In FORs 176 and 211, the Competition Department optimistically set the overall weight of the Tiger at 980 kg. Of course, this enthusiastic view of homologated vehicle weight was shared by all the main manufacturers, who, in practice, pared as much weight as possible off the rally cars to improve the power to weight ratios – but very rarely did any of them achieve the actual homologated weight in competition. In the last FOR 509, Rootes finally set the weight at 1147 kg, which was considerably closer to the production weight. In Appendix 8 – the Tiger performance figures - the weight of the standard Tiger under test is given as 2984 lb (1356 kg) and the rally Tigers as 25 cwt (2800 lb or 1272 kg) – so the level of calculated optimism is now clear to see.

Differences are notable in the total fuel capacities that the Tiger could carry. In all three forms the standard capacity is quoted as 52 litres (11.25 Imp gal), but in the three FORs the total fuel capacities, using standard and supplementary tanks, were quoted as 140litres, 117 litres and 87.6 litres (176, 211 & 509 respectively). Also the additional final drives that were homologated varied from six in FOR 176, to three in FOR 211 to finally one (3.77) in FOR 509. Similarly for camshafts, all three FORs had different valve lifts and different cam timing.

This appendix also includes, and starts off with, a set of homologation notes that the Rootes competition engineer, Des O'Dell, carried as an 'aide memoire'.

The 'homologations' in the USA were somewhat different and generally needed far fewer sales than the equivalent European requirement. For the USA 1965 season, it was necessary for the

Appendix 6

manufacturer's authorized optional equipment for the Tiger to have been offered for sale and at least 100 units produced in that preceding year (i.e. by December 1964).

The 1965 US Production Category Recognition Form is illustrated after the FIA Homologation Form. Whilst the reproduction is not the best – but just readable - it comes directly from Des O'Dell's original notes from Ian Garrad. The photographs are the originals (still stuck to the paper, although some are missing in the original sheets) and are included as they may be of some longer-term historical interest.

TIGER HOMOLOGATION

FORMS OF RECOGNITION ACC-US F.I.A. F.I.A. R.A.C. 176 F.I.A. R.A.C. 211 F.I.A. R.A.C. 509	SHELBY COBRA 30.11.1962 Ford V8 289 4727 Ltrs. Form of Recognition	SUNBEAM TIGER 11.07.1964 Ford V8 260 4260 cc Form of Recognition 176	TIGER ALPINE 260 01.08.1965 Ford v8 260 4260 cc Form of Recognition 211	SUNBEAM TIGER 01.01.1966 Ford V8 260 4261 cc Form of Recognition 509
Comp. Ratio	12:1	10:1	10:1	8.8:1
Bore	101.6 mm	96.5 mm	96.5 mm	96.5 mm
Stroke	72.9 mm	72.8 mm	72.8 mm	73 mm
Vol. of one combustion chamber	47.5 cc	47.5 cc	47.5 cc	66.4 / 702
Inlet valve diameter	49.25 mm	49.25 mm	42 mm	42.6 mm Max
Exhaust valve diameter	42.85 mm	42.85 mm	37 mm	37 mm Max
Carb. Type Make Model Number Choke	Down draught Weber 481DM 4 off 45 mm	Down draught Ford C 4 off - AL 4BBL 1 off 27 Primary 29.5 Secondary	Down draught Ford C 4 off - AL 4BBL 1 off 27 Primary 29.5 Secondary	Down draught Ford, 2 Barrel C4 DF 9510 - E 1 off Dia. of Venturi 25.65 mm
Alternative Carb.		Holley C4AF DAA 3LD 4 Choke Down Draught Choke Dia. Prim. 35 mm Sec. 35 mm Main Jet Ident. Prim. 76 Sec. 01	Ford Twin Choke Down Draught C4DF 9510E Choke Dia. 25.65 m Main Jet Ident. 44F	

Page 1 of Des O'Dells homologation 'aide memoire'.

Appendix 6

Engine and Car Performance				
Max. Eng. output				164 BHP at 4,400 rpm
Max. rpm				4,700 rpm 258 LB.F.T.A
Max torque				2,200 rpm
Max. Car speed				192 kmh 120 mph
Capacities				
Fuel Tank	140 Ltrs.	52 Ltrs. 11.25 galls	52 Ltrs. 11.25 galls	52 Ltrs. 11.25 galls
Radiator	17 Ltrs	8.2 Ltrs	15.3 Ltrs.	15.3 Ltrs. 27 pints
Sump	10 Ltrs	6.8 Ltrs	6.8 Ltrs	4.8 Ltrs. 8.5 pints
Supplementary Fuel Tank		Additional Tank Total Fuel - 140 Ltrs.	Additional Tank Total Fuel - 117 Ltrs.	Supp. Fuel Tank Kit 36.5 Ltrs 8.5galls All tanks 87 Ltrs 19.75galls
Oil Cooler		Radiator Type Add. 4 pints oil to sump	Radiator Type Add. 1.5 pints oil to sump Larger type available with increased capacity	
Trop. Radiator			Available with increased capacity	
Alternative Sump.		Available total oil capacity 10.2 Ltrs.	Available capacity 8 Ltrs.	

NB. S.U. Petrol pump used throughout. All batteries situated in luggage compartment

1966 Homologation Form: FIA Recognition No 509

F.I.A. Recognition No. **509**
Group **3.** ~~Grand~~ Grand Touring

ROYAL AUTOMOBILE CLUB

31, Belgrave Square, London, S.W.1.

Form of recognition in accordance with
Appendix J to the International Sporting Code of the

FEDERATION INTERNATIONALE DE L'AUTOMOBILE

Manufacturer... Rootes Group. Sunbeam Talbot Ltd.   Cylinder-capacity.. 4261 ...cm3... 260 ...in3
Serial No. of chassis. B.9470001   Model... Tiger
engine. 1000   Manufacturer... Sunbeam Talbot Ltd.
Recognition is valid from... **1st Jan 1966**   Manufacturer... Ford Motor Co. Ltd. U.S.A.
List.. **14**

The manufacturing of the model described in this recognition form was started on
..1st July.....19.64 and the minimum production of....500.......identical cars,
in accordance with the specifications of this form was reached on..31st.Oct..1964

Photograph A, ¾ view of car from front

F.I.A. Stamp

R.A.C. Stamp

Page 1

Appendix 6

No. 509

<u>Federation Internationale de l'Automobile.</u>
<u>Supplement to Form of Recongition.</u>

<u>Manufacturer:</u>   Sunbeam Talbot Limited.

<u>Model:</u>   Sunbeam Tiger.

1. Variation available in the form of detachable hard top :-

Photograph A, 3/4 view of car from front.

Photograph B, 3/4 view of car from rear.

1.

Appendix 6

Make Sunbeam   Model Tiger.   F.I.A. Rec.no. 509

Page 2

Appendix 6

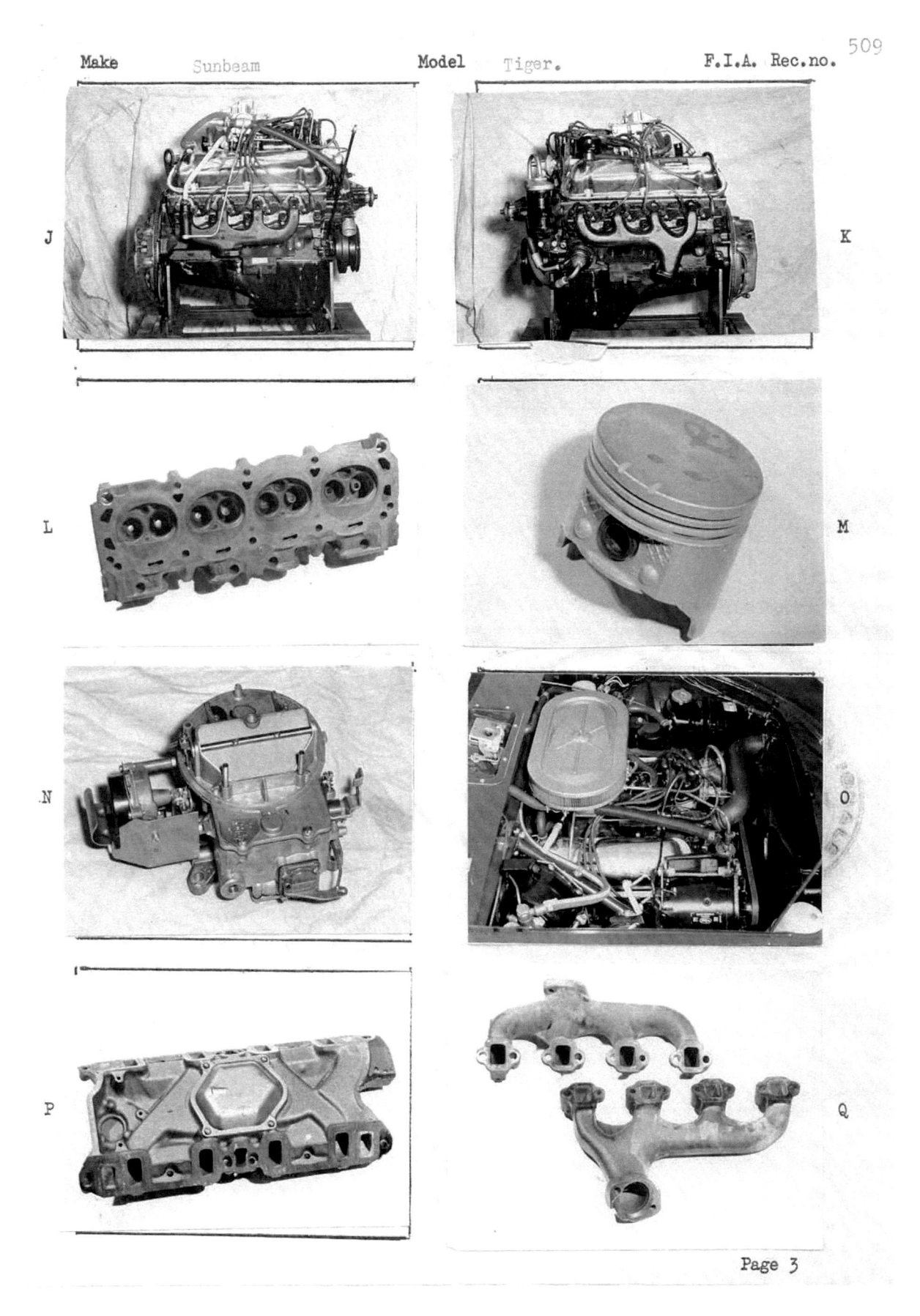

Make Sunbeam   Model Tiger.   F.I.A. Rec. no. 509

J

K

L

M

N

P

Q

Page 3

Make Sunbeam		Model Tiger.	F.I.A. Rec.no. 509

Drawing inlet manifold ports, side of cylinderhead. Indicate scale or dimensions and manufacturing tolerance.

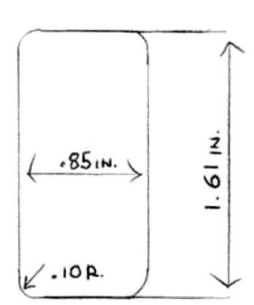

.85 IN., 1.61 IN., .10 R.

Cast in Manifold

Drawing of entrance to inlet port of cylinderhead. Indicate scale or dimensions and manufacturing tolerance.

.98 IN., 1.77 IN., .10 R

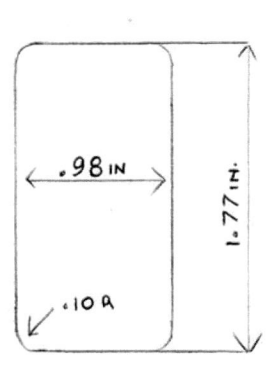

Cast in Cylinder Head

Drawing of exhaust manifold ports, side of cylinderhead. Indicate scale or dimensions and manufacturing tolerance.

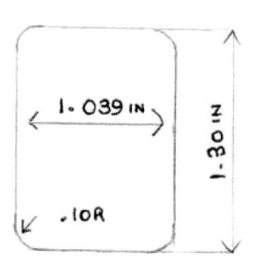

1.039 IN., 1.30 IN., .10 R

Cast in Manifold

Drawing of exit to exhaust port of cylinderhead. Indicate scale or dimensions and manufacturing tolerance.

1.015 IN., 1.035 IN., 10. R

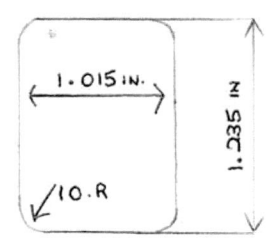

Cast in Cylinder Head

Page 4

Appendix 6

Make Sunbeam.   Model Tiger.   F.I.A. Rec.no. 509

<u>NOTE 1.</u>   All dimensions must be given in two measuring systems, see Note 3.
           <u>CAPACITIES AND DIMENSIONS.</u>

1.   Wheelbase   2184   mm   86   inches.
2.   Front track   1331   3. Rear track.   1229.3
     mm.   52.4   inches.   mm.   48.4   inches.

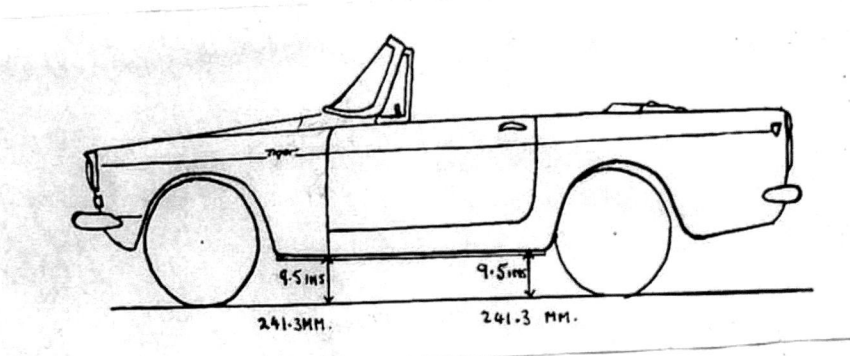

[Drawing of Sunbeam Tiger side view with measurements: 9.5 ins / 241.3 mm at front and rear]

4.   Overall length of the car   3962   cm.   156   inches.
5.   Overall width of the car   1537   cm.   60.5   inches.
6.   Overall height of the car   1308   cm.   51.5   inches.
7.   Capacity of fuel tank (reserve included)
            51.143 ltrs.   13.5 Gall.US   11.25 Gall.Imp.
8.   Seating Capacity   2.
9.   Weight. total weight of the car with normal equipment, water, oil,
     and spare wheel but without fuel or repair tools:

     1124.474 (soft top) kg.   2479 (soft top) lb.   22.1 (soft top) cwts.
     1147.154 (hard top)   2529 (hard top)   22.58 (hard top)

<u>NOTE 2.</u>

Differences in track caused by the use of other wheels with different
rim widths must be stated when recognition is requested for the
wheels concerned. Specify ground clearance in relation to the track
and give drawing of two easily recognisable points at front and rear
at which measurements are taken. These ground clearance dimensions
are only for information when checking the track and can in no way
affect the eligibility of the car.

<u>NOTE 3.</u>   <u>CONVERSION TABLE.</u>

     1 inch/pouce   - 2.54 cm.   1 quart US.   - 0.9464 ltrs
     1 foot/pied   - 30.4794 cm.   1 pint (pt)   - 0.568 ltrs
     1 sq.inch/pouce carre   - 6.452 cm2.   1 gallon Imp.   - 4.546 ltrs
     1 cubic inch/pouce cube - 16.387 cm3.   1 gallon US.   - 3.785 ltrs
     1 pound/livre (lb)   -453.593 gr.   1 hundred weight(cwt) 50.802 kg.

Page 5.

Appendix 6

Make   Sunbeam.   Model   Tiger   F.I.A. Rec. no. 509

CHASSIS AND COACHWORK (Photographs A, B and C)

20. Chassis/body construction : ~~separate~~ / unitary construction
21. Unitary construction, material(s)   Pressed steel with fibre hood.

SEPARATE CONSTRUCTION - MATERIALS

22. Chassis   23. Coachwork
24. Number of doors   2   Material(s)   Pressed steel.
25. Bonnet   Pressed steel   26. Boot Lid   Pressed steel.
27. Rear Window   I.C.I. 'Vybak'   28. Windscreen   Triplex laminated glass
29. Front door windows   Triplex safety (toughened) glass   30. Rear door windows   none.
31. Sliding system of door windows   Winding vertical
32. Material(s) of rear-quarter light   Safety-glass (on detachable hard-top variant only)

ACCESSORIES AND UPHOLSTERY

38. Interior heating : yes - ~~no~~   39. Air conditioning : ~~yes~~ - no
40. Ventillation : yes - ~~no~~
41. Front seats, type of upholstery   I.C.I. 'Ambla'.
42. Weight of front seat(s), complete with supports and rails, out of the car:

    11.34 kg.   25   lbs.

43. Rear seats, type of upholstery   nil.
44. Front bumper, material(s)   Chrome plated steel   Weight   7 kg.   15.24 lbs.
45. Rear bumper, material(s)   "   "   Weight   7 kg.   15.24 lbs.

WHEELS

50. Type   Disc
51. Weight (per wheel, without tyre)   5.76 kg.
52. Method of attachment   4 studs and nuts
53. Rim diameter   330.2 mm.   13   ins.
54. Rim width   114.2 mm.   4.5 ins.

STEERING

60. Type   Rack and Pinion
61. Servo-assistance : ~~yes~~ - no
62. Number of turns of steering wheel from lock to lock   3.1
63. In case of servo-assistance.   nil

Appendix 6

Make   Sunbeam   Model   Tiger.   F.I.A. Rec.no. 509

SUSPENSION

70. Front suspension (photograph D), type   I:F.S. S/L Wishbone
71. Type of spring   Coil
72. Stabiliser (if fitted)   Front - transverse Torsion Bar
73. Number of shock absorbers 2   74. Type   Telescopic
78. Rear suspension (photograph E), type   Orthodox, beam axle.
79. Type of spring   Semi-elliptic leaf.
80. Stabiliser (if fitted)   Panhard Bar.
81. Number of shock absorbers 2   82. Type   Direct acting Telescopic

BRAKES (photographs F and G)

90. Method of operation   Hydraulic
91. Servo-assistance (if fitted), type   Vacuum Servo
92. Number of hydraulic master cylinders   1

	FRONT		REAR	
93. Number of cylinders per wheel	2		1	
94. Bore of wheel cylinder(s)	54 mm.	2.125 inches	19 mm.	.75 inches
Drum Brakes				
95. Inside diameter	mm.	inches	229 mm.	9 inches
96. Length of brake linings	mm.	inches	218 mm.	8.6 inches
97. Width of brake linings	mm.	inches	44.4 mm.	1.75 inches
98. Number of shoes per brake 2	mm.	inches	mm.	inches
99. Total area per brake	mm2	sq.in.	194.8 mm2	30.2 sq.in.
Disc Brakes				
100. Outside diameter	250 mm.	9.85 inches	mm.	inches
101. Thickness of disc	12.7 mm.	0.50 inches	mm.	inches
102. Length of brake ~~linings~~ Pad Tapers	Max- 73.66 mm. 2.9 / Min- 53.34 mm. 2.1	inches	mm.	inches
103. Width of brake linings	52 mm.	2.05 inches	mm.	inches
104. Number of pads per brake	2			
105. Total area per brake	67.1 mm2	10.4 sq.in.	mm2	sq.in.

Appendix 6

Make   Sunbeam   Model   Tiger.   F.I.A. Rec.no. 509

ENGINE (photographs J and K)

130. Cycle   4   131. Number of cylinders   8
132. Cylinder Arrangement   90° in V
133. Bore   96.5   mm.   3.80 in. 134. Stroke 73   mm.   2.87 in.
135. Capacity per cylinder   532.6   cm3   32.5 cu.in.
136. Total cylinder capacity   4261   cm3   260   cu.in.
137. Material(s) of cylinder block   Cast iron.
138. Material(s) of sleeves (if fitted)   none.
139. Cylinder head, material(s) Cast iron   Number fitted   2
140. Number of inlet ports   8   141. Number of exhaust ports   8
142. Compression ratio   8.8 : 1
143. Volume of one combustion chamber   66.4 / 70.2   68.3   cm3   4.16 cu.in.
144. Piston, material Aluminium alloy Tin Plated   145. Number of rings   2 compression and 1 scraper
146. Distance from gudgeon pin centre line to highest point of piston crown
                                              40.665 mm.   1.601 in.
147. Crankshaft : ~~moulded~~ / Stamped   Cast   148. Type of crankshaft : integral/...Yes..
149. Number of crankshaft main bearings   5
150. Material of bearing cap   Cast iron.
151. System of lubrication : ~~dry sump~~ / oil in sump
152. Capacity, lubricant   4.83 ltrs.   8.5 IMP pts.   5 Quarts U.S.
153. Oil cooler : yes / no   154. Method of engine cooling Water (Pump)
155. Capacity of cooling system 15.3 ltrs. 27   pts. 16.2 quarts U.S.
156. Cooling fan (if fitted) dia.   355   cm.   14   in.
157. Number of blades of cooling fan   4

Bearings

158. Crankshaft main, type Steel shell implated copper lead.   Dia. 57.09/57.11 mm. 2.2482/2.2490 in.
159. Connecting rod, big end Steel shell copper lead alloy lined   Dia. 53.91/53.93 mm. 2.1228/2.1236 in.

Weights

160. Flywheel (clean)   9   kg.   lbs.
161. Flywheel with clutch (all turning parts).   18   kg.   40 lbs.
162. Crankshaft   17 kg.   37.25 lbs. 163. Connecting rod .6 kg. 1.33 lbs.
164. Piston with rings and pin   0.794 kg.   1.75 lbs.

Page 8

Appendix 6

Date   Sunbeam   Model   Tiger.   F.I.A. Rec.no. 509

FOUR STROKE ENGINES

170. Number of camshafts   1   171. Location   Centre of Vee.
172. Type of camshaft drive   Chain
173. Type of valve operation   Push Rod.

INLET (see page 4)*

180. Material(s) of inlet manifold   Cast iron
181. Diameter of valves   Min 42.2 mm.   1.661 ins.
                          Max 42.6   1.677
182. Max. valve lift 9.169 mm. .361 in.   183. Number of valve springs   1
184. Type of spring   Coil   185. Number of valves per cylinder   1
186. Tappet clearance for checking timing (cold)   2.083 mm.   0.082 ins.
                                                   3.861   0.152
187. Valves open at (with tolerance for tappet clearance indicated) 21° B.T.D.C.
188. Valves close at (with tolerance for tappet clearance indicated) 51° A.B.D.C.
189. Air filter, type   A.C. Paper Element.

EXHAUST (see page 4)

195. Material(s) of exhaust manifold   Cast iron.
196. Diameter of valves Min. 36.6   mm.   1.441 ins.
                       Max. 37.0   1.457
197. Max. valve lift 9.169 mm. .361 in.   198. Number of valve springs   1
199. Type of spring   Coil   200. Number of valves per cylinder   1
201. Tappet clearance for checking timing (cold)   2.083 mm.   0.082 ins.
                                                   3.861   0.152
202. Valves open at (with tolerance for tappet clearance indicated) 57° B.B.D.C.
203. Valves close at (with tolerance for tappet clearance indicated) 15° A.T.D.C.

CARBURETION (photograph N)

210. Number of carburettors fitted   1   211. Type   2 barrel
212. Make   Ford.   213. Model   C.4 DF. 9510 - E
214. Number of mixture passages per carburettor   4
215. Flange hole diameter of exit port(s) of carburettor   36.51mm.   1.4575 ins.
216. Minimum diameter of venturi/~~minimum diam. with piston at maximum height~~
                                                   25.65 mm.   1.010 ins.

INJECTION (if fitted)   nil.

220. Make of pump   221. Number of plungers
222. Model or type of pump   223. Total number of injectors
224. Location of injectors
225. Minimum diameter of inlet pipe   mm.   ins.

* For additional information concerning two-stroke engines and super-charged engines, see page 13.

Appendix 6

Make   Sunbeam   Model   Tiger.   F.I.A. Rec.no. 509

ENGINE ACCESSORIES

230. Fuel pump : ~~mechanical and~~/or electric.
231. No. fitted   1
232. Type of ignition system   Coil   233. No. of distributors   1
234. No. of ignition coils   1   235. No. of spark plugs per cylinder   1
236. Generator, number fitted   1   237. Method of drive   Belt
238. Voltage of generator   12   volts. 239. Battery, number   1
240. Location   In luggage compartment
241. Voltage of battery   12   volts

ENGINE AND CAR PERFORMANCES (as declared by manufacturer in catalogue)

250. Max. engine output   164   (type of horsepower; Gross B.HP.) at 4,400 rpm
251. Max. rpm   4,700   output at that figure   not available for publication.
252. Max torque   258 lb. ft.   at   2,200   rpm
253. Max speed of the car   192   km/hour   120   miles/hour

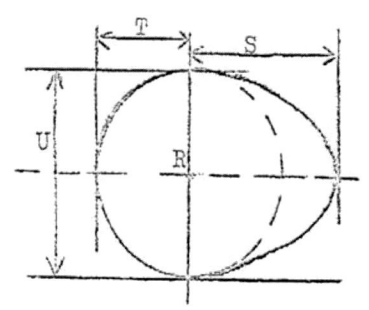

R = centre of camshaft.

Inlet cam
S = 24.676   mm. 0.9715 inches
T = 18.555   mm. 0.7305 inches
U = 37.465   mm. 1.4750 inches

Exhaust cam
S = 24.676   mm. 0.9715 inches
T = 18.555   mm. 0.7305 inches
U = 37.592   mm. 1.480 inches

Appendix 6

Make   Sunbeam   Model Tiger.   F.I.A. Rec.no. 509

DRIVE TRAIN

CLUTCH

260. Type of clutch Ford dry plate.   261. No of plates Single dry plate
262. Dia. of clutch plates   25.4   cm.   10   ins..
263. Dia. of linings, inside   17.145   cm.   6.75   ins.
                       outside   25.4   cm.   10   ins.
264. Method of operating clutch   Hydraulic with centrifugal assistance

GEAR BOX (photograph H)

270. Manual type, make   Ford type H E H - E
271. No. of gear-box ratios forward 4   272. Synchronized forward ratios 4
273. Location of gear-shift   Centre floor
274. Automatic, make   -   type -
275. No. of forward ratios -   276. Location of gear shift -

HEH C   HEH-B-

277.	Manual		Automatic		Alternative manual / automatic			
	Ratio	No.teeth	Ratio	No.teeth	Ratio	No.teeth	Ratio	No.teeth
1	2.32:1	$\frac{23}{25} \times \frac{32}{15}$			2.78	$\frac{30}{23} \times \frac{32}{15}$		
2	1.69	$\frac{23}{25} \times \frac{28}{18}$			1.93	$\frac{30}{23} \times \frac{31}{21}$		
3	1.29	$\frac{23}{25} \times \frac{25}{1}$			1.36	$\frac{30}{23} \times \frac{25}{24}$		
4	1.0	Direct			1.0	Direct		
5								
6								
reverse					2.32			

278. Overdrive, type   -
279. Forward gears on which overdrive can be selected   -
280. Overdrive ratio

FINAL DRIVE

290. Type of final drive   Semi floating. Hypoid (Salisbury 4 HA)
291. Type of differential   Double gears
292. Type of limited slip differential (if fitted)   -
293. Final drive ratio 2.88 : 1
     Number of teeth   49 and 17

Make Sunbeam   Model Tiger.   F.I.A. Rec.No. 509

<u>IMPORTANT</u> - The conformity of the car with the following items of the present recognition form is to be disregarded during the scrutineering, when the vehicle has been entered in group 2 (Touring cars) or 3 (Grand Touring cars): 41, 72, 80, 91, 142, 143, 144, 145, 146, 153, 156, 157, 160, 161, 162, 163, 164, 182, 184, 186, 187, 188, 189, 199, 201, 202, 203, 212, 213, 215, 216, 222, 225, 230, 250, 251, 252, 253, and photographs I, M and N.

During the scrutineering of cars entered in group 4 (sportscars) only the following items of the present recognition form are to be taken into consideration: 1,2,3,9,20, 21, 22, 23, 24, 25, 26, 70, 71, 78, 79, 90, 130, 131, 132, 133, 134, 135, 136, 137, 138, 139, 140, 141, 147, 148, 149, 150, 158, 159, 170, 171, 172, 173, 185, 200, 270, 271, 274, 275, 290, 291, 292 and photographs A, B, D, E, F, G, H, J, K and O.

The vehicle described in this form has been subject to the following amendments:

on..........19.. rec.no..........List.......on...........19.. rec.no..........List.....
on..........19.. rec.no..........List.......on...........19.. rec.no..........List.....
on..........19.. rec.no..........List.......on...........19.. rec.no..........List.....
on..........19.. rec.no..........List.......on...........19.. rec.no..........List.....
on..........19.. rec.no..........List.......on...........19.. rec.no..........List.....

Optional equipment affecting preceeding information. This to be stated together with reference number.

Page 12

Appendix 6

No. 509

FEDERATION INTERNATIONAL DE L'AUTOMOBILE.
SUPPLEMENT TO FORM OF RECOGNITION.

Manufacturer: Sunbeam Talbot Limited (Rootes Group).

Model: Sunbeam Tiger.

1. **Wheels.** Magnesium Alloy Wheels available, Part No. 5221007.

    50. **Type:** Ventilated magnesium alloy.

    51. **Weight:** (per wheel, without tyre), 4.08 Kgs. 9lb.

    52. **Method of Attachment:** 4 Stud with 1 spacer per wheel at front and 2 spacers per wheel at rear.

    53. **Rim diameter:** 330.2 mm. 13 inches.

    Resulting increase in track with magnesium alloy wheels:

    Front: 1330. mm. 52.44 inches.
    Rear: 1254.1 mm. 49.375 inches.

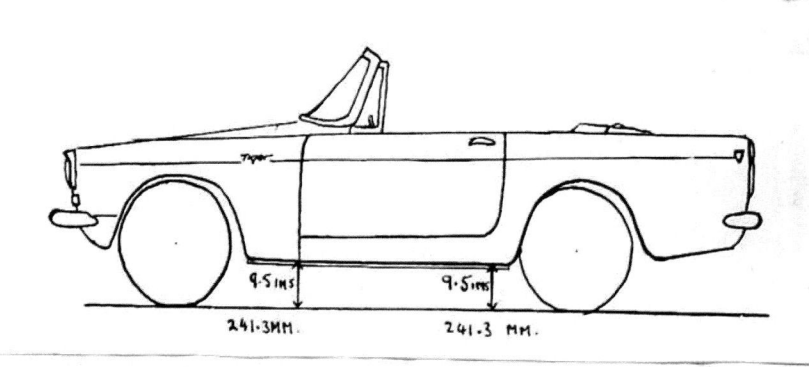

2. Limited slip differential available ; Part No. 1229810.

    292. Type: Salisbury Powr Lok.

3. Final Drive Ratio's: Part No. 5221008.
    293. Alternative final drive ratio: 3.77 : 1
    No: of teeth.

Appendix 6

TIGER.

Federation Internationale de l'Automobile.
Supplement to Form of Recognition.

Manufacturer: Sunbeam Talbot Limited (Rootes Group.)

Model: Sunbeam Tiger.

1. **Wheels.** Magnesium alloy wheels available, Part No. 5221007.

   50. **Type:** Ventilated magnesium alloy.

   51. **Weight:** (per wheel, without tyre), 4.08 Kgs. 9 lbs.

   52. **Method of Attachment:** 4 Stud with 1 spacer per wheel at front and 2 spacers per wheel at rear.

   53. **Rim diameter:** 330.2 mm. 13 inches.

   Resulting increase in track with magnesium alloy wheels:

   Front: 1340.6 mm.   52.781 inches.
   Rear: 1257.3 mm.   49.5   inches.

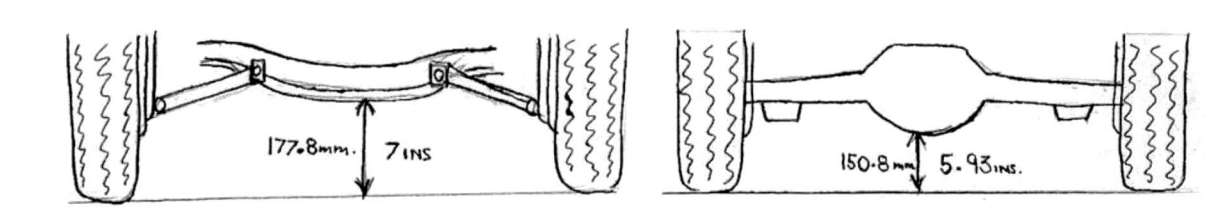

   [Diagram: Front axle showing 177.8mm / 7ins ground clearance; Rear axle showing 150.8mm / 5.93ins ground clearance.]

2. Limited slip differential available; Part No. 1229810.

   292. **Type:** Salisbury Powr Lok.

3. Final Drive Ratios: Part No. 5221008

   293. Alternative final drive ratio: 3.77 : 1

   No. of teeth : 49 x 13

Appendix 6

No. 509

FEDERATION INTERNATIONAL DE L'AUTOMOBILE.

Supplement to Form of Recognition.

Manufacturer: Sunbeam Talbot Limited. (Rootes Group.)

Model: Sunbeam Tiger.

The following optional equipment is available for this car:-

1. Steering.

    Alternative steering rack. Part No. 5221021.

    60. Type ; Rack and Pinion.
    61. Servo Assistance : No.
    62. Number of turns of steering wheel from lock to lock : 2.33
    63. In case of servo assistance : nil.

2. The following items are supplied when alternative camshafts are fitted.

    (i) Tachometer reading to 8,000 R.P.M. in place of 5,500 R.P.M. Part No. 5221020.

    (ii) Mechanically operated tappets fitted in place of hydraulic.

Amendment to Specification of Interior Coachwork.

Cars built after Chassis Number 382000001 are fitted with fixed leather-cloth rear squab and hood container in place of steel type previously fitted. No resulting change in weight of vehicle or exterior appearance.

The manufacture of the amended coachwork was started on 1st August 1965 and the minimum production of 500 identical cars was reached on 27th October 1965.

TIGER

No. 509

FEDERATION INTERNATIONALE DE L'AUTOMOBILE

Supplement No. 2 to Form of Recognition

Manufacturer: Rootes Group,
Sunbeam Talbot Ltd.

Model: Tiger

Optional equipment affecting preceeding information. This is to be stated together with reference number.

CAPACITIES AND DIMENSIONS

7. Supplementary fuel tank kit to be used in conjunction with existing fuel tanks. Part No. 1219175 A.

Capacity of fuel tank (reserve included)

   36.5 ltrs. 10.2 Gall.US. 8.5 Gall.Imp.

Total capacity of all fuel tanks

   87.6 ltrs. 23.7 Gall.US. 19.75 Gall.Imp.

Appendix 6

1964 Homologation Form: FIA Recognition No 176

Manufacturers Reference No. for Application

SUNTIG I

F.I.A. Recognition No. 176

ROYAL AUTOMOBILE CLUB
PALL MALL, LONDON, S.W.I.

Federation Internationale de l'Automobile.

Form of Recognition in accordance with
Appendix J to the
International Sporting Code.

Manufacturer: SUNBEAM TALBOT LTD.

Model: TIGER I   Year of Manufacture: 1964

Serial No. of Chassis: B9499991
Engine: B9499991

Type of Coachwork: OPEN 2 SEATER

Recognition is valid from: 11. 7. 64   In category: GRAND TOURING

liste 2/11

Photograph to be affixed here ¾ view of car from front right.

Stamp of F.I.A./R.A.C. to be affixed here.

Form: R.F.I.A.

Appendix 6

General description of car:

Specify here material/s of chassis/body construction

TWO SEATER SPORTS TOURER WITH REAR OCCASIONAL SEAT

TWO DOOR ONLY

HARD TOP OR SOFT TOP CAN BE FITTED

BODY CONSTRUCTION OF STEEL AND ALUMINIUM

Photographs to be affixed below.

¾ view of car from rear left.

Interior view of car through driver's door.

Engine unit with accessories from right.

Engine unit with accessories from left.

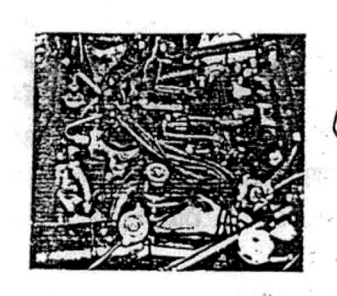

Front axle complete (without wheels).

Rear axle complete (without wheels).

Appendix 6

ENGINE

No. of cylinders __8__   in line __-__   in V __YES__

opposed __-__

Cycle __4 STROKE__   Firing order __15426378__

Capacity __4260__ c.c.   Bore __96.5__ m.m.   Stroke __72.8__ m.m.

Maximum rebore __1.524 m.m.__   Resultant capacity __4400__ c.c.

Material of cylinder block __CAST IRON__   Material of sleeves, if fitted __NONE__

Distance from crankshaft centre line to top face of block at centre line of cylinders __206__ m.m.

Material of cylinder head __CAST IRON__   Volume of one combustion chamber __47.5__ c.c.

Compression ratio __10:1__

Material of piston __ALUMINIUM__   No. of piston rings __3 PER PISTON__

Distance from gudgeon pin centre line to highest point of piston crown __46.99__ m.m.

Bearings:
- Crankshaft main bearings: Type __COPPER LEAD__ Dia __57.15__ m.m.
- Connecting rod big end: Type __COPPER LEAD__ Dia __53.975__ m.m.

Weights:
- Flywheel __9.3__ kg.
- Crankshaft __16.8__ kg.
- Connecting rod __0.63__ kg.
- Piston with rings __0.597__ kg.
- Gudgeon pin __0.17__ kg.

No. of valves per cylinder __2__   Method of valve operation __PUSHROD__

No. of camshafts __1__   Location of camshafts __IN BLOCK__

Type of camshaft drive __INVERTED TOOTH CHAIN__

Diameter of valves: Inlet __49.25__ m.m.   Exhaust __42.85__ m.m.

Diameter of port at valve seat: Inlet __46.0__ m.m.   Exhaust __39.75__ m.m.

Tappet clearance for checking timing: Inlet __.61__ m.m.   Exhaust __.61__ m.m.

Valves open: Inlet __28 BTDC__   Exhaust __72 ABDC__

Valves close: Inlet __72 ABDC__   Exhaust __28 ATDC__

Maximum valve lift: Inlet __13.3__ m.m.   Exhaust __13.3__ m.m.

Degrees of crankshaft rotation from zero to—

Maximum lift: Inlet __112__   Exhaust __248__

½ Maximum lift: Inlet __50__   Exhaust __136__

Valve springs:

	Inlet	Exhaust
Type	COIL	COIL
No. per valve	2	2

Carburettor: Type __DOWNDRAFT__   No. fitted __1__
(up or down draft, horizontal)

Make __FORD__   Model __C4OF - AL 4BDL__

Flange hole diameter __39.5__ m.m.   Choke diameter __27 PRIMARY__ m.m.

Main jet identification No. __52F__   __29.5 SECONDARY__

Appendix 6

Air filter: Type __PAPER ELEMENT__ No. fitted __1__

Inlet manifold:
  Diameter of flange hole at carburettor __40__ m.m.
  Diameter of flange hole at port __24 x 47__ m.m.

Photograph of combustion chamber to be affixed here.

Photograph of inlet manifold to be affixed here.

Diameter of flange hole at port __27 x 36__ m.m.
Diameter of flange hole at connection to silencer inlet pipe __52__ m.m.

Photograph of piston showing crown to be affixed here.

Photograph of exhaust manifold to be affixed here.

ENGINE ACCESSORIES

Make of fuel pump	SU	No. fitted	1
Method of operation	ELECTRICAL		
Type of ignition system	COIL AND DISTRIBUTOR		coil or magneto
Make of ignition	FORD	Model	C30F 3MB
Method of advance and retard	CENTRIFUGAL AND VACUUM		
Make of ignition coil	FORD OR LUCAS	Model	FAC 12029/HA 12
No. of ignition coils	ONE	Voltage	12
Make of dynamo	FORD OR LUCAS	Model	C40
Voltage of dynamo	12	Maximum output	30 amps.
Make of starter motor	FORD OR LUCAS	Model	M40
Battery: No. fitted 1 Voltage 12		Capacity	51 amp. hour
Oil Cooler (if fitted) type	RADIATOR	Capacity	4 pints

Appendix 6

Make: SUNBEAM Model: TIGER I F.I.A. Recognition No. _____
Manufacturers Reference No. of Application: SUNTIG

TRANSMISSION

Make of clutch: FORD Type: DRY
Diameter of clutch plate: 10" No. of plates: ONE
Method of operating clutch: HYDRAULIC AND MECHANICAL
Make of gearbox: BORG-WARNER Type: T34
No. of gearbox ratios: 4 FORWARD 1 REVERSE
Method of operating gearshift: MANUAL
Location of gearshift: CENTRE FLOOR LEVER
Is overdrive fitted?: NO
Method of controlling overdrive, if fitted: NOT FITTED

	GEARBOX RATIOS		ALTERNATIVE RATIOS					
	Ratio	No. of Teeth	Ratio	No. of Teeth	Ratio	No. of Teeth	Ratio	No. of Teeth
1.	2.33	36/17	2.33	36/17	2.20	36/17		
2.	1.61	29/20	1.75	30/19	1.63	30/19		
3.	1.20	25/27	1.40	24/23	1.31	29/23		
4.	1.0	DIRECT	1.0	DIRECT	1.0	DIRECT		
5.								

Type of final drive: HYPOID
Type of differential: 6 BEVEL PINION WITH POWER LOCKING
Final drive ratio: 2.88 Alternatives: 3.07 3.31 3.54 4.09 4.27 4.55 3.77
No. of teeth: 46/16 14/44 13/43 13/46 11/45 11/47 11/50 13/49
Overdrive ratio, if fitted: NOT FITTED

WHEELS

Type: PRESSED STEEL DISC Weight: 5.76 kg.
Method of attachment: FOUR STUD 7/16 UNF
Rim diameter: 330.2 m.m. Rim width: 116.5 m.m.
Tyre size: Front: 600 x 13 Rear: 600 x 13

BRAKES

Method of operation: HYDRAULIC
Is servo assistance fitted?: YES
Type of servo, if fitted: GIRLING VACUUM
No. of hydraulic master cylinders: 1 Bore: 22.1 m.m.

Additional information for cars fitted with two-cycle engines
System of cylinder scavenging: _____
Type of lubrication: _____
Size of inlet port:

Appendix 6

	Front	Rear
No. of wheel cylinders	2 PER WHEEL	1 PER WHEEL
Bore of wheel cylinders	54 m.m.	22.2 m.m.
Inside diameter of brake drums	— m.m.	223.6 m.m.
No. of shoes per brake	—	2
Outside diameter of brake discs	250.2 m.m.	— m.m.
No. of pads per brake	2	—

Dimensions of brake linings per shoe or pad (if all shoes or pads in each brake are not of same dimensions, specify each)

	Front	Rear
Length	77 m.m.	215 m.m.
	m.m.	m.m.
Width	54 m.m.	44.5 m.m.
Total area per brake	6645 m.m.²	19434 m.m.²

SUSPENSION

	Front	Rear
Type	WISHBONE	LIVE AXLE
Type of spring	COIL	SEMI ELLIPTICAL
Is stabiliser fitted?	YES	YES
Type of shock absorber	TELESCOPIC	TELESCOPIC
No. of shock absorbers	2	2

STEERING

Type of steering gear: RACK AND PINION
Turning circle of car: 10.36 m., approx.
No. of turns of steering wheel from lock to lock: 3

CAPACITIES AND DIMENSIONS

Fuel tank: 52 litres   Sump: 6.5 INC OIL FILTER litres
Radiator: 8.2 WITH HEATER litres
Overall length of car: 395 cm.   Overall width of car: 153.5 cm.
Overall height of car, unladen (with hood up, if appropriate): 135 cm.
Distance from floor to top of windscreen:
  Highest point: 92.7 cm.   Lowest point: 87 cm.
Width of windscreen:
  Maximum width: 122 cm.   Minimum width: 104 cm.
*Interior width of car: 128 cm.
No. of seats: 2
Track: Front: 131 cm.   Rear: 125 cm.
Wheelbase: 218 cm.   Ground clearance: 105 m.m.

*(To be measured at the immediate rear of the steering wheel, and the width quoted to be maintained in a vertical plane of not less than 25 cms.)

Overall weight with water, oil and spare wheel, but without fuel: 980 kgs.

Appendix 6

Additional information for cars fitted with two-cycle engines

    System of cylinder scavenging...

    Type of lubrication...

  Size of inlet port:

    Length measured around cylinder wall..m.m.

    Height...m.m.   Area..m.m.^{2}

  Size of exhaust port:

    Length measured around cylinder wall..m.m.

    Height...m.m.   Area..m.m.^{2}

  Size of transfer port:

    Length measured around cylinder wall..m.m.

    Height...m.m.   Area..m.m.^{2}

  Size of piston port:

    Length measured around piston..m.m.

    Height...m.m.   Area..m.m.^{2}

  Method of pre-compression...

  Bore and stroke of pre-compression cylinder, if fitted...m.m.

  Distance from top of cylinder block to lowest point of inlet port..............................m.m.

  Distance from top of cylinder block to highest point of exhaust port....................m.m.

  Distance from top of cylinder block to highest point of transfer port....................m.m.

                        Drawing of cylinder ports.

Supercharger, if fitted

    Make..   Model or Type No..

    Type of drive..   Ratio of drive...

Fuel injection, if fitted

    Make of pump..   Model or Type No..

    Make of injectors ....   Model or Type No..

    Location of injectors...

Appendix 6

Optional equipment affecting preceeding information:—

1. Alternative carburetion available twin choke down draft Ford Carburettor type No. C4DFE

   Flange hole diameter   36.5 m.m.
   Choke diameter   25.4 m.m.
   Main jet identification
            no.   44F

2. Alternative exhaust system available – all port dimensions identical with type originally specified.

3. Additional fuel tank available to bring fuel capacity up to 140 litres.

4. Engine oil cooler available.

5. Rear axle oil cooler with circulating pump available.

6. A bevel pinion differential available.

7. Alternative engine sump available giving a total oil capacity of 10.2 litres.

8. Magnesium Alloy Wheels available 330.2 x 127 m.m. giving tracks of front 141 cm. rear 135 cm.

9. Magnesium Alloy Wheels available 330.2 x 140 m.m. giving tracks of front 151 cm. rear 145 cm. With same fittings as original wheels.

Appendix 6

Manufacturers Reference No. for Application

SUNTIG.

F.I.A. Recognition No. 176.

ROYAL AUTOMOBILE CLUB
PALL MALL, LONDON, S.W.I.

Federation Internationale de l'Automobile.

Amendment to Form of Recognition

Manufacturer: SUNBEAM TALBOT LTD.

Model: TIGER I.

The chassis and engine nos. quoted on the homologation sheet are incorrect.

These should read Chassis B.9470001.
Engine 1000 E7 KL.

Alternative Carburettion now available 4 choke downdraught Holley Carburettor Part No. C4AF DAA 3LD.

Flange hole diameter 42 MM.

Choke diameter   Primary   35 MM.
                           Secondary. 35 MM.

Main Jet Identification

         Primary.   76
         Secondary. 01.

Stamp of F.I.A./R.A.C. to be affixed here.

Date amendment is valid from _____

Form: R.F.I.B.

Appendix 6

The Royal Automobile Club
Pall Mall, London, S.W.1

Please address all Communications to
THE SECRETARY
Quoting the following Reference:
C

Telegrams: AUTOMOBILE LONDON
Telephone: WHITEHALL 2345 (26 lines)

TIGER I

MANUFACTURERS REFERENCE NO: OF APPLICATION FOR HOMOLOGATION

SUNTIG I

I certify that in excess of 100 cars identical with the basic specification stated on the relevant form of recognition have been manufactured within a period of 12 months.

D. H. Delamont,
Manager, Competitions Department

RAC
MOTOR SPORTS
ASSN. LTD.

Appendix 6

The Royal Automobile Club
Pall Mall, London, S.W.1

Please address all Communications to
THE SECRETARY
Quoting the following Reference
C/RC

Telegrams: AUTOMOBILE LONDON
Telephone: WHITEHALL 2345 (26 lines)

3rd July 1964

Mr. Schroeder,
F. I. A.
8, Place de la Concorde,
Paris.

Dear Mr. Schroeder,

Since sending you the forms of recognition, we have received the part Nos on the nine items of optional extras for the Sunbeam Tiger. For your information they are as follows:

1. C4D59510E
2. 1219179
3. 1219175
4. A 267
5. 1219176
6. 1224887
7. C4026675A
8. 1219177
9. 1219178

We have already inserted these numbers on the two original copies we have left.

Yours sincerely,

Competitions Department

RAC MOTOR SPORTS ASSN. LTD.

Appendix 6

1965 Homologation Form: FIA Recognition No 211

Manufacturers Reference No. for Application

SUNTIG IA.

F.I.A. Recognition No. **211**

ROYAL AUTOMOBILE CLUB
PALL MALL, LONDON, S.W.I.

Federation Internationale de l'Automobile.

*Form of Recognition in accordance with
Appendix J to the
International Sporting Code.*

Manufacturer: SUNBEAM-TALBOT LIMITED.

Model: TIGER/ALPINE 260 (RIGHT OR LEFT HAND DRIVE.)   Year of Manufacture: 1965.

Chassis: B.9470001

Serial No. of Engine: 1000 Suffix E7.KL or L2.KA and subsequent Ford Motor Co.Ltd.series

Type of Coachwork: Open 2 Seater.

Recognition is valid from: ~~7 April 1965.~~ 1/8/65   In category: Grand Touring.

Photograph to be affixed here ¾ view of car from front right.

Stamp of F.I.A./R.A.C. to be affixed here.

Form: R.F.I.A.

Appendix 6

Make SUNBEAM Model TIGER/ALPINE 260 F.I.A. Recognition No.

General description of car:

Specify here material/s of chassis/body construction

Two seater sports tourer with rear occasional seat.
Two door only.
Hard top or soft top can be fitted.
Body construction : steel or aluminium.

Photographs to be affixed below.

¾ view of car from rear left.

Interior view of car through driver's door.

Engine unit with accessories from right.

Engine unit with accessories from left.

Front axle complete (without wheels).

Rear axle complete (without wheels).

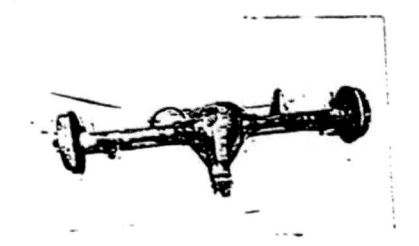

Appendix 6

Make: SUNBEAM Model: TIGER/ALPINE 260 Recognition No: _____

ENGINE

Cataloged B.H.P. _____ at R.P.M. _____

- No. of cylinders: 8
- in line: —
- in V: Yes
- opposed: —
- Cycle: 4 stroke.
- Firing order: 15426378.
- Capacity: 4,261 c.c. Bore: 96.5 mm. Stroke: 72.8 mm.
- Maximum rebore: 1.524 mm. Resultant capacity: 4,400 c.c.
- Material of cylinder block: Cast Iron. Material of sleeves, if fitted: None.
- Distance from crankshaft centre line to top face of block at centre line of cylinders: 206 mm.
- Material of cylinder head: Cast Iron. Volume of one combustion chamber: 47.5 c.c.
- Compression ratio: 10 : 1
- Material of piston: Aluminium. No. of piston rings: 3 per piston.
- Distance from gudgeon pin centre line to highest point of piston crown: 46.90 mm.

Bearings:
- Crankshaft main bearings: Type: Copper lead. Dia: 57.15 mm.
- Connecting rod big end: Type: Copper lead. Dia: 53.975 mm.

Weights:
- Flywheel: 9.3 kg.
- Crankshaft: 16.8 kg.
- Connecting rod: 0.63 kg.
- Piston with rings: 0.597 kg.
- Gudgeon pin: 0.17 kg.

- No. of valves per cylinder: 2 Method of valve operation: Pushrod.
- No. of camshafts: 1 Location of camshafts: In block.
- Type of camshaft drive: Inverted tooth chain.
- Diameter of valves: Inlet: 42 mm. Exhaust: 37 mm.
- Diameter of port at valve seat: Inlet: 39 mm. Exhaust: 33 mm.
- Tappet clearance for checking timing: Inlet: .508 mm. Exhaust: .508 mm.
- Valves open: Inlet: 25° B.T.D.C. Exhaust: 70° B.B.D.C.
- Valves close: Inlet: 70° A.B.D.C. Exhaust: 25° A.T.D.C.
- Maximum valve lift: Inlet: 7.5 mm. Exhaust: 7.5 mm.

Degrees of crankshaft rotation from zero to—
- Maximum lift: Inlet: 170° Exhaust: 170°
- ¾ Maximum lift: Inlet: 130° Exhaust: 130°

Valve springs:

	Inlet	Exhaust
Type	Coil	Coil
No. per valve	2	2

- Carburettor: Type: Down draft. (up or down draft, horizontal) No. fitted: 1
- Make: Ford. Model: C4OF AL.A.4CD.
- Flange hole diameter: 39.5 mm. Choke diameter: 27 Primary, 29.5 Secondary. mm.
- Main jet identification No: 52 F

Appendix 6

Make_____ Model_____ F.I.A. Recognition No._____

Air filter: Type __Paper Element.__ No. fitted __1__

Inlet manifold:
   Diameter of flange hole at carburettor __40__ m.m.
   Diameter of flange hole at port __25 x 47__ m.m.

Photograph of combustion chamber to be affixed here.

Photograph of inlet manifold to be affixed here.

Exhaust manifold:
   Diameter of flange hole at port __27 x 33__ m.m.
   Diameter of flange hole at connection to silencer inlet pipe __47__ m.m.

Photograph of piston showing crown to be affixed here.

Photograph of exhaust manifold to be affixed here.

ENGINE ACCESSORIES

Make of fuel pump	S.U.	No. fitted	1.
Method of operation	Electrical		
Type of ignition system	Coil and Distributor.		coil or magneto
Make of ignition	Ford.	Model	C 3CF 3 MB
Method of advance and retard	Centrifugal and Vacuum		
Make of ignition coil	Ford or Lucas.	Model	FAC 12029/HA 12
No. of ignition coils	1	Voltage	12
Make of dynamo	Ford or Lucas.	Model	C 40
Voltage of dynamo	12	Maximum output	30 amps.
Make of starter motor	Ford or Lucas.	Model	M 40
Battery: No. fitted	1 Voltage 12	Capacity	51 amp. hour
Oil Cooler (if fitted) type	Radiator.	Capacity	1.5 pints

Appendix 6

Make......SUNBEAM.   Model TIGER/ALPINE 260   F.I.A. Recognition No._____
                         Manufacturers Reference No. of Application___SUNTIG 1A.

TRANSMISSION
- Make of clutch......Ford.   Type......Dry.
- Diameter of clutch plate......10 inch.   No. of plates......1
- Method of operating clutch......Mechanical & Hydraulic.
- Make of gearbox......Ford.   Type......Synchromesh.
- No. of gearbox ratios......4 forward and 1 reverse.
- Method of operating gearshift......manual.
- Location of gearshift......Centre floor lever.
- Is overdrive fitted?......No.
- Method of controlling overdrive, if fitted......Not Applicable.

	GEARBOX RATIOS		ALTERNATIVE RATIOS					
	Ratio	No. of Teeth	Ratio	No. of Teeth	Ratio	No. of Teeth	Ratio	No. of Teeth
1.	2.32	23 x 32 / 25 15	2.78	30 x 32 / 23 15	2.33	36/17		
2.	1.69	23 x 28 / 25 18	1.93	30 x 31 / 23 21	1.61	29/20		
3.	1.29	23 x 25 / 25 21	1.36	30 x 25 / 23 24	1.20	25/27		
4.	1.0	Direct.	1.0	Direct.	1.0	Direct.		
5.	–	–	–	–				

- Type of final drive......Hypoid.
- Type of differential......6 Bevel pinion with power locking.
- Final drive ratio......2.88   Alternatives 3.31   3.54   3.77
- No. of teeth......46/16.   13/43 13/46 13/49
- Overdrive ratio, if fitted......Not fitted.

WHEELS
- Type......Pressed steel disc.   Weight......5.76......kg.
- Method of attachment......Four stud 7/16 UNF.
- Rim diameter......330.2......m.m.   Rim width......116.5......m.m.
- Tyre size: Front......600 x 13   Rear......600 x 13

BRAKES
- Method of operation......Hydraulic.
- Is servo assistance fitted?......Yes.
- Type of servo, if fitted......Girling Vacuum.
- No. of hydraulic master cylinders......1   Bore......12.1......m.m.

Appendix 6

Make: SUNBEAM Model: TIGER/ALPINE IA Recognition No. 262

	Front	Rear
No. of wheel cylinders	2 per wheel	1 per wheel
Bore of wheel cylinders	54 m.m.	22.2 m.m.
Inside diameter of brake drums	— m.m.	228.6 m.m.
No. of shoes per brake	—	2
Outside diameter of brake discs	250.2 m.m.	— m.m.
No. of pads per brake	2	—

Dimensions of brake linings per shoe or pad (if all shoes or pads in each brake are not of same dimensions, specify each)

	Front	Rear
Length	77 m.m.	215 m.m.
	— m.m.	— m.m.
Width	54 m.m.	44.5 m.m.
Total area per brake	6645 m.m.²	19484 m.m.²

SUSPENSION

	Front	Rear
Type	Wishbone.	Live axle.
Type of spring	Coil	Semi-elliptic.
Is stabiliser fitted?	yes	yes
Type of shock absorber	Telescopic	Telescopic.
No. of shock absorbers	2	2

STEERING

Type of steering gear: Rack and Pinion.
Turning circle of car: 10.36 m., approx.
No. of turns of steering wheel from lock to lock: 3

CAPACITIES AND DIMENSIONS

Fuel tank: 52 litres   Sump (including Oil filter): 6.8 litres
Radiator (with heater): 15.3 litres
Overall length of car: 395 cm.   Overall width of car: 153.5 cm.
Overall height of car, unladen (with hood up, if appropriate): 130.8 cm.

Distance from floor to top of windscreen:
  Highest point: 92.7 cm.   Lowest point: 87 cm.

Width of windscreen:
  Maximum width: 122 cm.   Minimum width: 104 cm.

*Interior width of car: 128 cm.
No. of seats: 2
Track: Front: 131.4 cm.   Rear: 125 cm.
Wheelbase: 213.4 cm.   Ground clearance: 104 m.m.

*(To be measured at the immediate rear of the steering wheel, and the width quoted to be maintained in a vertical plane of not less than 25 cms.)

Overall weight with water, oil and spare wheel, but without fuel: 980 kgs.

Model: TIGER/ALPINE 260. F.I.A. Recognition No. _____

...tional information for cars fitted with two-cycle engines

System of cylinder scavenging ....

Type of lubrication ....

Size of inlet port:
    Length measured around cylinder wall .... m.m.
    Height .... m.m.   Area .... m.m.^{2}

Size of exhaust port:
    Length measured around cylinder wall .... m.m.
    Height .... m.m.   Area .... m.m.^{2}

Size of transfer port:
    Length measured around cylinder wall .... m.m.
    Height .... m.m.   Area .... m.m.^{2}

Size of piston port:
    Length measured around piston .... m.m.
    Height .... m.m.   Area .... m.m.^{2}

Method of pre-compression ....

Bore and stroke of pre-compression cylinder, if fitted .... m.m.

Distance from top of cylinder block to lowest point of inlet port .... m.m.

Distance from top of cylinder block to highest point of exhaust port .... m.m.

Distance from top of cylinder block to highest point of transfer port .... m.m.

                Drawing of cylinder ports.

Supercharger, if fitted
    Make ....   Model or Type No. ....
    Type of drive ....   Ratio of drive ....

Fuel injection, if fitted
    Make of pump ....   Model or Type No. ....
    Make of injectors ....   Model or Type No. ....
    Location of injectors ....

Appendix 6

Make: SUNBEAM   Model: TIGER/ALPINE 260   F.I.A. Recognition No. _____

Optional equipment affecting preceeding information:—

1. Alternative carburettor available; twin choke down draft Ford, type No. C 4DF 9510E, flange hole diameter 36.51 mm, choke diameter 25.65 mm. Main jet identification number 44 F.

2. ~~Alternative exhaust pipe and manifold available, all port dimensions identical with type originally specified.~~

3. Additional fuel tank available to bring fuel capacity up to 117 litres.

4. Engine oil cooler available.

5. ~~Touring camshaft available.~~

6. Bevel pinion differential available.

7. Alternative engine sump available giving a total oil capacity of 8 litres.

8. Magnesium alloy wheels available – size 330.2 x 127 mm (5")
   Resulting tracks: front, 141 cm; rear, 135 cm.
   Same method of attachment as original wheels.

9. Magnesium alloy wheels available – size 330.2 x 140 mm (5½").
   Resulting tracks: front, 151 cm; rear 145 cm.
   Same method of attachment as original wheels.

10. ~~Alternative cylinder head available – all valve dimensions identical with type originally specified.~~

11. Tropical Radiator available increasing capacity.

Alternative exhaust manifold.

Alternative cylinder head.

Appendix 6

The Royal Automobile Club

Motor Sport Division,
31 Belgrave Square
London SW1

Telegrams: Motrace, London SW1
Telephone: BELgravia 8601

165044

Our ref: DM/GS
Your ref:

14th October, 1965.

Monsieur H. Schroeder,
Secretary, C.S.I.,
8 Place de la Concorde,
Paris 8.

Dear Monsieur Schroeder,

Homologation Application for November

Please find enclosed two new photographs of the Sunbeam Tiger/Alpine 260 to replace the existing photographs inserted on the Homologation Form which was not accepted at the last meeting.

Rootes have applied for an overall weight for this vehicle of 1,168 kgs.

We trust that you will find this satisfactory.

Regarding the modification to the Hillman Imp Homologation Forms sent recently, we would be pleased if you would kindly return these as the Rootes Group do not wish to continue.

Yours sincerely,

D. Mills,
Administrative Officer.

Appendix 6

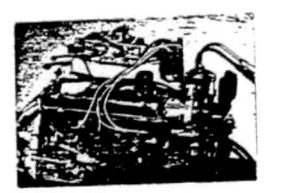

Photograph of engine unit with accessories from right.

Photograph of engine unit with accessories from left.

Appendix 6

Confidential

1965

PRODUCTION CATEGORY RECOGNITION FORM

SUNBEAM TIGER

FOR
SPORTS CAR CLUB OF
AMERICA.

Appendix 6

1965 Production Category Recognition Form

Manufacturer: **SUNBEAM TALBOT LTD.**

Model: **TIGER** PHOTO No. 1

Serial numbers of this series: **9470000**

Recognized by FIA in category **G.T.** as of (date) **1964**

THE FOLLOWING ARE THE NORMAL SPECIFICATIONS OF THE ABOVE LISTED AUTOMOBILE AS DELIVERED THROUGH REGULAR SALES OUTLETS:

Official Weight, Touring Trim: With water, oil, spare wheel, but without fuel or tools: **2400**. Be accurate.

Engine: AFFIX PHOTO **No. 2 and 2-A**
    Manufacturer: **Ford**
    Type: **V/8** (in line, V, opposed)
    Number of cylinders: **8**
    Cycle: **4**
    Firing order: **15426378**
    Bore: **3.80**
    Stroke: **2.87**
    Capacity: **4262 c.c.**
    Cylinder block, material: **Cast Iron**
        Sleeves, material: **iron**
        Main bearings: Type: **shell** No. fitted **5** Journal dia. **2.2486"**
        Connecting rod bearings: Type: **shell** Journal dia. **2.1232"**
    Cylinder head, material: **cast iron**
        No. valves per cylinder: **2**
        Method of operation: **pushrod - hydraulic or mechanical**
        Valve head diameter: Inlet: **1.582-1.677"** Exhaust: **1.381-1.457"**
        Valve spring type: **coil** (coil, hairpin)
    Camshaft:
        Number: **1**
        Location: **in block**
        Type of drive: **chain**
    Carburetor:
        Make: **Ford-Holly** Dia. of throat at butterfly valves **1.438-1.562"**
        Model: **C3OFAJ-C3OFAB**
        Type: **downdraft**
        Number fitted: **1 2-barrel or 1 4-barrel**
    Fuel Injection: **Not available**
        Injector: Make:
                Model:
        Pump: Make:
              Model:

(1)

Appendix 6

```
Supercharger:  Not available
    Make:
    Model:
    Type of drive:
    Ratio of drive:
Air Filter:  AFFIX PHOTO  No. 3
    Type:  Dry
    Number fitted:  1
Inlet manifold:  AFFIX PHOTO or DRAWING  No. 4 and 4-A
    Material:  Cast iron or cast aluminium
    Number fitted:  1
Exhaust manifold:  AFFIX PHOTO or DRAWING  No. 5
    Material:  Cast iron
Engine Accessories:
    Fuel Pump: Make:  S.U. Electric        No. fitted:  1
    Ignition system: Type:   Coil                (coil or mag)
        Distributor: Make:  Ford      Model:           No:  1
        Coil: Make:            Ford   Model: C4OF-12127A No: 1
        Dynamo: Make:  Ford  20F-0000-F  Model:   Voltage: 12
        Starter motor: Make:   Ford         Model: C.3OF-11001-B
        Battery: Voltage:  12

Transmission:
    Clutch:  Diameter:  10.4"
    Gearbox:  AFFIX PHOTO  No. 6
        Make:  Ford or Borg Warner
        Model:
        No. of gears:  Forward:  4    Reverse:  1
```

	GEARBOX RATIOS		ALTERNATIVE RATIOS					
	Ratio	No. of Teeth	Ratio	No. of Teeth	Ratio	No. of Teeth	Ratio	No. of Teeth
1	2.32		2.20		2.20		2.36	
2	1.69		1.63		1.48		1.63	17?
3	1.29		1.31		1.18		1.21	14?
4	1.00		1.00		1.00		1.00	
5								
Rev	2.32		2.20		2.20		2.36	

Handwritten margin notes (left): 2.77, 1.9, 1.35, 1.00
Handwritten margin notes (right): 2.33, 1.61, 1.20, 1.00

Handwritten: Ford. HEH/E   AEAD

Appendix 6

```
Overdrive:  AFFIX PHOTO --
    Make:       Not Available
    Model:
    Ratio:
Final drive:  Type:      Hypoid             AFFIX PHOTO No. 7
    Make:       Salisbury
    Model:      Type 44 or Type 23
    Standard ratio: 2.88   No. of teeth: Ring:_____ Pinion:_____
    Alternate ratios:  *   No. of teeth: Ring:_____ Pinion:_____
    Limited slip standard:_____ Yes:_____ No:_____
  * 3.07 - 3.31 - 3.54 - 3.78 - 4.09 - 4.27 - 4.53
Chassis:
    Wheelbase:
    Tread:  Front:    51"         Rear:    48.5"
```

Suspension: Photos - with wheel removed. No. 8 and 8-A

	Front	Rear
Type:	Independent	Beam axle
Type spring:	coil	Semi-elliptical
Size torsion bar:	--	
Stabilizer fitted? Size?	8"	5"
Type of shock absorber:	tube	tube
Number shocks fitted:	2	2

Brakes:

	Front	Rear
Method of operation:	disc	drum
Servo assistance:	yes	yes
Make:	Girling	
Model:		

```
Master cylinder(s):
    Make:     Girling
    Model:
    Number:   1
    Bore:     7/8"
Wheel cylinders:
    Make:     Girling
    Number:               2 per wheel      1 per wheel
    Bore:     .83"
Drums:  Where fitted?                      rear
    Inside diameter:                       9"
    Width:                                 2 and 1/16"
Shoes:
    Number per drum:                       2
    Width:                                 1.75"
Discs:  Where fitted:   front
    Make:     Girling
    Model:
    Disc diameter:      9.85"
    Disc material:      cast iron
    No. pads per disc:  2
    Piston size:        2.1"
```

Appendix 6

Wheels:
   Diameter: 13"
   Rim width: 4.5"

Capacities:
   Radiator: 10 qt. with engine
   Fuel tank: 13.5 gal.
   Sump: 5 quart

Steering:
   Make: Sunbeam
   Model: Tiger
   Type: Rack and pinion
   No. turns steering wheel from lock to lock: 3.2

Additional pertinent information or explanations:

The Sunbeam Tiger is offered for sale with two different horsepower ratings. The basic car is equipped with 2 BBL carburetion, hydraulic lifters and single point ignition. The slightly more powerful version has 4 BBL carburetion, solid lifters, dual point ignition, etc., etc. -- see attached road test from the November issue of Road & Track. Both engines are 260 C.I.D.

(4)

Appendix 6

-6

The following is a list of the manufacturer's authorized optional equipment for the model listed on page one, offered for sale through regular sales outlets, and of which at least 100 units have been produced by December 31, 1964.

Instructions: List part by name, part number, give complete description including sizes, capacities and any pertinent information for identification. If the item is a kit, give a complete itemization of the kit's contents, individual part numbers and dimensions. <u>Affix photo of each item</u>. If alternate items available or manufactured by different suppliers, give identification differences. Incomplete information will result in item not being considered for the approved option list. <u>AFFIX PHOTOS!</u> Use additional sheets as necessary.

IMPORTANT NOTE:

If optional wheels are listed, any resulting change in tread dimensions must be specified.

Option Name	Part Number	Description	Photo No.
Engine oil cooler	LAT23	--	9
Oil cooler (differential)	LAT24	--	10
Cold air scoop	LAT25	--	11 & 11-A
Large oil sump	LAT26	9 quart capacity	12
Intake valves	LAT28	Head diameter 1.62"	13
Exhaust valve	LAT29	Head diameter 1.43"	13
Competition exhaust manifolds	LAT27	--	14
Heavy duty radiator	LAT26	Capacity 14 quarts	15
Fan	LAT32	6 bladed	16
Gas tank	LAT33	Capacity 37 gallons	17
Engine compartment vents	LAT41	Heat extractor vents	18
Rear stabiliser rod	LAT40	--	19
Competition manifold	LAT38	For Holly 4-barrel carb.	20
4-barrel carburettor	LAT39	Holly carb. No. CAR-9510-DA Venturii size 1.087"	20
Limited slip kit which includes the following:			
Limited slip unit	LAT36	--	21
Axle shafts	LAT35	--	22
Differential plate cover	LAT34	Alloy cover	23
Knock off hubs	LAT42	Increases front track 1"	24
Alloy wheels	LAT31	13" x 6" and 13" x 7"	25
Safety hub kit which includes the following:			
Safety hubs	8133305	This increases track 1.5"	26
Rear end housing ends	LAT43	--	27
Fender skirts	LAT44	Rear fenders	28
Fender skirts	LAT45	Front fenders	29
Heavy duty springs	1365315	Front coil	30
Heavy duty rear springs	1365307	--	31
Competition rear shocks	1365307	Adjustable lever type	32
Rear disc brakes	LAT06	10" disc cast iron	33

(5)

Appendix 6

NOTE STOCK 2BBL 🚗 260. 2

2a NOTE - SOLID LIFTERS
SCREW IN STUDS

Appendix 6

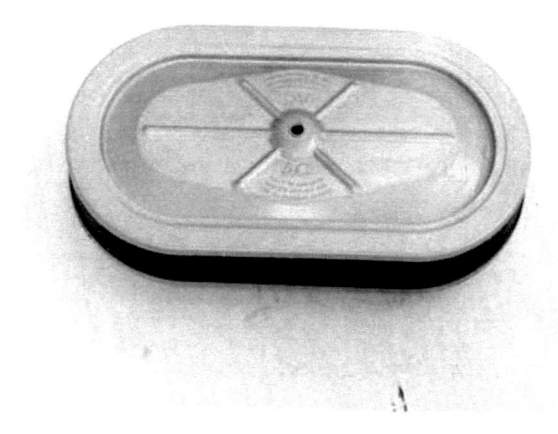

3

4

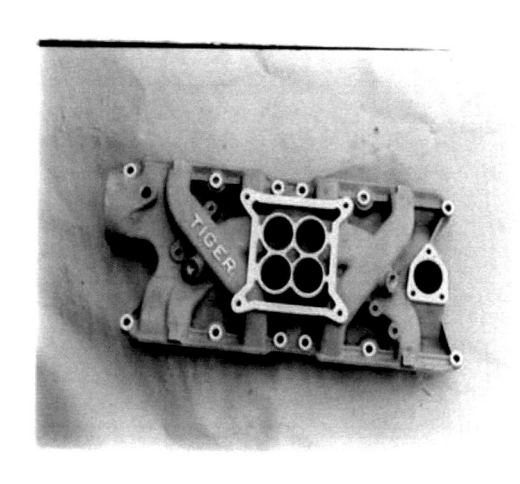

4a
STOCK 4BBL CAST
ALUMINIUM MANIFOLD.

Appendix 6

5 — STOCK ex HEADER. NO foto NECESSARY

6 — STOCK TRANSMISSION NO foto NECESSARY.

7

Appendix 6

8

8a

9 HEAVY DUTY OIL COOLER, WITH THERMOCOUPLING.

Appendix 6

10 — REAR AXLE OIL COOLER STOCK ALPINE.

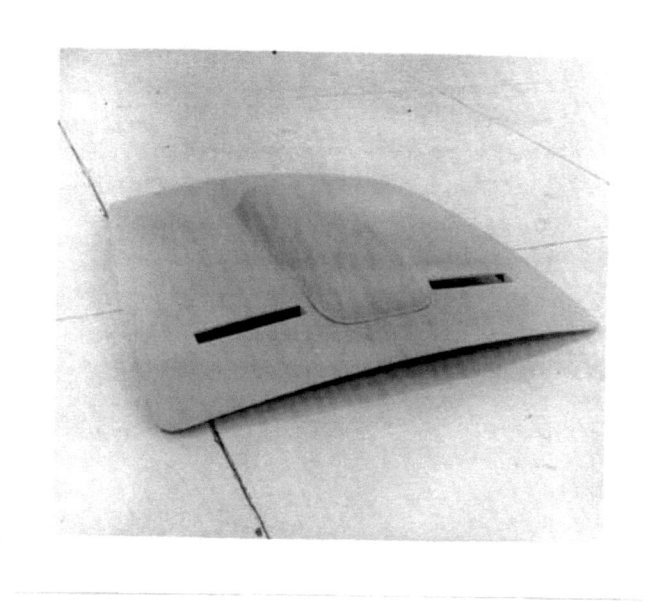

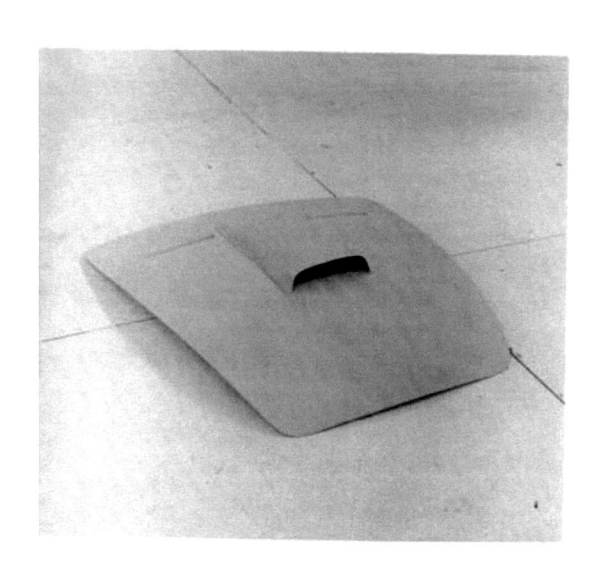

11

11a — NOTE - SUBJECT TO TEST THE HOOD SCOOP WILL POSSIBLY COME FURTHER FORWARD.

Appendix 6

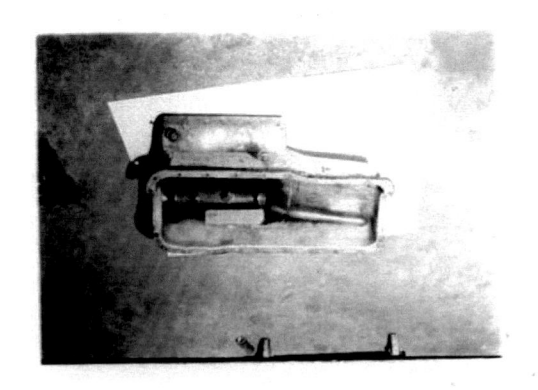

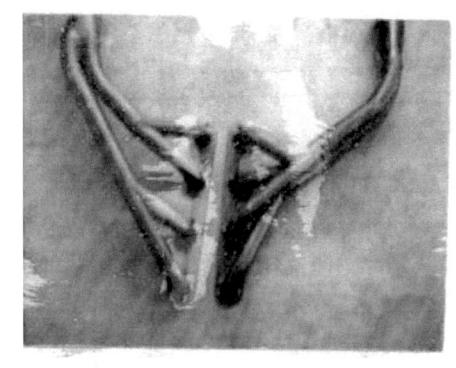

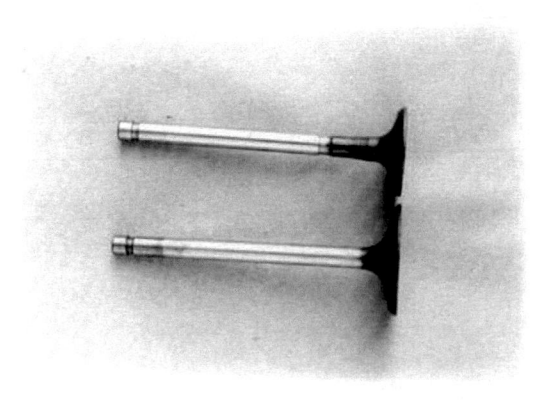

12

13

14

15

Appendix 6

16

17 TIGER —
JUST HOLE TO RELEASE HOT AIR

NOT
18

19   TWO DIFFERENT LENGTH
     PANARD BARS

345

Appendix 6

20 NOTE EXPERIMENTAL FORD HI-RISER MANIFOLD AVAILABLE JAN 65.

21

22 HEAVY DUTY AXLE - L.A. PRODUCT.

Appendix 6

23 NOTE. FOR TYPE 23 SALISBURY - ALU. COVER ALLOWS ADDITIONAL 1 QT OIL.

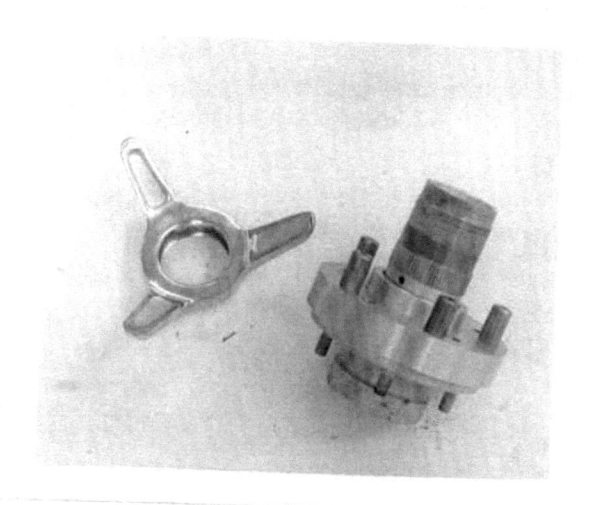

24

HALIBRAND WHEEL - BOLT ON OR KNOCK OFF 6" AND 7" AVAILABLE.

25

Appendix 6

26 - SAFETY HUB (AUSTIN HEALY TYP

28

29

Appendix 6

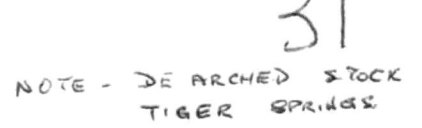

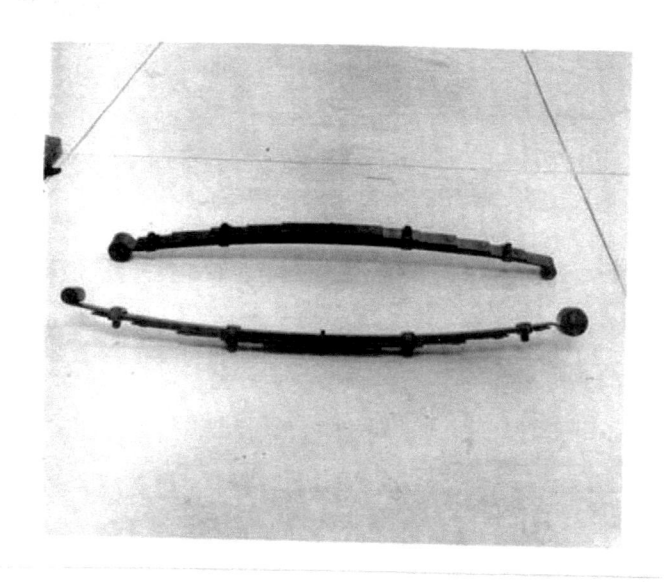

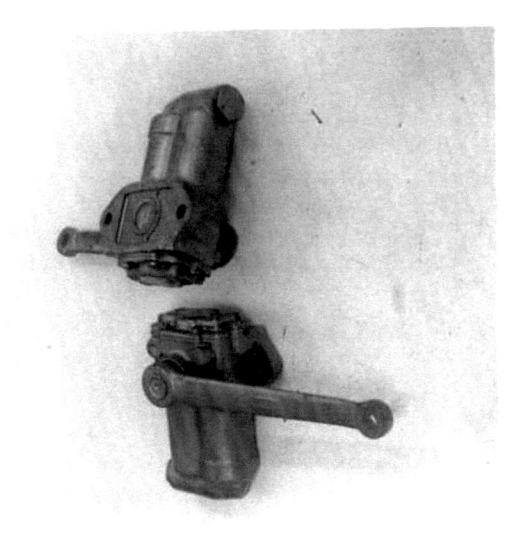

30

31
NOTE - DE ARCHED STOCK
TIGER SPRINGS

32
SERIES II ALPINE SHOCKS.

Appendix 6

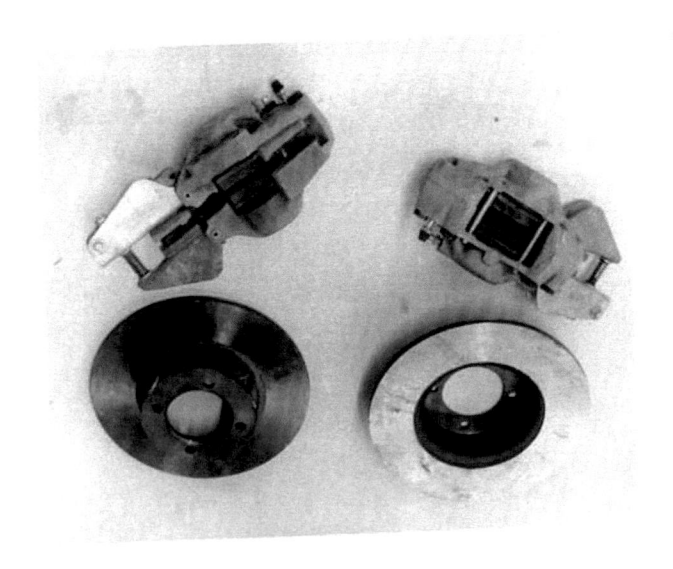

DAIMLER SP 250
DISC ASSYS.

33

17

Appendix 6

Appendix 6

352

Appendix 7: The FIA Appendix J Regulations

The regulations of Appendix J to the FIA International Sporting Code governed the classification and general build which motor vehicles had to meet to be able to compete in FIA run and sanctioned international motor events.

This allowed a wide range of motor vehicles – from standard high number production vehicles (Group 1 series Production cars) to the more exotic production sports cars (Group 3) and to the prototype cars that were road legal (Group 6) - to compete in international events.

The appendix also set out the minimum number of production vehicles that were required to meet the code and the basic components, dimensions and some aspects of the basic performance of the car (ground clearance, maximum turning circle etc.) that were similarly needed to fit within any one of the categories or groups.

Appendix J also set out those modifications allowed which made the basic car more adapted for competition (Group 2). Group 1 series production cars could thus be modified into Group 2 cars, but a minimum number needed to be produced in this state to meet the regulations – 1000 in the 1966 Appendix J.

Group 3 (Grand Touring) cars were meant to be for a lower production rate car and were generally sports cars from either a major, or less major specialist, manufacturer – but a minimum of 500 per annum was needed. The Tiger fitted this category.

The Appendix J shown here is for the 1966 season and governed the build of FRW667C and FRW668C. The previous Appendix J had been issued in 1964.

Appendix 7

APPENDIX 'J'
to the
F.I.A. INTERNATIONAL SPORTING CODE

CLASSIFICATION, DEFINITION AND SPECIFICATIONS OF CARS

CHAPTER I

CLASSIFICATION OF CARS

251—Categories and Groups

Cars competing in events shall be distributed into the following categories and groups:—

Category A: Recognised production cars (numbers between brackets are those of the required minimum production in 12 consecutive months).

Group 1 …	… Series-production touring cars	(5000)
Group 2 …	… Touring cars	(1000)
Group 3 …	… Grand touring cars	(500)
Group 4 …	… Sports cars	(50)

Category B: Special cars:

Group 5 …	… Special touring cars
Group 6 …	… Prototype sports cars

Category C: Racing cars:

Group 7 …	… Two-seater racing cars
Group 8 …	… Formula racing cars
Group 9 …	… Formula libre racing cars

CHAPTER II

DEFINITIONS AND GENERAL PRESCRIPTIONS CONCERNING CARS OF CATEGORIES A AND B

252—Definitions

(a) *Recognised Production Cars.* Cars of which the series-production of a certain number of identical (see definition of this word hereafter) cars, within a certain period of time, has been completed, and which are meant for the normal sale (see below) to the individual purchaser. This period of time is of 12 consecutive months. The checking of the existing minimum production enables the A.C.N. to apply to the F.I.A. for recognition (see this word below).

(b) *Special Cars.* Cars which have nothing or no more to do with a series-production vehicle, either that only one of the type has been built, or that an insufficient number of units has been built to enable recognition in Category A or that although they originate from a series-production car, they have been modified or equipped with new accessories to the point that their series-production nature no longer applies.

(c) *Racing Cars.* Cars manufactured solely for speed races on a circuit or a closed course. These cars are generally defined by the international racing formulae, the specifications of which are fixed by the F.I.A. for a certain period of time. Racing cars not being defined by any international formula are said of "formule libre" and their specifications must in that case be stated in the supplementary regulations of the event.

(d) *Identical.* By identical cars are meant cars manufactured as part of one same series and which consequently have the same coachwork (inside and outside) and the same mechanical components. The only differences allowed are those explicitly allowed by the present regulations and the limits of which are clearly specified for each group.

(e) *Minimum Production.* This minimum production, different for each group of cars, applies to perfectly identical cars, the manufacturing of which has been fully completed within a period of time of twelve consecutive months.

(f) *Normal Sale.* It means the distribution of cars to individual purchasers through the normal commercial service of the manufacturer.

(g) *Recognition.* It is the official checking made by the F.I.A. that a minimum number of cars of a specific model has been made on series-production terms to justify classification in group 1, 2, 3 or 4 of these regulations. Applications for recognition shall be submitted to the F.I.A. by the A.C.N. of the country in which the vehicle is manufactured and shall involve the drawing up of a recognition form (see below).

Recognition of a series-produced car will become void 4 years after the date on which the series-production of the said model has been stopped.

Recognition of a model may only be valid for one group. The transferring of a previously recognised model from one group to another will therefore nullify the effect of the said previous recognition.

(h) *Recognition Forms.* All cars recognised by the F.I.A. shall be subject to a descriptive form called Recognition Form on which shall be entered all data required to identify the said model.

To this effect only the standard recognition forms and standard additional form for "normal evolution of the type" and "variant" approved by the F.I.A. shall be used by all A.C.N's.

The production of the forms at scrutineering and/or at the start may be required by the promoters who will be entitled to refuse the participation of the entrant in the event in case of non-production.

In the case of any doubt remaining after the checking of a model of car against its homologation form, the scrutineers would have to refer themselves either to the maintenance booklet printed for the benefit of the make's distributors or to the general catalogue in which are listed all spare parts.

It will rest with the competitor to obtain the recognition form and, if need be, the additional forms concerning his car, from the A.C.N. of the manufacturing country of the vehicle.

Forms of cars of British manufacture are obtainable only from the R.A.C. at a fee of £1.10.0. Money must be submitted with the order.

(i) *Cylinder-Capacity Classes.* The cars shall be distributed into the following 13 classes, according to their cylinder-capacity.

1.	Cylinder-capacity inferior or equal to				500 c.c.
2.	,,	exceeding	500 c.c. and inf. or equal to		600 c.c.
3.	,,	,,	600 c.c.	,, ,,	700 c.c.
4.	,,	,,	700 c.c.	,, ,,	850 c.c.
5.	,,	,,	850 c.c.	,, ,,	1000 c.c.
6.	,,	,,	1000 c.c.	,, ,,	1150 c.c.
7.	,,	,,	1150 c.c.	,, ,,	1300 c.c.
8.	,,	,,	1300 c.c.	,, ,,	1600 c.c.
9.	,,	,,	1600 c.c.	,, ,,	2000 c.c.
10.	,,	,,	2000 c.c.	,, ,,	2500 c.c.
11.	,,	,,	2500 c.c.	,, ,,	3000 c.c.
12.	,,	,,	3000 c.c.	,, ,,	5000 c.c.
13.	,,	,,	5000 c.c.		

Regulations intended for specific events may provide one or several sub-divisions of class 13. There shall be no sub-division of the other classes.

The above-mentioned classification will only apply to non-supercharged engines.

Unless otherwise specified in special provisions set up by the F.I.A. for a certain category of events, the organizers are not bound to include all the above mentioned classes in the supplementary regulations, and, furthermore they are free to group two or more consecutive classes, according to the particular circumstances of their events.

(j) *Supercharging.* If the engine of a car includes a separate device used for supercharging it, the nominal cylinder-capacity will be multiplied by 1.4 and the car will pass into the class corresponding to the nominal volume thus obtained. The new cylinder-capacity of the car shall always be considered as the real one. This shall particularly be the case in order to classify the car according to its cylinder-capacity, its inside dimensions, its minimum number of seats, etc.

A dynamic air inlet meant for canalizing the air from the atmosphere into the engine feeding inlet will not be considered as having any supercharging effect.

(k) *Coachwork.* By coachwork is meant:
  Externally: All parts of the car licked by the air-stream and situated above a plan passing through the centre of the wheel hubs.
  Internally: All visible parts of the passenger compartment.
  Coachworks are differentiated as follows:—
  1. Completely closed coachworks.
  2. Completely open coachworks.
  3. Convertible coachworks: with a hood in either supple (drophead) or rigid (hard-top) material.

Coachworks of one minimum series shall be identical with the only exception of a "sun roof".

However, if a model has its coachwork equipped with a specific number of doors and has been recognised on the basis of a given minimum series, similar recognition may be granted to another coachwork with a different number of doors when its minimum production reaches 50% of the figure necessary for the recognition of the basic series, providing that both models have the following common characteristics:
  (i) A coachwork of similar shape, i.e., of which the general appearance is basically the same and to which only those minor alterations have been made to change from 4 doors to 2 doors (or vice-versa);
  (ii) exactly identical mechanical parts;
  (iii) the same wheelbase, track and number of seats;
  (iv) a weight at least equal;
  (v) the F.I.A. decision to recognise this variant coachwork involving the drawing up of an additional "variant" recognition form.

As far as convertible cars are concerned, these must comply in all respects with the specifications concerning closed cars if they run an event under this form, or with the specifications concerning open cars if they run with the hood down or the hard top removed.

(l) *Minimum Weight.* It is the real minimum weight of the empty car (without persons or luggage aboard) fully equipped and ready for delivery to the purchaser. It shall consequently include a spare wheel equipped with a tyre similar to the type mounted on at least 2 of the

Appendix 7

APPENDIX "J"

4 wheels, and none of the accessories normally mounted on the most economical model of the series concerned being removed, except for the normally supplied repair kit (jack, tool kit). All liquid tanks (of lubrication, cooling system, braking, heating system, if need be), except for the fuel tank, must be full.

The minimum weight of the car mentioned on the recognition form shall be strictly respected. Any lightening of the car by removal or replacement of parts, aiming at reducing its weight, is prohibited.

253—Prescriptions Common To All Cars of Categories A and B

(a) *Chassis, Ground Clearance, Steering Lock.* The car, supplied with enough fuel for starting the event, its oil and water tanks full, must be able to drive over—under the power of its engine and its driver at the steering wheel—a mass of 80×80 cm. and 10 cm. high.

The maximum steering radius shall be 6.75 m. which means that the car must be able to make a complete turn in any direction without the wheels going beyond two parallel lines 13.50 m. apart drawn on the ground.

(b) *Coachwork: Minimum Inside Dimensions and Minimum Number of Seats.* Cars shall be equipped with a minimum of two seats or a minimum of four seats according to the group in which they seek recognition and, within a same group, according to their engine cylinder-capacity.

For each group specified in these Regulations, the minimum number of seats is listed hereafter and the minimum inside dimensions for both cases are indicated in the following paragraphs.

1st Case (see diagram 1). Car equipped with 4 (or more) seats. The length (A) is measured from the centre of the brake pedal at rest to the vertical plane tangent to the back of the compressed rear seat.

The height at the front (B) is measured between the lowest surface of the front seat, compressed by a standard mass of 60 kgs. (see diagram 2) and the ceiling (the padding if any, being compressed).

If the front seats are separate, the measurement is made in the axis of the two seats. In case of adjustable front seats, the seats will be placed in medium position.
If there is a common front seat, the measurement is made at 25 cm. from the centre line of the car.

The height at the back (D) is measured between the lowest surface of the rear seat, compressed by the standard mass, and the ceiling (the padding if any, being compressed) at 25 cm. from the centre line of the car.

APPENDIX "J"

The width over the front seats (C) is measured along the vertical plane passing through the centre of the standard mass, 30 cm. above the compressed seat, and between the upper strip of each front door.

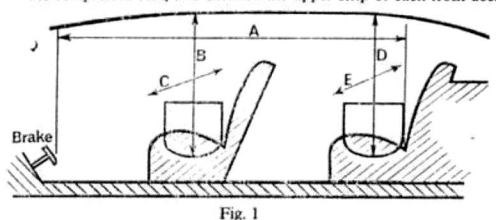

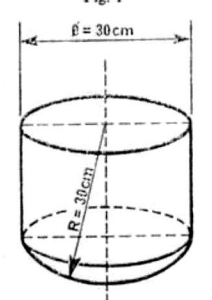

Fig. 1

Fig. 2
Standard Weight = 60 kgs ± 200 grms.

The width over the back seats (E) is measured along the vertical plane passing through the centre of the standard mass, 30 cm. above the compressed seat and between the upper strip of each back door, or at the same height as for the front seats when there are no doors at the rear.

The minimum dimensions (in centimetres) to determine that a car is a 4-seater are the following:—

Cylinder-capacity	A	B	C	D	E
Up to 700 c.c.	Free	85	100		
From 700 to 2000 c.c.	160	85	110	85	110
Over 2000 c.c.	170	90	120	85	120

APPENDIX "J"

2nd Case (see diagrams 3 and 4). Cars with a minimum of 2 seats. The two seats must be distributed equally on either sides of the longitudinal centreline of the car and at the same level, regardless of their normal play for adjusting them to the size of the driver. The location provided for placing or housing the seats must have a minimum of 40 cm. maintained all along the depth of the seat.

The "protected height" shall measure at least 85 cm. from the bottom of the seat compressed by the standard mass (see diagram 2) to the ceiling (any existing padding being compressed) in cars with closed coachwork, and at least 80 cm. from the bottom of the seat compressed by the standard mass (see diagram 2) to the upper edge of the windscreen, in cars with open coachwork (measure made vertically through the centre of the standard mass).

The minimum interior width over the front seats (see measurement C) shall be of 100 cm. in cars with a cylinder-capacity inferior or equal to 700 c.c., 110 cm. in cars with a cylinder-capacity varying from 700 c.c. to 2000 c.c. and 120 cm. in cars with a cylinder-capacity exceeding 2000 c.c. The minimum width of foot space (for each person) must be at least 25 cm. measured perpendicularly to the centre line of the car, plumb with the pedals.

(c) *Windshield—Windshield Wiper.* A windshield made of security material is compulsory. In all series-production cars it shall be made of the material originally provided by the manufacturer. It shall be equipped with at least one automatic wiper sweeping a sufficient area to enable the driver to distinctly see the road from his seat.

The windshield shall comply with the following requirements:—

(i) Be placed symetrically with regard to the centre line of the car;
(ii) have a minimum height of 25 cm., maintained between two points symetrically placed with regard to the centre line of the car and of which one is determined by the vertical line passing through the centre of the steering wheel. There must furthermore be at least 45 cm. between the two said points;
(iii) have a minimum width of 90 cm.; chord measured at half its vertical height.

Shall alone be considered as being the windshield, the glass area through which one has an entirely free vision towards the front, without being limited by any outside opaque projection apart from the bulge of the wings covering the front wheels.

(d) *Mudguards.* Mudguards shall be of permanent nature and firmly fixed.

They shall project over the wheels and provide efficient covering on at least one-third of their circumference, and at least the width of the tyre.

APPENDIX "J"

Width where the 'protected height' must be maintained

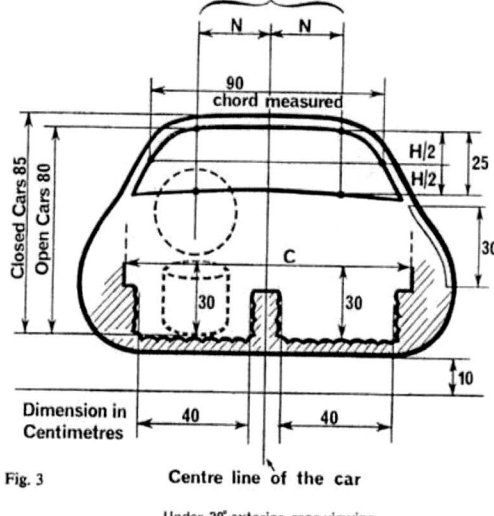

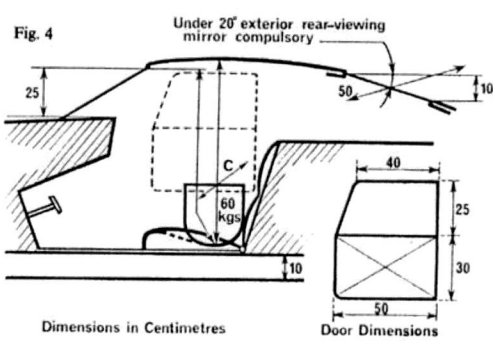

Fig. 3

Fig. 4

Dimensions in Centimetres

Door Dimensions

Appendix 7

APPENDIX "J"

In those cars where mudguards are entirely or partly overhung by the body structure, the combination mudguards-body or the body alone shall nevertheless meet the above protection requirements.

Mudguards must be solid with the body, there being no gap between them.

(e) *Hood.* Open or convertible cars shall be equipped with a hood fitting exactly, and without any intermediary device, to the windshield, the door windows or side panels, and the rear of the coachwork.

The hood may never interfere with the opening of the doors. It shall offer a rear window, the minimum dimensions of which are specified in the present article (see further on, at "rear window").

It must be liable to be used partially or permanently during the event. The supplementary regulations must specify in which state must run convertible body cars (as closed cars or open or at the discretion of the entrant) but the hood if not fitted on the car must always remain aboard the car during the whole of the event. The hood may be replaced by a hard top subject to the same conditions as for the hood.

(f) *Doors.* All vehicles shall be fitted with at least one rigid door on each side, with closing devices and hinges which may be located neither on the door-stile to the rear or on the door-sill. The dimensions of the door panel (part which is normally opaque) must be such as to enable a rectangle of at least 50 cm. wide and 30 cm. high being inscribed in. Cars with sliding-doors will not be allowed unless they comprehend a safety system enabling to quickly and easily empty the car of its occupants in case of an accident.

Cars with closed or convertible coachwork shall have doors equipped with mobile windows of the material provided by the manufacturer for the considered model, liable to be opened over at least one-third of their surface in order to provide for airing, each window having a minimum width of 40 cm. and a minimum height of 25 cm.

When opened, the doors must give free access to the seats. They must be made in such a way that they never restrict the lateral view of the driver.

(g) *Rear View.* It shall be secured by an inside mirror commanding a rear window measuring at least 10 cm. vertically maintained along a width of at least 50 cm. However, if the straight line connecting the upper and lower edges of the rear window opening makes by intersecting the horizontal line an angle inferior to 20 degrees, the car complying with the same specifications as those required for the checking of the ground clearance (see art. 253), the rear view will have to be efficiently obtained by other means (two outside mirrors or any other system of equivalent efficiency).

APPENDIX "J"

(h) *Luggage Trunk.* A covered space being an integral part of the coachwork but outside the space occupied by the seats provided for the passengers, shall be provided.

This space shall be such as to enable the placing without special difficulty, sheltered from rain or dirt, a variable number of suitcases (according to the cylinder-capacity of the engine equipping the car, see below) of the following minimum dimensions: 60 cm. × 40 cm. × 20 cm.

Cylinder-capacity inferior or equal to 2000 c.c.: 1 suitcase.
Cylinder-capacity superior to 2000 c.c.: 2 suitcases.

(i) *Starting.* Cars shall have to be equipped with a device for automatically starting the engine, with its source of power and liable of being actuated by the driver sitting at the wheel.

(j) *Fuel Tanks.* No recognition shall be granted to models of cars equipped with fuel tanks (main and additional) exceeding the following total capacities:—

Cars up to 700 c.c. of engine cylinder-capacity:	60 l.
Cars from 700 c.c. to 1000 c.c. "	70 l.
" 1000 c.c. to 1300 c.c. "	80 l.
" 1300 c.c. to 1600 c.c. "	90 l.
" 1600 c.c. to 2000 c.c. "	100 l.
" 2000 c.c. to 2500 c.c. "	110 l.
" 2500 c.c. to 3000 c.c. "	120 l.
" 3000 c.c. to 5000 c.c. "	140 l.
Cars exceeding 5000 c.c. "	160 l.

(k) *Spare Wheels.* All production and recognised cars shall be equipped with at least one spare wheel with its tyre occupying the position provided for by the manufacturer which may not encroach upon the space provided for luggage.

The spare wheel shall be equipped with a tyre of dimensions similar to those of the tyres fitted on at least two wheels of the car.

(l) *Muffler.* Even when the supplementary provisions of a group allow for the replacement of the original muffler, cars competing in an open road event shall always be equipped with an exhaust muffler complying with the road regulations of the country(ies) through which the event is run.

For events exclusively run on closed circuits, the supplementary regulations may authorise the modification, the replacement or the removal of the exhaust muffler.

(m) *Safety Devices.* For cars competing in speed races exclusively the following safety devices are provided:—

(i) For cars with an open coachwork: Compulsory mounting of a roll bar being 3 cm. higher than the driver's helmet and being wider than the driver's shoulders when seated at his wheel.

(ii) For cars with a closed coachwork: Optional fitting in of a roll cage improving the structure of the body and meant to prevent it from crushing in the event of a violent shock or a somersault. This roll-cage must be mounted in such a way that:—

It shall in no way interfere with getting into the seats and normally occupying them;

APPENDIX "J"

it shall not encroach on the volume occupied by the driver or any of the passengers;

the exact weight of the device shall be subject to a statement from the competitor, to be appended to the entry form.

(n) *Exhaust System.* The outlet pipes of the silencer shall be orientated either towards the rear or the sides of the car. If the outlet pipes are pointing rearwards, their ports shall be placed at a height neither superior to 45 cm. nor inferior to 10 cm.; they shall not protrude by more than 15 cm. beyond the overall length of the car. If the exhaust pipes are directed sideways, they must be located behind a vertical line passing through the wheelbase centre and may not project in any way beyond the coachwork plate. Adequate protection shall be provided in order to prevent heated pipes from causing burns.

(o) *Oil Catch Tank.* Cars participating in an event which only includes a speed race in closed circuit shall be equipped in such a way as to prevent the oil from spilling on the track. In cars of a cylinder-capacity inferior or equal to 2000 c.c., the oil catching device shall have a minimum capacity of 2 litres which shall be increased to 3 litres for cars with a cylinder-capacity exceeding 2000 c.c. This provision, binding in the case of circuit speed events, will be optional for the other events (hill climbs, rallies even those including classification tests run on closed tracks) and may be included in the Supplementary Regulations.

(p) *Limits of the Modifications Authorized.* Certain modifications to the original parts, certain additions and/or removal of accessories normally mounted by the manufacturer on the model concerned, are explicitly authorized by the present regulations. The limits of these modifications are explicitly mentioned for each of the 6 groups of categories A and B. All those not formally indicated as authorized for the group in which the car claims classification and which affect, even secondarily, the mechanical efficiency of the engine, the steering, the transmission, the road-holding and/or the braking, will imply the exclusion of the car from its group.

If these modifications or additions have been the subject of a previous statement by the entrant, the car may be allowed to compete in the event in one of the other groups provided in the supplementary regulations and with the prescriptions of which it complies.

Should there be however an obvious case of willful misrepresentation, the entrant would not be authorized to start or would be stopped if he had already started, with request to the A.C.N. concerned to pronounce his suspension for at least 12 months.

(q) *Fuel.* For rallies, commercial fuel of the countries traversed shall be used. For speed events, only fuel as Art. 297 is authorized.

APPENDIX "J"

254—Rule for Changing from one Group to Another and Authorized Amalgamation of Groups

Cars originally belonging to a certain group but which have been subject to duly declared modifications and/or additions that exceed the limits specified for the group concerned, may pass into a higher group, provided for in the supplementary regulations, with the prescriptions of which it complies and under the following conditions:—

Group 1 passes into group 2
Group 2 (or 1 + 2) passes into group 5
Group 3 passes into group 4
Group 4 (or 3 + 4) passes into group 6
Group 6 (or 3 + 4 + 5) passes into group 7

CHAPTER III

SERIES PRODUCTION TOURING CARS GROUP 1

255—Definition

Touring cars built on series production terms. These cars shall compete in events without having undergone any preparation likely to improve their performances or their conditions of use. The only working authorized is that which is necessary to keep the cars in running order, or to replace parts damaged through wear or accident. The modifications and additions explicitly authorized are mentioned hereafter under article 257. Except for what is explicitly authorized any part damaged through wear or accident may only be replaced by an original part which must be exactly the same as the one to which it is substituted.

256—Minimum Production and Number of Seats

Series-production touring cars shall have been manufactured at the rate of at least 5000 identical units within 12 consecutive months and offer at least 4 seats, except if their engine cylinder-capacity is inferior to 700 c.c., in which case the manufacturer may deliver them as two-seaters.

257—Mountings and Modifications Authorized

(a) *Lighting Devices.* All lighting and signalling devices must comply with the administrative regulations of the country where the event is taking place; cars from abroad must comply, in this respect, with the prescriptions of the Convention on International Road Traffic. Lighting devices supplied with the vehicle's standard equipment shall be those provided by the manufacturer for the model concerned.

It is permitted to add at the front only two extra lighting devices to those normally provided by the manufacturer and mentioned on the recognition form.

The mounting of reverse-lights is authorized provided police regulations are respected but not the fitting of manoeuvable search-lights on the roof or elsewhere.

Waivers may be granted to this specification on condition that they be explicitly provided for in the supplementary regulations of the event.

The mounting of additional headlights shall not entail any modification of the coachwork.

APPENDIX "J" 245

(b) *Fuel and Oil Tanks.* Must be those normally provided by the manufacturer for the model concerned, the capacities of which are mentioned on the recognition form. If, for the said model, tanks of different capacities are normally provided, only those mounted on the required number of cars necessary for recognition of the said model will be authorized.

The location and type of filling port for the fuel tank(s) may not be changed.

The use of a fuel tank with an increased capacity may be authorized by the A.C.N. with the F.I.A.'s agreement, in the case of events organized under particular climatic conditions (on desertic or tropical courses for instance).

(c) *Cooling Circuit.* If, for the said model, radiators of different capacities are normally provided, only those mounted on the required number of cars necessary for the recognition of the said car, will be authorized.

The addition of a radiator screen is authorized.

The use of a radiator with an increased capacity may be authorized by the A.C.N. with the F.I.A.'s agreement, in the case of events organised under particular climatic conditions (on desertic or tropical courses for instance).

(d) *Feeding.* The carburettor(s) or fuel injection pump(s) normally mounted on the recognised model and described on the recognition form may not be changed nor removed.

The elements which control the quantity of fuel taken into the engine may be changed, but not those which control the quantity of air.

(e) *Electrical Equipment.* The tension (voltage) of the electrical equipment may not be changed.

The make and capacity (amperage) of *battery* and *generator* are free. The manufacturer may provide for one same minimum series the use of either a dynamo or of an alternator on condition that this is explicitly mentioned on the basic recognition form or on an additional form.

The original battery may be replaced—by the manufacturer or the entrant himself—by another one of increased capacity provided however that the location remains unchanged. By location of the battery is meant the coachwork compartment in which the battery is originally mounted.

Ignition coil, condenser and distributor are free, subject to the ignition system remaining the same as that provided by the manufacturer for the model concerned, and the replacement of the said accessories not entailing any modification of the attachment system provided by the manufacturer for the model concerned.

Spark plugs. Make and type free.

246 APPENDIX "J"

(f) *Transmission.* For one same series of 5000 cars the following possibilities are given on the formal condition that they are those of the series-production and that they are normally sold to the purchaser and are entered on the recognition form.

Gear-box: Either two gear-boxes with the same number of ratios but different in their staging, or
two gear-boxes with a different number of ratios and different in staging provided that at least 50% of the required minimum number of cars have been equipped with either one of the two gear-boxes.

The fitting of an overdrive system in addition to the existing gear-box is authorised.

Final drive: Two different ratios.

Should the manufacturer have provided a greater number of gear-box ratios and/or rear axle ratios, he must, to obtain recognition, have to prove that he has achieved the required minimum production of the car as many times as he has submitted two different gear-boxes and two different rear-axle ratios. An automatically controlled gear-box is not taken into consideration. Recognition of it and of its particular rear-axle ratio will always be granted in addition to the two sets of manually controlled gear-boxes.

The gear-box lever will have to be located as provided by the manufacturer and mentioned on the recognition form. Form and length are free.

(g) *Shock Absrobers.* The make and type are free. However, no addition is allowed, and neither their original destination nor their number, nor their system of operation may be modified. By system of operation is meant: hydraulic or friction shock-absorbers, whether of the telescopic lever-type, whether the device has a double-acting or a simple-acting effect, and, in case of hydraulic shock-absorbers, whether there is or not an additional gas chamber. The original supports may not be changed in any way.

(h) *Tyres.* The make and type are free on condition that the tyres concerned are foreseen by the manufacturer to be fitted on the original wheels without any modifications of the original rims and without need of an intermediary device. Any special or additional non-skid device for snow or ice may also be fitted.

(i) *Brakes.* Must be those provided by the manufacturer. The replacement of worn linings is authorised and their system of attachment is free, provided the dimensions of inner friction surfaces remain unchanged, Servo-assistance is only permitted when duly recognised and at least 5000 identical cars having been made with this equipment.

(j) *Supplementary Accessories not Included in the Recognition.* Are authorised without restriction provided they have no influence whatsoever on the mechanical performance of the engine, such as those concerning the aesthetics or the inside comfort (lighting, heating, radio, etc.) or those enabling an easier or safer driving of the car (speed-pilot, windscreen wiper, etc.), provided they do not affect, even indirectly the mechanical performance of the engine, the steering, the transmission, the road holding and the braking.

The pedals must be those provided by the manufacturer (number, place, method of mounting), but it is allowed to change pedal pads or to fit heavier or wider pads.

APPENDIX "J" 247

(k) *Coachwork.* None of the normal elements of the coachwork (dashboard, all inside quiltings whatever their location), none of the accessories normally mounted by the manufacturer on the most economical model may be removed or replaced.

However, the modifications deriving from the mounting of the supplementary accessories authorised in the preceding paragraph, such as those necessitated by the adding of a windscreen washer (drilling of a hole into the bonnet) or of a speedometer (housing in the dashboard), will be allowed.

On same minimum series may comprehend various materials for seats, upholstery and inside quilting (cloth, leather, plastics, etc.) and two different types of front seats (bench type or separate seats). These variants must be stated on the recognition form and in particular the different weights resulting from the mounting of different seats must be specified.

Transparent parts must, in case of damages, be replaced by others made of a material identical to the original one listed on the recognition form. They shall be completely interchangeable with those originally mounted. They must be mounted on the original supports and their original opening system must be maintained.

(l) *Bumpers, Embellishers, Streamlining.* Bumpers are compulsory on all cars for which the manufacturer has normally provided them. Wheel embellishers may be removed. The addition of any protective device underneath the car is forbidden unless such a device is mentioned on the recognition form of the model in question or is authorised or made compulsory by the supplementary regulations of the event.

CHAPTER IV

TOURING CARS. GROUP 2

258—Definition

Cars of limited series-production which may be submitted to certain modifications aiming at making them more adapted to competition. The list of the modifications and additions explicitly authorised is given hereafter under article 260.

Moreover in this group may be classed cars of Group 1 which have been subject to modifications and/or additions exceeding the limits of Group 1. These cars will then enjoy the same freedom as provided for the present Group 2.

248 APPENDIX "J"

259—Minimum Production and Number of Seats

Touring cars shall have been manufactured at the rate of at least 1000 units and be equipped with at least 4 seats; however, if their cylinder-capacity is equal or inferior to 700 c.c. they may be delivered as two-seaters.

260—Modifications and Additions Authorised

All those already authorised in Group 1, plus the following ones:—

(a) *Lighting Devices.* The mounting of additional headlights is authorised provided that a total of 6 headlights is not exceeded (parking lights not included). Extra headlights may, if necessary, be fitted into the front part of the coachwork or into the radiator grille, but such openings as those needed in this case must be completely filled by the additional headlights.

(b) *Electrical Equipment.* The replacement of a dynamo by an alternator is authorised, provided the attachment system and the driving method remain unchanged.

(c) *Reboring.* Maximum tolerance: 1,2 mm., but the resulting increase in cylinder-capacity may not be such as to make the car pass into the above class. This reboring tolerance is valid for any type of engine (with or without sleeves).

(d) *Stabilizer.* The fitting of a stabilizer is authorised.

(e) *Fan.* Complete freedom.

(f) *Air-Filter.* May be changed or removed.

(g) *Fuel Pump.* A mechanically controlled pump may be replaced by an electrically controlled one or vice versa and the location of the pump may be different.

(h) *Oil Filter and Cooler.* An oil filter and/or oil cooler may be added when the model provided by the manufacturer has none, and/or the existing one may be altered.

(i) *Carburettor(s).* The carburettor(s) provided by the manufacturer may be replaced by another (others) of a different diameter, provided:
the number be the same as that provided by the manufacturer;
they can be mounted on the inlet manifold of the engine with no need of any intermediary device and by using the original attachment parts.

(j) *Springs* (valves, clutch, suspension, etc.). May be replaced by others of unrestricted origin, but with no modification of the number provided by the manufacturer and on condition they can be fitted without alteration of the original supports.

(k) *Transmission.* May be used on all gear-boxes, manual or automatic, and all final drive ratios provided and delivered by the manufacturer for the model concerned, which have been granted recognition and are entered on the recognition form. The replacement of a manually controlled clutch by an automatic one, is authorised, whatever its operating system may be.

(l) *Differential.* It may comprehend a device enabling to limit its normal functioning (limited slip control). This device must be entered on the recognition form or on an additional form (variant).

The use of a device which completely blocks the functioning of the differential may not be accepted unless it has been fitted on the same minimum number of cars as necessary for recognition of the basic model.

Appendix 7

APPENDIX "J" 249

(m) *Pistons and Camshaft(s)*. All modifications of pistons are permitted. They may be lightened, their shape may be altered and they may even be replaced by others supplied or not by the manufacturer.

The camshaft(s) may also be altered or replaced by others supplied or not by the manufacturer.

(n) *Cylinder Block and Head*. The increase in the compression ratio through machining of the cylinder head or block (or using a thinner gasket or removing it) is authorised.

(o) *Muffler*. The make and type are free, on condition that the original exhaust manifold—and particularly its outlet port—remains entirely identical to the original part. The silencing effectiveness shall not be diminished. It shall, in any case, remain within the limits provided by the police regulations of the country where the event is run.

By exhaust manifold is meant the part collecting together the gases from the individual exhaust ports.

(p) *Finishing Off*. All perfecting operations by finishing or machining the original mechanical parts, but not their replacement, except with regard to springs, pistons and camshaft(s) as specified above under paragraphs (j) and (m). In other words, provided it is always possible to ascertain unquestionably the origin of the series-production part, it may be rectified, balanced, lightened, reduced or modified with regard to the shape through tooling, to the exclusion of any addition of material or any mechanical extension or of any process involving a change of the characteristics of the molecular structure or of the surface of the metal.

(q) *Wheels and Rims*. Must retain the dimensions provided by the manufacturer for his series-production and be mentioned on the recognition form.

One basic series may comprehend wheels of different types (solid or perforated disc wheels, spoke wheels, etc.), and different rims. But even when the recognition form mentions such differences, all four wheels must have the same diameter.

(r) *Brakes*. The fitting of a dual pump or any type of device providing both have a simultaneous action on the four wheels and a divided action on the front and rear wheels is authorised.

The make and attachment system of linings are free, but not other change is authorised. In particular, the dimensions of inner friction surfaces must remain unchanged.

The mounting of a braking servo-assistance system is authorised.

(s) *Coachwork Elements*. The steering wheel and the front seats may be replaced, provided seats of at least the same weight as the original ones be substituted to them.

250 APPENDIX "J"

(t) *Cables and Lines*. It is allowed to entirely modify the arrangement and location of all cables and lines providing for the passage of fluid elements (air, oil, water, fuel, electric current, etc.)

CHAPTER V

GRAND TOURING CARS GROUP 3
Definition

261—Cars manufactured on a small series-production scale and designed for the drivers who seek the best possible performances and/or the greatest comfort without a special concern about cost.

262—Minimum Production and Number of Seats

Grand touring cars must have been manufactured at the rate of at least 500 absolutely identical units (unless authorisations, listed hereafter under article 263 specify otherwise) and be pped with at least 2 seats.

263—Modifications and/or Additions Authorised

Exactly the same as those authorised for Group 2 (touring cars).

CHAPTER VI

SPORTSCARS GROUP 4
264—Definition

High performance cars which must nevertheless include all equipments normally provided and legally required for vehicles using public roads.

265—Minimum Production and Number of Seats

Sportscars must have been manufactured at the rate of at least 50 units within 12 consecutive months, and be equipped with at least 2 seats (as defined under article 253).

266—Conditions Required for Recognition

The 50 cars shall be identical as regard the following points:—

(a) *Coachwork*. General line, materials of construction, shape of wings and bonnet, number of doors. Small modifications will be allowed when made necessary by the different uses of the car (circuit or road events), or by the mounting of supplementary equipments authorised by the present regulations.

(b) *Chassis*. Wheelbase and track.

(c) *Engine*. Cylinder head, cylinder block, number of cylinders, bore, stroke number and location of the crankshaft bearings, type of bearings and of all rotating parts; number, location and driving system of camshafts.

Number of valves and valve-operating system.

Number and location of the inlet and exhaust ports. (Free: Ignition including the number of spark plugs, feeding and exhaust; carburettor, filters, manifolds.)

APPENDIX "J" 251

(d) *Transmission*. Only one series of gears authorised, plus an automatic gearbox and its special final drive ratio. Complete freedom for all gearbox and final drive ratios.

(e) *Suspension*. Operating principle and function of its components.

(f) *Braking Systems*. The braking system (drum or disc, or drum and disc brakes) must be identical on all cars of the minimum series required for recognition. The braking system must be laid out in such a way that the brake pedal normally controls the four wheels. In case of a leak at any point of the piping or any failure in the braking transmission the brake pedal should continue to operate on at least two wheels.

(g) *Minimum Weight*. The weight of the sportscars shall be at least the one mentioned by their manufacturer on the recognition form of the model concerned, no reduction being allowed. This weight shall be at least equal to the inferior limits mentioned hereafter:—

Engine cyl.-cap. inf. or equal to 500 c.c. : 450 kgs.
" " from 500 to 600 c.c. : 460 kgs.
" " " 600 to 700 c.c. : 470 kgs.
" " " 700 to 850 c.c. : 480 kgs.
" " " 850 to 1000 c.c. : 500 kgs.
" " " 1000 to 1150 c.c. : 510 kgs.
" " " 1150 to 1300 c.c. : 525 kgs.
" " " 1300 to 1600 c.c. : 550 kgs.
" " " 1600 to 2000 c.c. : 575 kgs.
" " " 2000 to 2500 c.c. : 600 kgs.
" " " 2500 to 3000 c.c. : 650 kgs.
" " " 3000 to 5000 c.c. : 700 kgs.
" " exceeding 5000 c.c. : 750 kgs.

CHAPTER VII

SPECIAL TOURING CARS GROUP 5
Definition and Specifications

Vehicles deriving from cars recognised in groups 1 and 2, of which they have kept the original coachwork, but which have been submitted to modifications or additions not authorised under articles 257 and 260.

These alterations or additions may affect the mechanical parts of the engine, of the transmission, of the steering, of the suspension, the number of carburettors, the inlet and exhaust system, the braking system.

The re-boring of the engine whether sleeveless or fitted with sleeves, is authorised up to the limit of the class to which belongs the car according to

---

Since 1959 the Drivers' and the Formula 1 Constructors' World Championships have been won exclusively on

DUNLOP TYRES

---

252 APPENDIX "J"

its original cylinder-capacity. Furthermore, in consideration of the trend of technical evolution and the necessity of increasing the safety of cars whose high performances had not been initially foreseen by manufacturer, the improvement of the braking may be sought without any obligation of maintaining the original system. Thus, drum brakes may be replaced by disc brakes.

However, the fundamentals and general design of the car, of the engine and other mechanical parts must remain the same as those of the corresponding series-production car. The number and location of camshafts, the valve-operating system must remain unchanged. A feeding system by carburettor may be replaced by indirect injection, but not by direct injection. Neither the shape nor the original materials of the standard coachwork may be modified, the chassis may be reinforced but not lightened nor cut. The track and wheelbase must remain unchanged, excpet for small differences caused by simply changing the wheels.

The suspension and rear axle must remain of same type. All casings and blocks housing the mechanical parts must remain unchanged, except for the following:—

(1) Cylinder-head.
(2) Oil sump.
(3) Braking system.
(4) Gear-box and rear axle box, which may be subject to minor alterations to enable the modification of the gear-box ratios or the mounting of an overdrive.

The minimum weight must be that entered on the recognition form of the corresponding series-production touring car, but the tolerance granted when the weight is checked will be minus 3%.

All changes and additions not authorised under articles 257 and 260 shall be the subject of a written statement from the competitor to be appended to the entry form sent to the promoters.

N.B.—At the time of going to press additional regulations are awaiting approval by the C.S.I. They concern series-produced cars of a cylinder-capacity exceeding 5000 c.c. and especially prepared for being used in circuit races. In the United States, these cars are called "*stock cars*". For this reason, the numbering of the articles show a gap pending completion of Chapter VII.

Monte Carlo Rally ... Tulip Rally ... E. African Safari
—most of the great 1965 international events were won outright on

DUNLOP

Appendix 8: Performance Figures for the Rally Cars

The Rootes Competition Department, with Des O'Dell as the team engineer, carried out a number of performance tests on the rally cars. These were generally carried out at the nearby MIRA test track at Nuneaton.

The figures shown in this appendix are drawn from those MIRA tests in the form of data from Des O'Dell's notes, shown in this appendix, and from other MIRA data taken from Mike Taylor's book 'Tiger'.

As an interesting comparison with the then current competition in class, figures are also shown for the rally Healey 3000 (DRX258C) and these are taken from an Autocar 'Given the Works' road test of September 1965.

Figures for the standard 260 Tiger are also shown, tested by the Rootes Engineering Research & Development in March 1965 at MIRA, and also some data for the 289 Mk2 Tiger from Autocar June 26th 1969.

The first tests in February 1965 were on ADU312B, soon after the Monte Carlo Rally of that year. The acceleration through the gears is similar to its immediate rival, the works Healey 3000, and the superior torque of the V8 against the straight six shows in the top gear acceleration, although there is not a lot in it, and above 80 mph power gives way to aerodynamic drag and the cars are more equal.

The next three comparisons (Columns 2 to 4) are interesting in that they allow a more realistic comparison of fitting of competition parts, using the same car as a comparison vehicle.

The figures for AHP295B were taken after the Police Rally with John Gott and, after being used on the Alpine Rally Recce, tested at MIRA on, or around, 11 August 1965 (column 2). The car was to full rally spec, had Shelby heads, a compression ratio of 11:1, a 4 bbl Holley Carburettor, the newly homologated 'correct' size inlet and exhaust valves (42mm inlet, 37mm exhaust as homologated in FOR211), and weighed 25cwt (1227 kg). The acceleration through the gears figures are slightly better than ADU312B, particularly at the top end where the car is around 1 sec quicker to 80 mph, whilst the top gear accelerations are similar.

The car was then taken back to Humber Road and standard heads, but with polished ports and a standard compression ratio, fitted and the car tested a few days later under similar weather conditions. Interestingly the performance through the gears is not significantly different, and even allowing for the normal variations that occur in timing, the heads appeared to make little difference to performance in a rally car of this build, although there is some apparent improvement in the top gear 70 – 80 and 80 – 90 times, where power will count. That is not to say that the extra power, if any, from the Shelby heads and higher compression, would not be more noticeable in a racing environment.

A final comparison (col 4) uses the same cylinder head set up as column 3, but changes the carburettor and manifold to that which would be used for the 1966 regulations – a 2 barrel carburettor and standard manifold (in this case both off a 289 engine). The lack of relative performance can be seen in the acceleration through the gears figures, being some 3.7 secs slower to 90 mph and, perhaps more importantly, the 3rd gear acceleration figures are some 10% slower. Also in the standing ¼ mile figure, which gives a good idea of overall acceleration, the figures are again some 8% slower. However, a 0 – 60 mph time of 8 secs is not too bad for a fully laden rally car of the period, but shows well how important good breathing is on a V8. This was the set up that was used on FRW667C and FRW 668C for the 1966 season.

Appendix 8

The build state of the cars was as follows :

Column 1: ADU312B

Directly from the 1964 Monte Carlo and before rebuild.
Full rally spec, 3.77 Power Lok differential. 15 gallon fuel, spare wheel and jack.
Wind 0 to 8 mph Ambient 43 deg F Dull & Overcast, dry track
Driver: Jim Ashworth Observer: Des O'Dell

Column 2: AHP 295B directly from Alpine Rally Recce

Full rally Spec Full fuel tank (26 gallons) 3.77 Power Lock diff
Shelby cylinder heads, polished ports, 11:1 compression ratio
Holley Carburettors Chokes 172/173Jets 0.067inch, 0.078 inch
Inlet valve 1.65inch (42mm), Exhaust 1.45 inch (37mm)
Wind speed 0 to 8 mph S/E Ambient 70 degF Dry track
Tyres 175 x 13 Dunlop SP3 Weight 25 cwt
Driver: Des O'Dell   Observer: D Brown

Column 3: AHP295B as column 2 with standard & polished heads

Full rally Spec Full fuel tank (25 gallons) 3.77 Power Lock diff
Standard 260 cylinder heads, polished ports, standard compression ratio
Shelby high performance camshaft
Holley Carburettors Chokes 172/173Jets 0.067inch, 0.078 inch
Inlet valve 1.65inch (42mm), Exhaust 1.45 inch (37mm)
Wind speed 0 to 10 mph NW Ambient 71 degF Sunny Dry track
Tyres 175 x 13 Dunlop SP3 Weight 25 cwt
Driver: Des O'Dell   Observer: D Brown

Column 4: AHP295B as Cols 2 and 3 but with 2-bbl carb. & manifold

Full rally Spec Full fuel tank (25 gallons) 3.77 Power Lock diff
Standard 260 cylinder heads, polished ports, standard compression ratio
Shelby high performance camshaft
289 2 barrel carburettor 289 Cast iron 2 barrel manifold
Inlet valve 1.65inch (42mm), Exhaust 1.45 inch (37mm)
Wind speed 5 to 12 mph NW Ambient 70 degF   Dry track
Tyres Dunlop SP3   Weight 25 cwt
Driver: Des O'Dell   Observer: D Brown

Column 5: Standard production 260 Tiger

Standard compression ratio Ford dual carburettor Soft top Dunlop RS5 tyres (26/26 psi)
Mileage 4666   Weight 2984 lb (two up)
Wind speed 0 to 5 mph SE 46 deg F Damp

Appendix 8

Column 6: Standard 289 Mk2 Tiger

Autocar 26 June 1969

Column 7: Rally Austin Healey 3000 (DRX 258C)

Immediately post Alpine Rally 1965 (ex Morley Brothers class winner)
Autocar 3 Sept 1965 ' Given the Works' road test.

Appendix 8

A comparison of Tiger performance figures:

Parameter	1 ADU 312B Ex-Monte 11-Feb-65	2 AHP 295B Ex-Alpine Recce 11-Aug-65	3 AHP 295B 17-Aug-65	4 AHP 295B 1966 Spec 19-Aug-65	5 Std Tiger Eng R&D 27-Mar-65	6 Mk2 Tiger Autocar June-69	7 Rally Healey 3000 DRX 258C 3-Sep-65
0-30 mph	-	3.0	2.75	2.8	3.55	3.0	2.7
0-40 mph	-	3.5	3.55	3.95	5.0	4.2	4.7
0-50 mph	5.5	4.9	4.7	5.4	7.0	6.0	6.1
0-60 mph	7.5	6.8	6.45	8.0	9.2	7.8	8.2
0-70 mph	9.8	9.35	9.25	10.85	12.25	10.7	10.2
0-80 mph	12.4	11.4	11.5	14.1	16.27	13.7	12.9
0-90 mph	-	14.6	14.9	18.6	-	18.1	16.0
0-100 mph	-	19.5	19.0	-	-	22.6	19.2
0-110 mph	-	-	-	-	-	29.5	23.5

Top Gear

Parameter	1	2	3	4	5	6	7
30-40 mph	2.2	2.4	2.3	2.65	2.85	-	-
40-50 mph	2.2	2.3	2.25	2.45	3.15	30-50 5.7	30-50 6.3
50-60 mph	2.3	2.35	2.3	2.55	2.8	40-60 5.6	40-60 5.5
60-70 mph	2.5	2.45	2.4	2.9	3.43	50-70 5.9	50-70 5.4
70-80 mph	2.18	2.8	3.8	3.3	4.15	60-80 6.2	60-80 5.0
80-90 mph	3.1	3.2	3.8	3.9	5.22	70-90 9.8	70-90 5.3
90-100 mph	4.0	4.5	-	-	-	80-100 13.8	80-100 6.4
100-110 mph	-	-	-	-	-	-	-

3rd Gear

Parameter	1	2	3	4	5	6	7
10-20 mph	-	-	-	-	-	-	-
20-30 mph	-	-	-	-	-	10-30 4.8	10.30 4.6
30-40 mph	-	1.8	1.7	1.9	2.0	20-40 3.8	20-40 3.8
40-50 mph	1.8	1.7	1.65	1.85	2.3	30-50 4.0	30-50 3.4
50-60 mph	2.0	1.8	1.75	2.05	2.2	40-60 4.5	40-60 3.8
60-70 mph	2.4	2.1	2.15	2.35	2.9	50-70 5.9	50-70 3.8
70-80 mph	-	2.5	2.7	3.1	3.9	60-80 5.9	-

Parameter	1	2	3	4	5	6	7
Standing 1/4 (Secs)	15.4	14.8	14.7	15.9	21.7	16.1	15.6
(mph)	-	92	89	84	-	84	-
Flying 1/4 (Secs)	7.8	8.0	7.8	7.9	-	-	-
(mph)	115	112.5	115.3	113.9	-	-	-
Lap speed (MIRA (mph))	110	108	109	108	-	-	-
Max speed (mph)	-	-	-	-	118	125	120

Appendix 8

Tiger performance figures from Des O'Dell's notes:

MIRA PERFORMANCE TESTS — SUNBEAM TIGER

Sunbeam V8 260

27.03.1965
Standard Road Car
Engineering Dept. R & D
c.c. 4280: Mileage 4666
Compression: 8.18:1
Wind Speed: 0.5 mph Bar 2900
Dir. S/E, Amb. 46F, Damp
Weight: 2,984-lbs, 2 up
Soft Top,
Dunlop R5 5 Press F.26 R.26

Acceleration

	30-40	40-50	50-60
Top	2.85	3.15	2.80
	60-70	70-80	80-90
Top	3.43	4.15	5.22
	30-40	40-50	50-60
3rd	2.00	2.3	2.2
	60-70	70-80	
	2.9	3.9	

Thro.Gears: Change at 5,000 rpm
  0.30   0.40   0.50
  3.55   5.0   7.0
  0.60   0.70   0.80
  9.2   12.25 16.27
Standing ¼ mile 21.7
Maximum Speed: 125 mph

Ex-Monte ADU 312B

11.02.1965
Rally Car
Driver: J. Ashworth
Observer: D.F. O'Dell
3.77:1 Power Lock
15-gallon Petrol
Wind Speed: 0.8 mph Bar 29.90
Amb. 43F, Dull and Overcast
Full Rally Spec.
Ex-Monte before rebuild

Acceleration

	30-40	40-50	50-60	60-70
Top	2.2	2.2	2.3	2.5
	70-80	80-90	90-100	
Top	2.18	3.1	4.0	
	30-40	40-50	50-60	60-70
3rd	-	1.8	2.0	2.4

Thro.Gears:
  0.50   0.60   0.70   0.80
  5.5   7.5   9.8   12.4

Standing ¼ mile 15.4
Best flying ¼ mile   113 mph
Mean flying ¼ mile 417.8 = 115 mph
Lap Speed   92.0 = 110 mph

Ex-Alpine Recce AHP 295B

17.08.1965
Rally Car
Driver: D.F. O'Dell
Observer: D. Brown
3.77:1 Power Lock
26-gallons Petrol
Wind Speed: 0.8 mph Bar 29.80
Dir. S/E, Amb. 70F, Sunny
Full Rally Spec.
Shelby Heads, Comp. 11:1
Inlet Valve 1650 Ex. 1.450
Holly Carb. Jet .067 .078, Chokes 172/173
SP3 175 x 13 tyres

Acceleration

	30-40	40-60	50-60	60-70
Top	2.4	2.3	2.35	2.45
	70-80	80-90	90-100	
Top	2.8	3.2	4.5	
	30-40	40-50	50-60	60-70
3rd	1.8	1.7	1.8	2.1
	70-80			
	2.5			

Thro.Gears:
  0.30   0.40   0.50   0.60
  3.0   3.5   4.9   6.8
  0.70   0.80   0.90   0.100
  9.35   11.4   14.6   19.5

Standing ¼ mile   14.8 = 92 mph
Best flying ¼ mile   8.0 = 112.5 mph
Mean flying ¼ mile   8.1 = 112.1 mph
Lap Speed   94.0 = 108 mph
Max revs: 6,000
Weight: Front 12 cwt. Rear 13 cwt,
Total: 1 ton, 5 cwt-0 qr..

Team Tiger AHP295B

19.-7.1965
Rally Car
Driver: D.F. O'Dell
Observer: D. Brown
377 Power Lock
25-gallons Petrol
Wind Speed 0-10 Bar 2965
Direct NW Amb. 71F, Sunny
Full Rally Spec
Standard Heads
Valve 1.665 Ex 1450
Holly Carb. 4 Barrel
Jets .067 .078, Chokes 172/173
Shelby High Performance Cams
Standard Comp. Ratio

Acceleration

	30-40	40-50	50-60	60-70
Top	2.3	2.25	2.3	2.4
	70-80	80-90	90-100	
Top	3.8	3.8		
	30-40	40-50	50-60	60-70
3rd	1.7	1.65	1.75	2.15
	70-80			
	2.7			

Thro.Gears:
  0.30   0.40   0.50   0.60
  2.75   3.55   4.7   6.45
  0.70   0.80   0.90   0.100
  9.25   11.5   14.9   19.0

Standing ¼ mile   14.7 = 89 mph
Best Flying ¼ mile   7.8 = 115.3 mph
Mean flying ¼ mile   7.85 = 114.6 mph
Lap Speed   92.7 = 109 mph
Max Revs: 6,700
Weight:Front 12 cwt. Rear 13 cwt,
Total: 1 ton, 5 cwt-0 qr.

Appendix 8

...ze, above; machined wheels being anti-corrosion dipped

But although the Minilite success story is a legend in the motor industry, it was still an uphill struggle. Privateers started using Minilites in competition quite extensively (they were selling about 12 wheels a week then) but getting it accepted by the big manufacturers was much more difficult for the works teams stubbornly stuck to their steel wheels. Until the 1965 Monte Carlo Rally which was really Tech Del's big breakthrough. At this time, Marcus Chambers had big problems with the Rootes works rally Tigers which were losing wheel centres. The Tigers were the first works cars to be equipped with Minilites and that year won their class and immediately all the other works teams became interested. The next year the teams found that the use of the Minilites gave even greater returns for, as well as the increased strength, using Minilites gave savings in kerb weight — a boon when regulations were introduced to make cars carry all their spare wheels.

At that time, Tech Del's wheels were still sand cast by a small Welsh foundry and although they fulfilled all the engineering considerations, Derek was not happy with the appearance and quality of the rough casting. On rethinking the whole idea, he decided that the only way was to change founders and go over to die casting with Sterling Metals Ltd. Already they had many orders from all over the world but to carry out this changeover required suspension of all deliveries for six months. Even this early in their history their reputation was so good that not one single customer cancelled his order. From then on, Tech Del have hardly looked back; all the major UK teams use Minilites for rallies and in one year on the Monte they had no less than 1800 wheels in use. Production increased so enormously that in 1967 they vacated their original premises and moved to the present factory in

Appendix 9: The Press - Impressions of the Rally Cars

One of the main reasons for a manufacturer to get involved with national and international competition, either racing or rallying, was to gain publicity – hopefully attractive - to support production car sales. This had been successful when, for instance, BMC had won the Monte Carlo Rallies with their Cooper S's, and to support the results from the rallies, the various Competition Departments often loaned a works rally car to selected motor journals and journalists. For instance, Autocar regularly ran an article entitled 'Given the Works' and carried out performance and road tests on a number of works cars.

In 1965 Marcus Chambers, answering a question on "what's in it for the manufacturer?" noted "Well, first it's advertising – advertising before the event and advertising if you're successful after the event. Secondly, I think, national prestige, you're representing England and selling cars abroad, this comes into it and I think thirdly, the most important thing to us in this department, is the technical development and what we find out before and after the event."

The final article – 'It's All Go' – is from the year after the Tiger was retired from rallying and the Imp was in use as the front line rally car. However, it lucidly describes life in a service vehicle - a vital part of a rally team and exactly as it would have been in the Tiger days – less than 12 months previously – even down to the same service vehicles. Service crews were, and are, the unsung heroes of the rally team and, like the rally crews, could win or lose a rally in an instant.

A brief word on such service arrangements in the Rootes team.

Ian Hall was very much in charge of the service arrangements for the team and in an article written for the UK Sunbeam Tigers Owners Club (STOC) noted "On the Scottish I had been doing my proper job as distinct from co-driving Peter Harper and was co-ordinating the service arrangements and driving a service car. This varied according to the rally in question. On some events there were designated service arrangements at certain controls, such as at Chambery on the Monte Carlo, in Monte Carlo itself (near the railway station) before the Mountain Circuit, and 20 minutes were allowed at the end of each two-day stage of the Alpine Rally. Such set-ups were loosely on the lines of the scenes you see on TV on the 'office hours' so-called rallying they do today. But most of the time service cars were operating to our service plan, the devising and execution of which was very much my field of operations. Very often this would co-incide with other Teams such as BMC or Citroen and at these strategic spots we would work with Dunlops and hopefully others like Ferodo, Lucas and, if we were lucky, Shell. With the Tiger, petrol supplies in remote spots were a real headache as on fast rallies like the Alpine (road races in all but name) there was no time to queue up at filling stations. The Tiger could be down to 10 to 12 mpg in anger in the mountains.

"The service cars therefore carried Jerry Bags, inflatable heavy-duty rubber petrol containers which could be folded flat when not in use. Each held about 5 gallons and the Service Crews would have about ten of them on the roof! Who said 'Health and Safety'?

"For Service cars we had three Super Minx Estates, all carefully fitted out and with fixed racks on the roof and overhead flood-lights. They were very similar to the works Rapiers mechanically with overdrive on the intermediates. Tech-Del alloy wheels, telescopic dampers, rally brake pads etc. and rally type spot and fog lamps. On the RAC and winter rallies they were on lightly studded tyres.

"We sometimes used a Super Snipe Estate, a particular favourite of mine with automatic box and

Appendix 9

power steering (until the belt fell off one night in Scotland going very fast downhill and gave me the fright of my life).

"We had some dedicated ace mechanics who all deserved medals. They drove at high speed all over Europe in all conditions to be at the right place at the right time where they performed miracles of road-side mechanical wonders in no time flat. Gerry Spencer and Jack Walton were the established stars with dear old Ernie Beck the engine building wizard and Ernie Schofield the great improviser. Hard on their heels were the young enthusiastic ex-Rootes Apprentices – Derek Hughes, David Brown and Dick Guy. Chief Engineer Des O'Dell supervised all of them, made the big decisions and was an excellent roadside fettler himself.

"On most rallies Marcus Chambers, being in overall command, could, and sometimes did, alter the Service Plans to suit conditions or contingencies, as indeed so did I. Marcus often drove a service car. On one memorable Alpine he had a blue RHD hardtop Tiger in full rally trim but towing a large trailer full of petrol in Jerry-bags which, with his enterprising style of driving, was a sight to behold. I usually had a rally Imp with Des O'Dell or one of the young mechanics with a big bag of tools and spares and played a chase car role.

"On British forest rallies such as the RAC or the Scottish I would be a loose cannon getting to the end of as many stages as I could night and day with a map in one hand and the steering wheel in the other. In those days I would often be the only car around and spectators had not become a problem. We had many amazing incidents!"

The five following articles on the Tiger in this Appendix are from the press:

A Tiger for Rallying	Henry N Manney Road and Track	May 1965
Tigers can be Tamed	Doug Armstrong Modern Motor	June 1965
Sunbeam Tiger with Teeth	Car and Car Conversions	Dec 1966
No time for tantrums when you're the Mister	Jerry Sloniger	1967
It's all go	Hamish Cardno Motor	w/e May 13th 1967

Appendix 9

A Tiger for Rallying

As prepared for international rallying, Rootes' Ford-powered Tiger has even sharper claws

BY HENRY N. MANNEY

THE SUNBEAM ALPINE has long been referred to among its friends as the "Sports Husky," its chassis being derived from the utility van of that name, and thus there was some alarm when Rootes announced its intention of jamming a whacking great Ford V-8 therein. Boulevard sports, tired of rowing themselves along with the gear lever, applauded this decision but those with competition in mind had dark thoughts of the Dreaded Understeer. When the car actually appeared, it proved to be quite a pleasant automobile indeed, but even so the inclusion of three Tigers in the Monte Carlo Rally entry lists provoked much laughter. Collapse of stout party, as two of the three were among the select number of finishers, one made ftd on a special stage, and they wound up first and second in their GT class besides Peter Harper being fourth overall.

As to our mind this was the success story of the year, we made haste to contact the celebrated Marcus Chambers, COMCOMPROOTES, and try one of these diabolical devices. It turned out that Harper's would be available after he finished some Swedish ice racing and so it came to pass that in company with Gethin Bradley we tore ourselves away from a good cuppa tea and set sail for Stevenage and Mr. Harper's agency for guess which make of automobile. The Tiger was in what the used-car boys call "performance tested" condition with glass out of the headlights, a graunch on the rear wing (courtesy Pat Moss-Carlsson) a generous coating of Swedish dirt, rally plates, and a full set of Weathermaster snow tires with studs. This particular sort, explained Peter while he idly picked a few rusty ones out of the spare, wasn't too much use (they were all leaning at an angle of 45°), and he preferred the Scason type.

I then had the job of driving this studded monster to the works at Coventry while Gethers followed in the spacious and comfortable Humber wagon with which we had arrived, lunch then being scheduled with Marcus whilst proper tires were slammed on and a quick wash job was administered. As its conduct with studs on a dry road is not really relevant, I will content myself with saying that it showed a strong disinclination to deviate from a straight line and that it is easy to see why Peter and Andrew Cowan had to use the handbrake on all downhill hairpins to get the back end around. Combined with this tetchiness was an extremely short rear end ratio, which meant that if power were to be turned on in short corners in third in the amounts one would use, say, in my Lancia, one progressed in a series of zigs and zags. It says a lot for the soundness of the car, though, that it fired first kick, the only untoward mechanical noise was a slight tappet click, and the Ford 4-speed gearbox shifted as sweetly as ever.

Naturally enough, the rally Tiger differs in certain aspects from a street one, the chief external clue being an impression of bulk caused by the oversize 13 x 5 mag wheels and fat tires. The engine has been Cobra-ized, the clutch is also a Cobra unit and the box a Ford with special higher ratio internals as the Warner parts are not available in Britain. There is, of course, a Salisbury Powr-Lok limited slip diff which wore a 3.77:1 ratio for the Monte, and suspension consists of Husky export springs with Rapier rally dampers plus a 0.75-in. stabilizer bar. The brakes carry Ferodo DS-11 on the front and VG-95 at the rear, those back cylinders also being bored out to 0.875-in., a larger water radiator plus an oil radiator is fitted, a 26-gallon tank roosts in the boot to the exclusion of all else save a spare tire (a second spare parks on the lid), the exhaust system is higher up, and the electrical system boasts alternators to take care of all the iodine lights. There doesn't seem to have been much lightening of the bodywork which tends to be not over-heavy on the Alpine anyway, but even so the rally car must scale more than a normal one by virtue of the extra equipment.

Most of this is in the office, so important on international rallies, and it is extremely interesting to see just what is considered necessary. First off, since nobody can drive if he can't see the road, there are a multitude of switches controlling extra iodine driving lights and/or foglamps, sec-

Appendix 9

tional instrument lighting, the navigator's map light, the wire-heated screen front and rear, and de-icing squirts for the screen and driving lights too, no less. This last is because frozen snow cast up by cars in front forms on the lenses, causing an appreciable drop in illumination. Also fitted is a very handy plastic molded sheet nine inches high running closely around the inside of the screen to channel the defroster air. For the navigator's benefit, a pair of Heuers, one stop watch and one master clock, rest on a padded mount on the dash above the Halda twinmaster and, as an extra refinement, an additional rear-view mirror in case someone is following closely. The driver's side is more simple with a floor-mounted dip switch, a stalk flasher to the left of the wheel, a handy knee rest covering the window and door handles, and a tach in front of his eyes with "6000'" marked in red.

After lunch and inspection of the 998-cc rally Imps (one with a V-8 Ford poised nearby), Gethin and I stepped aboard and settled ourselves in the comfortable seats, finding out simultaneously that there was really more legroom than we needed and that we actually needed a cushion. Or else my overcoat, which I had had before. Clutching stop watch and Leica in hand, we then rumbled out through the works gate in second (such was the modest idle and low gears) and blatted off in the gap between two cloth-capped gents on bicycles en route to the pub. To say the least, the Tiger is a stimulating machine to drive in traffic as notwithstanding Shelby's trick cam there is a flattish power curve up to max revs (by which time you are too fast for traffic); just as well, too, for a peaky one would have been embarrassing on ice. Naturally enough the Tiger was a trifle noisier than the normal one due to the increased breathing and several squeaks, groans, and rattles brought on by the special stages, but I wouldn't say that an intercom was really necessary for those of normal hearing. Otherwise, its competition history did not reveal itself except for a rather heavy centrifugal clutch which needed to be pushed right down, a hardish ride, the brakes being a bit tired, and the front wheels bouncing a bit from weak shocks. None of these were terribly obtrusive and in fact the Tiger was dead simple to drive.

First off we went along some tricky bits so that we could get the odd picture; the handling seemed to be okay as far as we went (Marcus doesn't appreciate bent motor cars) but the slightly vague steering and dead handling characteristics made me wish that I had it for a week to gain more acquaintance. On fast swerves it went around all right if with a strong sensation of being propelled forcefully by the rear wheels, but there was no apparent understeer, oversteer, or anything—it just went. I suppose that one has to go a lot faster to find out its eventual behavior and on a damp road at 4 P.M. neither of us was prepared to do that. Suffice to say that the Tiger is not an understeering pig but lots of poke in a small package. Later on, in search of a suitable place to do acceleration figures, we negotiated several roundabouts and there the car did require some forethought to get the front end pointed away from the grass and into the corner. Reflections on the limited-slip diff and cures thereof produced the answer, though, and sundry squirts of throttle in third were found to do the trick. Like the heavier sort of front-driver, it very much liked the power on when any sharpish curve was contemplated.

Acceleration runs were lots of fun, as we would wait until some pursuing vehicle was within a hundred yards and then disappear into the distance. A moderate amount of throttle produced the best results on getaway as too little (below 2500) bogged it down and too much caused a bout of wheelspin with consequent sidewise attitude until the diff took hold. The back axle, much to our surprise, didn't begin to tramp and the most difficult bit was keeping one eye on the tach and the other out the windshield, as 6000 rpm came up far too quickly for comfort, by which time we were up the chuff of some unwary Mini. Top speed runs, limited by the redline as it was still accelerating vigorously at 6000 in top, showed that the Tiger was very steady at those speeds and was even steerable, the only indication of speed being a sizable amount of row from under the bonnet. The water temp rose to just under 100° C early on and stayed there, oil pressure was generally about 2.2 kg cm sq, and nothing smelled hot. Altogether quite a car and just what England needs with its crowded traffic conditions—good acceleration to reduce that awful time out passing Ford Zephyrs and heavy trucks while the oncoming column bears down. I've said it before and I'll say it again—there ain't any substitute for cubic inches. Please can we have it again, Mr. Chambers?

TIGERS CAN BE TAMED

BELOW: Oil check for the works rally Tiger Doug drove to Geneva. Seven headlamps turned night into day, but dipping wasn't easy. BOTTOM PHOTO: Journey's end. Note de-icing panel in back window, extra spare mounted on the boot.

Sunbeam Tiger V8s will soo

EVER since its introduction at the 1964 New York motor show, the Sunbeam Tiger V8 had been working solely for the Yankee dollar. In March this year, however, Rootes decided to remove the "U.S.A. only" tag and make their top glamor sports car available elsewhere.

"Elsewhere," they told me, would include Australia — and the Tigers would be released there in a matter of weeks. So I asked how soon I could have a car to trip-test for **Modern Motor**.

The request couldn't have come at a better time. The Geneva Salon was coming up, and Rootes wanted to exhibit the Tiger which Peter Harper drove into fourth place in this year's Monte Carlo Rally. Would I like to drive it over for them?

That's how I came to be standing at Lydd Airport one bitterly cold

Appendix 9

LEFT: Sunbeam Tiger under test. Maximum with stock-standard engine and gearing is 141 m.p.h., but rally cars are geared down to gain acceleration.

RIGHT: More instruments and controls than a Lancaster — all meant to be used. Floor shift works a Ford 4-speed box.

BELOW: 4.2-litre V8 with four-choke carby fits tightly into engine bay. It develops 164 b.h.p. in standard form.

be sold in Australia. Doug Armstrong has trip-tested one, tells you all about them

morning in March, waiting while the crew of the Bristol Airfreighter warmed up its engines.

My companion for the trip was Rootes P.R. man Gethin Bradley. As we waited, he filled me in on the details of the car I was about to drive.

The Sunbeam Tiger was developed from a most unlikely beginning—the underbody of the plodding, unglamorous Hillman Husky, which Rootes used as the basis for the 88 b.h.p., 100 m.p.h. Sunbeam Alpine sports car, introduced in 1959.

Then American high-performance machinery expert Carroll Shelby was called in to take the development a stage further. He replaced the Alpine's four-cylinder engine with a 4.2-litre Ford (Fairlane) V8 coupled to a three-speed automatic transmission, beefed up the rest of the car to suit, and the result was the Sunbeam Tiger.

The late Lord Rootes liked Shelby's prototype and approved it for production, except that he had the automatic drive replaced by a four-speed manual gearbox. This was before Rootes allied themselves with Chrysler — but the Ford V8 suits the car so well that it's expected to be retained.

The standard Tiger puts out 164 b.h.p. at 4400 r.p.m., and a staggering 258ft./lb. of torque at a mere 2200. Final-drive ratio is 2.88:1, producing 23.5 m.p.h. per 1000 revs in top gear — a theoretical maximum of 141 m.p.h., since the car's rev-counter is red-lined at 6000.

Acceleration isn't lacking, as you can imagine; but Rootes' Competitions Department wanted even more get-up-and-go for the rally, so the two cars prepared for it were modified accordingly.

The 4.2-litre lightweight Ford V8s were fitted with "Cobra kit" camshafts, heads and valves from Ford's 4.7-litre unit, plus enlarged and polished ports, heavy-duty valve springs and screwed-in rocker posts. Using a four-choke Holley carburettor in place of the standard two-choke, the rally engine gave around 200 b.h.p., and with 3.77:1 final-drive and Salisbury Powr-Lok diff it was quite a bomb—but a controllable one.

The new torque figure was never worked out — but although the diff ratio on Harper's Tiger was changed to 3.54:1 for our Geneva trip, there was still enough hurry-up left to snap your head back when accelerating, even at 90 m.p.h.

The Channel crossing took only 18 minutes — but the hour's difference

SUNBEAM TIGER

between Continental and British "winter time" meant it was 11.30 a.m. when we finally set out from Le Touquet, with 400 miles to cover to our night stop at Arbois, in France's Jura Mountains.

Peter Harper, who took this particular car to a class victory in the Monte, is an ex-R.A.F. pilot. After driving the Tiger for a couple of miles, I didn't think he could be anything else. The cockpit had more instruments than a Lancaster, and there was full safety harness for "pilot" and crew. Bradley and I were ringed with plastic tanks and electric motors to wash and defrost our windscreens —plus another to de-ice the headlamp glasses. The boot was so full of fuel tank (25 gallons) and spare wheel there was precious little space for anything else, and there were enough iodine-vapor lights fitted to land at 140 m.p.h. To complete the illusion, this Tiger would accelerate like a VC10—providing you could reach the clutch pedal.

I wouldn't have classed Harper as a very tall man but he must be all legs. His "long-arm" driving position, with the steering wheel down to the bottom of its column adjustment, suited me fine, but the pedals were only just in reach—and that clutch pedal was good and heavy.

The 3.54 diff ratio produced 19.25 m.p.h. per 1000 revs in top, representing a permissible maximum of 115.5 m.p.h.—and I found that red line on the tacho very useful, for the needle was only too willing to hit the 6000 mark. It got there so eagerly that I thought it wiser to sit around 5500 r.p.m. on long straights, considering 106 m.p.h. quite fast enough.

What really surprised me was the flexibilty of the rally engine. Top gear would take us through town traffic without snatch or fuss and the Tiger would accelerate like mad from as low as 10 m.p.h. — still in top gear, yet with never a ping.

The weather in France was filthy, and when we emerged from a half-hour lunch stop at Peronne, it was snowing heavily — a pleasant prospect, with another 300 miles to go!

On we went through Soissons, Chateau-Thierry, Troyes, and into the Seine Valley around Chatillon. The snow stopped and the Tiger pressed on. The hard-to-reach clutch pedal was a nuisance, but it brought out the V8's fantastic low and medium-speed pulling capabilities, for I found myself changing-down only when the car had almost reached the last chonk. Under all other circumstances it would pull like a train in top.

The other side of Dijon the terrain began to gain height. The roads were in a very bad state from the winter's frosts and snows, and the surface was a mass of potholes. For a car with only 7ft. 2in. wheelbase and competition suspension, the Tiger rode the bumps well — and there were times when we hit the holes pretty fast. The simple live axle was greatly assisted by the restraining Panhard rod—standard on the Tiger.

The potholes and puddles threw plenty of dirty water over the windscreen (which had not only a Triplex heating element built-in, but two "stick-on" heaters as well), but we had all the equipment to deal with it. A touch of one switch sent a stream of water over the glass, and another switch set off a squirt of glycol for de-icing. First time I switched on the washer, I was convinced I was driving an aeroplane, for the whirr of the electric motor (18in. away beneath the rear window) sounded for all the world as though the wheels were being retracted. I'm sure there was a bank-and-turn indicator among all those instruments somewhere!

Darkness began to fall soon after Dijon, and as we had neither amber headlights (requested, but not enforced, by the French) nor right-hand dipping arrangement, we worked out a special drill.

Iodine-vapor headlights are non-dippable, so the Tiger was wired with two separate pass-lights. We twisted the pass-lights to provide dip, and this arrangement worked well, for although the lamps were white, the French drivers didn't retaliate—and, believe me, I have been nearly driven off the road by "camionistes" (French for truckies) who hadn't liked the dip of my lights!

Racing the Clock

Time was marching on, and we had a date with a wonderful dinner at the Rotisserie de la Balance in Arbois. We decided to use all the incredible array of seven headlamps, including the central iodine-vapor "tar-melter" and the smaller spots on the bumpers. The central horror and the spots were controlled by switches on the Tiger's centre armrest/console, and the head dip by conventional foot switch. We would blind along with all lights blazing, then, at a shout from me, Gethin would douse the spots and the tar-melter, and I would dip the foot switch.

After the first two operations I learned the thing to do was dip and brake at the same time, for after seven lights with three iodine-vapor units, driving on two conventional pass-lamps was almost like being left in the dark.

We made Arbois by 7.45 p.m., despite a stop for coffee and cognac, and another for fuel. The Tiger returned just over 17 m.p.g. for an on-the-road average of 55 m.p.h. and objected not at all to the French "Super" (I use the inverted commas in their most literal sense). The Balance restaurant provided food and wine that were out of this world, and we fell into bed feeling all was well with the trip.

The Tiger slept out in the freezing temperatures but was away at the first touch of the button next morning, and a check on the rapier-like dipstick showed that oil consumption was nil.

It was really freezing as we thundered away in bright sunshine and began the ascent toward Pontarlier over the Cossonay Pass. As we got higher, the ice ruts became incredibly deep; at one point, I'm quite sure the Tiger was steering itself on its twin silencers. The roads were so narrow and iced that it was impossible to stop and take photographs.

Mindful that the car had to be exhibited on the Rootes stand in Geneva, I took it very gently. It would have been a shame to bend the model after having got so far. No, it was a case of hold that Tiger — and so intent was I on taking it easy that I motored over the pass, ice, snow and all, in top gear. What a fantastic machine!

A stop at the top for one last cafe-cognac, and we began the descent, to reach the French/Swiss frontier at Vallorbe at about 10 a.m. Down into Morges (next door to Lausanne), and we took the new Lausanne-Geneva autoroute. We averaged just on 100 m.p.h. down this 38-mile motorway, the Tiger shaking off a few Alfa drivers as they sped towards the city.

At 11 a.m. we checked in at our hotels, and the surprising amount of luggage we had managed to cram into the Tiger was unloaded. By afternoon, the Tiger was sitting on its show stand for all the world to see, and Rootes' publicity manager breathed a sigh of relief.

The car had given us a safe but exciting run to Geneva and had virtually done the journey in top gear. No oil was used, fuel consumption averaged out at 17.5 m.p.g., even though we'd done a lot of climbing and had seen 6000 come up on the rev-counter several times.

A real fire-breather, yet always docile and easy to drive. The standard 164 b.h.p. two-seater with 2.88:1 rear end should be a joy.

What does the normal Tiger cost? Basic U.K. price (without tax) is £1195 stg. for the roadster, so the Australian tag should be around £2400 tax-paid — or a bit over £2500 with the hardtop.

FOOTNOTE: I can foresee two further developments for the Tiger. 1.—Its 4.2-litre V8 differs from the 4.7-litre unit only in bore size — and Shelby has been getting a reliable 365 b.h.p. from the latter. What's the betting we'll see some 4.7-litre Tigers, perhaps in this year's Le Mans 24-hour race? 2.—Rootes may well go back to Shelby's original idea and offer the option of automatic drive on the Tiger; this would be in line with their general policy, since automatic Alpines are already available.

Appendix 9

FEATURE ROAD TEST

WORKS
SUNBEAM TIGER

A TIGER WITH TEETH

EVER dreamed of sitting behind the wheel of something really savage—something capable of spinning the wheels in top on a dry road, capable of leaving long black lines on the tarmac—something, in fact, which is the original hairy monster? So have we—and it doesn't matter how quickly the Mini can be made to go, it just ain't the same.

In fact, you can't really do it with a littl'un at all. What you want is lots of cylinders, lots of real poke and lots of lovely noise. For instance, you can do it beautifully in a Sunbeam Tiger of the right type—in this particular case, a works Tiger—Peter Harper's Tulip rally car, to be precise. A real brute of a car—not in fact as fast as all that but nevertheless juicing out a healthy increase in power over the standard 164 b.h.p., weighing, despite a lot of extra bits and pieces, probably a little less than the standard 22½ cwt., and one, way and another a car built for one purpose and one purpose only—competition. Not, in fact, the sort of car in which to take Auntie out for a Sunday afternoon's bluebell-picking.

From the outside it was pretty obvious that this was no ordinary Tiger. For a start, it was literally plastered with lights at both ends. Left-hand-drive, of course, which is usually favourite for continental events because it's easier for the bold intrepid pilot to overtake if he sits on the appropriate side—and in this car you do a fair amount of overtaking. The bodywork was standard, with the usual Tiger hard-top, apart from the holes to take all the lights, but the thing sat on Minilite wheels which were a dead give-away.

Hidden from the public eye, as you might say, were sundry other differences. For a start, the power unit—you know, the Ford V8 4,261 c.c. job which, under normal conditions, delivers 164.b.h.p. at four-four and the staggeringly high figure of 258 lb ft. of torque at only two-two (compare this with 260 lb. ft. for the 265 b.h.p. Jaguar engine if you like)—was equipped with a high-lift camshaft, solid tappets, single extra strong valve springs, polished ports and so on and had, of course, been fully balanced. Standard carbs and manifolding was retained, a competition distributor was fitted and the exhaust pipe was taken through the frame to stop it from being knocked off on the rough bits. Oh yes, and the car had an oil cooler on it. Not a lot, you might think, but enough to provide a healthy increase in power and still stay within the regulations. Balancing, port polishing and the camshaft meant that she would rev to six thousand, where the red mark was: the standard Tiger has a red mark on the tachometer at four-eight, so obviously something works differently!

The major snag with Tigers, in our experience, is the way they are stuck to the road—or not, as the case may be. Marcus Chambers and his men had sorted this little problem by fitting stiffer, high-rate front springs and stouter rear springs—in fact, those catalogued as export spring for the Hillman Husky. Laugh that off. Armstrong adjustable dampers all round appeared, from the ride, to be adjusted to the hard setting, too. Just in case all this took a bit of stopping, the brakes were fitted with DS11 front pads and VG95 rear linings, and a dual servo circuit had been arranged so that the standard under-the-bonnet servo unit operated on behalf of the front brakes, while a second servo, stuck behind the seats inside the car, looked after the back ones,

Appendix 9

A dirty great rev counter the driver can see amongst other things.

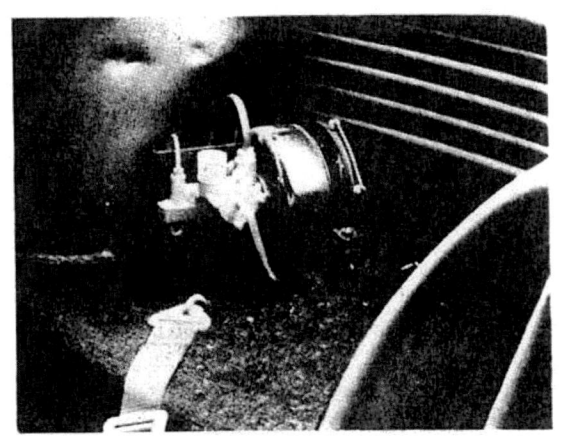

This is the only car we have tested with a duplicate brake servo fitted on the back seat.

which it did to the accompaniment of a great deal of puffing and blowing.

Finally, the Rootes Competitions men had fitted the beast with the ultra-low (by Tiger standards) final drive ratio of 3·7 to 1, and a Powr-Lok limited-slip diff. A fuel tank holding (though not for very long) 18½ gallons, plus a dirty big and very robust roll-over bar, laced around under the hard-top, completed the spec, and we were, as they say, off.

Off isn't just the right word here. To say that she was running a bit rich is putting it somewhat mildly. No choke, of course, so a cautious pump on the pedal. The electrical fuel pumps went mad, the starter whirred, as they say, and absolutely nothing else happened. Flooded, of course. Usual drill—throttle wide open and try again—still no sign of life. So we left her for a bit and then, very gingerly, tried again. This time the jackpot—eight cylinders all working, and great scads of noise hurtling out of the twin tail-pipes. We learnt after that no matter whether she was hot or cold, you just didn't touch the loud pedal until she had fired, which in nearly every other case she did at once.

With the engine running, and firmly settled in the driver's share of two very comfortable seats, there seemed to be no excuse for not going somewhere. Too bad about the audience—if you will park a thing like this in a public car park, etc. etc. . . . . Pole her into first, and see what happens when you let the clutch out. You've guessed it—we took off down that (empty, fortunately) car park like we were starting at Le Mans at about five-past-four. Something else we'd learnt—you could, and preferably did, start off from the mark at little more than tick-over revs unless you were in a hurry.

The fairly small degree of modding permitted by class regs for the Tulip had done nothing to impair the extraordinary flexibility you get from a big American V8, and it was *possible* to drive the thing very gently indeed. Of course, this was bit hard on the plugs, and it didn't want a lot of traffic driving to get her firing on not more than six or seven. A quick blast of the throttle—lots of black smoke out of the back, lots of lovely noise everywhere—was sufficient to keep 'em going, though, and once clear of what Mr. Wilson likes, for some obscure reason, to call a "conurbation" it didn't take long to see what works Tigering was all about. The controls of the Tiger take a bit of working out at first when the Comps Dept. has finished with 'em. For a start, the standard rev-counter is disconnected—at least, it wasn't working—and a monstrous great thing of a replacement is struck up on the top of the facia where you can't fail to see it. Lighting and wiper are located on the arm-rest between the front seats instead of on the dash, there are various extra switches and knobs labelled, in many cases, "iodines" in big bold letters; the speedo, not surprisingly on a left-handed motorcar, was in k.p.h. and the fuel gauge and the rev-counter were together equipped with the fastest-moving needles this side of an aircraft. The usual "rally gear"—pockets for maps documents, tools, and an Avanti navigator's light—were all built-in.

So you get all this sorted out, stoke up the fire and start the engine—carefully, this time, so as not to do that flooding bit all over again. Not exactly an ideal traffic car, this, for all its flexibility: the plugs and things aren't all that happy at under about two thousand revs, which means that for a good deal of the time urban motoring means third gear. Third itself is good for a ton at maximum revs, and the gearing is such, with a 3·7 to 1 top, that a LOT of Power is available at pretty well any point in the engine speed range. In other words, burbling along is fine so long as you don't press too hard on the pedal on the exits from roundabouts—especially if it's wet.

It is pretty noisy in there and becomes very noisy in there once you get a few revs on board. Full acceleration through the gears becomes a bit of an endurance test for the ears as the full chatter of gearbox whine, exhaust noise and the clack of tappets gets in amongst you. But by God you're going—the limited slip diff limits the slip all right, and instead of one wheel spinning both of them will, with no trouble at all. In the wet, the car moves sideways as easily as it does forwards and the quick take-off makes for a busy driver. It's all part of the excitement—especially when you relate it to an acceleration of the order of eleven seconds from a standstill to the legal limit—8·8 from nothing to sixty, and 26 seconds from rest to the ton. You can do fifty in bottom gear, the legal seventy in second, while third gives you ninety and top—well, we never had a chance to try it on full chat in top gear. The standard car does 121 m.p.h., mean of opposite runs, and this one is probably about the same although, with the low axle ratio, it would get there faster.

The ride is hard and businesslike, to say the least. Every bump in the road communicates itself to the driver's bottom—you would probably be able to tell if you drove over a match, but we didn't actually try it: we hardly ever went slow enough to see a match right down there on the ground. This makes for a remarkable degree of controllability—the car handles so much better than a standard Tiger, despite the increased power, that it is difficult to believe

Appendix 9

that they are the same car, only just a little bit different, if you follow.

The handling is entirely predictable: fast corners are taken in an attitude of understeer, and if you go too quickly round slower ones then you get oversteer and the behind comes round to meet the front. A quick flick of the command wheel and the situation is very largely under control again. In the wet, the car will adopt virtually any attitude you happen to want at a dab on the loud pedal—even in top, if you happen to be going quickly enough.

The brakes are pretty well twitched about, of course, and seem to be up to the job in hand. They don't, mark you, inspire confidence until they are warm—this is often the case with the "hard" friction materials but once you start using them they stop the car all right, and you never run out or even look like running out of anchors.

After dark—well, when the rest of the world is in darkness—you carry your own private daylight ration about with you. Standard headlights, plus a couple of small spots carried low down under the bumper, plus a pair of iodines for good measure tend to lighten the old darkness more than you might think possible. With the lot on it's a bit hard on anyone who happens to be looking towards you, and if you met an oncoming car under these circumstances you'd probably hear their screen melting. Still, the object of the exercise is to light the way, and it does this alright—you could land an aircraft down the "flarepath". In the same way, a whiff of iodines, to coin a phrase, is all that is necessary to move over the slower chap in front in daylight—if the worst comes to the worst, you simply give him a blast on the air-horns. If that doesn't move him, it would be no good trying dynamite—not loud enough.

Accepting, for a moment, that this tyre-squealing, rubber-burning snorting ball of 4·2-litre fire is all a young man desires to impress the birds (and, incidentally, himself) is there a snag? We don't count the racket, the harsh ride, the brutal acceleration—they are all part of the joy in this case. But there is, nevertheless, a snag. It's in that 18½ gallon tank, which needs filling up more often than the Editor's pint mug. The works Tiger is, to say the least, thirsty. This isn't much of a problem for Master Harper, of course, because one of the perks of being a works driver is that you don't have to buy the petrol. But it is a snag presumably for the likes of you and me, who do. Admittedly the car was running rich when we had it—probably a lot richer than it ought to have done. But even so, we boozed our way through the go-juice at the rate of a gallon of the stuff every fifteen British miles when driving normally, and about once in a dozen miles if you turned the tap on and went fast. Mr. Rootes Group says that this is too much, and that in proper trim it ought to do more than that.

All the same, though, given a pocket full of sufficient folding stuff to keep the beast's appetite satisfied, we can't think of a more exhilarating way to spend a journey than by doing it in this Tiger. Man alive, that beast's got real teeth!

Once again, your view.

Cars on Test

WORKS SUNBEAM TIGER

Engine: V8-cylinder, 96·5 mm. x 73 mm; 4, 261 c.c.; push-rod operated overhead valves; compression ratio 8·8 to 1; high-lift camshaft; solid tappets; stronger valve springs; polished ports, etc; twin choke-carburettor; competition distributor; fully balanced.

Transmission: Four-speed gearbox, synchromesh on all forward gears; 3·7 to 1 final drive; limited-slip differential.

Suspension: As standard Tiger, but with up-rated front springs; Hillman Husky special export rear springs; Armstrong adjustable dampers all round.

Brakes: As standard Tiger, but with separate circuits, dual servos and DS11 front pads, VG95 rear linings.

Dimensions: As standard Tiger.

PERFORMANCE

MAXIMUM SPEED:
Speeds in gears (at 6,000 r.p.m.)
First— 50 m.p.h.
Second— 70
Third—100

Fuel consumption: 12–15 m.p.g.

ACCELERATION
0– 30— 4·0 secs.
0– 40— 5·0
0– 50— 6·4
0– 60— 8·8
0– 70—11·0
0– 80—14·4
0– 90—19·5
0–100—26·0

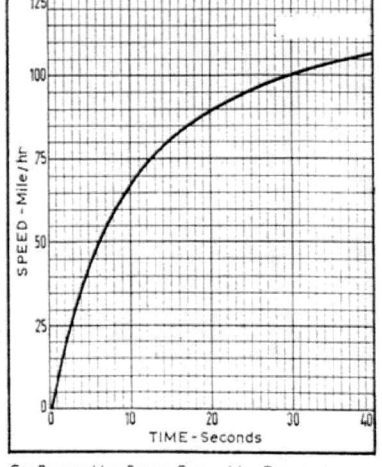

Car Prepared by: Rootes Competition Department, Coventry.

Appendix 9

No time for tantrums when you're the Mister

American journalist Jerry Sloniger, who covered this year's Monte Carlo Rally, reports on the life and times of a rally team manager—in this case Rootes Group's Marcus Chambers

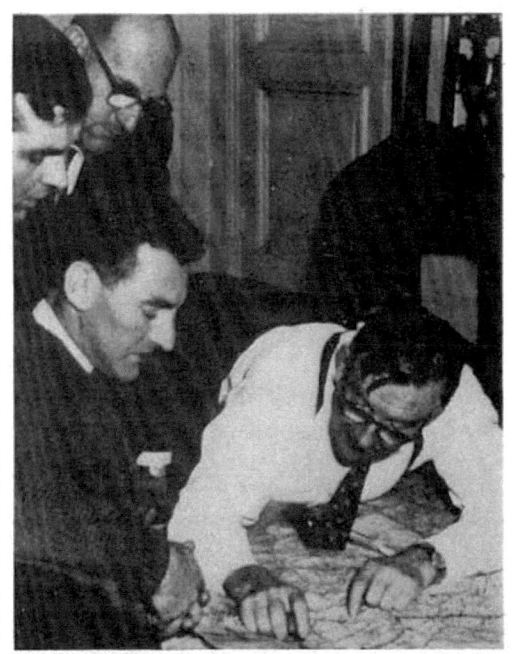

Marcus Chambers, on his stomach, discusses fuel points with his Monte Carlo Rheims starters. On his right is Peter Harper. Looking over Harper's shoulder is Tim Bosence, and on his left is "Tiny" Lewis

MANAGING A RALLY TEAM is partly application but mostly knowing when to bet on the lions and when to take odds on the Christians, You might even argue that the secret of rally management is stocking every conceivable item a team driver might want and anticipating where he'll ask for it—while the secret of winning is never being asked.

In addition to preparing the cars, pre-rally planning habitually runs to half-a-dozen legal-size pages detailing every move for your few precious service teams, from Channel crossing to hotel phone numbers. Actual service in the wilds of southern France then becomes largely a matter of knowing instinctively when to throw the programme away and improvise a schedule based on hope and experience.

Thinking back on a too-brief session with Marcus Chambers, Rootes' doyen of rally managers, I would guess that the good manager's twitch rate is inversely proportional to the emergencies he must solve. Like his master welder, who had to brew tea because there wasn't a single broken fitting to repair, Marcus got fretful only when nobody had need of a quick decision.

Chambers rumbles and steams quietly at the thought of spoilt team members—"never pamper a driver," he says, "they are like Oliver Twist, always wanting more." This same man will drive like hell in his Tiger to reach the finish before his Coupe des Dames crew. Why? "The girls like to see you there when they come in."

Taking her arm and giving her his gallant attention, Marcus will agree right down the line that Rosemary Smith needn't go out on the night test. She's absolutely right that no standard Imp could maintain those impossible averages—even the organisers don't expect any car under a litre to make the final roster of top sixty teams. Naturally he has a taxi ready to take her to the hotel. All this when a smiling, tired girl reaches Monte Carlo sick of the mountains. He merely grins the next day when she is raring to start the mountain test—"even if I can't possibly make more than four controls within the half-hour allowance."

The elegant and fur-coated Miss Smith, who took up his bet of a bottle of perfume if she got back under the limit, finished the test with two-thirds of her allowance unused. No command in the world, issued when she'd been driving for forty or more hours, would have bought that Coup des Dames the organisers later whipped again.

A tired team boss may mutter about "taking the Blue Train to Monte Carlo next year," but he knows you have to drive as far if not as fast as your drivers, meet them in improbable places and arrive looking like temperament doesn't happen in a well-bred rally team. Your tantrums are saved for the organisers.

Driving a car through France with numbers on the flanks guarantees you the plaudits. The sidewalk crowd doesn't know whether you are 59 minutes late and really retired or dead on time and fit. Incidentally, drivers like "Tiny" Lewis (of Imp fame) who breeze into a control grinning quietly are on time; the ones who arrive with all four wheels locked were likely over time two controls back anyway.

Service cars, tyre vans and team managers cover the same ground, without studs in many cases, and perhaps without a windsereen as well because "there's no time to fix that with our team cars running; we'll swap it later." Two days in an arctic wind tunnel won't get your name in the paper, or even surprise a dedicated rally mechanic, but it does impress the rally drivers who find you at every scheduled point on time.

Nobody doubts the very special talent it takes to navigate

375

Appendix 9

winding roads on the ignition key alone when your throttle cable breaks, yet *make up* five minutes on a tight schedule looking for time to fix things. "Tiny" Lewis and Tim Bosence did just that and won their class in the bargain. It takes as much dexterity of a very different sort to swap windscreens in minutes.

Rootes, carrying a spare screen, heard that a private driver was coming by—naturally tight for time—with a broken screen simply because he had started with the wrong kind. If that was simple, the solution was not. That spare was being carried against the one-in-a-hundred chance a team driver might need it. Can you justify fitting it to a non-team car early in the rally?

Marcus had already spent three days swearing, whenever asked, that he wasn't a nursemaid for privateers who wouldn't prepare. Rootes was proud of them, gave advice freely and offered what help they could—and that was all. Now one was paying for his folly. "We can't let him go on that way," Chambers decreed, and the precious spare was readied. If a team Imp needs one later you take it out of a service car. Drivers are expected to deal with cables but not carry spare glass.

The Swiss Imp team rushed into Pont Charles Albert check point, red eyes out on stalks from staring through a fine mesh and holding less than five minutes leeway on a very tight final section. The boys almost lifted driver and navigator out of their seats, shoved the granulated glass outside their car, cleaned the surround, slipped in the new screen and found time to clean it inside and out. The privateer, almost too tired and speechless to remember the English for "thank you," was off again with a safe bit of his five minutes left.

Versatility is a habit not a theory with rally mechanics, but as electrician Arthur Bird pointed out, he'd used a length of flex instead of cord to fit the rubber surround, so it was really within his field.

That was a job on schedule. Most rally service is only valid when it isn't used. The recent Monte—whatever we may think of its outcome—was properly scheduled to make any sort of service beyond helping the drivers with fuel and tyres impossible, apart from the occasional improbable act like that screen.

Tyres are a sore subject with any team manager, and reason enough for most of Marcus's curses. But you can't afford to shoe your cars improperly when all the others are using up to five different sorts. Even three options for each car—plain, part studs and whole studs—take up most of your logistical planning. Guess wrong on options before a crucial 20-mile test and you can throw away a 3,000-mile rally.

Any team boss would agree on the spot: two sets (ten) per car, branded at the start and dropped wherever you or the driver decide, but no more. Before the "safety" buffs rise righteously, I might point out that Rosemary Smith was the only lady to finish the entire course, while going fast enough to make the magic sixty finalists, a feat even the organizers doubted.

And she completed the whole first round on one set of tyres, without even using the spare.

Portable radios delivering automatic weather forecasts in four languages, a keen left ear for changing winds, and inspired guesses still rule a team manager's tyre allocations. Chambers swears he is one of the few people on earth who believes a weather report, "so long as it agrees with the

Turn to page 12

Peter Harper (left) takes an interest as mechanics fit new shock absorbers to his Sunbeam Tiger before the Rheims start. Below: Manager Marcus Chambers (left) makes sure the boys are checked in properley—in this case Tim Bosence (centre) and "Tiny" Lewis

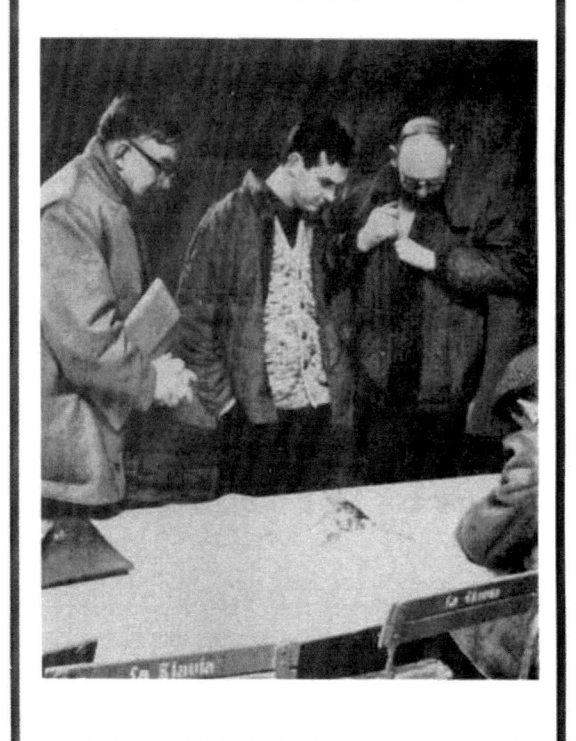

376

Appendix 9

No time for tantrums continued

direction the wind is blowing," but Houdini-style tyre shifts still rule. Some even prove necessary.

A case in point: with his schooled distrust of French petrol stations in the furthest reaches of the Alpes Maritimes, Marcus posted himself at Aups with eleven four-gallon jerry cans of super. On the drive there he realised that the rally route out of Aups was "dry tyre" territory. Whipping out a large-scale map and magnifying glass he ignored the obvious fact that collecting a set of five rubber-shod Tiger wheels from the nearest Dunlop van at Mont Ventoux would mean an all-night drive instead of sleep.

His eventual pre-dawn service point, in thirty degrees of frost, was complete, right down to a Pentastar to catch weary drivers' eyes. As Marcus growled on another occasion: "I have too many smart people working for me. They're always getting rid of me by handing over a sign to be waved up the road." None the less, he was ready in Aups with petrol for three team Imps and a Tiger; tyres extra to the plan.

One Imp was sadly retired before Aups, and the Tiger wheels weren't needed either. Rosemary whistled right past the marshalled ranks of petrol churns and into the control to make her schedule. That left Lewis and Bosence in their dark blue and white Imp who pulled up smartly and smiled. "No thanks, we just topped up at that petrol station back there; didn't realize you'd be waiting. But we will have a cup of coffee, thank you."

Five hundred miles is a long night of hurrying about roads that were often only second-class by courtesy to serve nothing but a cup of luke-warm coffee. The measure of rally service is having anything the crews might need—and not being asked. Everybody was happy when Rootes' chief technical arranger could find no other task for his welding torch than burning the bottoms out of tea kettles. With other tyre/petrol teams scattered across the mountains, Chambers was more than satisfied, though blasphemously chilled, to provide service that wasn't necessary.

Road distances between service crews can be five to ten driving hours, so the various units *have* to think for themselves. The ideal are men who invariably arrive at a common service point first and stake out the best location for quiet refuelling or a quick check, before competing crews arrive.

A certain amount of do-it-yourself psychology is implied here. As Marcus noted: "our boys like to work on winners; that's why they put out the extra bit now." The Mister, as his men call him, is a great hand for getting in a plug for the team—whenever they can't hear him.

When I unthinkingly praised a bit of fast action where the crew could conceivably overhear Marcus shot a sideways glare past his hornrims and rumbled: "that's why they're out here, to think; nothing special." When well out of earshot, he made sure the crew names were spelled right for proper credit.

Americans would call O'Dell the honcho of this team, the tech. rep. And you begin to think his credo is written on a cuff like a schoolboy's crib because his invariable answer to a tricky problem is: "Think, there is always a way." The service boys have heard this gambit before, because nobody thinks to make jokes about his perfection mania until later. Once their team cars were past a service point the crew could rag at will, while loading up that hundred pounds of unused tools— and tea kettles—to go and be redundant at some other obscure six-figure map reference.

You soon accept the Mister's flat statement that "our logistics are far worse than a GP team. They just put a little

Val Domleo (back to camera) supervises a wheel change while Marcus Chambers consults with Rosemary Smith

Time for a brew-up. There's practically no call for the welding kit, so master welder Des O'Dell puts it to good use

377

Appendix 9

car on a trailer and go to the race; we have men scattered all over France. Besides, it's just as hard to develop a rally winner as a Grand Prix car."

Aspiring rally team managers might take that to heart. You can't even give the cars long-range fuel tanks any more—in Group 1 where they run stock cars just like you and I drive. Tankage which might be more than enough on vacation looks pretty slim when driving flat out through the Alps at three in the morning.

Apart from obvious chores like scattering men across a thousand square miles with jerry cans at the ready, you have to carry sufficient licorice all-sorts, a fund of weather data and perhaps a spare thermos flask cup, ignore logical hours—and win classes or titles.

Bashing about the Alps at speed in the dark of night only looks glamorous if you don't absolutely have to make a rendezvous at the other end. Chambers is famous—if that's the word—among rally teams for his blinds between service points. There is even an authenticated case of a Marcus passenger arriving with white hair he hadn't got when he started, yet he insists that service cars be careful. A good part of the side planning that doesn't concern team drivers revolves around carefully staged daily distances so the crews arrive safely.

Of course, he doesn't travel by the same rule book, even with a two-wheel trailer following his Tiger—and you haven't lived until you try an articulated six-wheel drift on packed snow.

He gets away with this by being race trained, of course, but even more by knowing the French mountains like his own driveway. Tim Bosence is a first-rate navigator with private Monte experience (and a shoe emporium at home). Making his works debut for Rootes in the "Tiny" Lewis Imp he said flatly: "I thought I knew those maps—God knows I've studied them enough—but Marcus amazed me. He remembers *every* back road." And the maps Chambers knows so well require thirty sheets for France alone, not to mention the further reaches of Greece or Finland—depending on the event.

Does this begin to sound like a pæan to the team boss? Marcus will be the first to hook his belt below that permanent evidence of good eating around Europe, assume his wild-west sherriff's pose, and fix me with a twinkle over the glasses while he growls on about rally organisers, team drivers and fate—anything but managers. The book he has written covers that subject definitively, and he admitted to having trouble when paring it down to less than a three-volume compendium.

All right. One final comment and you get the last word, Mr. C. I would only note in passing that Freud didn't rally so far as we know. But only two female crews in international rally annuals have won major events outright, and for two of their victories a certain Marcus Mordaunt Bertrand Chambers lumbered about in the background making unobtrusive arrangements, shifting petrol churns and advising on special wine years over supper.

Those were winners, but what does the Mister say to drivers who drop the ball in the grass and then try to alibi that a co-driver let them down? "Don't tell me your navigator failed; you're the captain and ought to know both jobs—at least."

I have one question left over. Admitting that final truth about drivers, how many hats must a team manager own, let alone wear?

Marcus Chambers (on extreme right) holds the funnel while a serviceman pours fuel into a Sunbeam Tiger. Another stands at the ready with a second fuel can. Seconds count, and it's " all hands " at times like this

Appendix 9

Rootes competition manager Marcus Chambers in Service Car A—a heavily-laden Singer Vogue estate.

It's all go
A competition manager under the microscope

by Hamish Cardno

IF you think you could enjoy breakfast in a hotel on the coast of Holland, lunch in Frankfurt, dinner in Lausanne, then spend the night in a hotel in the west of France, you probably have about 10 per cent of the qualifications necessary to be competitions manager of a works rally team. After a week spent "shadowing" one of this elusive breed of sporting gentlemen, I think the other 90 per cent is made up of the dedication of a development engineer, the ability of a good mechanic, the tact of a diplomat, the stamina of a long-distance runner, and the constitution of a well-bred ox.

The subject of my scrutiny was Marcus Chambers, competitions manager of Rootes. He has the unique distinction of being the man who, while competitions manager of BMC, chose Stuart Turner as his assistant—a choice, he says with a wry grin, which he has sometimes regretted. We spent six days together—six days in which we managed only three nights' sleep, drove something like 2,000 miles, and visited six countries.

More people now write to competition departments asking to be competitions managers than works drivers—they must be mad. Works drivers usually have outside incomes so they are wealthier, they lead far more glamorous lives, don't have the same worries, and get more sleep. But there aren't any vacancies in that department either—if there were my name would be on the list!

Marcus Chambers started preparing for the Tulip Rally months before the event took place. It started for him when he decided, before the Rootes financial year began, which rallies they would enter, which cars they would use, which drivers and co-drivers would take part—and how much it would cost. The preparation became intensive in the month before the event, when two recce cars were prepared, travelling and currency arrangements were made for the teams and the service crews, and a thousand and one other details were attended to.

Rootes were fielding two cars for the event—a Group 3 998 c.c. Rally Imp for Peter Harper and David Pollard, and an Imp Sport for Andrew Cowan and Brian Coyle—and the two recce cars which the teams took over to the Continent 10 days before the event were "prototypes" in many ways of the competing cars. Exact notes were kept during all the practice runs on the various stages of shock absorber settings, tyre pressures, and the suitability or otherwise of the fittings inside the cars. At regular intervals the crews telephoned the factory at Coventry, and all their comments were noted, and the rally cars prepared to suit what they were finding to be best.

While the mechanics prepared the cars, a provisional service plan, based again on reports from the crews of where someone was likely to need attention, was drawn up. The Rally started on the Monday, but because of customs difficulties, the three service cars and two crews had to leave on Friday—the third service crew was Marcus Chambers and this inquisitive journalist.

On Saturday morning, Marcus and service mechanic Gerry Spencer drove the rally cars from Coventry to Southend Airport (where they were joined by aforementioned inquisitive journalist), and we flew across to Rotterdam. There Marcus had an appointment with Simon Heyndijk, a Dutchman who owns an Imp tuning firm, and who was the third member of the Rootes team, in a 998 c.c. Imp he had built himself.

Continued on the next page

Appendix 9

It's all go
continued

"No, no, you've got the engine at the wrong end." Topical tactics being discussed at scrutineering by Henry Liddon (left), Marcus Chambers (facing camera), and BMC's new competition manager Peter Browning.

While they talked shop, Gerry Spencer and I drove to Noordwijk, the seaside resort where the Rally starts, met the other members of the Rootes outfit, had lunch, and then found the garage of the local Rootes dealer where various adjustments were made to the rally cars. While the mechanics worked, the drivers gave "the guv'nor" brief details of how the recces had gone, how they expected to fare, and what differences there would be if the weather changed. Both Rootes and BMC were hoping for bad weather, as neither had much hope of catching the Porsches on dry roads, but bearing the Monte in mind, six inches of snow could make all the difference.

Then it was back to the hotel, where the co-drivers had been working on their pace notes, maps, and the provisional service instructions, and knew almost exactly where they would have time for a tyre-change, where they could manage to have the brakes checked, and where they would need fuel-stops—if everything went all right.

The service crews—Gerry Spencer and Ernie Beck, Derek Hughes and Brian Wileman—were then called in, their instructions revised, and all the service points marked on their maps. Then it was the turn of the third crew in the team—Heyndijk and his navigator Hans de Man, and Alan Fraser entrant Tony Maslen and navigator Martin Holmes—who were briefed on what to expect on the Rally, and what could be provided for them in the way of service.

By this time—it was nearly 10 p.m.—everyone was hungry, and the equipe retired to a local restaurant for a meal, highlighted by those "hairy" stories which circulate at all social gatherings of rally people. Then back to the hotel for some of the diplomatic stuff—chatting to some of the senior Rally officials whom a competition manager sees once or perhaps twice a year, but who on those particular occasions are Very Important People.

The next day, Sunday, was set aside for scrutineering, the very small items of last minute work on the cars, and discussing arrangements with representatives of petrol and tyre companies who were to help during the event. Immediately after the scrutineering the two main service crews set off, en route for their first service points: St. Maurice and Annecy, in France.

It is worth mentioning the service cars in a little detail. Rootes have for some time been quite famous (I think that's the word) for their rally service vehicles, which would appear to be the ultimate example of how to get a quart into a pint pot. In fact, it's all very scientifically done. Basically, the cars are Hillman Super Minx estate cars but, apart from the body shell the front seats and controls, there is little real resemblance to a Super Minx estate you might meet anywhere else. The rear seats are removed and large boxes containing spare parts are fitted. Larger parts which cannot be fitted into the normal containers are then added, plus rubber jerry-bags for carrying petrol, cans of oil, tool kits, jack, torches, batteries, the mechanics' luggage, food, a portable stove for making coffee and so on.

When the inside of the car is full, a roof rack is added. This carries spare wheels, an oxy-acetylene welding kit and—when they are full—the petrol bags. Each car is fitted with spot lights at the front and on either side of the roof rack, a powerful inspection light, power points, and a Halda Tripmaster. While the lights and tripmaster are useful to the service crews, their great advantage is that they can be interchanged for defective units on a competing car in a few minutes. To cope with this load—reckoned at about a ton—the cars have heavy duty springs, adjustable shock absorbers, highly modified engines and commercial vehicle clutch assemblies. Steel wheels were found to break under the loads, and now wide-rimmed magnesium alloy wheels with radial ply tyres

Loading one of Rootes' incredible service cars—Derek Hughes and Brian Wileman.

are used. The result is a car capable of carrying extraordinary loads at high average speeds; we were slightly less fortunate in that we had a straight-off-the-line Singer Vogue estate car which had none of the modifications, although it was to carry considerably less equipment. But it served the purpose more than adequately.

The scrutineering over, the roads books were issued, and to the astonishment of almost everybody, they contained a surprise selectif. Plans were quickly made. Service Car A (Chambers and Cardno) had been detailed to wait at the start until after the Rootes cars had gone, just in case there should be any trouble. As it was we left before 8 a.m.—and the first car—and drove through Germany and Switzerland to Annecy (where the competitors were to have 12 hours' rest), contacting the Rootes agent in Geneva on the way to arrange for an Imp to be waiting at Annecy when the drivers arrived on the Tuesday morning.

Lunch, as I've already mentioned, was in Frankfurt, dinner in Lausanne, and we booked into our hotel in Annecy just after midnight. A night porter (who is still convinced we are utterly mad) carried our bags to our rooms and then we dashed off again into the freezing night to recce a section of the mountain loop which the competitors were to try some 20 hours later. Annecy is less than 50 miles from the Swiss border, and fairly deep snow was lying over all the mountains, and right down to the edge of the road on the higher stretches. Melting snow had run across the road on three hairpin bends and one tunnel on the Col d'Aravice, which we negotiated downhill—the opposite way to the competitors—and ice had formed on these stretches. It was the ice in the tunnel, mentioned in last week's report, which was to create havoc among the competitors and reduce many cars to twisted and torn facsimiles of the shining models which had left Noordwijk.

We disturbed the night porter again shortly after 3 a.m., and retired to bed—to rise again just after 6 a.m. and head for the lakeside car park, where the control and *parc ferme* were already alive with officials. Here, too, was the man from Geneva with a standard Imp, who unwittingly accepted Peter Harper's offer of a run, when Harper set off to recce the new selectif, immediately after "clocking in".

We saw the other Rootes entries in, had a word with them and took them to the hotel —then the rest of the day was free. The service and re-fuelling plans for the next 24 hours were checked, our petrol bags filled, and the cars seen off from the *parc ferme* shortly after 9 p.m. Then it was off into the mountains for us, to our first re-fuelling point at Cluses just after midnight, and our second on the N202 shortly after 2 a.m. These went off without incident (although it was bitterly cold), and then we headed for Rumilly, the end of the loop, where there was an open park on which service crews could work if necessary.

And work *was* necessary. Peter Harper had arrived at the hotel there before us and, after a quick coffee with him, we returned to the car park where already there were several cars with signs of tunnel-itis. Then came our first victim, Andrew Cowan, who had bashed both front and rear offside wings. A front wheel was changed, and a rear lamp cluster replaced, before Tony Maslen limped in with the side of his Imp very much flatter than the designer intended. Some rapid work was done on his car, the drivers were wakened and the cars seen away before we headed for St. Maurice where there was to be another service point as the drivers made their ways north again.

No service was required here; in fact it was just a question of keeping in touch with the drivers and seeing how the Rally was going. We set off from there before 5 p.m., and headed north, through Luxembourg to Malmedy in darker (well it was when we were there) Belgium, where our cars were due in between 2 and 3 a.m. on Thursday. Only routine service and re-fuelling were needed here, and with the Rally almost over we set off again along the Belgian autoroute, into Holland and up to Noordwijk where the first car was due shortly after 8 a.m.

Service cars B and C were situated on the outside of Noordwijk to check light bulbs and any other minor detail which might catch the eyes of officialdom, and we were on the line ready for Peter Harper to come storming up the drive of the hotel on time, to finish third in the Group 3 classification and second in the under-1,600 c.c. GT class. Then came Heiyndijk, taking fifth place in Group 3, and it only needed Andrew Cowan to arrive and the entire team was in.

We waited and waited. Then suddenly a grim-faced Andrew was beside us. On foot. A stub axle on his Imp had sheared on the second last special stage—a tank testing ground—while he had been leading the 850-1,000 c.c. class by nine minutes. So that was it—one successful car, one successful private entrant, and a feeling of great disappointment that so little had come of so much work.

Still fancy the job?

What the competitions manager doesn't see but has on his mind—Andrew Cowan and Brian Coyle hurrying their Imp Sport through a bend on one of the selectifs.

The end of the road. A quiet word of congratulations for works driver Peter Harper from Marcus Chambers at the end of the rally.

Appendix 9

Appendix 10: Rally Car Build sheets

This appendix shows a selection of the original Rootes Competition Department work sheets, supplied from the dusty archives of Derek Hughes – one of the works mechanics for the whole history of the works Tigers and well beyond – with all of the details that are involved in the building and refurbishment of works vehicles.

The sheets are in chronological order and cover the period from June 1964 - after the International Police Rally - to preparations for the Tulip Rally recce in March 1966, and show an interesting insight into the detail of the works competition environment.

One of the later sheets shows, essentially, the complete build, to a works Tiger 1964/5 specification, for a good customer in the form of Gerry Tyack.

With the atmospheric costs of a modern rally, it is interesting to see the cost-of-build of the works Tigers. In 1965 Marcus Chambers was interviewed by ITN Presenter John Edwards and the following are excerpts from the transcript:

JE: What does Monte rallying cost a firm?

MC: Well, it's very difficult to say, but it can be anything up to £10,000, sometimes a little more, sometimes a little less depending upon the number of cars. But these days you can say a round figure of about £2000 per car, including everything.

JE: And what would that include? I mean what sorts of things?

MC: Well, that includes preparing the car beforehand, which will be probably three weeks to a month, fitting it out with additional equipment which is required to keep the crew – they're going to be about three and a half days in the car – comfortable, warm and prevent them from getting too tired. Equipment which will enable them to find out exactly where they are on the route to within 10 yards - so it has to be accurate measuring equipment - and a good engine, good brakes, good road holding naturally follow. After you've prepared the car you've got to consider giving the crews a reconnoitre, which will enable them to make pace notes, so they can find out whether they can drive corners fast or slow, and from pace notes, general navigation notes and after they come back to England we've got to lay on for the rally the best possible service which will look after the cars in the very limited time available.

Appendix 10

REPAIR ORDER CARD JOB NO. ....

OWNER'S NAME   Rootes Competitions
ADDRESS   Dept.
Ex Police Rally To leave on Friday
18th June on Recce for the Alpine
Date .... Tel. No. ....

Make .... Sunbeam
Model ... Tiger
Year 1964
Regn. No. AHP 295 B
Chass. No. ....
Eng. No. ....

Speedometer—Mileage .... Petrol Gauge ....

WORK INSTRUCTIONS

REPAIR SHOP 1/ Remove Sump Shield.
2/ Drain Engine, Gearbox and Rear axle.
3/ Refill Rear axle with oil <u>immediately</u>
4/ Remove Engine and Gear Box (Engine to
  Mr. E. Beck)
5/ <u>Gearbox</u>. First check oil seals for leaks.
Remove top lid. Flush out box, check visually
bearings, gears, selectors etc. Remove the
side change rods, check tightness of
lever and gate mechanism, lock this
mechanism with a ¼" drill in hole provided,
BODY REPAIRS & PANEL WORK ensure all 3 selector levers
are in neutral, adjust rod length
carefully. Remove rod (with split pins
not nuts), braze solid, recheck, if OK
assemble. Thoroughly check gear change,
especially no gritiness across gate. Tighten
all bolts.
ELECTRICAL REPAIRS 6/ Have car underside and engine
compartment Parafined and hosed down.
7/ Check chassis for breakages and cracks.
8/ <u>Rear axle</u> and <u>Rear Suspention</u>
Tighten all bolts, renew any suspect.
Check and record rear hub end float
GREASING and run out. Grease hub bearings,
check hub oil seals, examine wheel
studs. Check rear springs for breakage
or sag, clips, U bolts and shackles.
Spring Hangers and solid bushes and
frame this area. Prop shaft UJs
WASHING, POLISHING, ETC. and flange bolts.
9/ <u>Rear Brakes</u>. Fit new Wheel cylinders
and Brake Shoes. check and replace
drums if necessary. Check carefully pipe
run, pipe condition. Hose run, Hose condition.
Hand brake cable condition and run.

ALL TIME, SPARES AND MATERIAL TO BE LISTED OVERLEAF
Published by REDITE LTD., 36 Larkfield Avenue, Kenton, Middlesex. (Copyright)

Appendix 10

REPAIR ORDER CARD

CONTINUED

JOB NO. ....

OWNER'S NAME ROOTES COMPETITIONS
ADDRESS Dept

Date .... Tel. No. ....

Speedometer—Mileage .... Petrol Gauge ....

Make SUNBEAM
Model TIGER
Year 1964
Regn. No. AHP 295 B
Chass. No. ....
Eng. No. ....

WORK INSTRUCTIONS

REPAIR SHOP 10/ <u>Shock Absorbers</u> Check for fluid leak. Use these Shock absorbers again at the same setting, check mountings and mounting rubbers.

11/ <u>Front Suspension</u> Check main beam and fixing bolts. Inspect top and bottom wish bones, stub axles, wish bone pins. Remove Hubs, renew wheel bearing. Check anti-roll bar fixings.

12/ Inspect Front Shock absorbers, if OK use again 1 half turn stiffer.

BODY-REPAIRS & PANEL WORK 13/ <u>Front Brake</u> Inspect discs if OK check run out and record. Re-new pads check caliper seals hoses and pipe run and condition. Re new Brake Fluid.

14/ <u>Steering</u> Remove column and check splines at inner column end and

ELECTRICAL REPAIRS pinion end. Check U.J. Check track Rod ends and track Rods at ball ends. Fill with oil.

GREASING

WASHING, POLISHING, ETC.

ALL TIME, SPARES AND MATERIAL TO BE LISTED OVERLEAF
Published by REDITE LTD., 36 Larkfield Avenue, Kenton, Middlesex. (Copyright)

Appendix 10

REPAIR ORDER CARD   JOB NO. 87569

OWNER'S NAME: Competitions Dept
ADDRESS: (Alpine Recce)
(Delivery date 4/7/65)
Date: 22/6/65   Tel. No.

Make: SUNBEAM
Model: TIGER
Year: 1965
Regn. No. AHP 293 B
Chass. No. B 9470013
Eng. No.

Speedometer—Mileage _____ Petrol Gauge _____

WORK INSTRUCTIONS

REPAIR SHOP
1/ Change clutch unit & fit Competition
2/ Change back axle
3/ Re-line brakes V.G.95 rear, DS 11 front
4/ Fit Halda & single tripmaster.
5/ Change all oils.
6/ Check over car & chassis in general.
7/ Change clutch master cylinder.
8/ Fit flexible clutch pipe.
9/ Fit safety harness (Lap & diagonal.)

BODY REPAIRS & PANEL WORK

ELECTRICAL REPAIRS

GREASING

WASHING, POLISHING, ETC.

ALL TIME, SPARES AND MATERIAL TO BE LISTED OVERLEAF
Published by REDITE LTD., 36 Larkfield Avenue, Kenton, Middlesex. (Copyright)

Appendix 10

REPAIR ORDER CARD   JOB NO: 87364

OWNER'S NAME: Competitions Dept.
ADDRESS: (Alpine Recce)

Make: SUNBEAM
Model: TIGER
Year: 1965
Regn. No. AHP 295 B
Chass. No. B 9H7 6015
Eng. No.

Date: 30/6/65   Tel. No.

Speedometer—Mileage: Petrol Gauge:

WORK INSTRUCTIONS

REPAIR SHOP — Engine:-

1/ Rectify throttle linkage
2/ Fit elbow pipe to L/H oil cap.
3/ Oil leak L/H rocker cover.
4/ Check ignition point setting & timing
5/ Fit by-pass pipe and remove ~~header~~ pipe to header tank.
6/ Fit four row radiator
7/ Roughness at 4500 RPM and over, check exhaust for fouling (R/H baffle gone) hits floor on bumps.

BODY REPAIRS & PANEL WORK

8/ Change engine oil and fit Red filter.

Chassis
9/ Remove speed pilot and fit Twinmaster & rectify main speedo run

ELECTRICAL REPAIRS
10/ Tidy carpets & cockpit.
11/ Rear axle steering car (check)

GREASING

WASHING, POLISHING, ETC.

ALL TIME, SPARES AND MATERIAL TO BE LISTED OVERLEAF
Published by REDITE LTD., 36 Larkfield Avenue, Kenton, Middlesex. (Copyright)

Appendix 10

REPAIR ORDER CARD JOB NO. 37569

OWNER'S NAME: Competitions Dept
ADDRESS: (Alpine Recce)

Date: 1/7/65   Tel. No.

Make: SUNBEAM
Model: TIGER
Year: 1965
Regn. No. ERW 729C
Chass. No. 9472967 HRoFE
Eng. No.

Speedometer—Mileage   Petrol Gauge

WORK INSTRUCTIONS

REPAIR SHOP

Engine
1/ Change Engine oil and fit Red Filter.

Gearbox
2/ Check Gearbox linkage.

Chassis
3/ Rectify bonnet rubbing on radiator.
4/ Rectify bonnet hinge rubbing on oil cooler pipe.
5/ Fit full length of sorbo rubber at rear of bonnet.
6/ Mark water valve control lever's new position.

BODY REPAIRS & PANEL WORK

7/ Centre Steering Wheel.
8/ Fit Koni Shock absorbers.
9/ Mark red line on Rev. Counter at 6000 rpm.
10/ Clip petrol pipe in car away from throttle pedal.

ELECTRICAL REPAIRS

11/ Clip battery cable in car away from throttle cable.
12/ Secure wire away from heater.
13/ Fit larger buttons on bonnet fastener to secure bonnet.

GREASING

WASHING, POLISHING, ETC.

ALL TIME, SPARES AND MATERIAL TO BE LISTED OVERLEAF
Published by REDITE LTD., 36 Larkfield Avenue, Kenton, Middlesex. (Copyright)

Appendix 10

REPAIR ORDER CARD   JOB NO. 87569

OWNER'S NAME: Competitions Dept.
ADDRESS: (Alpine Race)

Date: 3/7/65   Tel. No.

Make: SUNBEAM
Model: TIGER
Year: 1965
Regn. No. AHP 293 B
Chass. No. B 9470013
Eng. No.

Speedometer — Mileage   Petrol Gauge

WORK INSTRUCTIONS

REPAIR SHOP:
1/ Fit Koni Shock absorbers all round.
2/ Fit latest type heater valve.
3/ Start clutch pedal ½" nearer driver and bleed system
4/ Change Wiper Blades

BODY REPAIRS & PANEL WORK

ELECTRICAL REPAIRS

GREASING

WASHING, POLISHING, ETC.

ALL TIME, SPARES AND MATERIAL TO BE LISTED OVERLEAF
Published by REDITE LTD., 36 Larkfield Avenue, Kenton, Middlesex. (Copyright)

Appendix 10

REPAIR ORDER CARD JOB NO. 87569

OWNER'S NAME: Competitions Dept
ADDRESS: (Athens Rally)

Make: SUNBEAM
Model: TIGER
Year: 1964
Regn. No.: ADU 312 B
Chass. No.:
Eng. No.:

Date: 13/7/65 Tel. No.:

Speedometer—Mileage: Petrol Gauge:

WORK INSTRUCTIONS

REPAIR SHOP

1/ Change starter Motor
2/ Adjust slave cylinder rod to ¼" free-play
3/ Carburetter trumpet requires nylock on retaining bolt, also pin rubber seal to trumpet.
4/ Check engine ie points, tappets, plugs, timing (No 7 lead) etc.
5/ Fit Red oil Filter & change oil.
6/ Rectify Speedo failure.

BODY REPAIRS & PANEL WORK

7/ Clearance Exhaust pipe from frame member
8/ More Bonnet clips inboard.
9/ Fit longer plastic hose to horn trumpets

ELECTRICAL REPAIRS

GREASING

WASHING, POLISHING, ETC.

ALL TIME, SPARES AND MATERIAL TO BE LISTED OVERLEAF
Published by REDITE LTD., 36 Larkfield Avenue, Kenton, Middlesex. (Copyright)

Appendix 10

REPAIR ORDER CARD   JOB NO. **87569**

OWNER'S NAME: Competitions Dept (Alpine Rally)
ADDRESS:

Make: SUNBEAM
Model: TIGER
Year: 1964
Regn. No.: ADU 312B
Chass. No.:
Eng. No.:

Date: 14/7/65   Tel. No.:

Speedometer—Mileage: Petrol Gauge:

WORK INSTRUCTIONS

REPAIR SHOP

1. Red line on Rev. Counter
2. Oil Pressure Gauge crooked in dashboard.
3. Blank rear end of air scoop.
4. 3/8" free play in slave cylinder rod (Max.)
5. Car steering badly (pulling left, steering dead & stiff, check geometry, loosen rack & tighten.)
6. Heater valve bracket loose.

BODY REPAIRS & PANEL WORK

7. Main coil lead loose in distributer.
8. Change to Ferodo Fan Belt.
9. Bonnet clips?
10. Change ignition switch.
11. Weld throttle linkage pedal.

ELECTRICAL REPAIRS

GREASING

WASHING, POLISHING, ETC.

ALL TIME, SPARES AND MATERIAL TO BE LISTED OVERLEAF

Appendix 10

REPAIR ORDER CARD JOB NO. 8668₹

OWNER'S NAME: Competitions Dept.
ADDRESS:

Make: SUNBEAM
Model: TIGER
Year: 1965
Regn. No. ERW 729c.
Chass. No.
Eng. No.

Date: 4/8/65   Tel. No.

Speedometer—Mileage   Petrol Gauge

WORK INSTRUCTIONS   Work Completed (Initial or Time)

REPAIR SHOP

1/ Carry out necessary work to insure that the car is in a road-worthy state.
2/ Check plugs, points & carburation
3/ Remove half-shaft en-float from rear axle (max 5 thou.)
4/ Fit steel wheels with Dunlop S.P.H/s. (Tyre press.
5/ Drain & refit Engine, Gearbox & Rear-axle oils.   30lb all round.
6/ Check clutch slave cylinder clearance (3/8")
7/ Remove rear brake drums and insure at least 50% lining, and check front pads for same.
8/ Tighten and check all bolts & nuts.
9/ Clean inside & outside of car.

BODY REPAIRS & PANEL WORK

ELECTRICAL REPAIRS

GREASING

WASHING, POLISHING, ETC.

ALL TIME, SPARES AND MATERIAL TO BE LISTED OVERLEAF
Published by REDITE LTD., 36 Larkfield Avenue, Kenton, Middlesex. (Copyright)

Appendix 10

REPAIR ORDER CARD   JOB NO. 87608

OWNER'S NAME: Shelly Motors
ADDRESS: Hawaii

Make: SUNBEAM
Model: TIGER
Year: 1965
Regn. No. Unrg
Chass. No. B382000030LRXFE
Eng. No.

Date: 8/9/65   Tel. No.

Speedometer—Mileage ___   Petrol Gauge ___

WORK INSTRUCTIONS

REPAIR SHOP

1/ Remove Steel Wheels from car, and take off the Tyres (including Spare)

2/ Fit Tyres of Tec Del Wheels and refit to car together with special hub caps

3/ Return Steel Wheels to Ryton

BODY REPAIRS & PANEL WORK

ELECTRICAL REPAIRS

GREASING

WASHING, POLISHING, ETC.

ALL TIME, SPARES AND MATERIAL TO BE LISTED OVERLEAF
Published by REDITE LTD., 36 Larkfield Avenue, Kenton, Middlesex. (Copyright)

Appendix 10

REPAIR ORDER CARD JOB NO. 87681

OWNER'S NAME Competitions Dept.
ADDRESS

Make SUNBEAM
Model TIGER
Year 1964
Regn. No. ADU 311 B
Chass. No. B 9470011
Eng. No.

Date 23/9/65 Tel. No.

Speedometer—Mileage Petrol Gauge

WORK INSTRUCTIONS | Work Completed (Initial or Time)

REPAIR SHOP

1/ Overhaul Engine unit to Mr O'Dell's instructions
2/ Modify front cross-member to Bagshot Spec.
3/ Fit tandem brake system
4/ Fit rear springs to Bagshot Spec.
5/ Examine & strength all weld on chassis
6/ Fit brake pipes inside car
7/ Fit new seals to all wheel cylinders & calipers
8/ Make up new undershield to Bagshot Spec.
9/ Remove diff. plug & fit "key" type
10/ Protect rear s/as adjusting knob.

BODY REPAIRS & PANEL WORK

ELECTRICAL REPAIRS

GREASING

WASHING, POLISHING, ETC.

ALL TIME, SPARES AND MATERIAL TO BE LISTED OVERLEAF
Published by REDITE LTD., 36 Larkfield Avenue, Kenton, Middlesex. (Copyright)

Appendix 10

REPAIR ORDER CARD JOB NO. 87681

OWNER'S NAME: Competitions Dept
ADDRESS:

Date: 4/10/65   Tel. No.

Make: SUNBEAM
Model: TIGER
Year: 1964
Regn. No.: AHP 295 B
Chass. No.
Eng. No.

Speedometer—Mileage   Petrol Gauge

WORK INSTRUCTIONS

REPAIR SHOP

1/ Modify front end of Stone Guard
2/ Check over car & prepare for Bagshot Test

WANTED FOR WEDNESDAY 6/10/65

BODY REPAIRS & PANEL WORK

ELECTRICAL REPAIRS

GREASING

WASHING, POLISHING, ETC.

ALL TIME, SPARES AND MATERIAL TO BE LISTED OVERLEAF
Published by REDITE LTD., 36 Larkfield Avenue, Kenton, Middlesex. (Copyright)

Appendix 10

REPAIR ORDER CARD JOB NO. 87681

OWNER'S NAME Competitions Dept.
ADDRESS (ex Bagshot car, prepare for sale)

Make SUNBEAM
Model TIGER
Year 1964
Regn. No. AHP 295B
Chass. No.
Eng. No.

Date 20/10/65   Tel. No.

Speedometer—Mileage   Petrol Gauge

WORK INSTRUCTIONS Work Completed (Initial or Time)

REPAIR SHOP
1/ Remove & replace front cross-member & assembly
2/ Replace S/A all round with new Konis

BODY REPAIRS & PANEL WORK

ELECTRICAL REPAIRS

GREASING

WASHING, POLISHING, ETC.

ALL TIME, SPARES AND MATERIAL TO BE LISTED OVERLEAF

Appendix 10

REPAIR ORDER CARD   JOB NO. 888044

OWNER'S NAME   Competition Dept.
ADDRESS   (Monte Carlo Rally Recce)

Make   SUNBEAM
Model   TIGER
Year   1964
Regn. No.   ADU 312B
Chass. No.
Eng. No.

Date   13/12/65   Tel. No.

Speedometer—Mileage   Petrol Gauge

WORK INSTRUCTIONS

REPAIR SHOP

1/ Change Gear-lever rubber. ✓
2/ Change S/A to Armstrong adjustable ✗
   A.T. 10
3/ Change bonnet to one less duct. ✗
4/ Fit anti-lift wiper blade on drivers side.   aB
5/ Carry snow-blades on arms inside car   aB

BODY REPAIRS & PANEL WORK

6/ Fit Servo cover.
7/ Fit Halda Trip-master ✓
8/ Fit map light. ✓
9/ Fit stop watch bracket. ✓

ELECTRICAL REPAIRS

10/ ~~Passenger~~ Drivers side demister tube missing.
11/ Fill screen washer bottle with de-icing fluid.
12/ Clip choke to manifold tube. ✓

GREASING

13/ Tidy up carpet around Throttle pedal.
14/ Fit cigar lighter* & drivers knee pad.   *aB
15/ Alternator over charging.   aB

WASHING, POLISHING, ETC.

FIT HEATER BARS   aB
FIT REVERSE LAMP SW   aB.

ALL TIME, SPARES AND MATERIAL TO BE LISTED OVERLEAF
Published by REDITE LTD., 36 Larkfield Avenue, Kenton, Middlesex. (Copyright)

Appendix 10

REPAIR ORDER CARD   JOB NO. ....

OWNER'S NAME Competitions Dept.
ADDRESS (on loan to Robin Turvey for Monte Carlo Rally)

Make: SUNBEAM
Model: TIGER
Year: 1965
Regn. No. ~~EWK~~ ERW 729C
Chass. No.
Eng. No.

Date 15/12/65   Tel. No.

Speedometer—Mileage   Petrol Gauge

WORK INSTRUCTIONS

REPAIR SHOP

1/ Change Engine & Gearbox oils. ✓
2/ Change oil Filter. ✓
3/ Check Brakes & adjust. ✓
4/ Check Gearbox linkage for fault (ie will not select gear properly.) ✓
5/ Wash, rear & clean interior. ✓

BODY REPAIRS & PANEL WORK

6/ Lift Tripmaster ✓
7/ Fill in grip handle in glove-box. ✓
8/ Fit new Fog Lamps ✓

ELECTRICAL REPAIRS

GREASING

WASHING, POLISHING, ETC.

ALL TIME, SPARES AND MATERIAL TO BE LISTED OVERLEAF
Published by REDITE LTD., 36 Larkfield Avenue, Kenton, Middlesex. (Copyright)

Appendix 10

REPAIR ORDER CARD

JOB NO. 89005

OWNER'S NAME: Competitions Dept.
ADDRESS: (Tulip Recce Car)

Make: SUNBEAM
Model: TIGER
Year: 1966
Regn. No. AHP 294B
Chass. No.
Eng. No.

Date: 15/3/66   Tel. No.

Speedometer—Mileage   Petrol Gauge

WORK INSTRUCTIONS

REPAIR SHOP

Prepare for Tulip Recce.

✓ 1/ Remove Engine & fit new unit.
✓ 2/ Check Front Wheel Bearings.
✓ 3/ Change Steering Arms.
✓ 4/ Check Front Crossmember ie Welds etc.
✓ 5/ Remove Cross-member fixings from Chassis.
✓ 6/ Check & reline all Brakes
✓ 7/ Check all Wheel Cylinders

BODY REPAIRS & PANEL WORK

✓ 8/ Change Windscreen
✓ 9/ Change Rear Springs.
  10/ Remove Gearbox top, flush & inspect Gears.
✓ 11/ Check Gearbox linkage. (Brazing)

ELECTRICAL REPAIRS

  12/ Check over all Electrics.
     Check over car Bolts, Lines etc.
? ✓ 13/ Std Petrol Pump. ~~And Line~~
✓ 14/ Reset St. Wheel.
✓ 15/ Repair Rear s/washer Bottle Brkt.

GREASING

Camber ¼° + N/S   Shocks Front 3
       ½° + O/S   Rear 1
Track ⅛" + toe in.

WASHING, POLISHING, ETC.

ALL TIME, SPARES AND MATERIAL TO BE LISTED OVERLEAF
Published by REDITE LTD., 36 Larkfield Avenue, Kenton, Middlesex. (Copyright)

Appendix 10

REPAIR ORDER CARD — JOB NO. 87420

OWNER'S NAME: MR. G. V. TYACK
ADDRESS:
Date: Tel. No.
Speedometer—Mileage: Petrol Gauge:

Make: TIGER
Model:
Year:
Regn. No. PDF. 331C
Chass. No. B 9472021 HROFE
Eng. No.

REPAIR SHOP — WORK INSTRUCTIONS

1. Remove & Polish Cyl. Heads.
2. Modify Rocker Post.
3. S/F New Valve Springs (RED).
4. S/F High Performance Camshaft
5. S/F Solid Tappets.
6. S/F 4 Barrel Manifold.
7. S/F 4 Barrel Holly Carburettor.
8. S/F Twin Point Distributor.
9. Modify oil pump pick up pipe.

BODY REPAIRS & PANEL WORK

10. Screw & plug oil gall.
11. S/F new Sparking plugs (BF601)
12. S/F Competition Clutch + Modify G/Box linkage
13. Fit Flex pipe to clutch
14. S/F Competition Exhaust
15. S/F S-U petrol pump (Double) + large bore pipe

ELECTRICAL REPAIRS

16. S/F DS 11 Front Pucks + VG 95 Rear lining
17. S/F 3¾ Rear wheel Cly + Amber fluid
18. S/F Husky Export front springs
19. S/F Husky Export rear springs
20. Fit anti tramp leaf + remove helper leaf

GREASING

21. S/F Competition shocks.
22. S/F ⅞ anti roll bar.
23. S/F 8'000 rev counter
24. S/F Speedo to suit 3-77 axle.
25. Remove rear axle + converted to 3-77.
26. Fit long studs to rear hub.

WASHING, POLISHING, ETC. 27. Modify wheel arches to take 5½" wheel

ALL TIME, SPARES AND MATERIAL TO BE LISTED OVERLEAF

Appendix 10

LABOUR							SPARES AND MATERIAL				
Fitter's Name	Hours Nor/O/T	Rate	£	s.	d.	Reqn. No. or Purchase O/No.	Qty.	Description	COST £ s. d.	RETAIL £ s. d.	
							1 set	DS 11 Front Pads			
							1 st	VG 95 Brake Linings			
							1	Rear wheel			
							2	Husky Rant Springs			
							2	" Front "			
							4	Shocks			
							1	Roll Bar			
							1	Rev Counter			
							1	Speedo			
								Valve Spring			
							1	Camshaft			
							16	Solid Tappet			
							1	Barrel Carb			
							1	Twin cont dist			

Total { Normal hours / Overtime hours }

TOTAL LABOUR COST

TOTAL COST of spares and material

Date completed

Appendix 10

REPAIR ORDER CARD JOB NO. ....

OWNER'S NAME ....
ADDRESS ....

Make ....
Model: Tiger
Year ....
Regn. No. ERW 729C
Chass. No. ....
Eng. No. ....

Date .... Tel. No. ....
Speedometer—Mileage .... Petrol Gauge ....

WORK INSTRUCTIONS | Work Completed (Initial or Time)

REPAIR SHOP
- ✓ Fit 2·88 Axle + Speedo Head ✓
- ✓ Fit STD Bonnet
- Reset Petrol gauge ✓
- ✓ Fit new set of Plugs. B4F 601
- Change Engine oil & filter unit (Super M)
- " Gear Box oil — EP 80.
- " Rear Axle — S640%.
- Reset tappets

BODY REPAIRS & PANEL WORK
- Petrol gauge — AB
- Horn — AB
- Noise Rear Axle — MB
- Change Rear Shocks — MB
- Remove Trip master — AB
- Balance Front Wheels — MB

ELECTRICAL REPAIRS

GREASING

WASHING, POLISHING, ETC.

ALL TIME, SPARES AND MATERIAL TO BE LISTED OVERLEAF
Published by REDITE LTD., 36 Larkfield Avenue, Kenton, Middlesex. (Copyright)

Appendix 10

REPAIR ORDER CARD   JOB NO. 87561

OWNER'S NAME: Rootes Autos
ADDRESS: Geneva.
Make: TIGER
Model: —
Year: 1965

Date: Tel. No.
Regn. No.:
Chass. No.:
Eng. No.:

Speedometer—Mileage: Petrol Gauge:

WORK INSTRUCTIONS

REPAIR SHOP
- Remove Engine unit ✓
- Modified Rocker Posts + fit red Springs ✓
- Fit solid tappets + High lift Camshaft ✓
- 4 Barrel Manifold (Cast iron) ✓
- 4 Barrel Carb (Ford) ✓
- Modify oil Pump Pick up. ✓
- Screw plug oil galleries ✓
- Fit BF.601 Sparking Plugs. ✓
- Fit Red oil Filter
- Fit Competition Clutch (Ford lining) ✓
- Fit 26 gall Tank + SU Pump with big piping ✓

BODY REPAIRS & PANEL WORK
- Fit Competition Exhaust Dual —
- Henge Bolts (STD. Gaskets.)
- Fit Competition Radiator + Bottom Hose
- Fit oil Cooler ✓
- Fit DS.11 Front Pads + VG.95 Rear linings ✓
- Fit Competition Front + Rear Springs with Anti tramp bar
- Fit Solid bushes ✓

ELECTRICAL REPAIRS
- Convert Rear Axle to 3·77 to 1 PL ✓
- Fit 8000 R.P.M rev counter
- Fit Speedo KPH to suit 3·77 axle.
- Fit Minilite Wheels + SP 41 Tyres
- Modify Wheel arches.

GREASING

WASHING, POLISHING, ETC.

ALL TIME, SPARES AND MATERIAL TO BE LISTED OVERLEAF
Published by REDITE LTD., 36 Larkfield Avenue, Kenton, Middlesex. (Copyright)

Appendix 10

Appendix 11: Competition Options from Humber Road and USA Factory Options

In the period, most of the manufacturers who were involved in national and international competition offered official tuning parts to the private owner. BMC had their Special Tuning Department at Abingdon for their Minis, Healeys and MGAs, Ford Competition Department at Boreham offered parts for their Cortina GTs and Lotus-Cortinas and Triumph for their TRs.

In those days tuning a rally car was relatively simple – even for the works cars. Normally a polished and modified cylinder head encouraged more air into the cylinders, a 'hairier' camshaft, better carburation and exhaust manifold provided the necessary performance and with a stronger clutch, better brake pads/shoe material and an uprated suspension, the car was ready for competition. The parts were generally offered in 'Stages'- Stage 1 tuning being the basic minimum and running up to Stage 3 or higher – the higher the 'Stage' the more potent the car.

It was all a bit simpler in the '60s – and a privateer could get very close to the build standard of a works car – all he then had to do was to match the skill and speed of the works crews.

From the heat of competition, the manufacturers found the weaker points on the cars and, as well as suitably modifying production parts, the competition departments offered the strengthened and modified parts to the private competitors – with resultant improvements in the reliability of the rally cars.

At the same time, of course, many tuning businesses were offering for sale their own ideas on improving the cars performance. This resulted in some commercial competition for parts and a variety of interesting themes in such areas as carburation, exhaust manifolding and camshaft design emerged. For international competition however, apart from the prototype categories, the cars had to be built to the correct specification laid out in detail in the Homologation Papers, and the manufacturers options would have met this criterion.

Homologation in America was a little different and not generally as stringent as that in Europe. Normally, in the USA, it was only necessary for the manufacturers authorized optional equipment for the Tiger to have been offered for sale and at least 100 units produced in that preceding year. This led to a number of options being offered for sale that would not be legitimate for some classes of International competition use under FIA rules. A typical, and widely queried, example for the Tiger is the use of Part number LAT 5 – Anti Tramp rods – and whilst the rods gave a significant advantage to the traction under acceleration, they could not be used in competition where the FIA rules applied. Quite legitimate in a road car - worldwide - but not for some levels of competition.

Appendix 11

COST OF MATERIALS FOR CONVERTING
SUNBEAM 260 TIGER TO COMPETITION SPECIFICATION.

The engine can be tuned in the following stages:

£. s. d.

STAGE I.
1. **High Performance Cam Kit.**

   Lift is .300", Timing duration 306°.
   This increases the stock 141 HP rating to
   approximately 161 HP.

   Kit includes: 1 Camshaft and 16 solid
   tappets. .... 25. 15. 0.

2. **High Performance Distributor Kit.**

   A twin point heavy duty distributor, with a
   competition curve, delivering a reliable
   spark at high r.p.m. Used with colder BF.603
   Sparking Plugs, there will be a gain of five
   horse power.

   Kit includes: 1 Distributor and 8 BF.601
   Sparking Plugs. .... 18. 10. 2.

3. **Heavy Duty Valve Springs - 16.**

   Advisable for speeds of over 5000 r.p.m. ...... ~~6. 8. 0.~~
   9. 18. 8.

   It is recommended that items 1, 2 and 3 be fitted
   as a single stage.

   STAGE II, WITH ITEMS 1 TO 3.
4. With the valve lift and duration allowing
   better breathing, it is now possible to increase
   the induction capacity by fitting the **Four Barrel
   Induction Kit,** giving a further 55 HP. .... 68. 4. 4.

   Kit includes: 1 Intake Manifold.
                  1 Four Barrel Carburettor.

5. To ensure adequate petrol supply at the
   carburettor, a **High Pressure Twin Barrel Pump**
   is fitted, with large bore piping. .... 13. 6. 6.

   Kit includes: 1 High Pressure Petrol Pump.
                  2 Pump Fixing Brackets.
                  Length of Petrol Pipe.

   STAGE III, WITH ITEMS 1 TO 5.
6. **Polished Cylinder Heads,** with flowed ports,
   gives further increase in horse power. .... 31. 10. 0.

7. **Heavy Duty Clutch Kit,** for increased efficiency
   at high r.p.m. .... ~~24. 11. 0.~~
                                                   28. 11. 0.
   Kit includes: 1 Pressure Plate Assembly.
                  1 Clutch Disc.

   Additional modifications to the engine, in the
   interest of reliability are:-

18.3.65.

Appendix 11

8. A competition sump, with anti-surge swing baffles, fitted giving increased capacity.   47. 5. 0.

9. Strengthened Oil Pump Pick-up Pipe.   1. 10. 0.

10. Fitting Threaded Valve Rocker Posts into cylinder heads, strongly recommended for high engine speeds.   25. 6. 4.

11. Removing pressed in oil gallery plugs and fitting threaded type (price when engine is stripped).   3. 15. 0.

12. Fitting a flexible pipe to the clutch slave cylinder.   3. 15. 0.

13. *Complete Engine Gasket set.   8. 10. 11.
    *Top Overhaul Gasket set.   6. 5. 9.

14. *Competition Exhaust System, giving an increase in power and more ground clearance, essential for competition work.   30. 0. 0.

    NOTE: The fitting of this item necessitates the modifying of the cross member holes and re-locating the petrol pump.

15. Engine Sump Guard.   17. 10. 0.

16. High Efficiency Radiator, of increased capacity.   50. 0. 0.
    An Engine Oil Cooler Kit,   35. 0. 0.
    Both items are essential for competition use.

    NOTE: The fitting of the above items requires extensive modification to the engine compartment front apron, and forward bulkhead.

17. *Revolution Counter, calibrated to 8000 r.p.m.   9. 15. 0.

18. 26 Gallon Petrol Tank kit.   37. 0. 0.
    Unit and Gauge.   3. 10. 0.
    Tank Retaining Straps.
    2 Sheets of Sorbo rubber.   1. 10. 0.
    5 Ply Board.   1. 10. 0.

    NOTE: The fitting of this item requires extensive modification to the boot.

CHASSIS.

19. *Brakes. It is necessary to fit competition brake linings and pads, and change to competition fluid.
    1 set of Rear Brake Shoes and Linings.   4. 1. 6.
    1 set of Front Brake Pads.   4. 0. 0.
    1 qt. of Brake Fluid.   18. 0.

Appendix 11

20. *<u>Front Suspension, Competition Springs and Shock Absorbers.</u>

    2 Front Springs @ £3.0.0.   6. 0. 0.
    2 Front Shock Absorbers @ £4.0.0.   8. 0. 0.

21. *<u>Rear Suspension, Competition Springs and Shock Absorbers.</u>

    2 Rear Springs @ £7.10.0.   15. 0. 0.
    2 Rear Shock Absorbers @ £4.10.0.   9. 0. 0.

22. <u>Rear Axle.</u>
    The following ratios are available and can be supplied with or without a limited slip differential (standard axle 2.88 to 1).

    3.31   3.54   3.77

    Exchange price for alternative ratios.   24. 0. 0.
    Exchange price for Powr Lok – all ratios.   35. 0. 0.

    <u>A rebate will be given depending on the condition of the exchange axle.</u>

23. *<u>Speedometer</u> for all ratios.   4. 17. 6.

24. Lightweight magnesium wheels, essential for competition use.

    5 Lightweight Magnesium Wheels.   71. 0. 0.
    1 Pack (18) Chrome Special Wheel Nuts.   6. 0. 0.
    2 Spacers for Front Wheels.   15. 0.
    5 Dunlop SP.41 Tyres @ £8.19.0.   44. 15. 0.
    5 Tubes @ 19.0.   4. 15. 0.
    Modification to the front and rear wheel arches, to offer extra tyre clearance.   3. 10. 0.

    It cannot be too strongly emphasized that the standard steel wheels are only suitable for road use, and it will be necessary to fit magnesium alloy wheels if the car is to be used for any form of competition. There will be an added charge for balancing.

    As a number of these parts are imported from abroad and are subject to variation in price and import duty, we reserve the right to change any prices without prior notice.

    Items so marked – Dealer normal discount applies.
    All other parts are nett.

Appendix 11

LABOUR AND MATERIAL CHARGES FOR TIGER CONVERSION WORK CARRIED OUT IN THE ROOTES GROUP COMPETITION DEPARTMENT.

ENGINE.	Labour.			Material.		
	£	s.	d.	£	s.	d.
STAGE I.						
1. High Performance Cam Kit.				25.	15.	0.
2. High Performance Distributor Kit.				18.	10.	2.
3. Heavy Duty Valve Springs.				6.	8.	0.
Top Overhaul Gasket Set.				6.	5.	9.
	22.	15.	0.	56.	18.	11.
STAGE II (with Stage I prices included).						
4. Four Barrel Carburettor Kit.				64.	4.	4.
5. High Pressure Petrol Pump.				13.	6.	6.
Small items - water piping etc.				2.	10.	0.
TOTAL STAGE I AND II.	33.	5.	0.	136.	19.	0.
STAGE III. Complete conversion.						
7. Heavy Duty Clutch Kit (Engine out of frame)	17.	6.		24.	11.	0.
9. Strengthened Oil Pump Pick-up Pipe.	2.	12.	6.	1.	10.	0.
10. Threaded Valve Rocker Posts.				25.	6.	4.
11. Threaded Oil Gallery Plugs.				3.	15.	0.
12. Flexible Pipe to Clutch Slave Cylinder.	1.	14.	10.	1.	10.	2.
13. Complete Engine Gasket Kit.				8.	10.	11.
14. Competition Exhaust System.	15.	15.	0.	30.	0.	0.
16. Radiator and Oil Cooler Kit.	43.	10.	0.	85.	0.	0.
17. Rev. Counter.	2.	12.	6.	9.	15.	0.
18. 26 Gallon Petrol Tank.	57.	15.	0.	43.	10.	0.
Removing and refitting engine.	21.	0.	0.			
CHASSIS.						
19. Competition Brakes.	3.	10.	0.	8.	19.	6.
20. Front Suspension Competition Setting.	1.	15.	0.	14.	0.	0.
21. Rear Suspension Competition Setting.	3.	10.	0.	24.	0.	0.
22. Rear Axle.	7.	0.	0.	35.	0.	0.
23. Speedometer.		17.	6.	4.	17.	6.
24. Wheels, Tyres, etc. Modifying wheel arches.	3.	10.	0.	127.	5.	0.
Engine oil and filter.				1.	18.	11.
Axle oil.					4.	2.
	£199.	4.	10.	586.	13.	3.

No exchange allowance made for standard parts removed, these remain the property of the customer.

```
82 - 1347  Koni Shock absorbers.   Front £6.7.6. each.
82 - 1348                          Rear  £6.7.6. each.
```

Appendix 11

Factory Options for Sunbeam Tiger Mk I as available through Rootes Motors Inc., USA, 1965-1966

Part No.	Description	List Price
LAT-1*	Super induction kit — (Hi-Rise manifold and Holley 4-bbl. carb.)	$140.00
LAT-2	Dress-up kit — polished aluminium rocker covers, chrome air cleaner. radiator and oil filler cap.	$69.00
LAT-4	Large capacity aluminium oil pan.	$86.00
LAT-5	Traction-Master anti-tramp rods.	$42.25
LAT-7	Steel N.H.R.A. & A.H.R.A. approved scatter shield	$100.00
LAT-8	Polished aluminium rocker arm covers.	$40.00
LAT-10	Tiger key chain.	$1.50
LAT-12	Tiger ash tray (for den or office).	$ .85
LAT-13	Tiger pocket lighter	$1.50
LAT-14	Tiger embroidered jacket patch.	$2.00
LAT-15	Tiger flag set.	$3.00
LAT-16	Tiger decals	$ .15
LAT-17	Men's Tiger "tee-shirts"	$1.70
LAT-18	Tiger rally jacket	$8.50
LAT-20*	Hi-lift camshaft kit — complete with $\frac{3}{4}$ solid lifter camshaft. 16 solid lifters, 16 outer, 16 inner valve springs. gaskets, one dual-point distributor.	$100.00

*The LAT-1 & LAT-20 kits are used on the 245 BHP engine.
The LAT-1 kit when supplied separately is fitted with a Holley No. 1-12-4-bbl. carburettor of 465 c.f.m. for use with the hydraulic lifter camshaft.
When the LAT-1 and LAT-20 kits are ordered as original equipment on the 245 BHP Tiger, the carburettor is a Holley R-3259-AS, 4-bbl. of 715 c.f.m.

Part No.	Description	List Price
LAT-21	Lightweight horns.	$15.00
LAT-22	7,000 R.P.M. tachometer	$55.00
LAT-25	Fibreglass hood air-scoop for fitting on standard hood.	$15.00
LAT-27	Cast-iron low restriction exahust manifolds	$65.00
LAT-48	Jacket pocket patch Tiger.	$ .75
LAT-50	Limited-slip differential (must use LAT-51, 52, 53, 54 ring gear and pinion set).	$110.00
LAT-51	Crown wheel and pinion 3.07:1 ratio.	$50.00
LAT-52	3.31:1 ratio set.	$50.00
LAT-53	3.54:1 ratio set.	$50.00
LAT-54	3.73:1 ratio set.	$50.00
LAT-58	Chrome silver Tiger tail stripe kit.	$3.50
LAT-60	Heavy-duty street clutch set, pressure plate and disc.	$50.50
LAT-63	Boy's "tee-shirt"	$1.50
LAT-67	Men's heavy sweat shirt.	$3.00
LAT-70	Polished aluminium 5.50x13 wheels, each:	$48.00
LAT-73	Competition header kit.	$140.00
LAT-74	Low restriction exhaust muffler kit.	$52.00
LAT-76	Hi-speed HD shock absorber — rear	$16.85
LAT-77	Hi-speed HD front shocks.	$16.85
LAT-79	Lightweight fibreglass hood, with air-scoop and engine heat exhaust outlets.	$135.00
LAT-80	Lightweight, fibreglass 6 blade engine fan, variable-pitch at high rpm for minimum drag.	

Appendix 12: Tiger Production Figures

TYPE	CHASSIS NUMBERS	YEARS	PRODUCTION
LE MANS RACE CARS	B9499997 - B9499999	3/64	3
'AF' PROTOTYPE + PRE-PRODUCTION	B9470002 - B9470010	1/64 - 3/64	9
MK I	B9470001 B9470011 - B9473762 B9473767	7/64 6/64 - 8/65 8/65	3,754
STYLING PROTOTYPES	B9479975 & B9479976	7/5/65	2
PHOTOGRAPHIC	PH650039 & PH650040	8/65	2
CKD S.AFRICA TIGERS	B9480001 - B9480073	1964 - 1967	73
MK IA (Modified numbering system)	B382000001 - B382002706	8/65 - 12/66	2,706
MK II PRODUCTION ANALYSIS	B382100001 - B382100002	12/66	2
MK II	B382100100 - B382100633	12/66 - 6/67	534
(Source STOC & T.I.R.O.S.T)			7,085

The above figures are based on analysis of the Jensen Motors Limited 'Ledgers' production records save for the CKD Tigers delivered to South Africa, which do not form part of the 'Ledgers'. It is unfortunate that Chrysler U.K. chose to destroy the entire Rootes Group archive bar engineering drawings. Consequently no production records of the Rootes Group for the Sunbeam Tiger survive. The Jensen Ledgers convey the following information for each entry:

1. Chassis (vin) number – They do not denote a market suffix descriptor, i.e. HROFE (Home market RHD), RROFE (Export markets RHD), LROFE (Export markets LHD), LRXFE (Export market Canada & U.S.A.)

2. JAL (body) number - JAL represents the 'Jensen Alpine Line' number affixed by Pressed Steel Limited on a alloy tag adjacent to the fixing point of the chassis plate.

3. Engine Number – The number given by Ford for production destined for Rootes.

4. Gearbox Number – Serial number and type.

5. Rear Axle – Salisbury Serial number.

Appendix 12

6. Key numbers – Ignition, doors and boot.

7. Rota number – Believed to be the Rootes sequence order number.

8. Jensen Date – Believed to be the date the build of each Tiger was completed.

The Jensen ledgers are imperfect as they carry several blank entries against certain chassis numbers known by enthusiast registrars (in the U.K. and U.S.A.) to have been manufactured. It is also clear that several Tigers did not reach showrooms as Rootes assigned them to the Experimental Department as well as the Competition Department. A series production total of 7,085 is widely believed to be accurate however.

The first production Tiger was B9470011 (ADU 311B) which was probably built by Jensen during the first week of June 1964. The last production Tiger was B382100633 HRO FE (HRS 121E) which was completed on the 27th June 1967.

Appendix 12

Prototypes & Pre-Production MK1 Sunbeam Tigers

Chassis Number	AF Nos.	UK Registration	Primary Assignment	Survives
B9499999	AF1	7734 KV	Project 870 + Le Mans development 'Mule'	Yes
B9203826	AF2	9274 KV	SIII body, 'pavé' & cooling tests	No
B9470002	AF4	5778 KV	De Dion suspension. 289 test bed	Yes
B9470003	AF3	NONE	Shelby Organisation = Race car 45B	No
B9470004	AF5	5393 KV	Endurance testing	No
-	AF6	-	Retained by Jensen	-
-	AF7	-	Brakes, cooling etc.	-
B9470005	AF8	TF 8264	New York Auto Show	Yes
B9470006	AF9	7415 KV	Pre-production testing	Yes
B9470007	AF10	7416 KV	Pre-production testing	Yes
B9470008	-	ADU 309B	-	Yes
B9470009	-	AWK 621B	-	Yes
B9470010	-	ADU 638B	289 test bed	Yes
-	AF11	-	1st right hand drive manual	-
-	AF12	-	2nd right hand drive manual + all disc brakes	-
B9470119 LRX	AF14	ARW 897B	260 automatic	Yes
-	AF15	EHP 51C	Road tests	-

Prototypes & Pre-Production MKII Sunbeam Tigers

Chassis Number	AF Nos.	UK Registration	Primary Assignment	Survives
-	AF201	-	Body structure after 'pavé' testing	-
AF202	AF202	EHP 170C	289 automatic + all disc brakes	Yes
AF203	AF203	EHP 621C	289 manual + 14" wheels + all disc brakes	Yes
AF204	AF204	EWK 322C	289 manual + 14" wheels + all disc brakes	Yes
-	AF205	-	Road test evaluation over 5000 miles	-
-	AF206	-	Performance + road testing	-
-	AF207	-	Sales and production technical literature	-
B382001322 LRX	PP1	FKV 357D	European specification, 13" wheels	Yes
B382001394 LRX	PP3	GDU 343D	US specification, 13" wheels	Yes
B382001519	PP4	-	-	-
B382001523 LRX	PP6	PGF 555E	US specification, 14" wheels, rear discs	Yes
B382001527 HRO	PP5	GDU 497D	UK specification, 14" wheels, rear discs	Yes
B382001528 HRO	PP2	GDU 498D	UK specification, 14" wheels, rear discs	Yes